Shadow, Self, Spirit

Shadow, Self, Spirit

Essays in Transpersonal Psychology

Michael Daniels

imprint-academic.com

Published in the UK by Imprint Academic
PO Box 200, Exeter EX5 5YX, UK

Published in the USA by Imprint Academic
Philosophy Documentation Center
PO Box 7147, Charlottesville, VA 22906-7147, USA

ISBN 1 84540 022 4

A CIP catalogue record for this book is available from the
British Library and US Library of Congress

Cover Image:
Baptism, banner in Aberdeen Cathedral Church
of Saint Machar, 1991, by Thetis Blacker©
Photograph: Mark Fiennes

For Penny and Lottie,
who may one day read this book and perhaps discover
something surprising about their Dad —
and something familiar about themselves.

Also, for Trina —
friend, soulmate and harmonizing influence.

Contents

List of Tables & Figures. vii

About the Author. viii

Acknowledgements ix

Preface 1

1. Approaching Transpersonal Psychology 11

2. Transpersonal Psychology and the Paranormal. 39

3. Holism, Integration and the Transpersonal 63

4. The Shadow in Transpersonal Psychology. 71

5. Towards a Transpersonal Psychology of Evil 94

6. Maslow and Self-Actualization 115

7. Self-Actualization, Myth and the Transpersonal. 130

8. A Psychohistory and Phenomenology of the Soul 159

9. The Transpersonal Self 177

10. On Transcendence in Transpersonal Psychology. 216

11. Contexts and Modes of Mystical Experience 234

12. Whither Transpersonal Psychology?. 263

Glossary 279

References. 317

Name Index 333

Subject Index 338

List of Tables & Figures

Table 1 Ascending and descending currents in
transpersonal thought and practice 29

Table 2 Ken Wilber's quadrant model. 33

Table 3 Areas of common interest in transpersonal
psychology and parapsychology 44

Table 4 Transpersonal experiences of a paranormal kind. . 48

Table 5 Transpersonal disciplines and parapsychology in
the quadrant model 60

Table 6 Zeitgeist and shadow in transpersonal psychology 78

Table 7 A taxonomy of transformative experiences 86

Table 8 A taxonomy of transformational practices. 87

Table 9 The quadrants of good & evil 110

Table 10 Concepts of the soul and spirit in religion and
philosophy. 161

Table 11 Wilber's structural-hierarchical model of self
development. 199

Table 12 Categories of mystical experience
(the '5 x 5' model). 254

♦

Figure 1 Suggested locations of major transpersonal
theorists on the ascending-descending dimension 31

Figure 2 The wheel of virtue and vice 103

Figure 3 Maslow's hierarchy of needs 117

Figure 4 Jung's model of the psyche 180

Figure 5 Assagioli's model of the psyche 186

Figure 6 The psychological-philosophical model of
Sri Aurobindo 194

Figure 7 Washburn's model of psychological development 206

About the Author

Michael Daniels, PhD is Senior Lecturer in Psychology and Co-Director of the Consciousness and Transpersonal Psychology Research Unit at Liverpool John Moores University (LJMU). A chartered psychologist and Associate Fellow of the British Psychological Society, he is also the present Honorary Secretary and Webmaster of the BPS Transpersonal Psychology Section (www.transpersonalpsychology.org.uk). He has taught in higher education for more than 25 years, mainly in the areas of humanistic and transpersonal psychology, counselling and psychotherapy, and parapsychology, and is joint Programme Leader for the MSc in Consciousness and Transpersonal Psychology at LJMU. His publications include journal articles and book chapters on observational methods, moral development, self-actualization theory, transpersonal theory, Jungian psychology and parapsychology. He is the author of *Self-Discovery the Jungian Way: The Watchword Technique* (1992) in which he introduces an innovative practical method of Jungian self-analysis based on word association, and he continues to run occasional workshops on this technique. He is a member of the Association for Transpersonal Psychology, Scientific and Medical Network, and Society for Psychical Research, and is on the editorial board of the *Transpersonal Psychology Review* and *International Journal of Transpersonal Studies*. For six years (1993–1998) he also trained and practised as an honorary psychotherapist within the National Health Service, using a psychodynamic orientation. Since 1996, he has maintained his own website that explores the areas of transpersonal psychology, parapsychology, and Jungian psychology (www.michaeldaniels.co.uk). He lives among the beauty and relative isolation of the North Wales mountains.

Acknowledgements

I would like to thank the editors of the *Transpersonal Psychology Review*, also Sage Publications, Inc. for permission to reuse material as follows:

Chapters 2, 3, 4, 5, 8, 9, 10, 11 are revised and updated versions of articles originally published in the *Transpersonal Psychology Review* from 1997–2003. Used with permission of the editors David Fontana and Ingrid Slack.

Chapter 7 is a revised and updated version of Daniels, M. (1988). The myth of self-actualization. *Journal of Humanistic Psychology, 28(1)*, 7–38. Used with permission of the publishers, Sage Publications, Inc.

Preface

A Personal Journey

Whenever I read a book on the transpersonal, I also try to discover something about the author. This is not simply nosiness, but rather reflects sensitivity to the fact that writing about the transpersonal cannot be divorced from a personal involvement or personal experience. All writers in this area are inevitably both enriched, but also limited, by the particular experiences they have had, and all of them, *without exception*, have their own personal equations, or personal agendas. In some cases this may be obvious to the reader from, perhaps, a heavy-handed or polemical style, or because the author is explicitly promoting a particular belief or ideology. In other cases, however, it is more subtle or disguised — especially the case, I think, with academic writers. It is important, therefore, that the reader should know a little about where I am coming from if only so that I may, perhaps, be unmasked from any disguise or guile that I may be tempted to perpetrate.

My own study of the transpersonal has its origins way back in early childhood (the 1950s), with an interest that was encouraged by some rare, wonderful, but essentially ordinary experiences of perfect days, perfect walks, perfect moments of lying in the grass and staring up at the clouds. Such experiences taught me, as no formal lesson or book could do, the reality of the human spirit and its mysterious relationship to the All. For me, these experiences contrasted heavily with those that I had when smartened up and dragged reluctantly off to Church (my uncle was a Church of England minister in another part of the country, and I presume there must have been something of a sense of family honour involved in keeping up Church attendance, even though my own family never appeared otherwise to be 'religious'). No doubt it was partly for this reason that during Church services I would often feel a distinct sense of hypocrisy among the congregation — accompanied also by a powerful intuition that there was, in fact, a great Truth or Mystery that lay concealed behind the veil of dead words and religious trappings. I must have been about four or five years old. Eventually, aged six, I was baptized by my uncle, but this did not seem to me a profound spiritual event.

In my later childhood I found myself interested in other mysteries — especially ghosts, psychism, spiritualism and flying saucers — and I read avidly in these areas. Although at first these phenomena did not particularly strike me as having any *spiritual* significance, they did clearly relate to some of the big questions: 'Where do I come from?' 'Who am I?' 'Where am I going?' 'Is death the end?'

The connection between spiritualism and spirituality came when I discovered Theosophy (at about the age of 12) and, from there, I was introduced to Vedanta and Yoga. A book that left a lasting impression on my developing thinking was Paramhansa Yogananda's *Autobiography of a Yogi* (originally published 1946) which excited me not only with its exotic tales of paranormal events and Yogic *siddhis*, but with the humility, sincerity, compassion and spiritual depth of the writing. It also reinforced my concerned intention to find a *guru*. Eventually I did find an Indian Yoga teacher (who was also a psychiatrist at a local hospital) and I studied Hatha and Raja Yoga intensively with him for two years (this was at a time when Yoga was relatively unknown and undeveloped in Britain). This relationship ended when I went to University, which also coincided with my increasing interest in the Western esoteric and magical traditions. At Leeds University I founded an 'Occult Society' and, as a result, came into contact with all sorts of charming and colourful, although sometimes very unsavoury, characters who variously styled themselves as psychics, ghost-hunters, spiritualists, mediums, witches, Wiccans, occultists, magicians, shamans and Satanists. This was a very interesting period in my life! At this time, I also studied closely for seven years with a teacher of magic (also a psychologist and educator) in a tradition that emphasized self-realization, including a one year period living in a small community he had established.

Studying psychology at University was something of a mixed experience at this time (the early 1970s). The research paradigm was essentially positivistic but the discipline was in something of a hiatus between a dying radical behaviourism and the gradually emerging cognitivism that now dominates academic psychology. Freud was discussed only in the context of the history of psychology, and Jung was hardly mentioned — and then with a barely disguised guffaw. There were, however, some chinks of light for someone, like myself, interested in inner experience, psychological development, and spiritual matters. One of these was George Kelly's Personal Construct Psychology, another was Jean Piaget's theory of intellectual development and Lawrence Kohlberg's related approach to moral development. For me, however, the most exciting of all was *humanistic psychology*, as represented in the work of Carl Rogers and, especially, Abraham Maslow (transpersonal psychology as a separate discipline had not yet become widely known in Britain). Maslow, in particular, dared to talk about spirituality, about transcendence and the transpersonal at a time when the prevailing culture in academic psychology was completely antithetical to such ideas.

Fortunately I was very lucky to have one or two tutors who were sympathetic to the humanistic perspective in psychology and, as a result, I undertook an independent undergraduate project on this which eventually led to my PhD (finally completed 1981) which examined Maslow's concept of self-actualization and its relationship with moral development and personality. From there, I stepped, relatively seamlessly, into a career in higher education which has continued in Liverpool since 1979.

I count myself very fortunate to have been able to develop my interest in the transpersonal in the context of an academic career in which I have been encouraged and supported by my host institutions (perhaps Liverpool really is the 'pool of life' referred to by Jung, 1983, pp. 223–224, in the interpretation of one of his dreams). Although, when I first proposed teaching an undergraduate module on 'humanistic psychology' (in 1980 I believe) I was made to run the gauntlet by certain members of the validating Board who feared that I would indoctrinate students with some kind of subversive new-age ideology, I am glad to say that reason won the day and I was allowed to proceed. Since that time, I have been able to devote more and more of my time to teaching and researching in the areas that most concern me — transpersonal psychology and parapsychology. Perhaps the most significant development in this respect has been the establishment of the MSc in Consciousness and Transpersonal Psychology at LJMU, as well as the enrolment of research students to PhDs in this area. These developments themselves only became possible due to the energies and efforts of colleagues at LJMU who, serendipitously, shared interests in the transpersonal and related fields.

The development of my thinking in the area of transpersonal psychology is shown in the articles I have had published that form the basis for this book. As well as being grounded in my reading of the transpersonal literature, my understanding has been informed by experience of various transpersonal practices which, in addition to Yoga and magic, have also included various forms of meditation (most notably *vipassana* and *zazen*), guided fantasy, and dreamwork. However, I now rarely practise any of these in a formal sense, but prefer to adopt a more 'casual,' unstructured and relational approach to transpersonal knowing. This change in approach began, I suspect, in the period leading up to the time of my second marriage and the birth of my two daughters (b. 1991, 1993). My interest in a more relational approach also expressed itself in my developing interest in Jungian psychology, counselling and psychotherapy which led to my undertaking six years' training and practice in psychodynamic (object relations) psychotherapy within the National Health Service. However, I discontinued psychotherapeutic practice in 1998 and have not returned to this. Most of my professional energies are now expended in teaching, research and writing.

The Purpose and Structure of this Book

In a literal sense, this book has been more than 20 years in the making. It has given me the opportunity to collate, revise and update a series of articles that I have had published during this time in the general area of transpersonal psychology. These articles themselves arose out of and supported my teaching of transpersonal psychology to undergraduate and postgraduate students. Such teaching, I should add, has been a most rewarding and enlightening learning experience for me and, I hope and believe, for many of the students I have had the privilege to work with during this period. I am truly indebted to the contributions they have made to my own thinking in these areas, and for the time, stimulation and support they have freely and generously given throughout my time in higher education. I should particularly single out the students who have undertaken the MSc in Consciousness and Transpersonal Psychology, which first began in 1994 under the perhaps more appealing but somewhat misleading title of 'The Psychology of Human Potential', and which now runs in both attendance and distance-learning modes. I have, without exception, enjoyed and learned from their committed and gracious presence on the programmes.

Because of the origins of this book in teaching and discussions with students, it will, I hope, be of particular value to those approaching transpersonal psychology for the first time as well as to those who wish to develop their understanding of the discipline to a level which broadly corresponds to that required for Masters' study. Because it also addresses important issues that are currently at the heart of theoretical debates in transpersonal psychology I also hope that it will be of interest to other academics in the field as well as to the wider general readership in these areas.

I should make clear at the outset, however, that this book almost exclusively addresses *theoretical* issues in transpersonal psychology. It is *not* a manual of transpersonal practice, and only indirectly addresses issues of concern to transpersonal therapists and counsellors (although I hope that both spiritual practitioners and therapists will find something of value in the pages that follow). My focus on theoretical matters does not mean that I dismiss the importance of experience, of practice, or of therapy, and I very much hope that it does not lead to my characterization as an 'ivory tower academic'. It does mean, however, that I consider theoretical issues (ontology, epistemology, methodology, conceptual understanding, etc.) to be of major importance to the field of transpersonal psychology at the present time and, in some sense, to be *primary*. In focussing on theoretical issues I also do not wish to give the impression that I devalue *empirical* research in transpersonal psychology. Indeed empirical research is sorely needed in this area (only a minority of articles published in transpersonal journals report empirical data). In our MSc in

Consciousness and Transpersonal Psychology, for example, students are required to undertake an empirical thesis. Many of these studies have been of outstanding quality and several have been published.

It has been an interesting and rewarding experience for me to develop what were essentially independent articles on different aspects of transpersonal theory into the format of a book. Particularly gratifying has been the realization that these various articles do tell a coherent story, although there are different emphases and sometimes varying perspectives presented in the different chapters that I hope will stimulate rather than frustrate the reader.

As part of the revision of these articles, I have striven to minimize repetition or unnecessary duplication of ideas. This has not always been possible, however, and in the interests of maintaining the coherence and flow of thought, and to maintain the integrity of each chapter, some repetition remains. For this I apologize and beg the reader's indulgence.

Chapter 1 of this book provides a general introduction to transpersonal psychology, including definitional issues, an historical overview, and a summary of the major theoretical approaches within the discipline. It ends with a description of some of the major resources in transpersonal psychology, including academic courses, journals, and organizations.

In Chapter 2, I consider two main questions: (1) What is the relationship between paranormal experience and transpersonal experience? (2) What is the relationship between transpersonal psychology and parapsychology? I look at examples of experiences that may be considered both paranormal and transpersonal and at how these two realms of experience have been associated throughout history and across cultures. I question whether distinctions need to be made between the paranormal and the transpersonal and examine potential pitfalls in various approaches that have been taken to understanding this issue. Finally, I discuss the differences between parapsychology and transpersonal psychology in terms of the contrasting perspectives and research paradigms that these disciplines take on paranormal experience. These approaches are considered in terms of Wilber's quadrant model (e.g., Wilber, 1997) in an attempt to understand how they provide alternative views that are complementary rather than opposed.

Chapter 3 discusses the meaning of 'holism' in spiritual and transpersonal circles. I argue that it is important to distinguish between three versions of holism: Holism 1 (New-Age Holism) involves the integration of *positive* aspects only of the Body, Mind and Spirit. Holism 2 (Psychological Holism) recognizes the importance of accepting and integrating the darker, *shadow* aspects of our being. Finally, Holism 3 (All-Quadrant Holism) proposes the need to integrate the individual body-mind-spirit (positive and negative) in the social, cultural and natural worlds. In arguing that transpersonal psychology should adopt the perspective of Holism 3, I note that an exclusively *psychological* approach to the transpersonal can never be sufficient.

In Chapter 4, I discuss the relevance of the archetype of the *shadow* for our understanding of transpersonal psychology, examining this in relation to two interdependent themes: (a) manifestations and implications of transpersonal psychology's own shadow, and (b) the importance of recognizing and incorporating our transformative experiences of the archetypal shadow. On the basis of this discussion I present a preliminary taxonomy of transpersonal experiences and practices that incorporates aspects of the transformative shadow. This taxonomy itself raises a number of important and largely ignored questions within transpersonal psychology, including that of the ontological status and psychological significance of the transcendental and of the archetypes of good and evil.

In Chapter 5, I examine the philosophical and psychological roots of moral evil, which I see as a potential that emerges alongside the development of ego consciousness and personality. In this way, ego development gives rise to the possibilities of both chosen (deliberate) and unchosen (characterological and projective) evil. I then examine the ways in which characterological and projective evil may be consequences of damaging socialization experiences in which there is a failure of empathic concern for the developing child. On this basis, I propose a model in which the various forms of human good and evil can be understood in terms of the two dimensions of (1) empathy vs. egocentrism and (2) benevolence vs. malevolence. The solution to human evil is the encouragement of both empathy (head) and benevolence (heart), together with the capacity for moral effectance (hands). Such development may largely depend upon the role that significant others can play in acting as empathic, benevolent and morally effective 'self-centres'. Finally I discuss the implications of Ken Wilber's quadrant model for our understanding of human evil before proposing a general transpersonal perspective in which moral good is seen in terms of an increasing expansion of empathy and moral concern. From this perspective, moral expansion is a critical feature in the process of self-realization, which may be viewed simultaneously as the realization of spirit.

Chapter 6 traces the development of Abraham Maslow's concept of self-actualization through four decades of his published writings. I argue that his views evolved both in content and sophistication, but that he never achieved a final coherent theory of self-actualization. I suggest that certain characteristics in Maslow's approach may have precluded the development of a satisfactory formulation.

In Chapter 7, I argue that the principal function of a theory of self-actualization is to establish a 'myth' or meaningful narrative account of human development that provides conceptual support for people seeking fulfillment and offers clear normative and practical guidance. Self-actualization theory should be evaluated primarily in terms of its effectiveness as myth rather than its logical precision or empirical confirmation. An effective myth, I suggest, must be believable, consequential, and morally defensible. An examination of Maslow's theory of self-actualization reveals inadequacies as a mythical interpretation of personal development. There are ambiguities and contradictions in the theory, and several conceptual elements may actually inhibit or corrupt the process of self-actualization. The failure of Maslow's theory is due, I suggest, to confusing the project with naturalistic science and to the adoption of biological metaphors and empirical methods that are fundamentally inappropriate. A more fruitful approach may be found in emphasizing a mythical perspective from which life becomes a shared quest for the human good.

Chapter 8 examines the development and experiential foundations of religious and metaphysical ideas about the soul. These ideas, I suggest, have profoundly influenced psychological approaches to the transpersonal self. A psychohistorical examination of the concept of the soul suggests that it encompasses a varied and complex set of aspects and meanings. The different aspects of the soul are, I suggest, based on interpretations of a wide variety of human experiences, including life and death, dreams, out-of-body experiences, hauntings, possession, self-reflexive consciousness, inspiration, and mystical experience. In general terms, concepts of the soul seem to have evolved from a primitive belief in a quasi-physical reality, through the later incorporation of psychological qualities, to what may be a relatively recent focus on spiritual experience. Conceptual difficulties can arise when we fail to recognize the differences between these levels of interpretation.

Chapter 9 focuses on a critical comparison of ideas about the transpersonal self as understood within nine major psychological theories — those of Abraham Maslow, C.G. Jung, Roberto Assagioli, Stanislav Grof, Sri Aurobindo, Ken Wilber, Michael Washburn, Peggy Wright and Jorge Ferrer. From an examination of these various approaches, I identify twenty distinct meanings of the transpersonal self. I suggest that it is not possible at this stage in the development of transpersonal psychology to select any one theory or conception as being the most adequate although I state my own preference for a concept that emphasizes the integrated, embodied spiritual life. It is important, I suggest, to learn from each of these interesting and very different perspectives.

Chapter 10 examines the meaning of 'transcendence,' distinguishing between the phenomenological and metaphysical uses of the term and considering various difficulties with the approaches to transcendence taken by Jung and Wilber. I suggest that transpersonal psychology should adopt a more phenomenological perspective on transcendence and should be more cautious and explicit in its metaphysical assumptions. Moreover, I argue that the transpersonal does not *depend upon* a conception of the metaphysical Transcendent and that, as a science, transpersonal psychology cannot be *based upon* such metaphysical assumptions.

In Chapter 11, I define mysticism as 'the individual's direct experience of a relationship to a fundamental Reality'. A review of the literature reveals many different conceptions and descriptions of mystical experience. I examine in particular the approaches of William James, Evelyn Underhill, R.C. Zaehner, F.C. Happold, Walter Stace, Rudolf Otto, Andrew Rawlinson, Ken Wilber and John Welwood. On the basis of this review, I propose a new framework for understanding mysticism (the '5 x 5' model) that identifies twenty-five distinct forms of mystical experience. These forms derive from the combination of five different *contexts* or objects of mystical experience (theistic, nature, social, mental, and monistic) and five different *modes* of experience (numinous, dialogic, synergic, unitive, and nondual). Assumptions and implications of the model are discussed.

Finally, in Chapter 12, I consider the current status of transpersonal psychology, including a summary of what I see as the major issues and controversies facing the discipline at this time. I also offer some suggestions for how transpersonal psychology might aim to develop a more integrative approach.

In this retelling of my intellectual journey in transpersonal psychology, several common and consistent themes emerge, many of which have been present in my thinking from the outset. In order more clearly to orientate the reader to my approach, I would, in particular, emphasize the following:

- A *humanistic* approach, which focuses upon the human origins, significance and value of transpersonal phenomena.
- The need to recognize, and to value, the full *range and variety of transpersonal experiences.*
- The close relationship between *paranormal and transpersonal experience.*
- A *pluralistic* approach that recognizes and values different perspectives on the transpersonal.
- A *pragmatic* approach to the transpersonal, in which the *transformative* function and potential of transpersonal experiences and events is primary.
- The need to develop adequate *narratives, myths and theoretical models* that are capable of guiding people towards transformation.
- The centrality of *morality* to human spirituality.
- The need for a *holistic* approach to spirituality that incorporates not only the shadow, but our relationship to other people, and the world in general.
- The importance of the *immanent* and the mundane.
- The need for transpersonal psychology to adopt a *scientific,* investigative approach that does not, however, preclude a normative agenda.

Chapter 1

Approaching Transpersonal Psychology

The Transpersonal, Spirituality and Religion

The word *transpersonal* literally means: beyond (or through) the personal. It refers to experiences, processes and events in which our normal limiting sense of self is transcended and in which there is a feeling of connection to a larger, more meaningful reality. For many people, religious or spiritual experience is seen as central to the transpersonal agenda, although the transpersonal can also be about extending our concern for (or our sense of identification with) other people, humankind in general, life, the planet, or nature (cf. Walsh & Vaughan, 1993a). The term 'transpersonal' therefore has greater scope than the more widely used concepts of 'religious' or 'spiritual'. It also has the advantage, noted by Walsh & Vaughan (*ibid.*), that it is metaphysically neutral (i.e., it does not necessarily imply a belief in the ontological reality of Spirit). Its major disadvantage, of course, is that at the present time the term is relatively unknown outside certain rather small intellectual circles. This means, in practice, that it needs to be *translated* in conversations with outsiders. In my experience this can be done in one of two ways:

a) The lengthy way, involving giving many examples of transpersonal experiences, processes and events. These might include unitive mystical states, numinous experience, ecstasy, states of absorption, near-death experiences, memories of previous lives, 'big dreams,' experiences of deep connection, empathy or merging with others, love, compassion, inner guidance, channelling, and creative illumination. At some point, the listener (bored or sufficiently illuminated) will say 'OK, enough!'

b) The short way, by (perhaps reluctantly) using the 'S' word. Thus the transpersonal may be said to be *more or less* about the *spiritual* dimension of life, or about human *spirituality*. I have found that most people, in fact, seem to be fairly satisfied with this translation, probably because it allows them to relate directly to their own experience and understanding of spirituality. For the reasons discussed above, using 'spiritual' as a synonym for the transpersonal is in many ways an oversimplistic cop-out but, in practice, it can be a convenient and useful one. When taking this strategy, it is important, however, to make a clear distinction between spirituality and religion (cf. Fontana, 2003). Although human spirituality often expresses itself in the religious impulse, which itself may become codified in one or other of the organized forms of religion, many people (like myself) who consider themselves to be spiritual, and who may report spiritual experiences, do not call themselves religious and do not follow any form of recognized religion. Some people even go so far as to argue for an *opposition* between genuine spirituality and organized religion. Thus Grof (2000, p. 211) suggests that '[o]nce a religion becomes organized, it often completely loses the connection with its spiritual source and becomes a secular institution that exploits human spiritual needs without satisfying them.'

If there is one common central theme to the concept of the transpersonal it is about the profound *transformation* of our usual egoic, self-centred existence to some ultimately more satisfying or valuable condition (cf. Caplan, Hartelius & Rardin, 2003; Ferrer, 2002; Lancaster, 2004). In other words, there is a normative, soteriological or salvational agenda to the transpersonal. This is not to say that such transformation is always pleasant or welcome when it happens — indeed precisely because our stable egoic structures are threatened with change, transpersonal experiences may often be frightening and painful (e.g., spiritual crises, hellish near-death experiences, states of possession). The concept of transformation does imply, however, at least the promise of a change for the better.

Transpersonal Psychology

Transpersonal psychology involves the psychological investigation of transpersonal experiences, processes and events. Because the transpersonal involves much more than the phenomena of religion, transpersonal psychology is not the same as the *psychology of religion* (e.g., Fontana, 2003; Spilka, Hood, Hunsberger & Gorsuch, 2003; Wulff, 1997). One way of viewing their relationship is to suggest that the psychology of religion may be included within the more general field of transpersonal psychology, although, in practice and for a variety of historical and cultural reasons, the two disciplines tend to remain largely separate. One of these reasons is that transpersonal psychology is a more *normative* discipline than the psychology of religion. In other words, transpersonal psychology addresses and promotes the need for transformation much more directly and proactively than does the rather more *descriptive* and restrained approach found within the psychology of religion.

One of the dangers in any normative approach to knowledge is that it may easily become *ideological* in the sense of promoting a belief system for which there may be little or no real evidence. Taking this route, transpersonal psychology may justifiably be dismissed (as it has been by many) as just some other new-age superstition, fad or cult. In my opinion, this can only be avoided by transpersonal psychology's clear commitment to a broadly *scientific* approach (cf. Friedman, 2002). Without wishing to get bogged down in arguments from philosophy of science, I suggest that a truly scientific transpersonal psychology must be based on (1) collection of all the relevant evidence, where possible using empirical methods (direct observation), (2) the attempt to understand transpersonal phenomena using terms, models and theories that emphasize the role of psychological factors, (3) putting these models and theories to critical test by examining whether their predictions are confirmed by further evidence, (4) communicating the knowledge obtained in appropriate ways to the scientific and wider communities. This model of a scientific transpersonal psychology is fully compatible, even identical, with that proposed by Tart (2004) in his description of what he calls *essential science* — itself the same, he suggests, as essential common sense. Thus essential science, Tart argues, consists in an iterative process involving stages of observation, theorizing, testing and sharing.

The transpersonal has, of course, been investigated for millennia, not least by spiritual practitioners, mystics, philosophers and theologians. It is indeed possible to understand some of these approaches (especially, perhaps, Buddhist teachings) as being forms of scientific transpersonal psychology according to the criteria given above. Thus there is a strong emphasis in Buddhism on direct personal experience (empiricism), detailed analysis of mental processes (psychological models), the testing of theoretical concepts in the light of spiritual practice and experience (hypothesis testing), and on sharing knowledge through the scriptures, commentaries, and oral teachings (communication). In general, however, most religious and philosophical approaches to understanding the transpersonal have preferred the authority of tradition rather than that of direct experience, the value of belief rather than sceptical inquiry, and an understanding that is based on mythological and metaphysical rather than psychological concepts. Even though academic philosophy, both East and West, has always emphasized the importance of sceptical inquiry and rational analysis rather than belief, its focus only on the logical relations among ideas often ignores the experiential, empirical and psychological dimensions. Philosophical discussions of personal identity, for example, often fail to take fully into account evidence from developmental psychology (e.g., theory of mind, stages of self), psychiatry (e.g., dissociative conditions), or parapsychology (e.g., evidence for personal survival).

What is important here is to attempt to distinguish transpersonal psychology as a scientific discipline based on psychological modes of understanding from other approaches to the transpersonal which themselves do not claim scientific or psychological status. These other approaches (which Friedman, 2002, suggests should be considered part of the broader field of *transpersonal studies*) include theology, religious studies, poetry, anthropological investigation, spiritual and folk traditions, and new-age belief. A similar argument is made by Walsh & Vaughan (1993a) and Boucouvalas (1999) who argue that transpersonal psychology (which focuses on psychological processes) should itself be seen as part of a broader, multidisciplinary *transpersonal movement* or *transpersonal orientation*. Although academic transpersonal psychology has itself developed within the domain of scientific psychology, it has always recognized the value of other disciplines in contributing to our understanding of the transpersonal. It is therefore quite happy to see itself as part of this larger transpersonal orientation that includes transpersonal approaches within, for example, anthropology, business, counselling, cultural studies, ecology, education, medicine, neuroscience, pharmacology, philosophy, politics, psychiatry, psychotherapy, religious studies, and sociology. Such a broad transpersonal movement represents not only the hope for an integral approach to knowledge, but also a commitment to widespread spiritual transformation in the individual, social, cultural and political spheres.

In arguing that transpersonal psychology is a science, this should not be taken to imply *scientism*, or the crude attempt to reduce all phenomena to a strictly materialistic and mechanistic explanation. The preferred mode of explanation in transpersonal psychology is *hermeneutic* (emphasizing understanding and interpretation) and should involve psychological rather than physical or physiological constructs. In other words transpersonal psychology focuses upon explicating the human meaning of transpersonal phenomena which, within the framework of a psychological discipline, can only be achieved using psychological discourse. Of course, this is not to say that transpersonal psychology cannot learn from neurophysiological studies (e.g., examining the brain processes that correlate with transpersonal experiences), but simply that a knowledge of brain processes cannot explain the irreducible phenomenological qualities (*qualia*) of the experiences themselves, nor their meaning and significance to the person (cf. Lancaster, 2004; Velmans, 2000).

Because of the normative, soteriological agenda inherent within the concept of the transpersonal, transpersonal psychology is best considered as an *applied* rather than pure science. If the knowledge we obtain has no practical application in the world, in terms of helping people to achieve the kinds of transformation we are investigating, then transpersonal psychology becomes an essentially irrelevant discipline. In this context I am reminded of Shotter's (1975) important distinction between two scientific psychological paradigms: (1) a value-free and essentially determinist *natural science of behaviour*, and (2) a value-laden and responsible *moral science of action*. Into the former camp fall the approaches of behaviourism, cognitivism and neurophysiological reductionism. In the latter camp we may include existential psychology, humanistic psychology, the psychotherapies and, I suggest, transpersonal psychology. This means that transpersonal psychology should be orientated not only to studying, but also to bringing about the kinds of transformation it examines — in the researcher, in other individuals, in the wider community and, ultimately, at the global, even cosmic, level. In practice, the first of these is perhaps a useful and, in fact, inevitable place to start. As Harman (1993, p. 139) puts it: '[t]he scientist who would explore the topic of consciousness ... must be *willing to risk being transformed* in the process of exploration' (italics in original). Of course this is not simply a risk, but also a wonderful opportunity. From the perspective of transpersonal psychology, therefore, it is vital that the researcher should *participate* in (rather than simply observe) the spiritual-transformational process. In this way personal transpersonal experience and practice serve to inform, ground and enrich the transpersonal psychologist's research.

A History of Transpersonal Psychology

In the modern world, *transpersonal psychology* may be said to have been born in 1901–2, when the eminent American psychologist William James (1842–1910) delivered the Gifford Lectures at the University of Edinburgh. In these lectures (published in 1902 as *The Varieties of Religious Experience*) James (brother of the novelist Henry James) approached the religious questions through a psychological analysis based on his study of individual people's direct personal experience. Religious experience, he argued, is the legitimate subject matter of psychology and may be investigated using empirical, scientific methods. Important in this respect, James coined the phrase 'radical empiricism' to extend the notion of empiricism beyond that of simple sensory observation of the external world, to encompass observation of internal mental states and processes.

William James was also an important pioneer of psychical research, which he believed to be of central relevance to understanding religious questions such as whether the human personality survives bodily death. His interest in religious experiences was also informed by his acquaintance with Swedenborgian doctrines, the American transcendentalism of Emerson, Thoreau and Whitman, Theosophy, Christian mysticism, Sufism, Buddhism, Vedanta and Yoga, as well as by his own experiments with the psychoactive nitrous oxide (laughing gas). James' experiences with nitrous oxide greatly influenced his own thinking about the nature of consciousness, reality and, as we would understand it, the transpersonal.[1]

> Some years ago I myself made some observations on this aspect of nitrous oxide intoxification, and reported them in print. One conclusion was forced upon my mind at that time, and my impression of its truth has ever since remained unshaken. It is that our normal waking consciousness, rational consciousness as we call it, is but one special type of consciousness, whilst all about it, parted from it by the filmiest of screens, there lie potential forms of consciousness entirely different. We may go through life without suspecting their existence; but apply the requisite stimulus, and at a touch they are there in all their completeness, definite types of mentality which probably somewhere have their field of application and adaptation. No account of the universe in its totality can be final which leaves these other forms of consciousness quite disregarded (James, 1902/1960, pp. 373–374).

The same year that James was giving his Gifford Lectures at Edinburgh (1901) also saw the publication of *Cosmic Consciousness* — a seminal and highly influential book about exalted and joyous experiences of our own deep connection to the whole universe, felt as a living and ordered Presence, written by the Canadian psychiatrist Richard M. Bucke (1837–1902). For Bucke, cosmic consciousness was a definite psychospiritual state in which:

---

1   James was, in fact, the first person known to have used the English term 'trans-personal,' in a 1905 Harvard course syllabus (Taylor, 1996).

a. The person, suddenly, without warning, has a sense of being immersed in a flame, or rose-coloured cloud, or perhaps rather a sense that the mind is itself filled with such a cloud or haze,

b. At the same instant he is, as it were, bathed in an emotion of joy, assurance, triumph, 'salvation' ...

c. Simultaneously or instantly following the above sense and emotional experiences there comes to the person an intellectual illumination quite impossible to describe. Like a flash there is presented to his consciousness a clear conception (a vision) in outline of the meaning and drift of the universe. He does not come to believe merely; but he sees and knows that the cosmos, which to the self conscious mind seems made up of dead matter, is in fact far otherwise — is in very truth a living presence. He sees that instead of men being, as it were, patches of life scattered through an infinite sea of non-living substance, they are in reality specks of relative death in an infinite ocean of life. He sees that the life which is in man is eternal, as all life is eternal; that the soul of man is as immortal as God is; that the universe is so built and ordered that without any peradventure all things work together for the good of each and all; that the foundation principle of the world is what we call love, and that the happiness of every individual is in the long run absolutely certain. The person who passes through this experience will learn in the few minutes, or even moments, of its continuance more than in months or years of study, and he will learn much that no study ever taught or can teach. Especially does he obtain such a conception of THE WHOLE, or at least of an immense WHOLE, as dwarfs all conception, imagination or speculation, springing from and belonging to ordinary self consciousness, such a conception as makes the old attempts to mentally grasp the universe and its meaning petty and even ridiculous (Bucke, 2001, pp. 87–88).

Bucke also describes cosmic consciousness as accompanied by a sense of immortality, distinct individuality, the loss of the fear of death and of the sense of sin. He further notes that the experience comes as a sudden illumination, like a lightning flash, that it depends upon the previous character and age of the person[2] and that the effect of the experience is to add charm to the personality and to change, even 'transfigure,' the person's physical appearance.

Bucke was both friend to and biographer of Walt Whitman whom many people, he says, believe 'was the greatest spiritual force yet produced by the race — which would mean that he is the greatest case of cosmic consciousness to date' (*ibid.*, p. 82–83). Bucke saw cosmic consciousness as essentially confirming Whitman's conception of 'My Soul' (the Oversoul or universal spirit of the American Transcendentalists). He also argues that cosmic consciousness has been known throughout the centuries by other names, such as 'Nirvana,' the 'Kingdom of God' or 'Kingdom of Heaven,' 'Spirit,' 'Spirit of God,' 'Christ,' or 'Gabriel,' and that the experience of cosmic consciousness in their founders accounts for the origin of all religion. In this sense he was an early advocate (as were the Theosophists) of the doctrine of the *perennial philosophy* (Aldous Huxley, 1947), i.e., the belief that all religions share a common doctrinal and experiential deep structure which recognizes the essential divinity of the human soul. Bucke also introduces an evolutionary dimension into his deliberations through his suggestion that the number of individuals who experience cosmic consciousness has been increasing throughout the ages and that the experience is also becoming more perfect and pronounced. In this way, he suggests, cosmic consciousness will, in the future, become more widely distributed and will occur earlier in people's lives, until this mode of consciousness finally characterizes the whole human race.

The phenomenological investigation and systematization of mystical experiences, pioneered by James and Bucke, was later refined and developed by writers such as Evelyn Underhill (1911/1995), Rudolf Otto (1917/1950), Walter Stace (1960), R.C. Zaehner (1961), Marghanita Laski (1961), Abraham Maslow (1968, 1973), Alister Hardy (1979), and Ken Wilber (e.g., 1995a, 1996a, 2000a). It is now a major area of research interest within transpersonal psychology, as represented in the classic work on altered states of consciousness by American psychologist Charles T. Tart (e.g., 1975) and also that of the Religious Experience

---

2   Unfortunately, but perhaps understandably given the times in which he was writing, Bucke suggests that cosmic consciousness occurs mostly in mature males of good intellect, high moral qualities, and superior physique.

Research Unit (now Centre) established by the distinguished British scientist Sir Alister Hardy in 1969 (www.lamp. ac.uk/aht/).

Another important impetus in the development of transpersonal psychologies came from the psychoanalytic movement. Like William James, the Swiss analytical psychologist C.G. Jung (1875–1961) had a lifelong interest in paranormal and religious experiences. At one time a close associate of Sigmund Freud, Jung became highly critical of Freud's uncompromising dismissal of the 'occult,' and Freud's belief that religion was essentially a form of neurosis. Instead of immature and unhealthy psychological projections, Jung viewed the religious impulse as the manifestation and projection of essentially healthy spiritual *archetypes* (universal patterns of human experience) that exist within our 'transpersonal' (überpersonlich) *collective unconscious*. Jung saw the goal of human life as *individuation* – essentially a spiritual quest for full humanness and psychological integration, or the realization of the archetype of the Self. Jung talked of the *transcendent function*, by which he meant the natural tendency of the psyche to creatively resolve oppositions and to unify unconscious and conscious contents. Because of the transcendent function, Jung believed that individuation could be facilitated by working creatively and imaginatively with dream images, symbols and myths that represent the process of spiritual transformation.

The Italian psychiatrist Roberto Assagioli (1888–1974) was a student of Raja Yoga and also of the esotericist Alice Bailey. Assagioli developed a theoretical and practical system of therapy and psychological development called *psychosynthesis*, which incorporates and emphasizes the spiritual dimensions of human experience and represents an attempt to integrate the discoveries of psychoanalysis with those of the spiritual traditions. Assagioli argued that Jung's concept of the collective unconscious does not adequately distinguish between 'higher,' 'middle,' and 'lower' realms of the unconscious. For Assagioli, psychological development involves the exploration and integration (synthesis) of all three realms. In exploring and working with the higher unconscious (the source of, for example, mystical experiences, higher intuitions and aspirations, moral imperatives, altruism, compassion, genius and illumination) Assagioli believed that we may contact the Higher Self (Transpersonal

Self) or the *Atman* (universal Self or Soul of the *Upanishads*). In learning to understand our higher nature and purpose, and to express and manifest the Higher Self, we move beyond personal psychosynthesis (the achievement of a well-integrated personality, centred on the personal ego) to spiritual or *transpersonal psychosynthesis* (the synthesis of personal ego and Higher Self). As a psychological-therapeutic system, psychosynthesis advocates various practical techniques, including meditation and visualization, as aids to transpersonal exploration and integration.

The American psychologist Abraham Maslow (1908–1970) is best known as the founder of humanistic psychology, which he saw as the 'third force' in psychology (the first two forces he identified as behaviourism and psychoanalysis). Humanistic psychology emphasizes human rationality, agency, consciousness, positive mental health, realization of individual potential, and self-actualization. It also seeks to recognize and study the 'higher' human experiences generally ignored or neglected by mainstream psychology. These include love, empathy, creativity, intuition, mystical experience, altruism and compassion. Maslow found that many self-actualizing people report experiences of transcendence (e.g., self-forgetting, 'peak,' or ecstatic experiences, and metamotivation or the desire to actualize universal values). Himself a mystical atheist, Maslow interpreted these transcendent experiences as expressions of our common (essentially biological) human nature. Because of their undoubted reality and significance, he suggested that a psychology should be developed to investigate these phenomena. In the late 1960s, together with his colleagues Stanislav Grof, Anthony Sutich, Miles Vich and others, he proposed the term *transpersonal psychology* for this 'fourth force'. To help realize such a force, the *Journal of Transpersonal Psychology* was launched in 1969, under the editorship of Anthony Sutich, and in 1972 the *Association for Transpersonal Psychology* was established, holding its first conferences the following year (see Sutich, 1969, 1976; Vich, 1990; Walsh, 1993).

Social changes in the 1960s had also contributed to the development of transpersonal psychology. These included the widespread use of psychedelic drugs among the affluent youth of America and Europe. Although this was often little more than a recreational activity, or a way of confirming an anti-establishment, alternative lifestyle and identity, LSD, mescaline and other hallucinogenics were viewed by some as facilitating valid states of spiritual consciousness. In *The Doors of Perception* (1954), the British writer Aldous Huxley had argued that mescaline could be a valuable aid in expanding human consciousness. Also in the 1950s and 1960s, the Czech psychiatrist Stanislav Grof (b. 1930) had pioneered the clinical use of LSD, for example in treating alcoholism and drug addiction. Grof (e.g., 2000) calls the LSD experience *holotropic*, meaning 'orientated towards wholeness' and his research suggests that by accessing and working through holotropic experiences, people are able to achieve greater self-understanding and psychological healing. This occurs not only by releasing biographical material (e.g., lost childhood memories) but, more importantly, by stimulating important and often traumatic *perinatal* experiences associated with various stages of the birth process. Grof also found that, especially with high doses of LSD, people would often report a rich and extraordinary variety of *transpersonal* experiences in which the sense of time, space and self, as well as the normal distinction between mind and matter were drastically altered. Just as William James had concluded from his experiences with nitrous oxide, Grof believed that LSD enabled people to experience 'transpersonal' realities normally hidden from our everyday consciousness. When LSD use became prohibited, Grof discovered that holotropic and transpersonal experiences could be induced using a technique he developed with his wife Christina called *Holotropic Breathwork*^{TM}, which involves lengthy sessions of altered breathing combined with loud evocative music and body work (e.g., Grof, 2000).

From his research on LSD and Holotropic Breathwork, Grof developed a very useful cartography of transpersonal experiences (e.g., Grof, 1988, 2000). Grof's transpersonal 'map' is based on distinctions between:

(a) Experiences that take place *within our consensual space-time reality* but that involve a transcendence of the usual limitations in our experience of space or time or external reference. Experiences involving the transcendence of *spatial* boundaries include identification with other people, with animals, plants, or the cosmos as a whole, consciousness of cellular, atomic or subatomic processes, clairvoyance and remote viewing. Those involving transcendence of *temporal* boundaries include ancestral, fetal, past-life and phylogenetic experiences, and precognition. Experiences involving a transcendence of external reference include physical introversion, states of absorption, and the narrowing of consciousness.

(b) Experiences that take place in a world or dimension that is *beyond consensual space-time reality*. These include spiritistic and mediumistic experiences, subtle-body phenomena, encounters with spirit guides, mythological and fairytale experiences, visits to parallel universes, experiences of blissful or wrathful deities, near-death and archetypal experiences. It is important to recognize that Grof believes that these experienced worlds or dimensions are ontologically real, and not mere subjective fantasies, illusions, or hallucinations (e.g., Grof, 2000).

(c) *Psychoid* experiences in which the normal distinction between mind and matter is transcended. These include synchronicities (meaningful coincidences between psychological and physical events), spontaneous psychoid events (such as supernormal physical feats, physical mediumship, poltergeist phenomena, UFO and alien abduction experiences), and intentional psychokinesis (e.g., ceremonial magic, healing and hexing, the Yogic *siddhis*, and laboratory psychokinesis).

Perhaps the most important contribution made by Grof's psychedelic-holotropic approach to understanding transpersonal experiences is his recognition of their extraordinary range, richness and variety. Transpersonal experience includes, but is not limited to, cosmic consciousness, or to other traditional categories of mystical or religious experience. Also, transpersonal experiences in many cases have no necessary or apparent 'spiritual' quality (for example, cellular consciousness or visits to other times and places) and they include the full gamut of paranormal phenomena (see Chapter 2).

For many people, however, *spirituality* continues to be the hallmark of the transpersonal. In the 1960s, at the same time as the psychedelic movement was at its peak, there was also an explosion of interest in eastern religions (especially Hinduism and Buddhism) and in eastern forms of meditation. Eastern teachings were seen by many westerners as both practical and psychologically sophisticated, and as offering the promise of direct spiritual experience often lacking in traditional occidental religions. These philosophies were not only absorbed into the popular counterculture of the time, but also increasingly came to dominate academic transpersonal psychology through the influence of writers such as Alan Watts, D.T. Suzuki, Sri Aurobindo, Ram Dass, and Chögyam Trungpa. Although Hinduism and Buddhism have had the clearest impact on theory and research in transpersonal psychology, other religious-mystical teachings have also been influential. These include Kabbalah, Christian mysticism, Gurdjieffian philosophy, Shamanism, Sufism, Taoism, Theosophy and Wicca.

From the early 1960s, meditation and other methods of personal transformation such as encounter groups, Yoga, psychodrama, Gestalt therapy, Holotropic Breathwork™ and body work, came to be taught at avant-garde 'growth centres' such as the Esalen Institute (www.esalen.org), which was established at Big Sur, California in 1962. These centres became the focus of what has been called the *human potential movement* — a diffuse, rich, eclectic mix of transformational approaches and technologies that in many ways represents the practical and experientially orientated wing of humanistic and transpersonal psychology.

A number of important developments have occurred in transpersonal psychology since its formal academic foundation in 1969. These include:

(a) Extensive research on altered states of consciousness and into the physiological and psychological effects of meditation (e.g., Murphy & Donovan, 1997).

(b) The attempt to define the nature and role of transpersonal psychology more carefully, including its relationship to other disciplines (e.g., Caplan, Hartelius & Rardin, 2003; Lajoie & Shapiro, 1992; Walsh & Vaughan, 1993a).

(c) The development of epistemologies and research methodologies that are more appropriate to its normative agenda and subject matter (e.g., Braud & Anderson, 1998; Ferrer, 2002).

(d) The creation of intelligible theoretical models of transpersonal states, processes and events (see discussion in the next section).

(e) Working to develop effective methods and practical guidance for people seeking to explore the transpersonal (e.g., Leonard & Murphy, 1995; Murphy, 1992).

(f) The development of transpersonal approaches to psychotherapy, counselling and psychiatry (e.g., Boorstein, 1996; Cortright, 1997).

Transpersonal psychology has also sought acknowledgement and acceptance from the psychological establishment. Although attempts to have Transpersonal Psychology accepted as a Division within the American Psychological Association have, to date, been unsuccessful, various aspects of transpersonal psychology are represented in other APA divisions, principally Division 32: Humanistic Psychology and Division 36: Psychology of Religion. However, in 1996, the British Psychological Society became the first professional psychological association to approve the formation of an academic section in Transpersonal Psychology (www.transpersonalpsychology.org.uk).

As well as the overlap between transpersonal psychology and both humanistic psychology and the psychology of religion, transpersonal psychology also shares much common ground with *consciousness studies* — a rich and rapidly developing area of research with its own history, approaches, methodologies, books and journals (see, for example, Lancaster, 2004; Velmans, 2000). Although some scholars (e.g., Lancaster, 2004) see a strong transpersonal-transformational agenda within consciousness studies (and hence a high degree of overlap with transpersonal psychology), other writers do not (e.g., Dennett, 1991; Velmans, 2000). Certainly the neurophysiological, cognitive and neuropsychological approaches which currently dominate consciousness studies do not seem to me self-evidently *transpersonal* in emphasis, despite Lancaster's (*ibid.*) and others' robust attempts to draw out connections with spiritual-mystical approaches. For this reason, the differences between the disciplines may be more apparent than the similarities. This is perhaps reflected in the fact that the British Psychological Society has a separate academic section in Consciousness and Experiential Psychology.

On the other hand, at Liverpool John Moores University, we have operated a successful and integrated Masters programme in Consciousness and Transpersonal Psychology for many years. A recent development has been the promotion by Martin Seligman (e.g., Seligman & Csikszentmihalyi, 2000; www.positivepsychology.org) of a scientific approach which he calls *Positive Psychology*. This focuses on the study and support of positive emotions (e.g., contentment, happiness, hope), positive individual traits (e.g., the capacity for love and work, courage, compassion, creativity, self-knowledge, self-control, wisdom), and positive institutions (e.g., social justice, teamwork, effective parenting). In many ways positive psychology may be seen as an attempt to re-launch and re-brand humanistic psychology (and aspects of transpersonal psychology) in a more modern, perhaps more corporately-friendly guise (cf. Taylor, 2001). Unfortunately positive psychology itself dismisses humanistic psychology (and by implication transpersonal psychology) as narcissistic, lacking a research tradition and being fundamentally anti-scientific. Taylor (*ibid.*) has shown effectively how these claims are both absurd and unhelpful, and he accuses Seligman of 'rushing to exclude on *a priori* grounds the very tradition his own theory represents' (*ibid.*, p. 13). A creative dialogue and co-operation between positive psychology and humanistic-transpersonal psychology may well become possible. Positive psychology can remind humanistic and transpersonal psychologists of the value of more traditional experimental and questionnaire-based methodologies. In return, humanistic-transpersonal psychology might expand positive psychology's epistemological and methodological straightjacket by emphasizing the value of phenomenological and qualitative research (*ibid.*).

Contemporary Theory in Transpersonal Psychology

The last thirty years have seen major theoretical developments in transpersonal psychology, with the last decade in particular focussing on what are major areas of controversy and disagreement between different theoretical approaches. All theories in transpersonal psychology have the common aims of clarifying our understanding of the nature of transpersonal, and accounting intelligibly for the process of transformation. Some of these theories take a strongly developmental position, in arguing for a sequence of age-related or experience-related stages in the transformational process. Others argue that it is sufficient to identify the basic qualities of transpersonal modes of being and to understand ways in which these may be fully realized in human consciousness and society.

The various theoretical approaches may conveniently be considered in terms of whether they favour (1) a predominantly *immanent, horizontal* or *descending* path of transformation, or (2) a *transcendental, vertical* or *ascending* path (see, for example, Fox, 1990, 1993, 1995; Wilber, 1995a, 1996a; Zimmerman, 1998).

The immanent-horizontal-descending position argues that transformation is to be sought through greater connection to the world of nature, to other people, the body, the feminine, or the dynamic ground of the unconscious. In many ways this tradition represents some of the assumptions behind what the philosopher of religion John Hick (1989) discusses as the *pre-axial* religions. These existed prior to the major and relatively sudden turning point in religious and cultural thought that occurred in the *axial period* (after Jaspers, 1949/1977) around 800–200 BCE with a change of emphasis from living in a state of natural harmony and communal well-being to that of seeking individual salvation and personal spiritual advancement. Pre-axial or primal religions such as animism and shamanism understood the goal of spiritual practice to be the maintenance or restoration of the individual's and group's relationship to the larger natural and supernatural order (individual physical and mental being, groups, nature and the supernatural were all seen as essentially connected). These cultures had no understanding of individual salvation separate from that of the community as a whole, no concept of 'rising above' nature, and no strong belief in evolution or 'progress'. The 'perennial' pre-axial philosophy was therefore basically that of the *interpenetration of the spiritual and natural worlds*. The world of spirit(s) was not, as the term 'supernatural' tends to imply, literally 'above' the natural world, but rather operated in parallel to nature, touching it intimately, even though it might be hidden from view behind a thin veil (cf. James' 'filmiest of screens,' op. cit.). If there is an appropriate symbol of perennial pre-axial philosophy it is probably best expressed as a *Great Circle or Web of Being*.

The axial period (which Jaynes, 1993, argues saw the first truly *self*-conscious persons) itself gave rise to the so-called 'major' organized world religions such as Hinduism, Buddhism, Judaism, Christianity, and Islam. For these post-axial religions, spiritual salvation (primarily of the individual) becomes the predominant concern. Furthermore, the achievement of such salvation is believed to involve the development of the person's supposed 'higher' intellectual and spiritual qualities. For Plato, this involved the full realization of the rational faculties. In Neoplatonism and on the Indian sub-continent, even 'higher,' more refined, mental-spiritual states were conceived. In its most extreme expressions (e.g., in Jainism and Gnosticism), spiritual advancement was seen as involving a complete separation from the material world, from the corruptibility of the body, and from the distractions of ordinary social living, of sensory experience, and of sex (meaning, in practice, of *women*, since spiritual practitioners in these traditions were generally male). In this way, from the perspective of the post-axial traditions, the perennial philosophy was no longer a Great Circle or Web of Being, but came to be conceived rather as a *Great Hierarchy, Ladder or Chain of Being*, from Matter (body, unconscious), to Mind (consciousness, rationality, personality), to Spirit (the transcendent Divine). Spiritual attainment thus essentially involved climbing up this ladder, leaving behind the 'lower' realms, ultimately to realize the sublime heights of Divine Consciousness (e.g., Nirvana, Enlightenment, Union with God, the 'One' of Plotinus). Most commentators on the perennial philosophy (including the early theosophists, Huxley, 1947, Smith, 1976, and Wilber, e.g., 1995a) generally take the *post-axial* version as standard. For this reason, they often find it difficult to appreciate pre-axial and contemporary indigenous religions (cf. Ferrer, 2002; Heron, 1998; Kremer, 1998; Wade, 1996, 2000).

Hence we have two fundamental historical-cultural traditions, paths or currents to contend with in trying to grasp the nature of the transpersonal and of spiritual transformation. Wilber (e.g., 1995a, 1996a) provides a very useful analysis of their differences and oppositions, and these are summarized, with amendments and additions, in Table 1. For convenience I shall, with Wilber, refer to these traditions by the short-hand terms 'ascending' and 'descending,' even though the latter term may perhaps seem pejorative.

Table 1. *Ascending and descending currents
in transpersonal thought and practice.*

ASCENDING	DESCENDING
Post-Axial	Pre-Axial
Organized Religion	Indigenous Religion
Hierarchy	Heterarchy
Vertical	Horizontal
Ladder	Circle/Spiral
Great Chain (Nest) of Being	Great Circle (Web) of Being
Power Over	Power For
Yang	Yin
The One	The Many
Other World	This World
Transcendence	Immanence
Evolving	Involving
Progress	Maintenance
Spirit	Body
Materialized (Entrapped) Spirit	Spiritualized Matter
Ascetic Mysticism	Embodied Mysticism
Head	Heart
Consciousness	The Unconscious
Wisdom	Compassion
Reason	Intuition
Ego	Eco
Solitariness	Relationship
Agency	Communion
Independence	Connection
Male	Female
Patriarchal	Matriarchal/Feminist
God	Goddess
Sky Father	Earth Mother
Wings	Roots

The distinction between ascending and descending currents can be useful when trying to understand the differences between the various theoretical approaches within transpersonal psychology. Jung, for example, through his emphasis on the collective unconscious, may be seen to advocate a more descending approach than Assagioli who talks about the higher unconscious and the higher Self. Maslow, it seems to me, represents more of a balance between the ascending and descending traditions (i.e., his interest in peak and other transcendent states is balanced by theoretically rooting these in human biology). Grof, on the other hand, is more clearly descending because of his emphasis on the perinatal roots of experience and the need to regressively access and work through unconscious material on the path to transformation.

It is not possible, I believe, to categorize theories as *either* ascending *or* descending. It may be possible and useful, however, to locate theories on an ascending-descending *dimension*. I have attempted this as shown in Figure 1. Also shown in Figure 1 are other major contemporary theoretical approaches in transpersonal psychology, to which I now turn.

The most influential (and controversial) contemporary theorist in academic transpersonal psychology is the American philosopher Ken Wilber (b. 1949) although Wilber has recently (2000b, 2002) renounced transpersonal psychology and now prefers to describe his own approach as 'integral'. In a series of brilliant books and articles, beginning with *The Spectrum of Consciousness* (1977), Wilber has developed a conceptual framework of extraordinary breadth, sophistication and wide-ranging application.

In his earliest presentation (1977) Wilber essentially argued for a Jungian model of transformation in which transpersonal development involves the healing of splits within the psyche (e.g., between consciousness and the unconscious) as well as those between mind and body, and individual and cosmos (these splits are believed to have been set up during the process of personality development). Wilber's model at this time was therefore relatively *descending* (see Fig. 1). However in 1980, Wilber rejected this Jungian formulation as failing to acknowledge that something distinctly new (and higher) is added at the transpersonal level. He now sees his own earlier view, and also Jung's approach, as examples of an elevationist *pre/trans fallacy*. This is based on the failure adequately to distinguish between what is prepersonal (e.g., the body, the unconscious), which exist *prior* to the development of personal, egoic consciousness, and what is truly transpersonal (e.g., spiritual structures), which only come

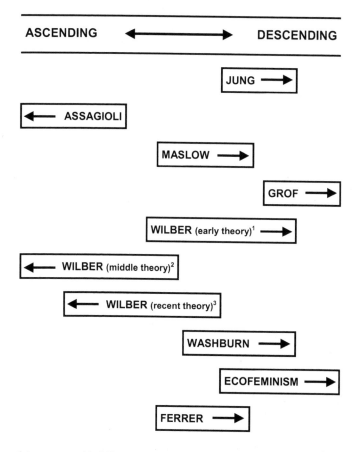

[1] As represented in Wilber (1977)
[2] As represented in Wilber's writings from 1980 to 1994.
[3] As represented in Wilber (1995a) and later writings

Figure 1. Suggested locations of major transpersonal theorists on the ascending-descending dimension.

into being *after* the development of personal structures. In the *elevationist* (retro-Romantic) version of the pre/trans fallacy, Wilber argues that prepersonal experience is elevated to the status of the transpersonal. The opposite *reductionist* version reduces all transpersonal experience to the level of the pre-personal (e.g., Freud).

Wilber's later theory proposes a primarily *ascending* model of transformation (Fig. 1) and is essentially based upon the post-axial version of the perennial philosophy. Thus, for Wilber, the perennial philosophy teaches the *Great Chain of Being* — i.e., the evolutionary relationship of Matter, Mind and Spirit. Wilber (e.g., 1995a) argues that this Great Chain is best understood using Arthur Koestler's (1967) concept of *holons* (wholes which are parts of higher wholes, as protons are parts of atoms which are parts of molecules, etc., or words are parts of sentences which are parts of paragraphs, etc.). Thus the Great Chain of Being is actually a Great *Holarchy* or Great *Nest* (like Russian dolls) of increasing levels of wholeness. In this way, Wilber sees Spirit as higher than but including Mind. Similarly Mind is higher than but includes Matter.

In psychological development (e.g., Wilber, 1996b), this evolu-tionary chain manifests as a progression from *prepersonal* con-sciousness (where there is no sense of self, or a very rudimentary physical one), through *personal* consciousness (involving a strong mental-egoic personality), to *transpersonal* consciousness (involving the expansion of identity beyond the personal, mental-egoic realm). Wilber also identifies successive stages at the transpersonal level. Transpersonal development, he argues, involves movement from *psychic* consciousness (paranormal experiences, nature mysticism) to *subtle* consciousness (e.g., experiencing imaginal, archetypal forms) to *causal* consciousness (formless experience, or transcendent Witnessing), to *ultimate* or *nondual* consciousness (in which the world of form reappears, but is now *directly experienced* as the play or projection of Spirit).

A further important development in Wilber's philosophy came in 1995 (1995a) with the suggestion that consciousness develops not only in the minds of individual persons. To explain his thinking, Wilber makes a distinction between (1) the interior and exterior aspects of any phenomenon, and (2) the individual and collective aspects. By combining these distinctions, Wilber comes up with four *quadrants,* as shown in Table 2. The interior-individual quadrant is that of private mental experience. The exterior-individual represents objective external observation of an individual's behaviour. The interior-collective refers to the worldview or shared understanding found among members of a community. Finally, the exterior-collective quadrant manifests as social systems, institutions, and organizational structures that are observable from outside.

Table 2. Ken Wilber's quadrant model

	INTERIOR	EXTERIOR
INDIVIDUAL	Intentional	Behavioural
COLLECTIVE	Cultural (worldview)	Social (system)

The importance of this model, for Wilber, is to emphasize that all approaches to knowledge and transformation must take into account all four quadrants. We cannot fully understand any phenomenon by looking only at the way it is expressed in one, two, or even three quadrants. Instead we need an 'integral' research agenda that recognizes all four quadrants (also all *levels* of development within these quadrants). In other words we need an all-quadrant, all levels (AQAL) approach. Wilber's current theory also recognizes relatively independent *lines* of development (e.g., intellectual, emotional, psychosexual, moral), different *states* of consciousness, and different *types* of personality. Therefore the AQAL approach is actually shorthand for 'all quadrants, all levels, all lines, all states, all types' (Wilber, 2003, p. xiii).

Wilber's integral approach has important implications for transpersonal psychology not only in regard to epistemology and methodology, but also, more fundamentally, for the way that we understand the process of transformation. Thus, to be integral, transformation must take place in all four quadrants, not just in private individual experience. In recognizing the need for collective-communal transformation (in the real world, in people's worldviews, as well as in social-political systems), Wilber's integral approach can perhaps be seen to represent in some sense a move towards a more descending understanding of spirituality. However, to the extent that Wilber maintains his belief in holarchical-hierarchical levels of development, his approach still remains predominantly ascending (Fig. 1).

In contrast to Wilber's structural-hierarchical model of transpersonal development, professor of philosophy Michael Washburn's model (e.g., 1990, 1994, 1995, 1998, 2003a, 2003b) is based on a *spiral-dynamic*[3] perspective. Washburn's theory essentially represents a reworking and extension of the Jungian and Grofian approach to the transpersonal. Washburn accepts, with Wilber, that there are three major phases in development, i.e. the prepersonal (preegoic), personal (egoic) and transpersonal (transegoic) but, according to Washburn, the transpersonal phase does not involve the formation of any new developmental *structures*. For Washburn there are just two structures involved in development. These are the dynamic ground (or nonegoic core) and the ego. The dynamic ground is the fundamental source of psychic energy, instincts, and creative imagination and it exists at the preegoic phase in a relatively undifferentiated and unconscious state. With the emergence of egoic consciousness, the dynamic ground becomes repressed by the ego (i.e., it then becomes the deep unconscious). The result of this is to cut off the ego from the potential energies and creativity of the dynamic ground. In the transpersonal phase, the ego turns back to face the dynamic ground and undergoes a spiralling, often disturbing, *regression in the service of transcendence*. This reconnects the ego to the dynamic potentials of the ground. With the full integration of ego and dynamic ground, the person becomes *regenerated in Spirit* and the dynamic potentials of the core are now expressed in their transpersonal forms. Washburn argues (2003a) that this spiral-dynamic perspective is not, as Wilber claims, based on an elevationist pre/trans fallacy because the dynamic ground contains only *potentially* transpersonal energies at the preegoic phase. These only become truly transpersonal when, following egoic development, they are re-experienced and integrated with the ego.

Recently Washburn (2003a) has conceded that the structural-hierarchical perspective of Wilber may be needed in order to

3   This should not be confused with 'Spiral Dynamics' (Beck & Cowan, 1996) which itself represents a structural-hierarchical approach to understanding the development of value systems within organizations and societies.

understand the cognitive and volitional aspects of ego development. However the spiral-dynamic perspective, he maintains, is better placed to explain dynamic potentials (e.g., emotion, creativity) and is 'the proper vehicle for explaining transcendence' (*ibid.*, p. 5). Washburn's theory therefore remains relatively descending in its approach.

Another important approach to transpersonal theory is that of transpersonal or radical ecology and, particularly, the closely related perspective of ecofeminism (e.g., Anderson & Hopkins, 1991; Chittister, 1998; Fox, 1993, 1995; Heron, 1998; Kremer, 1998; Metzner, 1999; Wright, 1995, 1998a; Zimmerman, 1994). Rather than focussing on stages of transpersonal development, these approaches emphasize the need to radically alter our ways of knowing and being in the direction of greater ecological awareness and responsibility, more sensitivity to women's experience of the sacred, and the recognition of the value of the spiritualities of indigenous peoples. The ecofeminists reject the post-axial version of the perennial philosophy (and structural-hierarchical models in particular) as patriarchal, androcentric and imperialist. In contrast, ecofeminists ally themselves more or less fully with the assumptions of pre-axial philosophy (i.e., the interpenetration of the spiritual and natural worlds; the Great Circle or Web of Being). This approach therefore represents an almost entirely descending approach to transformation.

The final theory I wish to consider here is that of Jorge Ferrer (2000, 2002, 2005). In his important book *Revisioning Transpersonal Theory* (2002), Ferrer provides a telling critique and deconstruction of transpersonal psychology. This deconstruction focuses particularly on what Ferrer sees as the errors of (1) *experientialism* (focussing on intrasubjective experiences and states of consciousness), (2) *inner empiricism* (the felt need to ground transpersonal inquiry in disciplined introspection and intersubjective consensus), and (3) *perennialism* (the assumption of a universally held core spiritual understanding). Ferrer argues forcefully that these three assumptions, while they may have once been useful, are now major obstacles to further progress in transpersonal theory. In their place, Ferrer advocates a *participatory vision* of human spirituality. By this he means that transpersonal phenomena are not essentially intrasubjective experiences, but rather *multilocal participatory events* (like a party) that are cocreated and arise not only in individual experience, but also in relationships, communities, and even places. Transpersonal phenomena are therefore created through our individual and collective interactions with the world. These phenomena arise not simply in each person's own experience but also in the space created by our interrelationships with each other and with the world.

The recognition of the participatory nature of transpersonal knowing is a useful antidote, Ferrer suggests, to the dangers of spiritual narcissism and the failure to integrate the transpersonal in everyday life. Indeed, for Ferrer, the essential hallmark of spiritual transformation is the *emancipation from self-centredness*. This in turn allows movement towards greater participation in the Mystery of existence which can result in a 'transconceptual disclosure of reality' (2002, p. 145). Most significant, perhaps, is Ferrer's insistence that there is no universal or perennial disclosure, but rather that we need to recognize a multiplicity of such disclosures. As he eloquently puts it: '*the Ocean of Emancipation has many shores*' (ibid., p. 147). Furthermore, 'the view that I am advancing here is that *no pregiven ultimate reality exists, and that different spiritual ultimates can be enacted through intentional or spontaneous creative participation in an indeterminate spiritual power or Mystery*' (ibid., p. 151, italics in original). Thus Allah, Jehovah, the Kingdom of Heaven, Tao, Nirvana, Enlightenment, Brahman, Atman-Brahman, the Original Self of Zen, etc. each represents a *different* spiritual ultimate that is cocreated within the context of a particular spiritual tradition through its participation in a spiritual power that remains essentially indefinable and mysterious (cf. Hick, 1989).

Ferrer's spiritual pluralism is not, however, entirely open ended, relativistic or value-free. Thus he argues that transconceptual disclosures and cocreated spiritual ultimates are themselves constrained by 'the spiritual power or Mystery out of which everything arises which, although indeterminate, does impose restrictions on human visionary participation' (Ferrer, 2002, p. 152). It is also possible, Ferrer suggests, to evaluate spiritual teachings and traditions on the basis of the degree to which they emancipate people from narcissism and self-centredness, and foster the quality of selfless awareness.

Ferrer's pluralistic and participatory vision is fully consistent with ecofeminist and indigenous epistemologies, and Ferrer himself acknowledges, for example, that self-centredness can be overcome through 'the commitment to visionary service and healing in many forms of shamanism' (*ibid.*, p. 145). In his openness to multiple ways of approaching the transpersonal (including both descending and ascending paths), Ferrer's perspective may be considered relatively even-handed on this dimension. Because of his primary emphasis on the *participatory* nature of transpersonal knowing, however, I have tipped the scales in Ferrer's case slightly in the direction of the descending current (Fig. 1).

These various contemporary theoretical approaches are evidence, I believe, for the growing maturity of the discipline, and its ability to acknowledge and discuss openly major differences of approach in epistemology, methodology and soteriology. There are, of course, no final answers to the debates that I have outlined here and no doubt each reader will have her or his own 'take' on the issues discussed. I hope that this brief outline has stimulated and kept your interest and that you will find the more developed and focussed discussions in the rest of this book to be of interest and value. For now, I shall finish with a few indications of opportunities for further study and other resources in transpersonal psychology.

Resources in Transpersonal Psychology

For people wishing to study transpersonal psychology, academic courses are taught at several universities and institutes (mainly in the United States and Britain), with postgraduate programmes being offered, for example, by the Institute of Transpersonal Psychology (www.itp.edu/), the California Institute of Integral Studies (www.ciis.edu/), Naropa University (www.naropa.edu/) , Saybrook Graduate School and Research Center (www.saybrook.edu/), John F. Kennedy University (www.jfku.edu/) and Liverpool John Moores University (www.ljmu.ac.uk). There are also training programmes in transpersonal counselling and psychotherapy offered by various independent organizations, including those based on Jungian, Buddhist and psychosynthesis approaches. Consistent with the general transpersonal ethic, an important feature of both academic study and professional training in transpersonal psychology is the way in which courses typically include an emphasis on students' own experiential learning and personal transformation. The major journals in transpersonal psychology include the *Journal of Transpersonal Psychology* (www.atpweb.org/journal.asp), *Journal of Humanistic Psychology* (www.ahpweb.org/pub/journal/menu.html), *ReVision*, the *Journal of Consciousness Studies* (www.imprint.co.uk/jcs.html), and the *International Journal of Transpersonal Studies* (www.saybrook.edu/about_saybrook/publications.asp?strMedia=ijts). The BPS section in Transper- sonal Psychology also produces the *Transpersonal Psychology Review* (www.transpersonalpsychology.org.uk/tpr.html).

Transpersonal psychology is also well represented outside mainstream academia. Organizations include the Association for Transpersonal Psychology (www.atpweb.org) and the European Transpersonal Association (www.eurotas.org). EUROTAS is itself a parent organization for transpersonal associations throughout Europe. Other organizations with a strong transpersonal approach include the Institute of Noetic Sciences (www.ions.org), and the Scientific and Medical Network (www.datadiwan.de/SciMedNet/home.htm).

Chapter 2

Transpersonal Psychology and the Paranormal

In this chapter I wish to consider two main questions:

1. What is the relationship between paranormal and transpersonal experience?

2. What is the relationship between transpersonal psychology and parapsychology?

In the course of this discussion I shall also re-address a number of related issues such as the nature of the transpersonal, the definition and purpose of transpersonal psychology, and the role and value of transpersonal experiences in the transpersonal life.

The Transpersonal and the Paranormal

To provide an initial reference point for the later discussion, I have selected two extracts of accounts of unusual experiences.

> Quite early in the night I was awakened ... I felt as if I had been aroused intentionally, and at first thought some one was breaking into the house ... I then turned on my side to go

---

This chapter is a revised and updated version of Daniels (1998)

to sleep again, and immediately felt a consciousness of a presence in the room, and singular to state, it was not the consciousness of a live person, but of a spiritual presence. This may provoke a smile, but I can only tell you the facts as they occurred to me. I do not know how to better describe my sensations than by simply stating that I felt a consciousness of a spiritual presence ... I felt also at the same time a strong feeling of superstitious dread, as if something strange and fearful were about to happen (E. Gurney: *Phantasms of the Living*, cited in James, 1901/1960, p. 76–77).

As I was looking on, she (Saint Teresa) was raised about half a yard from the ground without her feet touching it. At this I was terrified, and she, for her part, was trembling all over. So I moved over to where she was and I put my hands under her feet, over which I remained weeping for something like half an hour while the ecstasy lasted. Then suddenly she sank down and rested on her feet and turning her head round to me, she asked me who I was, and whether I had been there all the while (Anne of the Incarnation at Segovia, cited in Broughton, 1991, p. 53).

An interesting aspect of these experiences, to which I wish to draw attention, is the way in which each has elements that could be considered both 'transpersonal' and 'paranormal'. In the first account, for example, there is the sense of a presence, which is spooky and frightening and yet also 'spiritual'. In the second case, St. Teresa's spiritual ecstasy is accompanied by an apparently paranormal bodily levitation. This combination of spiritual and paranormal features seems to be a common feature of a whole range of extraordinary phenomena, from shamanic ecstasy to near-death experiences, UFO encounters and alien abductions (cf., for example, Braud, 1997; Grof, 2000; Grosso, 1997, 2001; Rao, 1997; Tart, 2004; White, 1997).

Throughout history, and in most cultures, the paranormal has been an important feature of human experience that has almost always been intimately connected in some way with religion and spirituality, whether considered an aspect of the divine and/or demonic. Some obvious examples of these connections are divination and oracles, voices and visions, stigmata, magic and miracles, hauntings and apparitions, spirit journeys, supernatural encounters, possession, and the wide range of mediumistic and spiritualistic phenomena.

It is only relatively recently that the realm of the paranormal has been largely stripped of its spiritual context in western industrialized culture. This has resulted, for some, in a complete sceptical dismissal of the paranormal, on the scientific materialist grounds that the world is a physical, rational place in which there is no room for either the spiritual or the 'paranormal' (which, almost by definition, cannot exist). For others, notably the parapsychologists, it has resulted in the attempt to view the paranormal as comprising a range of natural and lawful phenomena that exist as anomalies, just outside the current boundaries of scientific knowledge. From this perspective, parapsychology is promoted as a form of leading-edge scientific exploration.[1]

Yet despite this humanistic and scientific perspective, it has proved rather difficult, even in modern society, to divorce the area of the paranormal completely from that of religion. The early history of the Society for Psychical Research (founded 1882), the first organization devoted to scientific investigation of the paranormal, shows that, for a large number of the founder members, the primary purpose of such study was an attempt to prove the reality of religious belief in life after death. Thirteen of the nineteen members of the first Council were spiritualists, even though most of the research was carried out by non-spiritualists (Nicol, 1982).

Conversely, a significant number of the key figures in transpersonal psychology have had a serious interest in the paranormal or the occult. We may begin with William James, who as well as being one of the earliest pioneers of transpersonal psychology, was a member of the Society for Psychical Research, and himself carried out scientific investigations of the celebrated trance medium Mrs Leonora Piper (1859–1950) which he began in 1885 (Murphy & Ballou, 1961).

---

1 Ironically perhaps, this scientific and humanistic perspective on the paranormal was first proposed by Prospero Lambertini (1675–1758) who carried out extensive research into paranormal phenomena on behalf of the Church and who, in 1740, became Pope Benedict XIV (see Haynes, 1970). Lambertini concluded that most paranormal experiences are neither divine nor demonic but are simply unknown natural phenomena or the result of natural human abilities. This 'enlightened' view undoubtedly enabled and sanctioned later scientific studies of Mesmerism and other supposedly paranormal phenomena, even though most scientists then, as now, chose to ignore this area of research.

James, in fact, saw no fundamental distinction between the areas of the paranormal and religion. Thus he writes in his classic *The Varieties of Religious Experience* (1901/1960, p. 69):

> Were one asked to characterize the life of religion in the broadest and most general terms possible, one might say that it consists of the belief that there is an unseen order, and that our supreme good lies in harmoniously adjusting ourselves thereto.

James is careful to define the notion of an 'unseen order' in a way that includes phenomena generally associated with the area of the paranormal. For example, he goes on to recount a number of experiences of 'presence' and apparitions such as the one cited earlier, in which the paranormal aspects are at least as apparent as the spiritual or religious.

Another important figure in this context is Carl Jung, whose archetypal psychology remains one of the most influential approaches in the study of the transpersonal. Jung had a life-long interest in the paranormal and himself regularly experienced psychic phenomena, including visions and apparitions, weird synchronistic events, premonitions, telepathic communications, psychokinetic phenomena, and also a powerful series of visionary near-death type experiences in early 1944 which followed a heart attack.[2] Jung's doctoral dissertation (1902) was a study of the mediumistic trances of his fifteen-year old cousin Hélène Preiswerk, and one of the major reasons that Jung eventually broke with Sigmund Freud was the latter's uncompromisingly dismissive and aggressive attitude to the 'Occult'.[3]

---

2   After several weeks, Jung recovered and was allowed to sit up for the first time on 4th April 1944. On the same day, his doctor was taken ill and died a few days later. Jung felt, with considerable guilt, that he had himself somehow cheated death, and that the poor doctor had been taken in his place. For Jung, the numerological symmetry of the date (4.4.44) was also a profoundly significant synchronicity. His work in later years focussed extensively on exploring the archetype of the quaternity (the principle of four) which Jung understood to be an expression of wholeness, balance and self-realization (see Bair, 2003; Jung, 1983; McLynn, 1997).

3   The occasion of one of Jung's most interesting and celebrated paranormal experiences was a heated debate with Freud on the topic of precognition and parapsychology during Jung's second visit to Freud's home in Vienna. 'While Freud was going on this way, I had a curious sensation. It was as if my diaphragm were made of iron and were becoming red-hot —

In the modern era a number of important figures in transpersonal psychology also have a serious interest in parapsychology and the paranormal. These include Stan Grof, Willis Harman, Charles Tart and David Fontana who, as well as being Founding Chair of the BPS Transpersonal Psychology section, is past President of the Society for Psychical Research.

If we look beyond the personalities involved to the content of the two areas, it becomes clear that the realm of the paranormal continues to overlap extensively with that of the transpersonal. Rhea White, for example, prefers to abolish any clear distinction between paranormal and transpersonal by talking instead of the variety of *exceptional human experiences* (EHE) which 'is a global term for what have been called mystical, psychic, peak and flow experiences' (White, 1997, p. 83). Although EHEs come in five main classes (mystical experience, psychic experience, encounter-type experience, death-related experience, and exceptional normal experience), White (*ibid.*) argues that it is not possible to make clear distinctions between what is psychic/paranormal and what is mystical/spiritual. In practice this is readily confirmed by the large range of topics that are investigated by both parapsychologists and transpersonal psychologists (see also Neher, 1990). Among the most important of these we may note those listed in Table 3.

Of course, even though these topic areas are common to both parapsychology and transpersonal psychology, the particular research questions, approaches, epistemologies and methodologies of the two disciplines may be quite different. This is one of the issues that I wish to address in this chapter. Before we can understand this fully, however, we need to begin by digressing briefly in order to consider the definition of transpersonal psychology.

---

a glowing vault. And at that moment there was such a loud report in the bookcase, which stood right next to us, that we both started up in alarm, fearing the thing was going to topple over on us. I said to Freud: 'There, that is an example of a so-called catalytic exteriorisation phenomenon.'/ 'Oh come,' he exclaimed. 'That is sheer bosh.'/'It is not,' I replied. 'You are mistaken, Herr Professor. And to prove my point I now predict that in a moment there will be another loud report!' Sure enough, no sooner had I said the words than the same detonation went off in the bookcase ... Freud stared aghast at me.' Jung (1983), p. 178–179.

Table 3. Areas of common interest in transpersonal psychology and parapsychology

Auras and subtle energy systems

Channeling and mediumistic experiences

Experiences of Angels

Experiences of synchronicity

Lucid dreaming

Near death experiences (NDE)

Out of body experience (OOBE)

Past life memories

Possession

Prophecy and precognition

Reincarnation experiences

Sense of Presence

Shamanic experience

Spiritual healing

Stigmata, and other bodily transformations

Telepathy, clairvoyance and the 'siddhis'

Trance

Experiences of UFOs, alien contact or abduction

Psychokinetic phenomena

Witchcraft and magic

The Transpersonal and Transpersonal Psychology

As we have seen, the term 'transpersonal' first became widely used in the late 1960s to refer to areas of human experience which seem to take the person beyond the normal boundaries of the personal domain to the realm traditionally associated with religion, spirituality, meditation and mysticism.

From a comprehensive survey of 40 definitions published from 1968–1991, Lajoie & Shapiro (1992) identified five key themes or concepts that they believe characterize transpersonal psychology. These are:

* An interest in states of consciousness.
* A concern with humanity's highest or ultimate potential.
* The notion that human experience may develop beyond ego or personal self.
* The related notion of transcendence.
* The importance of the spiritual dimension in human life.

On this basis, Lajoie & Shapiro (*ibid.*, p. 91) define transpersonal psychology as:

> ... concerned with the study of humanity's highest potential, and with the recognition, understanding, and realization of unitive, spiritual, and transcendent states of consciousness.

However, as Walsh & Vaughan (1993a) argue, states of consciousness do not define the field. For example, prayer, compassionate action, selfless love, and spiritual healing, may be considered to be transpersonal phenomena, but they are not precisely 'altered states of consciousness,' if only because they clearly involve a strong behavioural component. Rather, as Ferrer (e.g., 2002) argues, transpersonal phenomena are better understood as participatory *events* rather than inner experiences. Furthermore, the notion of 'highest potential' is problematic. For example, how can we ever know what is the highest unless we impose some *a priori* perspective? There is also the related problem that such a definition makes particular metaphysical assumptions, for example about the existence of a transcendent spiritual reality or the importance of 'unitive experience'.

Walsh & Vaughan (1993a) also make the important point that, in practice, much of the concern in transpersonal psychology is patently not with the highest or even the 'spiritual'. For example, there is a growing interest in 'trough' rather than 'peak' experiences, such as the spiritual emergencies, or the dark night of the soul (e.g., Grof, 2000; Grof & Grof, 1995; Hale, 1992; Steele, 1994). Also there are many realms of experience that may be 'transpersonal' in the sense that the person appears to be taken 'beyond the self' but in other respects could be considered to be primitive or regressive. Perhaps the clearest examples may be seen in Grof's (e.g., 1988, 2000) comprehensive list of transpersonal experiences, based on his work with LSD and Holotropic Breathwork. Thus Grof includes in his list:

- Identification with Animals
- Identification with Plants and Botanical Processes
- Experience of Inanimate Matter and Inorganic Processes
- Embryonal and Fetal Experiences
- Ancestral Experiences
- Past Incarnation Experiences
- Phylogenetic Experiences
- Spiritistic and Mediumistic Experiences
- Experiences of Animal Spirits

The important question here, of course, is whether such experiences should be counted as genuinely transpersonal, or whether they are, as Wilber (e.g., 1980, 1996c, 1997) would argue, largely *prepersonal*. I shall return to this issue in a moment, but in the meantime wish to observe that there is a danger in Lajoie & Shapiro's position that we may be tempted to smuggle in our own religious preferences and prejudices and to consider only certain sorts of experiences as genuinely 'spiritual'. Thus certain forms of experience may be rejected because, for example, they do not conform to a particular theological or metaphysical view. In this way indigenous, shamanic, mediumistic or spiritist experience may be dismissed by some as primitive forms of religion that have no genuine or 'higher' spiritual or transpersonal value (cf. Kremer, 1998). It may be further argued by such people that transpersonal psychology should study only the kind of exalted and refined states of consciousness achieved by the Christian, Jewish or Sufi mystics or by certain advanced Yogis or meditators.

Because of these kinds of difficulties in the definition of the transpersonal, Walsh & Vaughan (1993a) prefer to approach this from a position that makes as few metaphysical and evaluative assumptions as possible. Their own preferred definition is:

> *Transpersonal experiences* may be defined as experiences in which the sense of identity or self extends beyond (trans.) the individual or personal to encompass wider aspects of humankind, life, psyche or cosmos (*ibid.*, p. 203, emphasis in original; cf. Walsh & Vaughan 1993b. p. 3).

In my view this definition provides a useful 'neutral' position from which to approach this whole area. It also provides a context for considering the central issues addressed in this chapter concerning the relationship between the transpersonal and the paranormal.

The Transpersonal and the Extrapersonal

Grof's (e.g., 1988, 2000) list of transpersonal experiences includes a considerable number of experiences of a clearly 'paranormal' kind (Table 4).

Although Grof accepts these paranormal experiences as genuinely transpersonal, several influential writers seek to disagree or to reformulate the problem. John Rowan (1993) develops a distinction made by Green & Green (1986) between the transpersonal and the 'extrapersonal'. Rowan's main purpose in doing this, it seems, is to attempt to distance transpersonal psychology from certain tendencies that he identifies with the popular new-age and other related movements. Rowan illustrates this distinction with some examples of approaches and experiences that he divides into the two camps. Extrapersonal, he suggests, includes spoon bending, levitation, ESP, dowsing, working with crystals, fire-walking, OBE, fakirism and mind over matter. The transpersonal, on the other hand, includes the higher self, inner teacher, high archetypes, creativity, the soul, the superconscious, upper chakras, and subtle energy systems.

At first sight, and at one level, I can see what Rowan is getting at here, and I accept that it is important to try to make some such distinction. However, I do not agree with the way that Green & Green, or Rowan, attempt to conceptualize the matter. Green & Green argue that the difference is basically between the divine and non-divine (spiritual vs. non-spiritual). This is a problematic position to adopt for many reasons. Firstly, as argued above, much of the interest that many of us have in transpersonal psychology is manifestly not with the divine or spiritual as generally conceived, or is only arguably so (e.g., trough experiences, lucid dreams, creative inspiration, experiences of love and merging). Secondly, as Rowan recognizes, this view is difficult because it could be argued (as does Wilber, 1997) that nothing is really non-divine.

Table 4. Transpersonal experiences of a paranormal kind
(after Grof, 1988)

Past incarnation experiences

Psychic phenomena involving transcendence of time

Spiritistic and mediumistic experiences

Energetic phenomena of the subtle body (chakras)

Experiences of animal spirits

Encounters with spirit guides and suprahuman beings

Visits to other universes and meetings with their inhabitants

Synchronistic links between consciousness and matter

Supernormal physical feats

Spiritistic phenomena and physical mediumship

Recurrent spontaneous psychokinesis (poltergeist)

Unidentified flying objects (UFO phenomena)

Ceremonial magic

Healing and hexing

Siddhis

Laboratory psychokinesis

Despite this reservation, Rowan is tempted to concur with the thrust of Green & Green's position although he prefers to psychologize the matter using Wilber's (e.g., 1996b) distinction between the 'low subtle' (psychic) and the 'high subtle' (archetypal-divine) levels of the spectrum of consciousness. Yet, paradoxically, this seriously undermines and confuses the distinction between transpersonal and extrapersonal. According to Wilber (e.g., 1996b), the 'low subtle' level is (by definition and within the framework of the spectrum model) *transpersonal* — i.e., it is beyond the 'Centaur' level of existential authenticity and individuation and is therefore of legitimate concern to transpersonal psychology. Rowan may quite justifiably claim that his own interest in the transpersonal goes beyond the psychic or low subtle level, but that does not mean that the low subtle is somehow extrapersonal rather than transpersonal and therefore outside the brief of transpersonal psychology.

As mentioned above, in my view a distinction between extra-personal and transpersonal is important, but I believe that it needs to be conceptualized in different terms from those proposed by Rowan, or Green & Green.

Transpersonal, Psychic and Religious Experience

If, following Walsh & Vaughan's (1993a) example, we define the area of the transpersonal in terms of experiences where the sense of identity or self extends beyond the individual or personal, then this has certain important methodological and conceptual implications. Perhaps most important is the need to approach the transpersonal from the perspective of the experiencer rather than from any *a priori*, external set of assumptions or beliefs. Thus if, for the individual, an experience has the consequence of extending his or her sense of identity or self beyond the purely personal, then such an experience is, according to this definition, transpersonal. This is true irrespective of the particular trigger, content or context of the experience. It could, for example, be the result of a telepathic experience, or a UFO encounter, or visiting a clairvoyant, or walking over live coals, or even watching a spoon mysteriously bend on a TV show. If the effect of this experience is in some way to transform the person's sense of self to encompass a wider or deeper reality, then I would argue that the experience is genuinely transpersonal.

In this way, I am attempting to define the distinction between the extrapersonal and transpersonal not in terms of its manifest content, but in terms of its form — i.e., the *transformational meaning or effect* that it has on the person (cf. Ferrer, 2002; Lancaster, 2004). For this reason it is not possible, I believe, to draw up precise lists of experiences that are extrapersonal and/or transpersonal, based purely on considering the phenomenological content or context of the experience. In this sense, therefore, there is a basic flaw in the approach adopted by Rowan.

In my opinion, a psychic experience may be genuinely transpersonal-transformational (although my guess is that most are not). Conversely, apparently 'spiritual' or religious activities such as prayer or meditation may, for many people, have absolutely no transformational effect whatsoever. In these cases we should not, I believe, consider such experiences to be truly transpersonal, even though the content and context of the experience is religious or spiritual.

This is one important way in which transpersonal psychology may be considered quite distinct from the psychology of religion (cf. Fontana, 2003). For example, the question of what social factors influence people to engage in religious practices, or how religious belief develops in childhood, or the different psychological patterns of religious behaviour, are the legitimate concern of the psychology of religion. They are, however, of only incidental interest in transpersonal psychology, because they do not directly address the issue of transformation of the self beyond the purely personal. Conversely, transpersonal psychology will take an interest in the processes by which the sense of identity can develop beyond the personal, irrespective of whether or not this transformation occurs within a religious or obviously 'spiritual' context. If people are transformed in this way by watching movies or TV soap operas then, as transpersonal psychologists, we should be interested. If we are not, then I fear that we simply reveal our own prejudices and spiritual snobbery.

The Pre/Trans Fallacy

It should be clear that I am not arguing that *any* kind of personal transformation equates with transpersonal development, but only transformation that extends our sense of identity beyond the personal to encompass a wider reality. In other words the kinds of profound personality transformations that may result, for example, from degenerative disease, strokes or other brain damage are not (generally) transpersonal. In this way I believe it is important to recognize, *in some sense*, the distinction emphasized by Wilber (e.g., 1980, 1996c) in his discussions of the 'pre/trans fallacy'. Wilber argues that theoretical and practical confusion arises in this area if we do not acknowledge the difference between prepersonal and transpersonal phases of development. The prepersonal phase exists before the individual has fully achieved a stable sense of selfhood and personal identity, or has permanently regressed to more primitive, childlike states. In contrast, the transpersonal phase represents a genuine progressive evolution beyond the personal level. One important way of recognizing the difference is that at the prepersonal, the individual has no clearly defined sense of self to draw on and therefore is fragile and unintegrated in experience. At the transpersonal, on the other hand, the sense of self is transcended (and may be *temporarily* suspended in mystical states) but is not permanently lost or destroyed. One way of putting this is to suggest that, with transpersonal development, the person no longer exclusively *identifies* with the mental ego or 'personality' but instead the ego-personality system becomes a vehicle for the expression of transpersonal potentials. In practice this means that the person who has developed transpersonal awareness operates from the position of a stable, integrated self that is, however, also in touch with a deeper or more extended reality. The transpersonal therefore transcends and includes the personal, whereas the prepersonal is a primitive anticipation or permanent reversion that excludes the personal.

The Prepersonal and the Paranormal

One of the reasons that Rowan and others may be tempted to dismiss the 'psychic' and paranormal is the belief that these represent primitive or prepersonal modes of experience which, for this reason, are not genuinely transpersonal. The problem with this argument, however, is that it is based solely on examining the content or context of the experience, rather than its underlying structure, meaning or form.

I agree with Wilber (e.g., 1996a, 1996b, 1996d) that many forms of magical and mythical thinking are prepersonal because the sense of self has not yet fully differentiated from the body, the natural world and from social roles.[4] This is true whether these modes of thought are manifested ontogenetically in early childhood, or phylogenetically in the course of human evolution. There is a danger in this view, however, that we may be tempted to attribute any and all experiences of a seemingly transpersonal nature that occur in childhood, or in earlier periods of history, or in present day indigenous societies, to prepersonal structures of magical or mythic thinking (cf. Ferrer, 2002; Kremer, 1998).

Wilber himself recognizes this danger (e.g., 1996d, 1997) and he is careful to argue that some forms of at least quasi-transpersonal experiences are possible in childhood (i.e., before the stable sense of personal identity has been achieved). In such cases, however, these are either temporary states (i.e., not integrated structurally into the personality) or else represent the 'trailing clouds of glory'[5] of the 'eternal indestructible drop' that, in Buddhism, is believed to continue from our previous existences. In

---

4   'Differentiated' means that the self is no longer completely (sub)merged or identified with the body, natural world, or social roles. At the personal phase of development the achievement of such differentiation can lead to a dissociation of the mental ego from the body, world or other people which can produce a sense of alienation (cf. Washburn, 1994, 1995). Transpersonal development (according to Washburn) involves overcoming this dissociation and alienation in the achievement of an integrated relationship between mind and body, conscious and unconscious, self and Other (*ibid.*). This helps us to understand, I think, the important difference between (1) prepersonal (superstitious) magical thought and practice and (2) genuinely transpersonal forms of archetypal-intuitive experience. The former (prepersonal) is based on the failure to understand the distinction between self and world, or between subjective and objective realities. The latter (transpersonal) is based on appreciating the distinction between but also recognizing the *subtle interconnectedness* or mutual relationship of self and Other. As Washburn (2003a) points out, however, both magical-symbolic (primary process) and archetypal (tertiary process) cognition may represent the different prepersonal and transpersonal expressions of 'a single dynamic potential: the autosymbolic process or symbol-producing imagination' (*ibid.*, p. 13).

5   From a line in Wordsworth's poem *Intimations of Immortality from Recollections of Early Childhood* (1807): 'Not in entire forgetfulness, / And

the latter case, therefore, transpersonal experiences in childhood may reflect a kind of karmic trace memory of transpersonal achievements from another life, carried forward into this life via the eternal indestructible drop, 'soul,' or 'psychic being' (cf. Aurobindo, 1970; Dalal, 2001).

In the course of human evolution, the matter is rather more complicated. Wilber (e.g., 1996d) argues that we must distinguish between (1) the ordinary mode of consciousness generally achieved by individuals within a particular stage of evolution, and (2) the advanced mode of consciousness that this evolutionary stage makes possible for the more enlightened members of the society. Wilber's argument is complex, detailed and controversial but, for example, he believes that even in the animistic and magical hunter-gatherer societies of the Palaeolithic period, experiences of psychic awareness and shamanic ecstasy were possible (the low subtle). However, experiences of blissful union with the archetypal-divine (the high subtle) were not — these became possible only with the development of settled farming communities in the Neolithic and Bronze Age periods. Causal consciousness (formless Witnessing), he argues, arose for the first time not until the Iron Age.

One point that I want to emphasize from this is that 'magical thinking' is not the same as psychic or paranormal experience. Magical thinking (as understood by Wilber) is prepersonal because it is based on a failure to fully differentiate the self from the natural and social worlds. Psychic experience, on the other hand, is an aspect of the low subtle which is transpersonal in the sense that it implies an opening up to a *relationship between self and an unseen reality* that exists beyond the purely material, personal or social worlds. It is possibly true that psychic awareness and shamanic ecstasy (rather than states of mystical union with the archetypal-divine) originated in earlier stages of human evolution but nevertheless they are (at least potentially) transpersonal-transformational and, as transpersonal psychologists, they are worthy of our serious consideration. Indeed one way of reading Wilber's spectrum model is to conclude that psychic experience (the low subtle) may be a primary or initial gateway to the transpersonal. This is true, I believe, for many people

not in utter nakedness, / But trailing clouds of glory do we come / From God, who is our home'.

in our society today, for whom psychic experiences may be more common and more profound than the more abstract, refined and often seemingly unattainable states reported by long-term meditators, high Yogis or Christian saints.

If someone experiences telepathic communication, or has an out-of-body, or near-death experience, or receives a chanelled message from their long-deceased mother, or experiences healing, then this may very well make them consider the meaning of their life and current preoccupations in a different light. This might then lead to the kind of fundamental personal transformation that, I believe, is the true hallmark of the transpersonal. In the case of the near-death experience, there is considerable evidence that such transformation is quite typical. People who have these experiences therefore often report that the experience has changed their life in a transpersonal direction — for example, it has made them more interested in spiritual matters, or less materialistic, or more compassionate, or less afraid of death, or simply a 'better' person (e.g., Fenwick & Fenwick, 1995; Irwin, 2004; Van Lommel, van Wees, Meyers, & Elfferich, 2001).

The Low Subtle and the Siddhis

It is important to realize, however, that a psychic or other 'paranormal' experience is not necessarily transformational and, in fact, may be rarely so. In this sense, therefore, even though technically within Wilber's model, psychic experiences are 'low subtle' (and hence transpersonal) this does not, in my opinion, mean that they are necessarily transpersonal-transformational in their effects. This is a general problem with Wilber's model and also, I believe, with other approaches that attempt to define the transpersonal in terms of obtaining certain experiences or the achievement of specific states of consciousness (e.g., Grof, 1988; Tart, 1975). If a 'transpersonal' experience has no transformational effect, then it has simply been an entertaining diversion. This is true, I believe, no matter how extraordinary, ecstatic, delightful, or profound the experience may seem to be. (cf. Ferrer's, 2002, powerful critique of *experientialism* in transpersonal psychology). A useful way of reinforcing this is to draw a parallel with a distinction that is made by Schechner (1988) in relation to the functions of dramatic performance. Schechner suggests that theatre may induce either temporary *transportations* of consciousness in performers and audience, or permanent *transformations*. In exactly the same way, I believe, paranormal experiences (or other altered states) may be either transportative or transformative. Only if they are truly transformational, I suggest, should they be considered genuinely transpersonal.

In this context we may note a warning that is routinely issued to transpersonal practitioners within many traditions about psychic experiences. Thus the Yogi or meditator is cautioned on the dangers of being seduced by the *siddhis*, i.e., the psychic and paranormal powers that are believed to result from the practice of Yoga or meditation. It is important, it is taught, to renounce or let go of these siddhis in order for further spiritual development to become possible. This may well be true, but unfortunately it can come across as a specific prejudice against the paranormal (perhaps this also lies behind Green & Green's and Rowan's rejection of the extrapersonal). In my opinion, a similar warning needs to be given at every level of the spectrum. John Rowan, for one, recognizes this. Thus he writes (e.g., 1993) that the major challenge of each stage of development is to dare to let go of the attractive and seductive features of one's current stage. For example (in crude terms) the challenge of the transpersonal (low subtle) is to relax one's grip on our rigid sense of personal identity. At the high subtle, the challenge is to let go of the fascination with the psychic and paranormal (low subtle), whereas at the 'causal' (mystical) level, the challenge is to let go of our attachment to our symbols and to blissful states of union with spiritual archetypes. At the 'ultimate' level, perhaps, the challenge is to let go of our attachment to everything.[6]

Wilber (1995a) argues that the psychic and paranormal level represents the lowest manifestation of the transpersonal because it is still closely related to the world of conventional reality. In other words, the low subtle is relatively 'gross' in comparison to the increasingly refined high subtle and causal levels (see Wilber, 1995a, p. 607–610). Although I would not frame it in

---

6   Such 'letting go' of our current fascinations may be important whether or not we accept the *sequence of levels* implied by Rowan (after Wilber). As I will argue later, there may be problems with Wilber's characterization of the stages or levels of transpersonal development.

exactly these terms,[7] I agree with Wilber and Rowan that it is important to recognize and encourage development beyond the level of fascination with the transportations that may be provided by the low subtle. In this respect, the challenge to renounce the psychic and paranormal may be particularly difficult for many people, precisely because these areas can be so fascinating and seductive.

Yet this should not lead us to underestimate, devalue or dismiss the relevance of the low subtle realm. For many people, experiences of the low subtle may be the critical factor that can promote structural development to the level of the transpersonal. Thus many of the 'spiritual emergencies' discussed by Grof & Grof (1995) involve encounters with the low subtle realms such as NDE, past-life memories, kundalini awakenings, shamanic crises, possession states, ESP, channelling, and UFO experiences. As Grof and Grof (*ibid.*) show, such experiences may often be crucial in leading the person towards profound personal and spiritual transformation, or spiritual *emergence*.

The Dangers of 'Dabbling' with the Paranormal

This discussion helps also to place into context the warnings that are often given about the low subtle, for example the spiritual dangers of dabbling with the paranormal and the occult. In my view these very real dangers result when (as may often happen) paranormal experiences lead to regression into prepersonal modes of being. Thus for many people, a paranormal experience may not encourage transformation to the level of the transpersonal but rather produces a retreat into prepersonal superstitious and magical thinking, or even into psychosis (Grof, 2000; Grof & Grof, 1995). As a direct consequence the person may then become open to abuse and exploitation by unscrupulous or dangerous people who are desirous and capable of manipulating this regressive and vulnerable position.

---

7   There is also a danger in Wilber's formulation that the ordinary world of personal and social experience may be considered relatively unimportant. In my opinion the transpersonal is not fundamentally separate from the ordinary world. It is therefore important always to bring the transpersonal into our everyday lives and, in this way, to 'ground' our mystical experience.

In my opinion the answer to this problem is not to make people afraid of the paranormal with undiscriminating or fundamentalist warnings about the dire consequences of any such involvement since, counter-productively, this only serves to bring about or reinforce a retreat into superstitious and magical thinking. Rather it is important, I believe, to encourage people to face up to their paranormal experiences, to find a way of integrating them meaningfully into their life and, ultimately, to allow them to lead towards development beyond the self. Indeed this is very much the approach taken by Grof & Grof (1995) in their discussion of how to work with spiritual emergencies (see also Clarke, 2001; Grof, 2000).

Transpersonal Psychology and Parapsychology

I wish finally to turn to the question of the relationship between transpersonal psychology and parapsychology. I have shown how many topic areas are common to both transpersonal psychology and parapsychology, and have discussed how the paranormal may be understood from a transpersonal perspective. This raises the question of how a parapsychological approach to these topics differs from that of transpersonal psychology.

From the perspective of transpersonal psychology, paranormal experiences are of interest if they can promote the kind of transpersonal development that I have been emphasizing. From the perspective of parapsychology, on the other hand, paranormal experiences are of interest only to the extent that they are able to demonstrate objectively the reality of paranormal phenomena and/or lead to an understanding of the paranormal processes involved. These are quite different, although potentially related agendas.

Consider, for example, the case of the near-death experience. To a parapsychologist, these experiences are studied as a potential source of scientific evidence for post-mortem survival of the personality. The question that parapsychological research wishes to answer is 'does the near-death experience provide convincing evidence that the human personality survives bodily death?' To the transpersonal psychologist, on the other hand, the near-death experience is of more importance in the context of its potential transformational effects. For example, the transpersonal psychologist is interested in the extent to which the person may be led to take a wider or deeper, less personal and more transcendent view of life. In a sense, therefore, the issue of whether the NDE provides objective proof of survival is of relatively less concern than the subjective experience, beliefs and behaviour of the experiencer. The point is that the NDE may be a valid and profound experience, which can transform the person's life to a more transpersonal basis even if the experience does not itself *prove* survival of the personality. Even more critically, the NDE can be transpersonally valid even if survival of bodily death does not actually occur in any objective (evidential) sense, i.e., even if the NDE is a kind of illusion.[8]

Another way of making the same point is to realize that the parapsychologist is not directly interested in the subjective meaning that the NDE may have for the experiencer. The parapsychologist is therefore less likely to explore in detail the phenomenology of the experience, or the impact that the NDE may have on the individual's life, unless this could provide evidence for paranormal features. As a result, the kind of methodologies used by the transpersonal psychologist and the parapsychologist will be very different. The parapsychologist is mainly concerned with collecting data that are capable of objective verification. The transpersonal psychologist, on the other hand, is primarily interested in the phenomenology, subjective interpretation and structural consequences of the experience, irrespective of whether any objectively verifiable information may be obtained.

Let us consider a concrete example. A feature of the advanced stages of the NDE is an encounter with deceased relatives, or other figures. Typically the person may receive a message, for example that it is not time to die and that it is important to return because there is some significant purpose to fulfil in life (e.g., Fenwick & Fenwick, 1995; Irwin, 2004). To the transpersonal psychologist, such encounters are of direct interest in their own right, particularly as these profound and moving experiences may lead to a significant change in the person's sense of identity and spiri-

---

8   In my opinion, however, the evidence from research on NDEs very much supports some kind of 'reality' to these experiences. Of course, although these experiences may powerfully suggest survival, they do not prove it, if only because in all cases the person has not actually (irreversibly) died. Also survival is only one of several possible explanations for NDEs.

tual outlook. To the parapsychologist, however, such a message is of no real interest, because it contains no information that can be directly checked with objective facts. If, on the other hand, the message was that it was important to return to life because there was a chest of money hidden in the brickwork of the house which should be used to help the poor, then this would provide the para-psychologist with potentially verifiable information.

This difference in approach between transpersonal psychology and parapsychology echoes the basic difference discussed by Allport (1955) between the humanistic (hermeneutic) and positivistic (experimental) camps in psychology. Thus the transpersonal psychologist is interested in meaning and in per-sonal significance; the parapsychologist is interested in informa-tion and in statistical significance. Another very useful way of understanding this difference in approach is to relate it to Ken Wilber's quadrant model (e.g., Wilber 1995a, 1997). According to this interpretation, transpersonal psychology (at least in its more narrow sense) is primarily an *interior-individual* discipline, although it may also extend to the interior-collective. For exam-ple a transpersonal psychologist may study the phenomenologi-cal and structural aspects of the NDE (interior-individual) but may also be interested in how the NDE is experienced in various cultures (interior-collective).[9] Parapsychology, on the other hand, is principally an *exterior-individual*, positivistic discipline in which phenomena are validated against publicly verifiable data. (Table 5).

Towards an Integral Approach

One of the major implications of Wilber's quadrant model is the importance of honouring all four quadrants and, ultimately, seeking an integration of the different approaches to knowledge. In terms of the relationship between transpersonal psychology and parapsychology, perhaps the most crucial initial advance would be for each discipline to acknowledge the validity and value of the other's contribution. For example, transpersonal psychologists can only benefit, I believe, by becoming informed about parapsychological research in their areas of interest. In

---

9   It is important also to recognize the role that other transpersonal discip-
     lines might play, for example transpersonal sociology or transpersonal
     anthropology (Boucouvalas, 1999; Walsh & Vaughan, 1993a).

Shadow, Self, Spirit

*Table 5. Transpersonal disciplines and parapsychology
in the quadrant model*

	Interior	Exterior
Individual	Transpersonal Psychology Some parapsychology (e.g., research on apparitions)	Parapsychology (especially laboratory research)
Collective	Transpersonal Psychology Transpersonal Sociology Transpersonal Anthropology	Transpersonal Sociology Transpersonal Anthropology Some parapsychology (e.g. research on hauntings, poltergeists)

particular, although it is rarely, if ever, conclusive, the evidence from parapsychological research can open up people's minds to the existence of possible realities that cannot be easily explained from a purely *materialistic* perspective, and in this sense parapsychology can support a transpersonal perspective (cf. Tart, 1997, 2004). More specifically, research evidence from parapsychology may be capable of suggesting likely avenues for future investigations on the transformational aspects of paranormal experiences. For example, the evidence for psychokinetic effects induced by the participation of large numbers of people in the kind of shared consciousness that is triggered by major world events (e.g., Radin, 1997; http://noosphere.princeton.edu/) may prompt transpersonal psychologists to investigate the *transformative effects* that participation in these events may produce.

Similarly, parapsychologists may benefit from a fuller understanding of the phenomenological, structural and spiritual aspects of the experiences they investigate since this may not only suggest methodological refinements but may also lead to further suggestions for empirical studies. For example, the evidence from transpersonal psychology on the transformational effects of Yoga, meditation, prayer, ritual or guided visualization may encourage parapsychologists to investigate further whether these kinds of activity may produce conditions in which paranormal phenomena may occur.

Charles Tart is one of the very few contemporary researchers who have achieved prominence in both parapsychology and transpersonal psychology, and he has been a major force in the attempt to bridge the gap between these two disciplines (e.g., Tart, 1997, 2004). He argues (e.g., Tart, 2004) that parapsychologists have generally shunned the spiritual aspects and implications of their research (and transpersonal psychology) in their attempt to achieve recognition by the scientific community.[10] In return, transpersonal psychologists have often dismissed parapsychology because of its emphasis on methodology at the expense of meaning. But transpersonal psychology, he suggests, needs parapsychology in order to ground its speculations in reality. In this way, parapsychology may help to curb any tendency within transpersonal psychology to wild, unsupported metaphysical fantasy. Parapsychology also needs transpersonal psychology to point out the larger meaning and significance of its data. In this way '[w]e will get a parapsychology that is rigorous but much more meaningful and a transpersonal psychology that is meaningful but has a base of more rigorous and scientifically-based findings, making it more effective and discriminative' (Tart, 2004, p. 89).

Conclusions

I have argued that the paranormal is an aspect of human experience that has the potential for promoting transpersonal development. Paranormal experiences can lead to such transformation by encouraging the individual to consider the significance of the wider or deeper reality beyond the world of the ordinary self and its concerns.

In most cases, however, paranormal experiences (though they may be *transportative*) will have no *transformational* effects on the individual, or may possibly lead to regression to primitive modes of superstitious or magical thinking. Because of this it is not possible to say whether a paranormal experience is prepersonal or transpersonal simply by assessing the phenomenological content or context of the experience. Rather the distinction

---

10   Yet, interestingly, Tart (2003) also discovered that many parapsychologists came into this field because of spiritual interests.

needs to be made by considering the prepersonal or transpersonal consequences that the experience may have for the experiencer.

Transpersonal psychology and parapsychology differ widely in their philosophical and methodological approaches to paranormal phenomena. However, each discipline may be enriched through mutual recognition and understanding of the contribution that can be made by the other.

Chapter 3

Holism, Integration and the Transpersonal

'Holism' is one of the catchwords of the humanistic, transpersonal, complementary health, and 'new age' movements. In the popular mythology of these movements, holism is generally considered a self-evidently 'good thing,' representing the notion that various divisions or splits may be resolved, healed, or transcended in some kind of higher-order integration. Indeed such integration is often equated with health and maturity, whether this is in personal, social or political realms.

Ken Wilber (e.g., 1995a, 1996a) provides a useful analysis of the general mechanisms involved in holistic (or 'holarchical') processes. According to Wilber (1996a, p. 29), 'all evolutionary and developmental patterns proceed by holarchization, by a process of increasing orders of wholeness and inclusion'. New wholes become possible when a principle emerges that is capable of uniting formerly separate and conflicting elements.

It is not my intention in this chapter to deny the validity of the general concept of holism or holarchy. Indeed I generally support much of Wilber's holarchical analysis. What I wish to question, however, is the extent to which specific commonly-held notions of holism are useful and valid.

This chapter is a revised and updated version of Daniels (1997)

Holism 1 (New-Age Holism)

Perhaps the most popular version of holism is the belief in the integration of body, mind and spirit. Ideologically, this is often taken to mean the basic indivisibility of the person's physical, mental and spiritual being (though these may in some cases be viewed as hierarchically related, for example in the Great Chain of Being). Therapeutically, it refers to the importance of treating the 'whole' person as well as to the healing that results from the personal integration of the three aspects.

This powerful and appealing metaphor has been enthusiastically promoted by many who proclaim the new paradigms in health and psychology. In my opinion, however, it is limited and often deeply flawed. One of the main reasons for this is that, within the various new paradigms, it is largely synonymous with an exclusively 'positive thinking' approach that is itself polarized and unintegrated. Art Levine (1985) caricatures this as the 'Pollyanna paradigm' and Michael Marien (1983) has written a more considered critique of what he calls the 'sandbox syndrome' — essentially a puerile, utopian, blinkered approach in which everything is or can become perfect and wonderful. This kind of holism therefore generally promotes the possibility of what is seen as a perfect integration of the healthy body, positive mind and divine spirit. This is revealed, for example, by the way that the new paradigms usually focus upon and idealize youthfulness, physical beauty, imagination, creativity, love, empathy, happiness, self-actualization, enlightenment, peak experiences, ecstasy, and peace.

I shall call this kind of holism 'Holism 1,' or 'new-age holism'. Its problem is that it is simply not holistic enough. Rather than being truly integrative, Holism 1 reinforces basic splits of, for example, good vs. evil, life vs. death, youth vs. old age, health vs. illness, beauty vs. ugliness, imagination vs. logic, love vs. hate, and ecstasy vs. pain. In this way it inevitably denies, represses or demonizes what Jung would call its 'shadow'. It is an approach which, as Rollo May (1982) has pointed out, is incapable of fully acknowledging or dealing with the so-called 'negative' aspects of human experience such as illness, anxiety, hostility, stagnation and death. For this reason it cannot, I believe, offer a truly integrative or holistic vision.

Holism 2 (Psychological Holism)

A more holistic approach must therefore attempt to integrate and heal the splits that are implicit within Holism 1. As in psychotherapy, this will involve the recognition, owning, and in some sense *acceptance* of the shadow. This implies the possibility of a higher-order integration of 'positive' and 'negative' in which the shadow is seen not as our enemy, but as fundamental to our own nature.

Such an approach (which I will call 'Holism 2' or 'psychological holism') is nothing new. It is to be found in existentialist thinking as well as in much psychotherapeutic (especially psychodynamic) theory and practice. Unfortunately, Holism 2 is much less evident in the new paradigms. In their often zealous attempts to establish their unique identities and to differentiate themselves from the 'old paradigms' (as, for example, in Maslow's 'third force,' or Seligman's 'positive psychology'), these approaches have generally identified with what they see as the positive side of the split while simultaneously projecting much of the negative side onto their opponents. This inevitably produces a fragmented and incomplete vision.

Holism 2 recognizes the need to integrate the seemingly negative, darker aspects of human nature. If we apply this principle to the body-mind-spirit metaphor, then this means acknowledging and coming to terms with the shadow as it manifests in each of these areas. In relation to the body, this implies an acceptance of pain, illness, aging and death. At the level of mind, we need to own and come to terms with anxiety, depression, jealousy, anger and other seemingly negative emotions, as well as the rational, analytical, and conceptual thinking that is often devalued and neglected within the new paradigms. Spiritually, we need to find a way to acknowledge and reconcile ourselves with meaninglessness, tragedy, human weakness and fallibility, loss of faith, existential guilt, the dark night of the soul, and the problem of evil.

If we turn our attention specifically to transpersonal psychology, then Holism 2 has a number of important implications and recommendations. Most importantly, perhaps, is the need to be on the lookout for polarized, idealistic tendencies in our approach to the transpersonal. In practice, these may often be recognized by their secondary characteristics such as dogmatism or cult-like certainty, charismatic enthusiasm, hubris and spiritual one-upmanship. In contrast, a little self-doubt and humility is not only refreshing, but, I believe, essential in anyone approaching the transpersonal. Second, we should give much greater consideration in our experience, thinking, and research to the *transpersonal shadow* (cf. Vaughan, 1985). We should, for example, attempt to balance our interest in self-actualization, peak experiences, ecstasy, and the 'positive' effects of meditation with studies that focus upon spiritual failure, trough experiences, the 'dark night' and the dangers inherent in psycho-spiritual practice. Finally we should attempt, both personally and as a discipline, to develop ways of integrating our experience of the transpersonal in all its manifestations.

Holism 3 (All-Quadrant Holism)

Is Holism 2 the final answer? To the extent that it implies that integration may be carried out as a purely individual endeavour, then no. This is, of course, a further major problem with the body-mind-spirit metaphor. Where do other people, social and cultural systems, the physical world and ecosphere figure in this model? How does it understand the relationship between the individual and these other realities?

One of the important debates within transpersonal psychology at the end of the 20th century has concerned the relationship between 'other-worldly' and 'this-worldly' approaches to the transpersonal (e.g. Ferrer, 2002; Fox, 1990, 1993, 1995; Wilber, 1995a, 1995b, 1996a; Zimmerman, 1998). Fox (e.g., 1990, 1993) argues that the 'other-worldly' approach that has dominated transpersonal psychology is essentially egocentric and anthropocentric in its aim to promote the person's 'vertical' ascent to higher forms of spiritual consciousness. Fox himself advocates a 'this-worldly' or 'horizontal' view of transpersonal development — a 'transpersonal ecology' or, 'deep ecology' (after the Norwegian philosopher Arne Naess, 1973) which is fully biocentric or ecocentric, and which emphasizes the importance of expanding our concern and sense of self outwards to achieve a wider and deeper identification with the natural world or Gaia.

Although Fox is surely right to alert us to the importance of the horizontal dimension and to the limitations of a purely vertical approach, he unfortunately reinforces polarized thinking in this area. Fox provides neither the means nor clear motivation to integrate the horizontal and vertical approaches to the transpersonal, but presents the horizontal mainly as an alternative to the vertical. For these reasons, transpersonal ecology fails to provide a truly holistic vision (see also Stavely & McNamara's, 1992, critique of Fox's transpersonal ecology). In the 1990s, this debate was greatly advanced by Wilber's (e.g., 1995a, 1995b, 1996a) elegant analyses. Wilber recognizes the need to develop our understanding of, and ultimately to integrate, both the 'ascending' (vertical, other-worldly) and 'descending' (horizontal, this-worldly) paths. Unlike Fox, Wilber also acknowledges the importance of the collective, social-cultural world. He thus proposes that we need to find ways to respect and integrate all four quadrants. In this way, Wilber's model clearly moves beyond both an individually-orientated Holism 2, and Fox's polarized deep ecology, which Wilber dismisses as an ecoromantic, limiting, 'flatland' (mono-dimensional) approach (see, for example, Zimmerman, 1998).

Wilber's arguments imply what I shall call 'Holism 3,' or all-quadrant holism — the integration of the individual body-mind-spirit (positive and negative) in the social, cultural and natural worlds. However, as Wilber (1995b, p. 118) himself points out 'as of yet, there has historically been no "holism" that actually embraces all four quadrants in all their levels ... this is one of the central aims of general transpersonal studies'. Wilber's own recent work, particularly his emphasis on an integral all-quadrant, all level (AQAL) approach to knowledge undoubtedly marks a major advance towards the development of Holism 3, but it is important to realize that the kind of formal analysis that Wilber offers can only provide a general schematic programme. There is a vast difference between being able to understand that Holism 3 requires an integration of ascending and descending currents, or the interior-exterior and individual-collective dimensions, and actually being able to achieve this integration. This is the difference that Wilber (e.g., 1995a, 1996a) himself acknowledges, between the map and the territory. Holism 3, like the other holisms, ultimately has to be achieved through our living experience, not through our models. The establishment by Wilber of the Integral Institute (www.integral institute.org) aims to develop not only the kinds of integrated knowledge implied by an AQAL approach, but also practical applications of this knowledge. It will be interesting to see how successful and influential this particular initiative may be.

Although models have their limitations, they can help to point the way forward. Certainly the concept of Holism 3 has some important implications for transpersonal psychology. One of these, of course, is that an exclusively *psychological* approach to the transpersonal can never be sufficient (essentially the formal reason for Wilber's 2000b, 2002 renouncing of transpersonal psychology). While I do not advocate an abandonment of the psychological approach to the transpersonal, transpersonal psychology should never be considered as a totally separate, discrete discipline, but should be supplemented and ultimately integrated with, for example, transpersonal sociology, transpersonal anthropology, and transpersonal ecology (cf. Boucouvalas, 1999; Walsh & Vaughan, 1993a). A related practical message is the need to balance our interest in possible universal 'psychological' features of transpersonal experiences and processes with a careful examination of the social-cultural influences on them, and on the meanings that people attach to them. Put simply, social- cultural differences may be just as interesting and revealing as universal commonalities.

Holism 3 also helps us to clarify the meaning of the transpersonal and to identify certain problems that may arise in our spiritual practice. A common paradox in this area is that transpersonal experiences may be presented as something that the person may actively seek, or may look forward to enjoying. If we are to be genuinely transpersonal then surely we need to develop beyond the personal desire for our own enlightenment or self-realization? In this sense, I believe that Fox is correct in his observation that there is something essentially egocentric in elements of the transpersonal movement's thinking and practice. A real danger, if we are not vigilant, is therefore that transpersonal psychology may develop models and practices that serve only to sustain and reinforce what Chögyam Trungpa (1973) calls 'spiritual materialism' — a form of self-deception in which spirituality becomes a subtle means to fulfil egocentric (or anthropocentric) desires. Ferrer (2002) also provides a similar powerful critique of such 'spiritual narcissism'.

One important advantage of Holism 3 is that it offers a perspective that takes us beyond self-centred spiritual materialism, or spiritual narcissism, without, however, repressing or denying the significance of personal-individual being. Holism 3 therefore leaves open the possibility of synergistic (integrated) relationships between personal and transpersonal, horizontal and vertical, ascending and descending, interior and exterior, individual and collective, this-world and that-world. Such relationships imply that we may enjoy and gain satisfaction from the transpersonal path, and may experience profound states of consciousness, even though we are not on the path for fun, or personal fulfilment, or to notch up experiences, and even though much of the time it may be bewildering, difficult, demanding, tedious, unrewarded, and even hellish.

From the perspective of Holism 3, the true meaning of 'transpersonal' is not 'beyond the personal,' or even 'beyond the ego,' although, as recognized by Ferrer (2002), it certainly implies 'beyond person-centredness' and 'beyond egocentrism'. More crucially, perhaps, it signifies 'beyond the polarization of personal and trans-personal, or of egoic and transegoic'. In practice this makes possible a perspective in which there is no fundamental difference between the spiritual and mundane paths. The transpersonal journey may therefore be undertaken through our everyday life experience rather than being seen as separate and dissociated from ordinary living. This perspective is fundamentally consistent, I believe, with Ferrer's own vision of a truly participatory spirituality.

Conclusions

'Holism' is a seductive but tricky concept that means different things to different people. In distinguishing between three main holistic approaches, I hope to have clarified some of the problems associated with certain perspectives. In advocating an approach that I have termed 'Holism 3' (all-quadrant holism), I have tried to resolve some of these problems in a way that accurately reflects the direction of current thinking about the transpersonal and also offers some useful pointers to possible future developments within transpersonal psychology.

There is much in this chapter that may seem critical of the new paradigms in general and of the transpersonal movement in particular. However it is not my intention to strangle the baby at birth and I remain personally committed to, and basically optimistic about, the future of transpersonal psychology. Although as a formal discipline, transpersonal psychology is relatively new, William James' (e.g., 1901/1960) pioneering work makes transpersonal psychology almost as old as psychology itself. Furthermore, the great advances in transpersonal thinking that have occurred in the last quarter of the 20th century mean, I believe, that transpersonal psychology is no longer an infant, but is fast developing a maturity that makes it tough enough to withstand constructive criticism and debate. Indeed I believe that this is very much what the discipline needs at this time in order to further define and refine its approach and to deepen our understanding of the transpersonal

Chapter 4

The Shadow in Transpersonal Psychology

'If my devils are to leave me, I am afraid my angels
will take flight as well.'   (Rainer Maria Rilke)

The Shadow Archetype

At 11 am on 11th August 1999,[1] I was standing, wet and cold, on
a rocky hillside on the West Coast of Cornwall, near the prehis-
toric monument of Men-an-Tol. Ten minutes later, the long-
heralded shadow of the Moon swept silently in over a sinister
sky, heavy with cloud cover. A fleeting two minutes of distant
amber and the light returned, allowing a fresh glimpse of the
strangely unmoving faces of anoraked onlookers. There was
brief applause, then most of those present quietly collected up
their things and made their way back down the path in single
file, as if in trance.

What did it all mean? Was this what I had consciously waited
more than 40 years to experience? Was this what I had driven
seven hours through the night to witness? Was it worth it? Had
anything changed? Questions that floated in the air like the

This chapter is a revised and updated version of Daniels (2000)

---

1   The day of a total solar eclipse over Southern Britain and Europe.

retreating clouds before me. The Earth did not move, but an answer eventually came. This was one of the most significant and memorable days of my life.

The image of the shadow is highly evocative, especially when considered in the context of spirituality and the transpersonal. These domains so regularly employ the metaphor and symbolism of light that it is perhaps surprising that more consideration is not given to its complement, i.e., darkness. Darkness is implied by light. Light not only has the property of illuminating the dark places, but it also, by its sheer brilliance, casts dark shadows when contacting the ordinary world of form that we inhabit.

In Jungian analytical psychology, as also in many other traditions, light is considered to be a symbol for consciousness. Light illuminates our world and brings it into awareness, thereby enabling us to act with intention and rational intelligence. Darkness is primarily a symbol for that which is not illuminated in consciousness — the unacknowledged, hidden, unconscious reality that moves silently in the depths. Darkness therefore represents a level of our own being that is outside our conscious knowledge and control.

In Jung's model of the psyche, the shadow is the complement to our conscious persona. It is, metaphorically, the shadow thrown when the light of our persona (our consciously expressed public personality) meets the larger reality of our total being. Most of us have been brought up to acknowledge and express only a limited, socially acceptable portion of our total personality. The other, socially unacceptable, parts remain unacknowledged, generally either deeply repressed in our own unconscious minds, or projected outwards onto certain others who thereby come to represent for us all that is dark, unpleasant or evil.

At this point, it is perhaps useful to mention that there are two main ways in which the Jungian archetype of the shadow may be understood. Firstly, and principally, we may conceive the shadow as those aspects of our own being that are not illuminated by the light of awareness; those parts of us that we do not, cannot or dare not acknowledge. In this sense, the shadow is morally neutral or ambiguous. For example, while one person may find it difficult to acknowledge anger, domination, or lust, another may find it equally difficult to experience or express sensitivity, gentleness or compassion. In other words, there is such a thing as the 'positive shadow' (Firman & Gila, 1997, p. 111ff), comprising submerged goodness and creative potentials. However, to the extent that most of us are brought up to express a socially acceptable, conventionally 'good' persona, the shadow will typically (and hence archetypally) come to represent those qualities deemed unacceptable or 'bad'. In this way, the archetype of the shadow comes to acquire its secondary, negative meaning, i.e., that which is evil and reprehensible in our own psychological being.

Despite the important distinction between the positive and negative shadow, in practice our personal shadow will tend to be subjectively apprehended or experienced as bad, whether positive or negative, because it represents those aspects of our personality that we have learned should not be expressed. For example, the person who cannot express sensitivity or gentleness would consider it wrong or unacceptable to do so. The shadow is thus always in some sense bad from the relative perspective of the individual. However, in absolute terms, or from the perspective of the larger Self, the shadow is neither good nor bad — it is simply there (or rather, it is right *here*).

For Jung, one of the most important primary goals of therapy was to enable individuals to begin to acknowledge and own their shadow. As long as the shadow remains unconscious, kept out of awareness by defence mechanisms such as repression or projection, it will inevitably cause psychological and interpersonal difficulties. Or when, at times of stress, intoxication or crisis, there is an uncoordinated 'return of the repressed,' the unexpected emergence of the shadow into awareness will typically lead to intense feelings of guilt and unworthiness, or to personally and socially destructive forms of acting out behaviour.

The operation of defence mechanisms against the shadow also prevents the kind of higher order functioning of the personality that may become possible when previously unaccepted aspects are fully acknowledged, truly owned, and put into perspective in the context of our total being. If we continue with our principal metaphor for a moment, Jung is arguing that we need to begin to shine the light of consciousness down into those dark places that our upbringing will have made us afraid to explore. Only in this way can we begin our psychological journey towards completion, wholeness and individuation.

According to Jung, there is another important dimension to the shadow — its collective manifestations. Jung is referring here to the darkness that may be found as an undercurrent in all human groups, whether families, tribes, organizations, movements or large civilizations, as well as in human nature generally. For example, in the same way that the personal shadow is the dark complement of an individual's persona, a culture's dominant *zeitgeist* will cast its own dark, antithetical, collective shadow. At the collective level, the shining light of our self-professed and sometimes expressed humanity is complemented and counterbalanced by a very dark side to human nature. We rightly react in horror and disgust at the brutality and inhumanity of the Holocaust, or of Rwanda, Kosovo and Sudan. But the real horror is that we are all capable of such atrocities — especially, it seems, if we are male. It is very much a case of 'There, but for the grace of God, go I'. Or, as Jung (1958a, p. 96) puts it: 'we are always, thanks to our human nature, potential criminals … None of us stands outside humanity's … collective shadow'.

Transpersonal Psychology:
Persona and Shadow

As we have seen, humanistic and transpersonal psychology first arose as collective movements in America in the 1960s and 1970s from the pioneering efforts of Abraham Maslow, Anthony Sutich, Miles Vich and Stan Grof. Maslow himself coined the phrases 'Third Force' (humanistic psychology) and 'Fourth Force' (transpersonal psychology). At the time, these movements were seen as a necessary reaction against the two then dominant forces in psychology, i.e., Freudianism and behaviourism, which Maslow criticized for their negative and reductionistic tendencies. At the outset, therefore, both humanistic and transpersonal psychology were distinguished and identified by their advocacy of a positive, optimistic view of human nature, in direct contrast to the view of the Freudians and behaviourists. Maslow's own writings are typical of this positive approach, with their self-conscious, studied emphasis on self-actualization, human potential, creativity, love, humanistic education, peak experiences, and metamotivation (e.g., Maslow, 1970, 1973).

Such an overtly positive agenda also, of course, characterizes the 'positive psychology' of Martin Seligman (e.g., Seligman & Csikszentmihalyi, 2000).

The consequence of this reaction against the perceived negativity of the prevailing psychological paradigms has been that humanistic and transpersonal psychology have sometimes been promoted enthusiastically as an alternative paradigm in which the shadow side of human nature can seemingly be ignored, cast out, or overcome. This is well exemplified in Marilyn Ferguson's influential book *The Aquarian Conspiracy* (1980) and has become almost a defining characteristic of the human potential, alternative health, and 'new age' movements.

An implication that can often arise within this new paradigm is that personal and transpersonal development involves a wonderful, joyful, entertaining, illuminating, 'happy-clappy', always forward-moving, easy journey of discovery and spiritual advancement. This journey begins when we learn to cast off and leave behind all personal negativity and darkness, adopt an attitude of 'positive thinking', make appropriately positive affirmations, and orientate ourselves and gravitate towards the light, like moths to a flame.

This optimistic perspective is perhaps most evident in some of the more popular manifestations of new age thinking, yet it is also found and often directly promoted within humanistic and transpersonal psychology. Most obviously, are the unrelentingly cheerful theories of Carl Rogers and Abraham Maslow. Furthermore, research in transpersonal psychology has tended to focus largely on what we may loosely call the 'positive' aspects of transpersonal experience such as ecstatic mystical states, creative inspiration, human kindness and compassion, wholeness, and enlightenment.

In my view, this can lead to a naïve and simplistic view of transpersonal development that is both wrong and deeply unhelpful. It does not accord with my own life experience or that of many other people with whom I have been privileged to discuss these matters. Furthermore, if taken literally or seriously, such a view can produce a number of unfortunate, even dangerous consequences for the transpersonal movement (cf. Chapter 6). Many of these are encapsulated in certain myths (or, as I prefer to call them, 'dangerous partial truths') that are very commonly encountered in this area. Among these, we may note the following:

- Transpersonal development may be achieved by seeking out ecstatic and other exciting altered states of consciousness.
- Enlightenment makes you happy.
- Spiritually advanced people are joyful, dynamic and charismatic.
- Spiritual development can be achieved by adopting an 'enlightening' doctrine, or by discipleship to an enlightened Master.
- Ignore evil — perhaps it will go away.
- The spiritual path can be followed in a self-centred way, by focussing on our own personal and transpersonal development.

These myths are dangerous, I believe, because they can encourage both projected authority and spiritual materialism. Projected authority, according to John Heron (1998), is the tendency to invest spiritual authority in some external source (e.g., a teacher, book, doctrine, or group). This can lead not only to the denial of our own internal authority, but also, in its more extreme forms, to the kind of blind adherence to external authorities characteristic of certain religious movements, both ancient and modern. Spiritual materialism, as described by Chögyam Trungpa (1973), represents an attitude of pleasure-seeking, spiritual greed and passive consumerism. From such a perspective, the spiritual life is reduced to a demanding quest for gratifying subtle 'experiences' and new wonders (cf. Ferrer's, 2002, critique of experientialism and spiritual narcissism). Inevitably those who hold such a spiritually materialistic attitude lay themselves open to exploitation from the ever-growing and ever-regenerating band of smiling, smooth-talking salesmen and saleswomen of the new age. In this context we should perhaps heed Nietzsche's plea in *Thus Spake Zarathustra*:

> I conjure you, my brethren, to remain faithful to earth, and do not believe those who speak unto you of superterrestrial hopes! Poisoners they are, whether they know it or not (Zarathustra's Prologue, Verse 3).

These approaches to the transpersonal remind me again of Art Levine's (1985) caricature of the Pollyanna paradigm in humanistic psychology — the ingenuous belief that by looking on the bright side, everything can be made OK. Many others, including May (1982), Friedman (1976), Smail (1984), and Ferrer (2002) have added their own criticisms to the naïve, self-serving optimism that characterizes much of the human potential movement. Michael Marien (1983) delivers perhaps the most scathing attack on this attitude, which he terms the 'sandbox syndrome' because it reminds him of the attitude of children innocently amusing themselves in their sandbox, playing at changing the world, while the world itself goes about its business, untouched and unconcerned. As transpersonal psychologists, many of us undoubtedly believe that we are engaged in valuable and significant work. But perhaps we should occasionally stand back, take the perspective of an outsider, and reflect on whether transpersonal psychology may itself demonstrate features of the sandbox syndrome. To what extent are we a community of like-minded people, playing at being important, while real life itself continues in its own course, largely unaffected by our precious or puerile vanities?

The solution to the problem of the sandbox syndrome, according to Michael Marien, is for the humanistic and transpersonal movements to grow up — personally, socially and politically. We need to swallow our pride and start to deal with some of the real issues and challenges facing ourselves and the world around us. In my view, an important way forward in this respect is for transpersonal psychology to begin to face its own shadow.

One way of approaching this shadow is to examine features of the dominant persona or *zeitgeist* of transpersonal psychology and to consider what may thereby be neglected, ignored or devalued from this viewpoint. In my view (cf. also Ferrer, 2002; Heron, 1998; Kremer, 1998) transpersonal psychology today is dominated by a zeitgeist that tends to emphasize the characteristics shown in the left-hand column in Table 6. Transpersonal psychology's neglected shadow may therefore be understood to involve explicit or implicit opposites to these dominant tendencies, i.e., the characteristics shown in the right-hand column.

Table 6. Zeitgeist and shadow in transpersonal psychology

Dominant Zeitgeist	Neglected Shadow
Ascending current (cf. Table 1)	Descending current (cf. Table 1)
Transcendence	Immanence
Masculine experience of the spiritual	Feminine experience of the spiritual
Perennial philosophy (post-axial version),	Non-perennialism, or a pre-axial version of the perennial philosophy
Cartesian dualism / Idealism	Fully embodied spirituality
American optimism	European realism
Mysticism	Magic
Eastern metaphysics and spiritual practice (especially that of Buddhism and Vedanta)	Non-metaphysical approaches to the transpersonal; Western theology and religious practice; indigenous religions
Belief in individual salvation	Commitment to collective salvation
Individual-interior quadrant	All-quadrant knowledge and practice
Primacy of consciousness	Integrated participation in the world and with the Mystery of Being
Unmediated ('pure') experience	Mediated (contextualized) experience
Achievement of causal states (transcendent Witnessing)	Psychic and subtle experiences
Ecstasy	Suffering
Spiritual tradition	Spiritual innovation
Absolutist (often dogmatic) spiritual perspective	A more pluralistic conception of spirituality

Of course, there are problems with any attempt to dichotomize tendencies in this way. In drawing up these polarities I do not wish to caricature transpersonal psychology, nor to imply that what I have identified as the 'shadow' side is totally unacknowledged within the discipline. That is clearly untrue and most serious writers on the subject recognize many of these dialectics in their own work. However, in my view, there is still a distinct tendency within much current transpersonal psychology, to overemphasize the features that I have identified as the dominant zeitgeist.

If nothing else this suggested distinction between the dominant persona/zeitgeist of transpersonal psychology and its neglected shadow serves to identify dialectical themes and issues that have been addressed in different contexts by a number of critics and commentators. These include Ken Wilber (e.g., 1995a, 1996a, 1997, 1999a, 2000a), John Heron (1998), John Rowan (1993), James Hillman (1977), Warwick Fox (1990, 1995), Michael Washburn (1995), Peggy Wright (1995, 1998a), Michael Zimmerman (1998) and Jorge Ferrer (2002). Wilber is in something of a difficult position in this regard, since for many people he is the primary representative of the 'Wilber/Buddhist/Male' approach within transpersonal psychology (Heron, 1998). However, Wilber's writings (e.g., 1995a, 1996a, 1997, 1999a, 2000a) have themselves identified several of the important polarities presented in Table 6. Furthermore his quadrant model and his related notion of integral studies do seek to provide a conceptual framework within which it becomes possible to recognize and discuss these complex and challenging issues (cf. Zimmerman, 1998).

I do not have the space to rehearse all the arguments that have been put forward by Wilber and his critics (see Rothberg & Kelly, 1998, for a lively discussion; also Visser, 2003). The point I wish to make here is simply that transpersonal psychology must find appropriate ways in which it can begin to acknowledge, honour and perhaps integrate these different perspectives if it is not to breed factionalism, partiality and endless cross-party bickering. Only in this way will it become possible to come to terms with the apparent contradictions within and between paradigms. We may not agree with Wilber's analyses but he is, in my opinion, making an honest attempt, in his own way, to provide an inclusive perspective on the transpersonal.

If I have one general criticism of Wilber, it is that despite his aim to recognize and integrate the different perspectives, he seems to remain committed to the idea that everything can be tied up and tidied up in a grand, over-arching conceptual scheme. My own experience tells me that life, self, relationships, and spirituality are fuzzy, fluid and rather messy, and that they resist all attempts to be parcelled up into neat packages. In this respect I have considerable sympathy for the position of James Hillman (e.g., 1977). Hillman, for example, rejects the Jungian and humanistic notion of the healthy, integrated self in favour of his deliberately ambiguous and undefined concept of the 'soul'. For Hillman, soul emerges as our experience of the world is deepened and made meaningful through imagination and fantasy. Soul is not a fixed given, but is a fluid, imaginative response to life. Furthermore, although soul is experienced as we imaginatively create myths and narratives to connect us with the archetypal, there is a danger in all such myths and narratives that they can become fossilized conceptual schemes that restrict and deaden the soul with their literalness. The life, the soul, is in the myth *making*, not in the mythical form itself, which must constantly be regenerated as soul emerges afresh. This essentially *creative* approach to the transpersonal is also reflected in Ferrer's (2002) important notion of cocreative participation in life's essential Mystery.

This implication of this for transpersonal psychology is, I believe, that we should not expect nor seek final answers to the apparent contradictions posed by these different approaches and perspectives. To aim to do so would be like imagining there was a final answer to the 'problem' of the relationship between the sexes. In most cases, it seems to me, those who claim an answer usually find it by attempting to impose their own one-sided perspective on the other, either directly or guilefully. As with sexual relations, we should, perhaps, each seek ways of constantly discovering our own personal meanings in this creative, challenging and fascinating melee, while at the same time listening to and honouring the differing views and experience of others.

In this respect it is not satisfactory, I suggest, to argue that these differences of approach can be fully encompassed and explained in the context of a model that recognizes the differences, but seeks to prioritize one approach over the other. (cf. Ferrer, 2002). This seems to me a clear feature of Wilber's model in which, for example, causal (formless) transpersonal experiences are believed to represent a higher mode of consciousness than subtle (image-based) experiences. In this way Hillman's notion of soul-making through imagination, myth and fantasy may be too easily dismissed by some as 'merely' subtle. By implication, therefore, soul-making itself needs to be transcended in the movement to causal consciousness. While such movement may indeed be prototypical in particular spiritual traditions, such as the path of Buddhist meditation, in my view Wilber has yet to prove that it is a universal feature of transpersonal development (cf. Chapter 11).

The Shadow and Transformation

I define transpersonal experiences, after Walsh & Vaughan (1993a), as those in which our sense of identity is transformed beyond the limited boundaries of the ordinary personal self. In my opinion, this is consistent, if not precisely identical, with Hillman's notion of soul making, or the deepening of human experience. As already mentioned, there appears to be a common presumption in much of the new-age and some transpersonal literature that such transformation or deepening is a wonderful, exciting, ecstatic joy ride of personal and transpersonal discovery. From here it is easy to become drawn into the belief that transpersonal progress can be measured by the number and variety of altered states of consciousness experienced, the number of workshops or retreats attended, the number of hours spent in meditation, or the range and depth of one's spiritual reading.

I call this essentially consumerist agenda the 'exotic' approach to the transpersonal and it does not accord well with my own experience. In my time I suppose that I have had certain experiences that might be deemed mystical or paranormal. I have also undertaken certain exotic practices, followed several systems of spiritual and esoteric training, and have read quite widely in the area of spirituality and the transpersonal. I have found almost all of this to be of interest and significance, and it has undoubtedly contributed to my appreciation and understanding of life and of the transpersonal. If I am honest with myself, however, I could not say that all of this has been profoundly *transformational* in the sense in which I have defined transpersonal experiences. In fact the opposite may sometimes be true. There is a real danger, not only for myself but for others in this area, that such experience can become, through an attitude of spiritual materialism or narcissism, yet another way of sustaining and promoting the self rather than transforming it. In the language of my youth, the transpersonal can easily become an 'ego-trip' for many. It can also be a good career move for some. In case it may seem that I am being unduly harsh on others, let me say that I am the first to stand up and plead guilty in this respect. For example, I am one of the small but increasing number of people lucky enough to be able to combine an interest in the transpersonal with my own professional development. In truth, however, I often experience a *conflict* between the demands of career development (which by nature requires an active, agentic approach), and my own spiritual preferences (which are more relaxed and relational).

If I look back on those events and experiences in my life that have truly transformed me — challenged the sense of who I am, given me an expanded or deepened sense of reality, or perhaps made me a better, more aware, more alive, or more compassionate person — they are, almost without exception, quite prosaic. They include the Arts, conversation, sexual love, death of friends and relatives, hill walking, tracing my family history, humanitarian crises, personal therapy and therapeutic practice, creative writing, divorce, intense experiences of isolation and of community, depression and, perhaps most important, the struggle, joy and sacred trust of becoming a parent.

I call this the 'mundane' approach to the transpersonal and I believe that it is much more widespread and significant than is generally acknowledged. At the present time it remains one of the shadow areas within transpersonal psychology, neglected by commentators and researchers who are still largely caught up in the delights of the exotic transpersonal.[2]

Another aspect which I am forced to recognize is that, with the exception of moments of temporary enrapture, the important transformations in my life have generally been slow, difficult, painful or unpleasant. Lasting transformation, in my experience, is rarely a sudden ecstatic turnabout, accompanied by bells, whistles and instant acclaim. It is rather a gradual, often unwel-

---

2   James Horne (1978) is one of the few writers to have recognized explicitly these mundane experiences of the transpersonal, which represent aspects of what he terms 'casual mysticism'. Horne contrasts this with 'serious mysticism' based on intentional practice (see also Rowan, 1993, p. 97–98). Other advocates of a more mundane approach to the transpersonal include John Welwood (e.g., 1991) who promotes the value of intimate relationship as spiritual path, and Jenny Wade (e.g., 2000) who argues that a more widely accessible path to transpersonal experience may be found through sex.

come, dawning of awareness, typically occurring at a time of considerable personal difficulty, stress, suffering or tragedy.

It seems to me rather paradoxical that transpersonal psychology should emphasize 'positive'[3] experiences of transformation to the relative neglect of 'negative' experiences, given the focus in many of the World's religious traditions on the significance of suffering, death, spiritual struggle, penitence and evil. In recent years, however, there has been an increasing awareness within transpersonal psychology of the importance of emotionally negative experiences such as illness, depression, tragedy, trauma, confrontation with death, loss of faith, alienation, negative near death experiences, and even alien abduction. These experiences have been conceived and characterized in a variety of ways by different writers, among which I note the following:

- Metapathology (Maslow, 1973)
- Existential crisis / existential neurosis
- Existential vacuum / noogenic neurosis (Frankl, 1967)
- Self-renewal through trauma (Jaffe, 1985)
- Psychopathology (e.g., Hillman, 1977)
- Catharsis
- Shamanic crisis (Harner, 1980)
- Crises / psychological disturbances (Assagioli, 1993)
- Dark night of the soul (St John of the Cross, 1991)
- Dark night of the self (Hale, 1992)
- Creative illness (Ellenberger, 1970)
- Renewal process (Perry, 1974, 1976)
- Night sea journey (Jung, 1967)
- Spiritual emergency (Grof & Grof, 1995; Grof, 2000)
- The 'wounded healer' (Jung, 1954)
- Healing of the Primal Wound (Firman & Gila, 1997)

One of the most significant features of these experiences is the way in which they are typically described as having profoundly transformational consequences, either in themselves, or when

---

3   In this context I use the terms 'positive' and 'negative' to refer to the affective quality of the transformational experience, rather than its consequences.

worked with in a particular fashion. A major reason for this may be that these 'negative' experiences *demand* transformation in a way that the more pleasant, 'positive' experiences may not. If we are privileged to experience ecstatic states, these may be taken as reinforcing current trends and behaviours — a kind of spiritual reward or grace, and a sign that we are doing things right. As such, while they may encourage various efforts to repeat the experience, they are perhaps less likely to produce genuine personal transformation, or a true deepening of experience. On the other hand, if we are suffering, or in a state of spiritual emergency, then transformation may be our only solution. Hillman (1977) argues, for example, that psychopathology is our primary route to the emergence of soul:

> Through depression we enter depths and in depths we find soul ... The true revolution begins in the individual who can be true to his own depression (*ibid.*, p. 98–99).

From the time of the classical Greeks, tragedy has been recognized not only for its cathartic effects, but also for its capacity to reveal the depth and nobility of human existence. Without tragedy, it might be said, life would be banal. For many people, Ken Wilber's most significant book is *Grace and Grit* (1991): a complex, moving, and at times brutally honest account of life during his wife Treya's five year struggle and eventual death from breast cancer. Wilber writes towards the end of the book:

> In the last six months of her life, it was as if Treya and I went into spiritual overdrive for each other, serving each other in every way that we could. I finally quit the bitching and moaning that is so normal for a support person, a bitching and moaning that came from the fact that I had, for five years, set aside my career in order to serve her. I just dropped all that. I had absolutely no regrets; I had only gratitude for her presence, and for the extraordinary grace of serving her (*ibid.*, p. 405).

Incorporating the Transforming Shadow

An important challenge for transpersonal psychology is, I believe, to provide a framework within which the significance of both mundane and negative transpersonal experiences can be acknowledged, honoured and understood. As a first step in this direction it is perhaps useful to draw up a rudimentary working

taxonomy of transformative experiences that incorporates both
the mundane and the negative. Table 7 presents such a taxonomy.
In drawing up this list, I have found it helpful to distinguish also
between introverted experiences in which the direction of attention or energy is principally inwards, focussed within the Self, and
extraverted experiences in which the direction is principally outwards, focussed on the Other (cf. Horne, 1978).[4]

Table 7 is not intended to be an exhaustive or definitive list.[5]
Rather it is offered as a simple introductory guide, or aide-
memoire, to stimulate thinking and research in these areas and
as a corrective to those taxonomies that ignore the mundane and
the negative. I recognize also, that there is some ambiguity and
overlap between both classifications and exemplars. This echoes
my earlier caution about the difficulties and dangers of seeking
too much clarity and order in these untidy and fluid realms of
human experience.

This taxonomy of experiences also helps to provide a perspective on the variety of transformational *practices* that are found in
the transpersonal field. Many of these practices seem particularly suited to inducing, developing or (especially with the negative) *working with* specific types of experience. Practices may
therefore themselves be roughly grouped according to the same
scheme of classification. Table 8 provides some preliminary suggestions for such a taxonomy of transformational practices.
Again there is inevitably some ambiguity and overlap.

---

4   The taxonomy presented in Tables 7 and 8 also has interesting parallels
    with the model of spiritual traditions developed by Andrew Rawlinson
    (1997, 2000). Rawlinson distinguishes between hot and cool traditions.
    Hot traditions emphasize the importance of relationship with a
    transcendent Other, whereas cool traditions assert that the essence of
    spirituality is within the Self. Rawlinson's hot traditions are comparable to
    the outer-directed exotic, whereas his cool traditions show similarities
    with inner-directed mundane. Rawlinson's model also makes a useful and
    interesting combining distinction between traditions that are structured
    (specifying a particular route to the spiritual goal) and those that are
    unstructured (arguing that the goal is already present and available,
    therefore there is no route to attainment). As with the model presented in
    Tables 7 and 8, Rawlinson acknowledges much overlap between
    categories.

5   Cf. also the '5 x 5' model of mysticism that I present in Chapter 11.

Table 7. *A taxonomy of transformative experiences*

Positive			
Mundane		**Exotic**	
Introverted	**Extraverted**	**Introverted**	**Extraverted**
Plateau experience	Inspiration	Peak experience	Peek / glimpse experiences
Flow experience	Love	Ecstasy	Psychic awareness
'Just this'	Creativity	Orgasm	Divine inspiration
Simple awareness	Action	Enstasy	Divine Grace
Suchness	Connection	Nirvana	Mystical Union
Peace, quietude	Compassion	Pure consciousness	Channelling
Innocent cognition	Simple enjoyment	Joy, rapture	Visions and voices
Negative			
Mundane		**Exotic**	
Introverted	**Extraverted**	**Introverted**	**Extraverted**
Trough experience	Tragedy	Negative Void	Archetypal Terror
Depression	Suffering, trauma	Loss of faith	Possession
Existential crisis	Illness	Bad trip	Confronting Evil
Existential angst	Stress	Dark night of the soul	Spirit attachment
Emptiness	Ageing	Night sea journey	Alien abduction
Alienation	Failure	Catharsis	Shamanic crisis
Deadness	Dying, bereavement	Confronting own death	Negative NDE

Table 8. A taxonomy of transformational practices

Positive			
Mundane		**Exotic**	
Introverted	**Extraverted**	**Introverted**	**Extraverted**
Samatha	Compassionate action	Raja Yoga	Worship, devotion
Focussing	Karma Yoga	Kundalini Yoga	Bhakti Yoga
Tai Chi	Politics	Holotropic therapy	Ritual magic
Relaxation	Service	Psychoactive drugs	Psychism, spiritism
Quietism	Creative work	Schutz Encounter	Some healing
	Some healing	Vision quest	Metta
	Parenting	Zazen	Sexual mysticism
Negative			
Mundane		**Exotic**	
Introverted	**Extraverted**	**Introverted**	**Extraverted**
Psychotherapy	Tonglen	Transpersonal therapy	Exorcism/ Deliverance
Counselling	Meditation on suffering	Jungian analysis	Spirit release therapy
Existential therapy	Hospice work	Psycholytic therapy	Sadomasochism
Logotherapy	Nursing, caring	Holotropic therapy	Confession/ self-abasement
	Bereavement work	Bioenergetics	Some Tantra
	Working with survivors		

Table 8 is useful, I believe, if only to indicate those areas of interest which individuals and groups may tend to express in their transpersonal practice. For example, it can help to demonstrate our own particular preferences and predilections in the transpersonal field, and enable us to compare these with other people's experience and practice. In this way we may better understand, and therefore be better placed to respect, the experiences and practices of others. Table 8 might also suggest to us ways in which our own developmental needs may be met by the application of particular practices. For example, a person who is experiencing alienation might well benefit from logotherapy. Perhaps Table 8 may even challenge us to consider the ways in which our own transpersonal practice may be limited and might be further developed by exploring alternative approaches. I am not explicitly suggesting that it is necessary or advisable to explore self-consciously and deliberately all these areas (for example, I am not advocating exorcism). However, I do believe that, for some people, spiritual development can become closeted and restricted by sticking rigidly to any one approach or practice. In this sense the taxonomy I am presenting might be used as a basis for developing a more integral practice (cf. Leonard & Murphy, 1995; Wilber, 2000a).

Another point that I should perhaps emphasize in this context is that the classification in Tables 7 and 8 is in no way intended to imply any *hierarchy* or universal developmental sequence. In my opinion all eight categories of experience are capable of leading to transformation and the various types of practice may have value for different people at different times in their lives, according to their own individual developmental priorities. I would strongly resist any attempt to superimpose a hierarchical structure such as Wilber's spectrum model on this scheme.

The Question of 'Evil'

I am aware that there is a most important question begged by the analysis that I have presented. This concerns the question of evil, in my opinion one of the great ignored or side-stepped issues in transpersonal psychology. In our current post-modern climate we simply do not have the conceptual wherewithal to consider effectively the nature of evil. We therefore generally assume that evil does not exist — that, like God, it represents a quaint remnant of an archaic theological dualism. So with the death of God, the Devil is also cast out of our equations. Wilber, for example, has comparatively little to say about evil. Although he claims to be a realist who recognizes the existence of manifest 'relative evil' (which should be lessened rather than eradicated) he rather conveniently argues that both good and evil can be transcended by adopting his own nondual perspective (e.g., Wilber, 1995a, p. 645; 1999b, p. 223).

The Jungian concept of the collective shadow goes some way towards an acknowledgement of evil. Yet for Jung, the collective shadow is simply the antithesis of the dominant collective zeitgeist, an essentially *relative* reality that is dark or hidden, but not in and of itself necessarily evil. When Jung addresses the issue of evil directly (e.g., Jung, 1969) he argues that both God and evil exist, but that these are essentially psychological structures, having no knowable transcendental reality. God and evil, in other words, are fundamental archetypes although, for Jung, they are no less real for that.[6] Whether or not we agree with Jung on this matter, his position is reasonably clear and coherent, and perhaps can provide an answer to the horrors of the Holocaust, Rwanda, Kosovo and the other many examples of humankind's inhumanity.

Transpersonal psychology, however, does not generally adopt this Jungian view and therefore cannot easily utilize his sophisticated psychological metaphysics. For the majority of writers on the transpersonal, the transcendental is accepted as having some kind of metaphysical reality of its own, beyond the human, psychological realm. It perhaps behoves these transpersonal psychologists to explain as clearly as possible their own particular metaphysical view, especially as this relates to the issue of good and evil. In practice very few appear to do so.

Wilber is one of these few and his position, as I understand it, seems to be that good and evil emerge as relative realities in the human-psychological-subtle realm. The ultimate transcendental reality, however, is beyond all duality, and therefore beyond good and evil. On the other hand, Wilber, like most Ascenders, also believes that this transcendent, nondual realm is somehow

---

6   Jung's writings and statements are often ambiguous and can be interpreted as implying that the archetype of God suggests the actual existence of a genuinely transcendent God. For a fuller discussion, see Chapter 10, also Stevens, 1990, pp. 247-254.

accessible to human consciousness and is also a prize worth considerable personal effort to attain. Whether in fact such a transcendent, nondual realm of experience is actually worth the candle is, however, a matter of some current controversy (see, for example, Heron, 1998).

An alternative, more fundamentalist and perhaps less fashionable view in transpersonal psychology, is that the transcendental realm is itself dual. In other words, there is both transcendental Good and transcendental Evil. God and Devil exist in their own right, and not just as archetypal images in the human mind.

Grof (e.g., 1998, 2000) adopts essentially this position. Although agreeing with Wilber that at the level of Absolute Reality (which is prior to creation) there is no good or evil, Grof argues a basically Gnostic position that these arise in the process of creation as *metaphysical* realities — the two faces of God:

> Good and Evil as separate entities come into existence and manifest in the initial stages of creation when the dark and light aspect of the Divine emerge from the undifferentiated matrix of the Void and Absolute Consciousness (Grof, 1998, p. 117).

Moreover, in Grof's scheme, metaphysical Evil is a *necessary* evil, since without it there would be no manifestation of the Good and 'the absence of metaphysical evil would drastically reduce the need for religion, since God without a powerful adversary would become a guaranteed commodity that would be taken for granted' (*ibid.* p. 116). The metaphysical realities of Good and Evil may, according to Grof, be directly experienced in holotropic states, but it is also possible, in the highest transpersonal experiences, to completely transcend Good and Evil in the achievement of nondual Absolute Consciousness (cf. Wilber). From this perspective, Good and Evil are seen as purely relative realities, themselves essential features of the 'cosmic game', 'virtual reality' or 'movie' of manifest existence, but of no ultimate concern.

> [N]one of the events from our everyday life, and, for that matter, none of the situations that involve suffering and evil, are ultimately real in the sense we usually think about them and experience them (Grof, 1998, p. 126).

In my view, these *metaphysical* questions and answers about the transcendental status of good and evil may be largely unimportant as far as human existence is concerned. For me, as for Jung, good and evil are very clear *psychological* and *experiential* realities, which is possibly all that matters. I do not necessarily wish to deny outright the reality of an absolute transcendental realm, but the direction my argument is taking me is towards the Kantian position that this noumenal realm may not only be ineffable, but perhaps also unknowable and unthinkable. As such it is of no immediate concern to human beings, who live and seek meaning in the phenomenal realms of psychological and interpersonal realities.

There is a very real danger, however, for those who accept the reality of the transcendental, but at the same time deny the reality of transcendent Evil (e.g., Wilber). This is that they may also be led to deny, or may become blind to, the real psychological and social evils of our time. If we believe that evil can be transcended in states of nondual or 'One Taste' consciousness (Wilber, 1999a), then why should we worry about tackling manifest evil in any direct way, whether in others or ourselves? Wilber himself recognizes this potential danger:

> This becomes a bit of a nightmare … because once you get a strong glimpse of One Taste, you can lose all motivation to fix those holes in your psychological basement (*ibid.*, p. 138).

Grof also points out the apparently disturbing implications of any transcendence of good and evil:

> At first sight, seeing the material world as 'virtual reality' and comparing human existence to a movie seems to trivialize life and make light of the depth of human misery. It might appear that such a perspective denies the seriousness of human suffering and fosters an attitude of cynical indifference, where nothing really matters. Similarly, accepting evil as an integral part of creation and seeing its relativity could easily be seen as a justification for suspending any ethical constraints and for unlimited pursuit of egotistical goals. It might also seem to sabotage any effort to actively combat evil in the world (Grof, 1998, p. 128).

Wilber's answer to this problem is to argue that nondual consciousness, although the 'highest estate imaginable' (Wilber, 1999a, p. 139) is not sufficient. From a truly integral perspective, he argues, we still have a need and also a moral duty to work at the 'lower levels' of our being. The moral duty, for Wilber, is entailed in the *bodhisattva* vow to 'communicate One Taste to all sentient beings' (*ibid.*, p. 139).

Grof's answer, more simply, is that:

> practical experience shows that the awareness of the emptiness behind all forms is not at all incompatible with genuine appreciation and love for all creation. Transcendental experiences leading to profound metaphysical insights into the nature of reality actually engender reverence toward all sentient beings and responsible engagement in the process of life (Grof, 1998, p. 128).

I agree with Grof's observation and also with Wilber's emphasis on the necessity for integral work. However, I question their assumption that nondual consciousness necessarily represents the most advanced and desirable achievement of the human condition (I do not doubt that it can be experienced). In arguing that personal experience of One Taste must be complemented by work at 'lower levels,' Wilber himself recognizes the necessity of some developmental advance *beyond* One Taste consciousness. His argument that the purpose of this complementary work is to communicate One Taste to others provides internal consistency in his position, but may simply be based on an ideological premise. More simply, we may suggest that spiritual understandings need to be fully integrated into our lives and relationships.

In my view, the dramas of human existence and the transpersonal take place against a rich psychological and social backdrop of good and evil. If we deny the *psychological and social realities of evil*, then how can we partake fully or deeply in life's drama? This does not mean, however, that we must therefore accept the existence of transcendent Evil, in the sense of a metaphysical ontological reality. For me, and this is crucial, the transpersonal does not necessarily imply, nor depend upon, the metaphysical transcendent (cf. Chapter 10). Transpersonal means simply the transcendence of ego boundaries. This does not necessarily involve the experience of a transcendental metaphysical realm or the transcendence of our normal human, psychological or interpersonal realities. Transpersonal development involves becoming more fully and more deeply human, not rising above our humanity. As Jung argues, we can only know or experience that which is in the psyche. Even if metaphysical Good or Evil exist as transcendent realities (noumena), we could only experience and know these *psychologically* (as phenomena).

In order to reclaim and enrich our humanness it is necessary, I believe, to acknowledge fully the shadow side of human nature, both personal and collective, and to find meaningful, creative, *soulful* responses to the challenges that this awareness will bring. As human beings who happen to be transpersonal psychologists, we should also realize that there is an important shadow side to the transpersonal that must be understood and responded to.

Conclusions

In this chapter I have discussed several aspects of this transpersonal shadow and suggested ways in which we might attempt to respond meaningfully to some of the issues raised. There have been many encouraging signs in recent years that transpersonal psychology is beginning to grow up and step outside the sandbox of its own making. In so doing, the movement is showing, for example, an increasing awareness that there is a dark and sinister side to the transpersonal that needs to be acknowledged and addressed. One manifestation of this is the sexual, emotional and physical abuse of children and adults in spiritual groups, or by religious authority figures (e.g., Heron, 1998; Langone, 1995; Storr, 1997; Welwood, 1983). Another manifestation, though still largely ignored in transpersonal psychology, is the rise of racist, fascist and terrorist organizations claiming spiritual or transpersonal authority, as well as of a variety of Satanist-styled groups of somewhat dubious status and purpose. For those who wish to explore some of these areas in more detail, the Internet is a particularly rich, if rather unreliable, resource.

In my opinion we cannot as transpersonal psychologists, nor as human beings, ignore the activities of those who would act in evil fashion, especially if they do so in the name of spirituality. Part of the process of stepping out of our sandbox into the real world is that we are willing to take on a mature, responsible, socially, politically and spiritually aware approach to the problem of evil, whether this exists in ourselves or in the activities of others. This does not mean that we lack compassion. In fact the ability to deal firmly with evil is itself an act of compassion. It means that we are no longer flakes.

Chapter 5

Towards a Transpersonal Psychology of Evil

In this chapter, I wish to explore more fully the concept of evil, particularly as it may be understood from the perspective of transpersonal psychology. 'Evil' is, of course, a difficult word. A major problem is that the concept of evil has become unfashionable in intellectual circles, including transpersonal psychology. This is partly because the word has been increasingly commandeered by the horror buffs, the tabloid press and by bishops, religious fundamentalists and ideological fanatics. These people all tend to use the word in a populist, often careless and sometimes hysterical way that sees evil as an absolute, substantial, perhaps demonic 'other' reality that can 'possess' certain people and make them absolutely wicked. As a result, these evil persons are perhaps beyond human understanding and compassion. They are also beyond redemption other than through divine or supernatural intervention, aided perhaps by rites of exorcism or 'deliverance ministry', or by conversion to a new set of religious values and beliefs.

In contrast, post-modern thought suggests that moral evaluations are relative and culture-specific. Our judgements of good and evil are made simply on the basis of personal or social values

This chapter is a revised and updated version of Daniels (2001a)

that are, in the final analysis, arbitrary and parochial. The implication is that neither good nor evil exist in any absolute sense — that what is good for one person or one society may be considered evil by another. Although we can morally evaluate actions within the confines of a particular ideological or social system, we cannot justifiably extrapolate our views and opinions to other societies and cultures.

The fundamentalist position is that evil is an absolute and substantial reality. For the relativist, evil is simply a point of view. But do we have to choose between these two polarized positions? Is there a way of accepting the absolute reality of evil, without simply asserting a set of restricted cultural values, or invoking questionable religious or ideological premises, or falling into the common trap of romanticizing evil? In other words, can we come to a rational and scientific understanding of evil that does not radically deny its existence? In my view, the answer is 'yes'. Furthermore, this understanding may also point the way towards some possible solutions to the problem of evil.

I shall begin by explaining that I use the word 'evil' principally in its descriptive or adjectival sense. Importantly, this contrasts with the use of 'evil' as a noun that refers to some kind of hypothetical reality such as a force, substance, intelligence or supernatural entity. In my view, there is no physical or metaphysical substance in evil. 'Evil' simply describes certain things, whether these are actions, events, persons, values, beliefs, processes or other phenomena. This use of 'evil' as a descriptor implies, of course, that a moral judgement is being made. Indeed the word 'evil' is reserved as the most extreme term of moral condemnation. Good and evil therefore only exist as a result of humankind's moral consciousness and our resulting ability to make moral evaluations. We have tasted the fruit of the tree of knowledge of good and evil and there is no turning back or away from our moral awareness. Indeed to do so would be to renounce our spiritual heritage.

Despite what the post-modernists may argue, moral evaluations are not simply relative. On the contrary, our moral consciousness is capable of making universal judgements of goodness and evil. In this, I very much follow the American moral philosopher John Kekes in his important book *Facing Evil* (1990). For Kekes, moral judgements are based firstly on the rational assessment of the human value of certain 'goods' and 'harms'. There are certain things that are intrinsically and universally good — the things that all rational persons agree will facilitate a good life. These include life itself, food and shelter, financial security, living in a stable and just society, being loved and respected, and being able to exercise one's talents and capacities. In contrast, 'harms' refer to those things that prevent a good life. These include prolonged pain, disease, untimely or unwelcome death, fear, depression, extreme poverty, rape, brutalization, captivity, contempt and social ostracism.

It is important here to distinguish these simple universal or intrinsic goods from those more complex relative goods that are merely defined or asserted as such by a particular individual, group or ideology. These relative goods may include material wealth, fame, racial purity, control of feelings, conformity, or religious devotion. In practice, as I will explain in more detail later, many of the manifest evils in this world are the direct result of promoting and imposing these relative and ideological goods in favour of (and usually at the expense of) simple, universal goods.

The tragedy of human life is that we sometimes suffer harm when we do not deserve it. In many cases, harm is due to contingency, in other words to natural causes such as epidemics, earthquakes, hurricanes, tidal waves, pestilence, or attacks by predators. Although we may refer to these as 'natural evils,' the occurrence of such natural harmful events has, I believe, no moral implications. I say this despite the tendency in many societies and in various philosophies, both traditional and new age, to interpret these events as deserved — in other words as some kind of punishment for, or inevitable consequence of, moral or religious transgressions, meted out by some supernatural intelligence, or as the inevitable reaping of karmic seeds. This is not to say that human beings do not have the moral capacity and duty to respond to such natural events, simply that the events themselves are amoral.

There is also, however, another fundamental type of undeserved harm — that which is inflicted by human beings. This is the essential domain of *moral evil*. Indeed, according to Kekes, moral evil may be defined as *undeserved harm caused by human beings*. At this point it might be objected that the harming of a person is never deserved or justifiable, and therefore that moral evil occurs whenever people cause harm. However if we have a serial killer in our midst, then it is not only morally justifiable, but also imperative, that we seek to apprehend this individual and to restrict his or her freedom to roam the streets and to exercise this particular talent. But in saying that the serial killer deserves to be harmed by imprisonment we must be clear about the principles by which we morally justify this action. If we are not very careful then the idea of deserved harm can easily become a platform for justifying revenge and for all manner of disproportionate, undeserved harm — in other words, it can become a platform for evil.

Kekes is clear that the only possible moral justification for inflicting harm is that it serves the interests of morality, defined as a commitment to human welfare.[1] However, Kekes is rather broad in his understanding of deserved harm, seeming, for example, to justify the punishment of offenders for punishment's sake. I offer a more specific and perhaps less controversial formulation that is, I believe, generally consistent with Kekes' main agenda. In my view deserved or justifiable harm may be defined as *the minimum harm that prevents a greater undeserved harm*. According to this definition it is morally justifiable to imprison offenders if their presence in the community would constitute a greater threat of undeserved harm to themselves or others. In contrast, it is not morally justifiable to execute a petty thief. All punishment must be reasonable and proportionate in relation to preventing greater harm.

One important consequence of distinguishing between the concepts of deserved and undeserved harm is that it reveals that there are certain actions for which there can *never* be any valid moral justification. This is because they cannot possibly prevent a greater undeserved harm. These actions are, in other words, absolutely and undeniably evil. They include the major evils of rape, physical and sexual abuse of children, mutilation and torture, as well as comparatively minor evils such as vandalism and the propagation of computer viruses and worms. In contrast, certain forms of theft and killing are, in my opinion, sometimes

---

1   Many people, notably the deep ecologists, would wish to include animal or planetary welfare in this definition, and I shall briefly return to this issue later.

morally justifiable (for example the theft of food for the starving, or of killing in defence of self or others).

It will be noted that in the definition of moral evil as 'undeserved harm caused by people,' there is no reference to the conscious intention, choice or decision to cause harm. This is, in fact, a most important and deliberate omission. It is commonly assumed that an action is morally good or evil only if the person has chosen to perform it. However, as Kekes effectively demonstrates, much moral evil is, in fact, *unchosen*. Kekes is referring here not so much to accidental harm, such as the unintentional shooting of someone while cleaning a firearm, but rather to evil that results from harmful personal characteristics or vices such as selfishness, jealousy, cowardice, cruelty, or avarice. People with these vices do not necessarily choose consciously to enact evil, rather their behaviour follows inevitably from their flawed character structure.

At this point, we have begun to step beyond a purely philosophical analysis to a consideration of the psychological causes of evil. What motivates people to commit evil? How is character formed? Are some people fundamentally evil? If so, are they born evil, or do they become evil? Can we prevent evil, or rehabilitate its perpetrators?

I shall begin with the question: '*When* do human beings become capable of evil?' The answer, which follows from our definition of moral evil, is as soon as the individual is capable of causing undeserved harm. Babies are, in my experience, harmless and totally vulnerable beings. I have never seen an evil baby, except in the distorted imaginations of Hollywood filmmakers. On the other hand, as many of us can attest, quite young children are capable of violent destructive tantrums and of inflicting undeserved pain and suffering on animals and siblings. At this point, it becomes meaningful to understand their actions as morally wrong ('evil' is probably too extreme a term in most cases). In fact it is vital that we see their actions in this way. Only by so doing will we seek to stop the present harm, prevent its reoccurrence, and take the necessary steps to begin to inculcate moral consciousness in the child.

The reality seems to be that children become capable of moral evil (and good) at precisely the time when ego consciousness and the sense of self are starting to emerge. This enables moral good

and evil to be considered primarily as *ego functions* and as character traits (or, virtues and vices) that may be encouraged or dis-
couraged in the child's developing personality. Although good
and evil exist as potentialities within every infant, these potentialities become actualities only with the emergence of ego consciousness and the development of character traits. To the extent
that neither animals nor babies possess a sense of self, they are
amoral beings. They have a nature but no character. They are
therefore capable of neither unchosen (characterological) nor
chosen (deliberate) moral evil.

For the same reason, human nature and the human unconscious must be considered to be fundamentally amoral — in
themselves neither good nor evil. The capacity for human
aggression is undoubtedly innate, as it is in many animals. In
animals, for the reasons outlined, aggression has no moral status
whereas, in humans, it may be used for either good or evil.
Aggression becomes morally evil when it is either a conscious
choice, or a character trait that produces undeserved harm —
either chosen or unchosen evil. Freud was partly right when he
postulated the *Thanatos* instinct (1920) — human beings do have
an innate capacity for evil and destructiveness. But he was
wrong to argue that Thanatos is an evil and destructive drive
within the unconscious. On the contrary, our innate capacity for
evil, and also for good, is a consequence of the human species'
programming to develop ego consciousness and character.

In contrast to Freud's view of the unconscious, I find Jung's
formulations (e.g., 1966) to be much more valuable and instruc-
tive. For Jung, the unconscious can be dangerous, but it is not
basically evil or destructive. However, there is one important
functional component of the unconscious that, in certain circumstances, can become a source for much of the evil that human
beings create in the world. This component is the *shadow*.
According to Jung, the shadow is the dark complement of the
consciously expressed personality (or persona). The shadow
represents those personal qualities and characteristics that are
unacceptable to the ego, which consequently defends against
them. The most important of these ego defences are repression
and projection. When we repress, the ego pushes the unacceptable tendencies down into the unconscious, where they remain
as shameful personal secrets. Such repression requires psychic

energy and may therefore cause us harm as a consequence of the general depletion in our psychological reserves. Repression can also harm us because the shadow may contain unacknowledged and unexpressed positive and beneficial qualities such as the capacity for joy, love and creativity.

Much more dangerous and potentially evil, however, is the defence mechanism of *projection*. With projection, the unacceptable shadow characteristics are cast out from the self and are perceived as being located in something external — usually in other people. Thus, for example, our own unacknowledged anger, hatred, jealousy, selfishness or lust are falsely experienced as qualities possessed by another person or group. This unconscious phantasized projection will generally cause a corresponding conscious moral devaluation of its object, which in turn leads us to behave towards the innocent person or group in harmful ways. In practice this may range from the comparatively minor damage caused by a snub or hurtful comment to the major evils of rape, torture, murder and ethnic cleansing.

According to Jung, this results from the fact that the shadow both complements and compensates for the conscious persona. Therefore to the extent that our persona is evaluated by us as 'good', the shadow will be apprehended as evil. If this 'evil' shadow is then projected onto others, these people will be defined and experienced as evil, and our moral enemy, and we will thereby feel consciously justified in the harm that we might cause them, which is cleverly interpreted by the ego as *deserved* harm. In this way evil (undeserved harm) is mistakenly seen as good (deserved harm). Such is the moral double-talk that projection can produce.

In identifying an important source of human evil with the unconscious shadow, this does not contradict the view expressed earlier that the capacity for evil develops alongside the emergence of ego consciousness. This is because the shadow is itself a by-product of conscious personality development. The shadow is thus formed from those characteristics of the whole self that cannot be accepted into the conscious persona. Because these characteristics are unacceptable to consciousness, they become defended against and submerged into the unconscious, where they constellate together as the shadow system.

However, in addition to the evil that may be caused by unconscious shadow projections we also need, as Kekes (1990), M. Scott Peck (1997) and Erich Fromm (e.g., 1947, 1964, 1973) have all importantly recognized, to acknowledge the reality of *character evil*. In this, it is the ego-persona system that is the principal, direct cause of evil, not the shadow. In other words, the individual develops a sense of self and a conscious personality structure that is itself evil, in the sense that it becomes the source of undeserved harm to self or others. In this way we develop character traits that are vicious, in the literal sense that they are full of vice. How is such a vicious development of the self possible? The simple answer, of course, is that personality development is the result of socialization and enculturation. By introjecting the behaviours, views, values, expectations and opinions of others, communicated via rewards and punishment, behavioural example, language, ideology and cultural mores, the child acquires a socialized self-system, persona, and self-concept. If these introjects are themselves vicious, then the child will inevitably develop a potentially evil-producing character structure. If brought up in a damaging, dysfunctional family or society where violence, spite, greed and selfishness are both modelled and encouraged, or in which it is considered normal and acceptable to exhibit sexist and racist attitudes, children will develop a self-system that incorporates and expresses these harmful characteristics. The resulting selves will cause evil in the same way that dogs bark — it is simply what they do. Moreover when such people themselves come into a position where they may influence the next generation, whether as parents, teachers or role models, then the whole vicious, damaging cycle is repeated.

According to Firman & Gila (1997), in their excellent book *The Primal Wound*, although this damaging process of socialization may be typical, it is not inevitable or natural, but represents a basic failure of empathic concern for the developing child that often results in neglect and abuse. They argue that children are traumatized into developing a false self, or survival personality, because of the failure of adult caretakers to empathize with and mirror accurately the child's own experience. In this way, the child is unable to acquire an authentic self-system, based on reflected knowledge and acceptance of its own total Being. In its place, the child develops a false-self system, based upon adapting to the non-empathic behaviours, values and opinions of the caretakers.

In this failure to empathize with the child's experience, the adult treats the child as an object or thing rather than as a subject or person. In Martin Buber's terms (1970) the child becomes an It rather than a Thou and therefore is seen as something to be moulded according to the wishes and views of the adult. Of course parents and teachers must set limits on children's behaviour, and provide examples of good and effective behaviour. But these adult interventions must always be led by a deep understanding of the child's true needs and experience; in other words on deep empathy with the child. This kind of 'good-enough' parenting, which leads to the development of authentic selfhood, is very different from the damaging, wounding manipulation caused by the failure to empathize with the child's experience.

According to Carl Rogers (e.g., 1959), adults achieve this manipulative moulding though their conditional love and conditional approval of the child. In this way the child gradually learns how it must think, feel and behave in order to receive the love and approval of its parents and other significant figures. These imposed 'conditions of worth' are eventually incorporated into the child's self-concept and thereby become characteristic features of its persona, or survival personality. The remedy for this damaging process, according to Rogers, is for the adult's attitude to the child to be based on unconditional love or unconditional approval, which Rogers calls 'unconditional positive regard'. Only if love and respect are unconditional will the child experience a psychological and social atmosphere in which it is possible and safe to become what he or she truly is.

In my view, the failures of empathy and unconditional love are not simply features of the primal wounding of the child, but are general characteristics of the psychology of evil. Thus moral evil results when people treat others (or themselves) as things or objects, or when there is a failure of concern for their welfare. If we truly empathize with people, treating each person as a Thou, rather than an It, and if we simultaneously show them moral regard and concern, then personal moral evil (or, character evil) is simply not possible. If either of these conditions is not met, then various kinds of moral evil can occur.

Figure 2. The wheel of virtue and vice

This argument is illustrated in Figure 2. Here I distinguish firstly between empathy and egocentrism. In empathy, there is understanding of the experience and needs of another (or of the larger reality of the whole Self), whereas from an egocentric or narcissistic position, there is awareness only of one's own limited egoic experience and needs. Secondly, I distinguish between benevolence and malevolence. Benevolence is essentially having good will towards oneself or others, wishing them well, and showing concern for their welfare. Malevolence is ill will, or wishing someone harm. The diagram recognizes that egocentrism and empathy, and benevolence and malevolence, can exist in varying degrees; also, importantly, that these two dimensions seem to be more or less independent. In other words, a high degree of empathy can coexist with either benevolence or malevolence. The various combinations and degrees of egocentrism-empathy and benevolence-malevolence give rise to different potentials for good and evil. If there is both empathy and benevolence, then moral good is the likely outcome, whether expressed as compassionate action, care, sympathy, or interest in others. If both egocentrism and malevolence predominate, then we have the potential for the evils of neglect, antipathy, abuse and enmity.

Other kinds of evil are possible, however, when egocentrism is combined with benevolence, or empathy with malevolence. Consider, for example, the infatuated lover or smothering parent who, despite what may be intense feelings of good will and concern for the other, is unaware of the actual experience of their partner or child and instead projects their own needs onto the relationship. Such narcissistic projection is inherently damaging to the other person because it is non-empathic and distorting. Then there are those forms of evil in which the person seems to understand certain aspects of another's experience, but is malevolently envious, or seems to delight in the other's suffering. In sadism, for example, the enjoyment would appear to be all the more delicious precisely *because* the sadist is able to empathize with the pain of the victim. There would be little point to sadism if the victim were an actual object that could not experience the terror and suffering — for example if she or he became unconscious. Although it is true that the sadist is almost certainly unaware of the larger reality of the victim's experience (in other words, the sadist empathizes only with the immediate pain), sadism is perhaps not so much a failure of empathy as of compassion. Thus in the sadistic trance there is no moral concern whatsoever for the victim, who becomes simply the object of the perpetrator's desires.

Although I have emphasized the dimensions of empathy-egocentrism and benevolence-malevolence in determining the potentialities for good and evil, an additional factor in the manifestation of these potentials is personal effectance, or the power to act. In practice a person may be both empathic and benevolent, but may lack the power, capacity or skill to effect beneficial action. Similarly, a person may be non-empathic and malevolent, but is fortunately prevented from engaging in evil action through personal weakness or by strong social controls.

According to this model, the basic solution to character evil lies in the development of empathic understanding and benevolence, characteristics that may be conveniently symbolized by the *head* and the *heart*. In order to actively promote moral good, we also need to encourage personal effectiveness and a *hands*-on approach in our moral dealings with other people. To do these things, we need to replace the vicious circle of non-empathic primal wounding and malevolent socialization with a virtuous circle of empathic responding, benevolence and moral effectance. To see how this may be done, we need to understand more clearly the function of significant others in creating and defining the self. Heinz Kohut (1977) calls these significant others 'selfobjects' and psychosynthesis refers to them as 'unifying centres'. In object relations theory they are known simply as 'objects'. In this discussion I shall use the term 'self-centre' to refer to these defining and unifying selfobjects.

Self-centres are often individual people, but they also include groups, norms, customs, values, roles, beliefs, ideologies and worldviews. Since the self exists, and can exist, only in relationship, these self-centres reflect and re-present the individual's experience, and in this way serve to define and maintain the self-system. Because they are fundamental to the self's very existence, representational images of external self-centres are incorporated psychologically and thereby come to function as internal centres with which the subjective self maintains an interior relationship. Thus, for example, we may form internal images of the loving carer or strict head teacher that become abiding reassuring or fearful presences, and with whom we maintain an inner, often unspoken dialogue. Then there are also the relationships we have with other internalized self-centres, such as our inner representations of the values, roles, beliefs and ideologies that have influenced us throughout our lives. In this way, we may, for example, engage in inner debates with our conscience, or experience conflict with our internalized sexual or ethnic identities.

The assumption in all this is that if external self-centres are distorting, damaging or malevolent, they will produce distorted self-systems and damaged or malevolent characters. We actually know quite a lot about the ways in which manifest evil results from people's relationships to significant others that are either non-empathic or malevolent, or both. There is extensive research, for example, on the traumatizing and damaging effects of inadequate or abusive parenting, or of growing up in an emotionally disturbed and conflicted family environment. Social psychological studies have also shown that people are less likely to act to help a victim when they observe other people who fail to act, and will themselves inflict what they believe to be life-threatening pain when ordered to do so by someone in authority.

Furthermore, members of groups will conform to harmful behaviours and, when occupying a social role that permits and normalizes actions that harm others, people will often act in ways that fulfil this malevolent role. Here the actions of others, or the authority of the leader, or group ties, or a social role, act as non-empathic or malevolent self-centres in relation to which the self often becomes seemingly incapable of empathic and benevolent moral action.

Another important consideration in this is the learned and progressive nature of human evil. When people cause harm, their behaviour can become an acquired habit, learned simply by doing. In his book *The Roots of Evil*, Ervin Staub (1989) has shown that a pattern of harm-doing often starts out in relatively minor forms, such as name calling or ostracism. However, when perpetrators begin to harm people in these ways, then further harm becomes more likely and often more extreme. Sadistic killers, for example, often have a history of inflicting pain to animals when children, from which they gradually progress to the killing of animals and eventually to murder, often of an increasingly horrific nature. In the Nazi Holocaust there was a similarly evil progression from the boycotting of Jewish businesses to the eventual attempt at the Final Solution in the death camps of Auschwitz, Dachau and Treblinka. As Staub points out, one of the most effective ways in which we can, in practice, prevent great evil is by speaking or acting against the smaller evils that precede it. Evil, it seems, can be nipped in the bud. Social psychological studies have shown, for example, that bystanders — the witnesses of evil — can themselves have tremendous influence for good or ill, depending upon whether or not they are prepared to take appropriate action in times of crisis. These bystanders may be either individuals witnessing an attack in the street, or the international community that witnesses large-scale brutalization or ethnic cleansing.[2] All this confirms the point made earlier concerning the need for a hands-on approach to the problem of evil.

In the processes whereby human evil becomes possible, we should not underestimate the significance of social norms, customs, values, beliefs, myths, and religious or political ideologies.

---

2   Of course I am not necessarily condoning military intervention — as indicated earlier, we should always aim at the *minimum* necessary harm.

As we have seen, these provide important self-centres in relation to which personalities are created and maintained. If we understand evil as the causing of undeserved harm then it is undeniable that certain of these norms, customs and so on are themselves evil because they encourage, justify or condone undeserved harm. By way of example, we may note the following:

- Social norms such as ignoring the starving beggar in the street.
- Customs such as female circumcision or the murder of female offspring at birth.
- Values of male sexual conquest or of personal success at any cost.
- Beliefs such as the just world view that victims of circumstance have deserved their fate.
- Myths of racial or ethnic superiority.
- Religious doctrines such as that women or black people have no soul.
- Political ideologies that are fascist, despotic or that permit slavery.

A characteristic feature of many of these evil systems of valuation, belief or practice is their moral distinction between ingroups and out-groups, between 'us' and 'them'. Moral concern, or benevolence, is restricted to ourselves, our family, tribe, nation or race, whereas outsiders and strangers are seen as potential threats or enemies that may deserve to be harmed, perhaps simply because they are different, or because of perceived harms they have caused us in the past.

Not only is the enemy the legitimate object of conscious malevolence, but he or she also becomes the appropriate target of unconscious shadow projections, both personal and collective. In this way undeserved harmful action towards our enemy is often due to a complex mix of both conscious and unconscious malevolent motives. As mentioned earlier, one of the most pernicious aspects of this process is the way in which these evil value systems are themselves used to justify morally the harm done to our enemies. Thus the enemy is defined as evil and therefore it is seen as not only justifiable but also our moral duty to inflict the harm we cause, even to the point of genocide. The tragic and devastating irony of this, as history clearly attests, is that moral and religious systems are themselves among the greatest causes of human evil.

Ervin Staub's (1989) analysis of human evil demonstrates that the scapegoating and harming of enemies is particularly likely to occur in conditions of hardship, threat, stress and frustration. These difficult conditions may be economic, personal or social. A common feature, however, is that there is a perceived attack on the sense of self. This assault on the self and self-concept leads to a response that Heinz Kohut (1978) calls 'narcissistic rage' and to a lust for revenge. At such times our fury may be so powerful and destructive that we become oblivious even to our own welfare. The threat to which we are responding in this narcissistic rage is that to our very existence. Something fundamental to whom we are has been violated and we respond with a primitive fury that, according to Firman & Gila (1997), reveals the depths and damage of our own primal wounding and our fear of non-being.

It is important to realize that this kind of narcissistic rage can occur in response to a threat to *anything* that is central to the self, in other words to any of the self-centres that define and maintain the self-system. These may be our own body, our friends or family, our gender or ethnicity, our football team, our nation, our heartfelt values, our religious and political beliefs, or our ideals and heroes. In this rage our motivation is both to dissociate from the wounding pain to the self and to destroy the enemy who violates us in this way.

In the personal sphere we may note not only the relatively recent phenomenon of 'road rage,' but also the profound rage often experienced by those whose bodies have been violated, whether by disfigurement, illness or rape. In groups, there are the manifestations of narcissistic rage often exhibited in fights between street gangs or between rival football supporters. In the political arena, too, as Staub and others have shown, we may also see how ethnic cleansing, genocide and war are often the result of a profound wounding to the self-concept of a group or nation, whether current or historical. At these times, as for example in the Germany of the 1930s, people may look to a strong leader to provide a stable centre in relation to whom the violated sense of shared identity may be recovered. As is well understood by political analysts, a country will generally rally around its leaders when threatened with attack, no matter how unpopular these leaders may have previously been. Astute leaders will then commonly exploit this phenomenon by directing the people's desire for revenge towards an appropriate target, whether this is the actual aggressor or a convenient scapegoat.

What, then, is the solution to human evil? Because the issue is so complex there can be no simple or single response to this question. In my opinion, there is certainly no final answer communicated to us from a transcendent source and we have no alternative but to struggle as human beings, as *whole* beings, with the reality of our own evil. However, the analysis I have outlined goes some way to providing at least partial answers. Perhaps the most important implication is the centrality of empathy and benevolence in the moral equation, and of the need for a relationship with external and internal self-centres that represent and express these qualities, thereby enabling the self to experience its connection to the total reality of its Being. In practice, such empathic and benevolent self-centres may include:

- Significant others such as empathic and benevolent parents, friends, mentors, therapists, or spiritual teachers.
- Universal moral values and principles.
- Religious, social and political ideologies that express values of universal empathy and benevolence.
- Internal archetypal images of empathy and benevolence, such as the Realized Self, Buddha, Christ, the Virgin Mary, Krishna, God or Goddess.
- For those who have been able to discover these within the self, perhaps as a result of spiritual practice, there is also the *soul*, which I understand as the benevolent spiritual Heart, and the *witness*, or our empathic spiritual Head.

Only in relation to these empathic and benevolent self-centres, can the self begin the process of healing the damage caused by the influence of non-empathic and malevolent centres. As is suggested above, such healing can be viewed as a process of self-knowledge and self-realization, an important component of which is the acknowledgement and integration of the personal and collective shadow. This process may involve personal therapy, the further development of moral consciousness, fundamental changes in relationships or in religious or political affiliation, or spiritual practice of one kind or another.

It is also important, however, not to see the phenomenon of evil as a purely personal or psychological problem. This would open us up to the charge of psychologism. Ken Wilber's quadrant model (e.g., Wilber, 1995a, 2000a) provides one important way forward in this respect. If we apply this model to the phenomenon of evil, then we might come up with something like that illustrated in Table 9.

Table 9. The quadrants of good & evil

	INTERIOR	**EXTERIOR**
INDIVIDUAL	Self & identity	Drug treatment
	Moral development	Behaviour therapy
	Psychotherapy	Token economy
	Meditation & spirituality	Psychosurgery
COLLECTIVE	Myths	Laws and customs
	Cultural values	Institutions
	Ideology and religion	Language and propaganda
	World View	Economic system

Firstly, we have the individual-interior quadrant. This is the quadrant of inner psychological experience. In relation to morality and evil it is the quadrant of moral and spiritual consciousness, of empathic awareness, of the development of moral judgement, character and personality, and of psychotherapy and self-realization. One of the ways in which we can seek to promote human goodness and tackle moral evil is by working directly on these aspects of our Being. For many people, especially psychologists and psychotherapists, this may seem the most important quadrant to address. However, the important implication of Wilber's quadrant model is the need to examine also the other three perspectives.

In the exterior-individual quadrant we look at individuals from the outside and respond to their external behaviours. In the moral sphere, this is the quadrant that addresses the question of how we should attempt to control the person who is behaving in an evil fashion, and how we might seek to replace antisocial with prosocial behaviour. This quadrant seeks external solutions to individual evil, such as restraint or imprisonment, the imposition of training programmes or regimes of reward and punishment, or the use of medication or psychosurgery to control aggressive behaviour.

Next we have the interior-collective quadrant. Here we look at groups, societies and cultures from the perspective of the insider who has a shared understanding. In terms of morality, this is the quadrant of cultural values, beliefs, myths, ideologies and worldviews. As we have seen, many of these aspects of collective experience are manifestly evil and the demands of morality require that they should change. However, because this is a quadrant of interior experience, it is not possible to alter this from the outside, or to impose alternative, morally better perspectives in any direct way. Instead, change must develop from the inside, perhaps as a result of the efforts of enlightened and brave members of the community who dare to challenge the dominant evil consensus.

Finally, there is the exterior-collective quadrant. This refers to those social structures that are observable from the outside. These include laws and customs, institutions, the use of language to maintain shared perspectives or as a means of propaganda, and the economic system. In many cases, these social structures support a system that is itself evil or provide the social context in which evil is nurtured. Although it may be hard to break customs or change the way in which people use language, governments do have powers to propagandize, to pass laws, to reform institutions and to modify the economic system. In fact this is perhaps the most immediate and direct way in which evil can be tackled within society. Thus, for example, the establishment in Britain of the National Heath Service and the introduction of laws against racial and sexual discrimination are undoubted victories for good. Equally, however, governments can, and often do, use their powers for evil, for example in the passing of the Nuremberg Laws defining the status of Jews in Nazi Germany. Another important element in the exterior-collective approach to evil, as Ervin Staub's (1989) careful analysis has shown, is the importance of eliminating the social conditions that produce hardship, stress and frustration since these are the conditions in which evil can propagate. Although once again this may be in the hands of those with political power, it is not only governments who have the ability to instigate changes in social structures. In this respect we should not underestimate the power of pressure groups, NGOs, the media and political commentators. Neither should we forget that we all also live in micro-societies such as family groups, clubs and organizations in which many of us have the power to bring about significant social change, either for good or ill.

My purpose in identifying and describing these quadrants is to emphasize that the solution to evil should ideally work on all four quadrants. It is not enough to enact laws if we do not also attend to people's values and beliefs. Nor can we expect evil to disappear in the world by devoting ourselves to a life of purely personal development, whether through psychotherapy or spiritual discipline, if in so doing we ignore urgent social and political realities such as suffering and injustice. And, of course, it will never be sufficient to rely solely on an approach that simply advocates locking up or punishing offenders or subjecting them to psychological or medical treatment.

The mistake entailed in each of these perspectives is that of ignoring the value and importance of the others. The significance of each is its own unique contribution to the total picture, which must be seen from an all-quadrant perspective. There is still much work to be done towards understanding the ways in which development occurs within each quadrant. However, according to Wilber, there may be very close parallels between the evolutionary patterns or waves of development that may be seen in each quadrant. At its simplest, as we have seen, there seems to be a general three-stage evolution from the prepersonal and presocial, to the personal and social, to the transpersonal and spiritual.

I want to end by exploring briefly the implications of this evolutionary and transpersonal perspective for our understanding of moral development and of the nature of good and evil. Although Wilber (e.g., 1999) provides more extensive analyses of development, the three general phases of prepersonal/presocial, personal/social and transpersonal/spiritual are sufficient, I believe, to understand the ways in which the capacities for good and evil may develop. In the first phase, to the extent that consciousness is essentially *egocentric* (non-empathic), there is very little capacity for moral good even if, as Carl Rogers believes, the child is naturally benevolent. In the second phase, moral good and evil emerge as expressions of character development and shadow projections. At this phase, however, the capacity for moral good is limited not only by the unintegrated influence of the shadow but also because of the continuing *self-centredness* of personal consciousness (i.e., its focus on 'me and mine'). Such self-centredness can only be radically overcome, I believe, by developing to a transpersonal phase in which there is not only an acknowledgement, owning, and integration of the shadow, but also an opening up of the head (our capacity for empathy) and heart (our capacity for benevolence) to something beyond the personal self and those close to the self (cf. Ferrer's, 2002, notion of *emancipation from self-centredness*).

In simple terms, empathy is present whenever a person moves beyond an egocentric perspective to an understanding of the experiences of others (or of the larger self). Yet empathy may have a lesser or a greater span. Thus some people may be able to empathize only with their immediate family or friends, others also with members of their own gender or peer group, or with those who share the same tribal identity, nationality or ethnicity. Perhaps a minority is capable of extending the capacity for empathy to all people. Here we see empathy as something that may *expand* during the course of development in a way that itself parallels the general evolutionary movement from individual-egocentric to personal-social to global-transpersonal. In a similar way we can perhaps also understand the development of benevolence as involving an increase in moral span, in other words an expansion in the number and range of people for whom we show moral concern and whom we consider as a Thou rather than an It. At the highest levels of transpersonal development, as the deep ecologists and Wilber (e.g., 2000a, Chart 5c) argue, moral consideration may extend beyond the human realm to encompass all sentient beings or even the whole of reality.

From this transpersonal perspective, good is brought into the world and evil is countered through the development of our human capacity for moral consciousness, as expressed in all four of Wilber's quadrants. Yet consciousness is not enough, for we also need the ability and willingness to *act* directly and effectively in accordance with our moral consciousness. In other words, we also need skilful and willing *hands*. Good and evil arise in the human head and heart, and our moral destiny is literally in our own hands. There is no other solution. Evil is not a mysterious, unknowable, demonic reality that possesses or infects us. Evil is a part of the human equation. It is as familiar to us as our own face. Indeed it *is* the human face, as seen at our most non-empathic, malevolent or ineffectual moments. Moral evil arises as a result of our human capacity for ego-consciousness and personal being. It exists because we exist. The radical solution to evil can only be for human consciousness in all its manifestations to develop beyond egocentrism and the wounded self-system towards a truly transpersonal foundation based upon an ever-expanding empathy and benevolence, and an increasing capacity to act according to our conscience. In this way we pave the way for the true realization of the Self — in the sense of the whole person connected to the whole of reality. In my opinion such realization of the Self is simultaneously the realization of the human spirit. Indeed it is this spirit, I believe, that is the deep source of our moral consciousness and the true Ground of empathy and benevolence.

Chapter 6

Maslow and Self-Actualization

Although Abraham Maslow did not originate the term or concept of self-actualization, interest in this field derives largely from his work. Maslow died in 1970, yet many of his writings are still in print and are widely read, not only by psychologists and students, but by educationalists, managers, nurses, social workers, counsellors and broad sections of the general public. Furthermore, Maslow's seminal role as one of the founders of both humanistic and transpersonal psychology has made him extremely influential in both disciplines and has contributed to his standing as one of the key figures in the larger history of psychology.

Abraham Maslow was born in 1908, in Brooklyn, New York, the son of Russian Jewish immigrants. Colin Wilson (1972) has suggested that the fact of being Jewish influenced Maslow's later thinking: 'He speaks about his Utopianism, "yearning for the good world" which is a Jewish tradition' (p. 136). According to Wilson, by the time Maslow enrolled at the University of Wisconsin to major in psychology, he was an idealist socialist who had become 'bowled over' by Watsonian behaviourism, which he saw as offering a practical way of improving people and society. While Maslow later became disillusioned with both social-

---

This chapter is a revised and updated version of Daniels (1981, 1982) ism and behaviourism, idealistic fervour and utopianism were to remain consistent features of his approach.

Maslow's undergraduate training was primarily in the classical laboratory methods of animal research. While at Wisconsin, Maslow worked with Harry Harlow and together they wrote research papers on primate behaviour. After graduation, Maslow was briefly a research assistant to E.L. Thorndike at Columbia University before obtaining a teaching post at Brooklyn College. In 1951, Maslow moved to Brandeis University, where he remained until 1969, when he accepted a fellowship at the Laughlin Foundation in California. It was at Brooklyn College that Maslow's intellectually formative years were spent. While in New York, Maslow sought out and was influenced by a number of eminent psychologists, many of whom had fled to America from Nazism in Europe. These included Max Wertheimer, Alfred Adler, Erich Fromm, Karen Horney, Kurt Goldstein, and the anthropologist Ruth Benedict. Together they extended Maslow's intellectual horizons beyond the American traditions of behaviourism and functionalism, and introduced him to Gestalt and Freudian theories. Wertheimer encouraged the holistic approach that was to characterize Maslow's later research. Adler prompted Maslow's interest in dominance, while Fromm reinforced his humanism. It was from Horney, Goldstein and Benedict, respectively, that Maslow acquired the key terms real self, self-actualization, and synergy.

Early Attempts at Theory (c. 1942–1949)

Maslow first introduces the concept of self-actualization as part of a broadly-based theory of motivation, the well-known 'hierarchy of needs' model (Figure 3):

> There is a hierarchy of five sets of goals or purposes or needs which are set in the following order of prepotency. First, satisfaction or gratification of body needs ... Second, the safety needs ... Third, love, affection, warmth, acceptance, a place in the group. Fourth, desire for self-esteem, self-respect, self-confidence, for the feeling of strength or adequacy ... Fifth, self-actualization, self-fulfillment, self-expression, working out of one's own fundamental personality, the fulfillment of its potentialities, the use of its

capacities, the tendency to be the most that one is capable of being (Maslow, 1943a, p. 91).

The description of self-actualization in this statement clearly indicates the direction of Maslow's thinking, but conceptual problems are immediately apparent. Maslow fails to specify, for example, whether he views self-actualization as a state of ultimate satisfaction and fulfilment, a state of need, a process, or merely a tendency to this process.

In a presentation of his full theory of human motivation, Maslow (1943b) begins by suggesting that self-actualization is something there is a need *for* — an end-state, goal or ultimate satisfaction. He then attempts to specify exactly what sort of goal is implied, proposing that 'what a man can be, he must be' *(ibid.,* p. 382). Maslow does not generally consider the possibility that a person may become any one of several alternatives, depending upon upbringing, circumstances, opportunities and active choices. He implies, in contrast, that there is only one possible

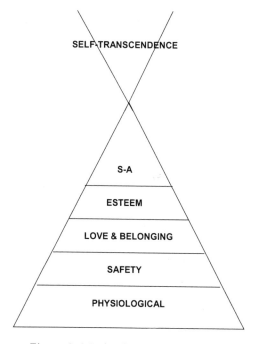

Figure 3. Maslow's hierarchy of needs

end-state (or ideal end-state) for each person, and thus that there is only one way in which an individual may truly self-actualize. Maurice Friedman (1976) has pointed out that 'the concept of self-realization has its earliest philosophical roots in Aristotle's doctrine of entelechy, according to which every individual being needs to realize his or her own telos, or goal' (p. 5). Maslow's statement appears to indicate that he has himself adopted this essentially deterministic Aristotelian conception.

Maslow's position is more fully explicated when he goes on to suggest that a person's self-actualization refers to 'the tendency for him to become actualized in what he is potentially. This tendency might be phrased as the desire to become more and more what one is' (Maslow, 1943b, p. 382). This is one of the first indications of Maslow's leaning towards what Gordon Allport (1955) has termed a 'homunculus' theory of personality. The assumption behind Maslow's statement thus seems to be that normally people do not fully express or actualize their true natures or fundamental personalities. In other words, there exists a *real self* (cf. Horney, 1950) which lies unseen behind the everyday facade. This real self, for Maslow, presumably consists in the sum total of the person's potentialities and capacities, for to become what one is means to 'become everything that one is capable of becoming' (Maslow, 1943b, p. 382).

It might appear from this that Maslow avoided a consideration of the role of opportunity or choice in the actualization of potentialities because he believed that it is possible to actualize all capacities. Such a belief is clearly untenable, and it is inconceivable that Maslow seriously maintained this position. What seems more likely is that he had rejected the end-state conception of self-actualization. If self-actualization is simply the process of becoming everything that one is capable of becoming (or, perhaps, merely the need, desire or tendency for such a process), then there is no implication that the individual can or will ever achieve total fulfilment.

Due, perhaps, to the conceptual difficulties encountered, or to the lack of an empirical base for his speculations, Maslow next turned from a theoretical analysis of human motivation to a consideration of self-actualization as a personality syndrome. Maslow's change in approach is indicated by a statement that 'we may expect to find in people living at the higher need level a larger number and greater degree of the qualities found in self-actualizing people' (Maslow, 1948a, p. 436). Here he is clearly suggesting that the concept of self-actualization may be approached in terms of both motivational level and personality syndromes. This is done by arguing that need gratification is central to the formation of character. Individuals at different motivational levels are thereby assumed to differ in their basic expressions of personality. Furthermore, the personality syndromes associated with the various motivational levels are assumed to differ in terms of psychological health, or 'gratification health' (Maslow, 1948b, p. 409). Self-actualization, which implies gratification of all lower needs, thus comes to be equated with a personality syndrome exhibiting ideal health.

Empirical Researches into Self-Actualization (primarily 1950)

Maslow (1973, pp. 43–44) describes how he conceived of a characterological study of self-actualization from his acquaintance with two of his 'teachers', Max Wertheimer and Ruth Benedict. Whatever self-actualization was, Maslow believed that these two people exemplified it. Furthermore, Maslow became convinced that the informal notes that he had made on Wertheimer and Benedict described not the characteristics of two individuals, but rather those of one *type* of person. Self-actualization indeed appeared to exhibit the properties of a personality syndrome. Spurred on by this success, Maslow looked to identify other self-actualizing people, in order to examine the syndrome more exactly and fully. Selection was from three populations: (a) personal acquaintances and friends, (b) public and historical figures, and (c) college students. The basis for selection reflected Maslow's belief that self-actualization represented the highest level of psychological health, and also the full utilization of talents and capacities. The criteria he used therefore

> had a positive as well as a merely negative side. The negative criterion was an absence of neurosis, psychopathic personality, psychosis, or strong tendencies in these directions ... The positive criterion for selection was positive evidence of self-actualization ... loosely described as the full use and exploitation of talents, capacities, potentialities, etc. (Maslow, 1950, p. 12).

Unfortunately, Maslow does not specify in sufficient detail how either criterion was assessed. In particular, it is not clear how a subject's full utilization of talents and potentialities was determined. What is apparent, however, is that the criteria were applied in such a stringent manner as to generate an extremely select sample. Maslow (e.g., 1950, 1970) includes among his named cases and partial cases Einstein, William James, Schweitzer, Aldous Huxley, Thoreau, Beethoven, Freud, Spinoza and F.D. Roosevelt. Furthermore, when Maslow applied his criteria in a screening of 3000 college students, he was able to identify 'only one immediately usable subject and a dozen or so possible future subjects' (Maslow, 1950, p. 12), and he was forced to conclude that 'self-actualization of the sort I had found in my older subjects perhaps was not possible in our society for young, developing people' (Maslow, 1970, p. 150). This is rather circular reasoning, however, for if such young people are developing it is difficult to conceive how they could exhibit the necessary full utilization of talents and capacities.

Maslow himself recognized the select nature of his sample, and he concedes that his generalizations grew out of 'my selection of certain kinds of people ... people only from Western cultures, people selected with all kinds of built-in biases' (Maslow, 1973, p. 44). Moreover, Maslow's empirical method was essentially to form his own global impressions of his subjects, a procedure that is likely to emphasize any subjective bias. Such, however, was Maslow's belief in the importance of his studies of self-actualizing people that methodological doubts did not deter publication.

Maslow's descriptions of self-actualizing people (e.g., Maslow, 1950, pp. 14–33; Maslow, 1970, pp. 153–180) seem to indicate a coherent personality syndrome, and several characteristics are consistent with the notion that self-actualization represents optimal psychological health and functioning (e.g., self-acceptance, lack of defensiveness, autonomy, spontaneity, profound interpersonal relations). This, however, may be largely self-fulfilling, given that psychological health was a criterion for selection.

The publication of the 1950 paper marked the beginning of Maslow's empirical researches into self-actualization, yet it also heralded a move away from the empirical method. His later writings are mainly theoretical and philosophical sequels to this brief research study.

The Psychology of Becoming (c. 1950–1965)

One gratifying aspect of Maslow's later writings is his willingness to address the difficulties and inconsistencies in his earlier formulations. One of the first indications of this is when he confronts the issue of whether it is more fruitful to consider self-actualization as a process or as a state:

> Self-actualization ... tends to be seen as an ultimate or final state of affairs, a far goal, rather than a dynamic process, active throughout life ... If we define growth as the various processes which bring the person toward ultimate self-actualization, then this conforms better with the observed fact that it is going on all the time in the life history (Maslow, 1955, p. 9).

In this statement, Maslow suggests that growth (a process) brings the person towards ultimate self-actualization (a state). This suggestion would be acceptable if Maslow were to remain consistent; unfortunately, his writings tend to use the terms 'growth' and 'self-actualization' interchangeably.

The concept of growth involves certain assumptions, as Maslow appreciated. Thus he had argued in 1949 that self-actualization is 'intrinsic growth of what is already *in* the organism, or more accurately of what *is* the organism itself' (p. 263), implying that it is essentially a maturational process in which the formative parameters are biological. Maslow's thought was always characterized by a rejection of the developmental origin of the real self and by a general disregard of the symbolic-interactionist approach. Like Karen Horney (e.g., Horney, 1950), Maslow tended to believe that any formative influence of social interaction produces an idealized *pseudo-self*, a pastiche of roles and performances behind which the *real self* is hidden or repressed (see, for example, Maslow, 1956, pp. 41–42). According to Maslow, the real self is primarily a biological 'given':

> We have ... an essential inner nature which is intrinsic, given, 'natural' ... I include in this essential inner nature instinctoid needs, capacities, talents, anatomical equipment, physiological balances, prenatal and natal injuries, and traumata to the neonatus (Maslow, 1965, p. 307).

Implicit in this formulation is the assumption that self-actualization is encouraged to the extent that the real self is available to consciousness. Thus Maslow (1965) argues that 'authentic selfhood can be defined in part as being able to hear these impulse-voices within oneself' (p. 309). Self-actualization occurs, by implication, through following ones 'natural' impulses and desires:

> It is ... best to bring out and encourage, or, at the very least, to recognize this inner nature, rather than to suppress or repress it. Pure spontaneity consists of free, uninhibited, uncontrolled, trusting, unpremeditated expression of the self ... with minimal interference by consciousness (Maslow, 1965, p. 309).

Moreover, according to Maslow, the process of growth is governed by the principle of pleasure: 'Growth takes place when the next step forward is subjectively more delightful, more joyous, more intrinsically satisfying than the last' (Maslow, 1956, p. 36). This occurs, he suggests, when the organism is satiated with 'lower' pleasures. If, however, as a result of defensiveness, individuals forfeit their own subjective experiences or inner signals and adopt instead the opinions of other people, then growth is prevented. Thus Maslow (1956) concludes that 'the primal choice, the fork in the road, then, is between others' and one's own self' (p. 42).

On the basis of such a model of growth it is easy to confuse self-actualization with abandon, sensuality, hedonism, narcissism and self-seeking, as many have done. It is also clear, however, that Maslow did not wish to foster this conception. Thus he argues that 'my impression is that impulsivity, the unrestrained expression of any whim, the direct seeking for 'kicks' and for non-social and purely private pleasures ... is often mislabelled self-actualization' (Maslow, 1966, p. 109). At the same time he recognized certain limitations in his conception of growth. He reports, for example, (1955, p. 15) that the sort of growth he is interested in is future oriented, even future motivated. Self-actualizing growth thus appears to be teleological, not merely in the sense that there is a *final cause* of such growth, but in the sense that it is governed by the conscious plans and goals that people set themselves. The self, as Maslow (1965, p. 308) concedes, is therefore not solely a biological given, but is also partly self-constructed, and 'many of the tasks of self-actualization are largely intrapersonal, such as the making of plans, the discovery of self, the selection of potentialities to develop, the construction of a life-outlook' (Maslow, 1955, p. 22). However, when discussing such tasks, Maslow felt obliged to return at all times to the biology of the organism as final arbiter. In this way our biology, he suggests, imposes essential constraints on the processes of choice and self-construction. He thus states categorically that he would:

> reject entirely Sartre's kind of arbitrariness. I think it's a profound mistake to think of us as being confronted only with arbitrariness, with choices we make by fiat, by sheer, unaided acts of will, and without any help from the nature of reality or from the essential nature of human nature (Maslow, 1967a, p. 155).

As well as recognizing the dangers and limitations of a purely hedonic and Aristotelian interpretation of growth, and the possible role of a moderated quasi-existential choice, Maslow also appreciated that, up to this point, his theoretical analyses appeared to leave out much that his empirical research had suggested was of importance in self-actualization — values, ideology, ethical principles, the 'mystic experience' or 'oceanic feeling', and the sense of mission. Maslow's final series of theoretical papers was written largely in an attempt to incorporate these features, to resolve some of the inconsistencies in his approach, and to rid self-actualization of its hedonistic and self-centred connotations.

The Psychology of Being (c. 1960–1970)

Maslow's concern with states of *being* developed from studies of the love and sexual experiences of self-actualizing people, and of other 'moments of highest happiness and fulfillment I shall call the peak-experiences' (Maslow, 1959, p. 45). These studies led Maslow to the conclusion that a special kind of cognition characterizes such peak experiences, which he dubbed *Cognition of Being*, or *B-Cognition*. Cognition of Being, Maslow (1959) reports, exhibits qualities of, for example, exclusive attention to and holistic perception of an object, self-forgetfulness, passive or 'Taoistic' receptivity, and resolution of dichotomies and conflicts. This was in contrast to normal cognition, organized by the deficiency needs of the individual (D-Cognition), which is characterized by diffused attention, partial awareness, egocentrism, active organization by the perceiver, contradiction and dissociation.

Maslow (1959) argues that many of the characteristics of B-Cognition imply that 'in the peak experience the nature of reality *may* be seen more clearly and its essence penetrated more profoundly' (p. 51, italics in original). Moreover, since in B-Cognition the world is also *valued* quite differently from normal, and if the world is more clearly apprehended, then perhaps 'we perceive *its* values rather than our own' (Maslow, 1959, p. 51, italics in original). Maslow thus came to believe that in the peak experience it was possible objectively to perceive absolute and universal values. He called these the *Values of Being*, or *B-Values*. Common to most religious and philosophical systems, the B-Values include Truth, Goodness, Beauty, Unity, Aliveness, Perfection, Justice, Order, and Meaningfulness (Maslow, 1967b, pp. 108–109).

From a theoretical point of view, one of the most interesting consequences of Maslow's concern with peak experiences and B-Cognition is that it made possible a redefinition of self-actualization. The rationale for this was a suggestion that:

> any person in any of the peak experiences takes on temporarily many of the characteristics which I found in self-actualizing individuals. That is, for the time they become self-actualizers ... This makes it possible for us to redefine self-actualization in such a way as to purge it of all its static and typological shortcomings (Maslow, 1959, p. 62).

Self-actualization thus becomes equated with peak experiencing, or B-Cognition — i.e., with a temporary subjective state. It is therefore no longer strictly possible to distinguish self-actualizers from non-self-actualizers, except on the quantitative and relative basis that self-actualizing people may have more frequent peak experiences. Maslow recognized, however, certain difficulties with this attempted redefinition of self-actualization. Most importantly was evidence that major characteristics of the peak experience are passivity and self-forgetfulness (or ego-transcendence). This seemed to contradict the earlier notion of the active fulfilment of the individual self. Maslow's initial solution to this apparent contradiction was to add *transcendence of identity* to the top of his motivational hierarchy (Figure 3):

> The goal of identity (self-actualization, autonomy, individuation, Horney's real self, authenticity, etc.) seems to be simultaneously an end-goal in itself, and also a transitional goal, a rite of passage, a step along the path to the transcendence of identity (Maslow, 1961, p. 260).

According to this interpretation, self-actualization (the actualization of the real self) is conceptually distinct from, and *precedes*, self-transcendence (transcendence of identity in the peak experience).

In an attempt to develop his theory, Maslow (e.g., 1966, 1967b) suggests that self-actualizers are motivated by the B-Values rather than by lower deficiency needs. In other words, they are *metamotivated*. Furthermore, these B-Values become defining qualities of the self.

> These motivators of self-actualizing people are different in some ways from basic needs and deficiency-motives. For one thing, they are identified with by the person, interiorized, introjected, taken into the self. Indeed they *become* the self, for they become defining-characteristics of it (Maslow, 1966, p. 111, emphasis in original).

This statement is revolutionary with respect to Maslow's previous conceptions. Thus the self is defined, at least partly, by its B-Values, which are also *the* B-Values. Self-actualization may therefore be interpreted as the actualization of these universal B-Values. According to this view, the real self of talents, capacities and potentialities is no longer the central creative source and object of self-actualization, but is merely the channel or medium whereby objective B-Values may become actualized. Here, therefore, is another sense in which we may speak of self-transcendence: going beyond the biological real self in the fulfilment of absolute B-Values.

While Maslow had earlier argued that self-transcendence and self-actualization were distinct, with self-transcendence representing a higher level, this new interpretation suggests that self-actualization is the same as, or implies, self-transcendence. Responding to a critical paper by Viktor Frankl (1966) who argued that self-actualization (the actualization of the individual's potentialities) is not a goal, nor even a transitional state, but is rather the *by-product* of self-transcendence (the actualization of meanings and purposes that go beyond the self), Maslow (1966, p. 109) agrees that self-actualization is to a great extent dependent upon, and bound up with, self-transcendence.

Maslow was, however, seemingly unwilling to commit himself fully to this transcendent interpretation of self-actualization, for he did not wish to renounce his earlier concern with the inner biological core. He also felt it necessary to explain why he believed that the B-Values were absolute and universal. Maslow's solution involved a synthesis of the apparently incompatible notions that (a) self-actualization is the actualization of an inner biological core, or real self, and (b) self-actualization is the actualization of universal values and meanings. This synthesis was effected by postulating that the absolute B-Values have their source in the biology of the human experience. In what may be viewed as an anticipation of modern sociobiological thought (or as a biological reduction of Jung's concept of archetypes), Maslow argues that values, ultimate meanings and the religious or spiritual life are essentially biological phenomena, while culture provides merely the backcloth and stage:

> The value-life (spiritual, religious, philosophical, axiological, etc.) is an aspect of human biology and is on the same continuum with the 'lower' animal life (rather than being in separated, dichotomized, or mutually exclusive realms). It is probably therefore species-wide, supracultural even though it must be actualized by culture in order to exist (Maslow, 1967b, p. 113).

In this way Maslow attempts to transcend the dichotomy between self-actualization and self-transcendence: 'The spiritual life ... is part of the Real Self ... To the extent that pure expressing of oneself, or pure spontaneity, is possible, to that extent will the metaneeds also be expressed' (Maslow, 1967b, p. 113). Actualization of one's biological real self therefore involves actualizing absolute values and meanings that take the person beyond the self. Self-actualization and self-transcendence therefore turn out to be simultaneous and equivalent, or *synergic* (collaborative).

Maslow's last major contribution as a theorist was, however, to shatter this apparent synthesis of self-actualization and self-transcendence. This was the discovery that there were individuals who were clearly self-actualizing in every other respect, but who appeared not to exhibit the peak experience or the other characteristics of transcendence. According to Maslow (1969a, pp. 31–32), non-transcending or 'merely healthy' self-actualizers are essentially practical and down-to-earth 'doers' who are actualizing their own personal capacities. 'Transcending' self-actualizers, on the other hand, are more aware of the realm of Being, are more metamotivated, and have more B-Cognitions in the form of peak (climactic) or plateau (serene, contemplative) experiences. This distinction between transcending and non-transcending self-actualizers threw Maslow's theory into comparative disorder, and he bemoans (1969a, p. 31): 'it is unfortunate that I can no longer be theoretically neat at this level'. Maslow might have regained coherence by returning to his earlier view that self-transcendence was the next level above actualization of self, but Frankl (1966) had caused him to reject this possibility. Moreover, Maslow had also found '*non*-healthy people, non-self-actualizers who have important transcendent experiences' (Maslow, 1969a, p. 31). Maslow never managed to resolve these conceptual difficulties and he was content, in his final years, to provide descriptive data on the differences between transcending and non-transcending self-actualizers (e.g., Maslow, 1969a), and to discuss various philosophical issues concerning the concept of transcendence (e.g., Maslow, 1969b).

Conclusion

That Maslow never developed a comprehensive and coherent theory of self-actualization may simply reflect the complexity of the subject. Alternatively, it is possible that certain characteristics in Maslow's approach may have precluded the development of a satisfactory formulation.

With the exception of the very late distinction between transcending and non-transcending self-actualizers, Maslow's researches seem to represent a growing commitment to a *transpersonal* interpretation of self-actualization. According to this interpretation, self-transcendence (the actualization of absolute values and meanings, apprehended in B-Cognition, via a mission in life) is primary, whereas the actualization of personal talents and capacities is always *for the sake of* the vocation or call.

The self-actualizing person exhibits both characteristics, as Maslow (1966) recognized, because in order for individuals to transcend themselves in the fulfilment of their metamotivated missions, they will generally be required to actualize certain of their personal capacities and talents.

Maslow's failure fully and consistently to adopt such a transpersonal interpretation, and his belief in non-transcending self-actualizers, may have been the result of his commitment to a biological organismic theory, in which self-actualization was viewed as the actualization of an intrinsic real self. Thus, according to such a theory, non-transcending self-actualization should be possible. If, on the other hand, self-actualization is interpreted as self-transcendence — going beyond the self in the fulfilment of absolute meanings and values — then persons who are simply actualizing *themselves* are not recognized as true self-actualizers but, perhaps, as 'sub-geniuses' (Otto, 1968). While this may turn out to be a purely verbal argument, it has important practical and ethical implications. Self-actualization theory has been criticized on several occasions for appearing to advocate self-seeking and personal gratification. Frankl (e.g., 1966) was clearly aware of this possibility. Ansbacher (1971), speaking of the conception of self-actualization as the actualization of the individual's potentialities, has succinctly outlined the dangers of such a view for the humanistic movement:

> With self-actualization as the ideal, the movement can easily be mistaken for a cult of the self. It would thus attract self-seeking, immature persons who wish to avoid responsibility toward their fellow men, and who are not prepared to contribute to the whole, exemplifying the pampered style of life (Ansbacher, 1971, pp. 60–61).

Friedman (1976) has further argued, like Frankl, that any such conscious and deliberate aiming at the self is, in any case, essentially self-defeating, while Maslow himself notes (1966, p. 109) that people who seek self-actualization personally and selfishly fail to achieve it.

I suggest that the theory of self-actualization must recognize and emphasize its essentially transpersonal nature, while research should explore this nature in greater depth. Such emphasis is implicit in Maslow's later writings, and his own studies of B-Cognition and metamotivation may turn out to be his most important contribution. Maslow's organismic approach, his negative attitude to social influence and his rejection of existential functioning led him to argue that transcendence, the value-life and the realm of Being have their source in human biology.

While this is an important suggestion, the possibility must be considered that the values and meanings which metamotivate the self-actualizer emerge in transactions between the individual and the natural, social and cultural environments. In this respect it may be argued that self-actualization refers not so much to qualities of an individual but to qualities of the *relationships* a person has with the world, or to the qualities of the person's participation in the Mystery of being (cf. Ferrer, 2002). It may indeed be precisely these qualities that Maslow studied in his investigations of B-Cognition and metamotivation. Furthermore, commitment to B-Values and ultimate meanings, via the sense of mission, may be the result of an existential process of free, responsible, authentic choice. Only such a conception may be capable of taking Maslow's theory beyond Aristotelian and hedonistic principles towards a coherent formulation in terms of self-transcendence.

Chapter 7

Self-Actualization, Myth and the Transpersonal

Toward a Mythical Perspective

A clear understanding of the concept of self-actualization is of personal and practical as well as academic importance. Recognizing the role of social scientists as creators of active myths, Phillips, Watkins and Noll (1974) point out that self-actualization theory 'not only identifies individuals as mentally healthy, fully human, etc., but also creates a rationale or personal philosophy for achieving the state or process of what is described' (p. 61). In other words, many people are going to orientate their lives in terms of psychologists' conceptions of self-actualization. For this reason, if for no other, it is vital either that theories of self-actualization can be shown to be valid, or else that the assumptions underlying them are clearly delineated and made explicit.

Unfortunately, the psychological study of self-actualization continues to face a crisis that extends to both theoretical and practical issues. The theory of self-actualization has been criticized frequently and variously (e.g., Ellis, nd; Ferrer, 2002; Frankl, 1966; Frick, 1982; Friedman, 1976; Geller, 1982, 1984; Smith, 1973).

This chapter is a revised and updated version of Daniels (1988)

Furthermore, the practice of self-actualization, as exemplified in the Human Potential Movement and psychological interest in transpersonal methods, wisdom traditions, and religious cults, has become diverse, eclectic, and often, perhaps, degenerate (Friedman, 1976; Hendlin, 1983; Koch, 1971; Welwood, 1983).

The major reason for the eclecticism and degeneration of the practical approach is, I believe, the lack of an accepted and valid system of constructs that may serve to guide those who seek to assuage the vague hunger or disquiet that many of us feel within our being and that we may loosely term 'the need for self-actualization'. Maslow (1967a, p. 156) describes his own approach to research as one of 'determined naivete,' in which the importance of clear conceptual formulations is denied on the grounds that differences in theory are immaterial as long as they 'do not obscure or deny the facts' (Maslow, 1966, p. 109). Perhaps for this reason, Maslow was never particularly systematic in his theorizing.

Although we may deny the necessity of any such theoretical framework by claiming the priority of direct experience through practical work, this fails to recognize that experience must be *interpreted* if it is to have any lasting influence — it must mean something — and that practical work can be futile or inefficient if we are not sure what we are doing or why we are doing it. Theoretical and conceptual issues are of primary concern, and many of the problems and difficulties that arise in practice may be the direct result of inadequate theory or conceptual misunderstandings. In the absence of any such overarching framework we become naked and vulnerable; our sense of direction and our powers of discrimination are limited to a reliance upon what 'feels right,' and we are consequently ripe for manipulation and exploitation by those who would seek to capitalize upon our uncertainties.

The Moral Imperative

As we have seen, Maslow's writings reveal many different conceptions of self-actualization. These include the realization of individual talents and potentialities, positive mental health, the ability to listen to 'inner signals' or 'impulse voices,' the development of an integrated life style, 'peak' or mystical experience, existential authenticity, or the actualization of universal values and transcendent meanings. Rather than immediately pitting these conceptions against each other, we should perhaps begin by asking: To what fundamental issue do all these views relate? Put another way: What type of question are we asking when we inquire into the nature of self-actualization?

All approaches to self-actualization, as Peters (1960) and Geller (1984) have pointed out, are basically concerned with assumptions about a person's ultimate good or essential purpose and with the *right* ways in which to live. In other words, the notion of self-actualization addresses questions of *moral philosophy* as much as it does those of psychological science. This has been concealed by the majority of writers in the field, including Abraham Maslow and Carl Rogers, by an emphasis on the relationship between self-actualization and psychological health. Szasz (1974, p. 101) comments that our age 'prefers the rhetoric of medicine to the rhetoric of morals' and he has argued forcefully (e.g., 1972, 1974) that the concept of 'mental illness' has been used as a metaphor and disguise for moral reproof. Humanistic psychologists, it seems, may have used the concept of self-actualization in a similar manner, but as a metaphor and disguise for moral approbation (see Smith, 1969, 1973). Speaking of the end-states discussed by Maslow and others under the general label of 'self-actualization' or 'self-realization', Peters (1960, p. 135) notes, for example, that 'perhaps the only common denominator of such postulated end-states would be that they are states that are commendable, states that we think people ought to enjoy'.

Geller (1984) has used the diversity evident in interpretations of the ultimate end or purpose of human existence, together with the failure of each interpretation to provide a convincing justification of its own perspective, to argue that the concept of self-actualization is meaningless. Geller concludes that 'self-development' must be understood to be multidimensional, involving the pursuit of excellence in whatever aspects of the self an individual wishes to emphasize.

I have sympathy with aspects of Geller's attack on self-actualization, and I agree that personal development is not a simple unidimensional process. However, I cannot accept his form of subjective relativism, mainly because it misses entirely the import of the concept of self-actualization, which is to imply something holistic (unitary rather than unidimensional) and, in some sense, universal. Unlike Geller, I am also unwilling to dismiss out of hand all attempts to establish a nonrelative status for the concept of self-actualization. My intuition is to believe in some objective basis for the idea, while reason leads me to recognize that the concept with which we are dealing is subtle, elusive and challenging. Our understanding is therefore almost inevitably vague and tenuous — yet this need not mean that we must deny all comprehension simply because we are unable to express or justify it fully and formally.

A major reason for our difficulty is, I believe, the assumptive position of contemporary moral debate, and of modern culture itself. MacIntyre (1981) has argued that in our own 'advanced' society there are no rationally agreed ways of reaching moral consensus because arguments are based upon rival premises that are merely assertions of personal preference. This underlying post-modern perspective of *emotivism*, he believes, has become so deeply rooted within our liberal individualistic culture that any attempt to justify rationally an objective, nonrelative moral position is often immediately dismissed as foolish and unworkable. MacIntyre argues that modern emotivism is the consequence of the Enlightenment rejection of the classical 'Aristotelian' or teleological tradition of thought, in which morality is seen as functional in the achievement of the *telos* or goal of human life. The essential feature of this classical tradition is the distinction between human life *as it is* and human life *as it may ideally become*. With the decline of the kinds of social context that supported the notion of human life as functional and teleological, morality lost its essential purpose and meaning. The failure of the Enlightenment attempts to establish a new teleological or categorical status for morality (e.g., utilitarianism, Kantian ethics) has, according to MacIntyre, led inexorably to our modern fall into emotivism and moral relativism.

If MacIntyre's analysis is correct, then Geller's (1984) dismissal of all teleological accounts of self-actualization may be placed in its rightful historical context. Ironically, although Geller (1982) is himself highly critical of what he takes to be the dehumanizing individualistic assumptions of self-actualization theory, his own rejection of teleology is itself a symptom of a post-Enlightenment, liberal individualistic perspective.

MacIntyre's important contribution to moral theory has been to argue that the teleological tradition may be reinstated in a version that provides a rational and viable alternative to emotivism. In the final analysis we must choose between these two irreconcilable positions. As MacIntyre puts it: Nietzsche or Aristotle? Although philosophers may debate at length the relative merits of the two viewpoints, as individual human beings we are forced to decide the issue one way or the other because our decision determines the kinds of persons we become. Thus MacIntyre (1981, p. 112) points out that this is 'an inescapable question in that an answer to it is given *in practice* in each human life'.

Self-Actualization and Ideology

To the extent that people adopt either a liberal individualistic (emotivist) or a teleological life-position, we should expect their understanding of, and reaction to, self-actualization theory to differ markedly. It is a consequence of both Geller's and MacIntyre's arguments that the concept of self-actualization can have meaning only within some version of the teleological tradition. Geller dismisses this tradition and therefore, for him, self-actualization is meaningless or has to be redefined beyond all recognition. MacIntyre's considered defence of a *form* of teleology encourages me, however, that the issue is not foreclosed as Geller believes. For this reason it seems to me justifiable to continue with attempts to explore and clarify the teleological meaning that may be attached to the concept of self-actualization. We should continue, moreover, not simply in the interests of fair play, but because of the central practical and functional role that a theory of self-actualization may have for those who would adopt a teleological perspective on their lives.

Over the years I have talked to many people about self-actualization and have introduced humanistic and transpersonal psychology to many groups of students. People I have met appear to fall into distinct categories in terms of their personal response to self-actualization theories. Some are bemused, others critical. A third group, however, shows an almost immediate response to, grasp of, and facility with the concepts and terms of humanistic and transpersonal psychology. Such people often report that these theories are referring to issues that are personally relevant. Their reactions may be expressed as a feeling that they knew these things all along and are now being reminded of something elusive that they had half forgotten or had lacked words to articulate. For such people, then, a theory of self-actualization seems more like a living, personal ideology than a set of dry academic propositions.

This indicates, I believe, the nature of the project that faces those who would develop a theory of self-actualization. This project is not primarily to undertake formal conceptual analysis or empirical research, but rather to provide guidance and support for those seeking fulfilment. A theory of self-actualization should therefore be clearly normative and heuristic (see Geller, 1982, 1984; Maslow, 1973, chap. 15; Phillips, Watkins & Noll, 1974). If there are, or appear to be, conceptual difficulties in the theoretical structure, we would be foolish to abandon it in its entirety, simply because our intellect refused to entertain this unreasonableness. We might then be left in such an impoverished situation that development may become impossible. In our search for an adequate theory we should instead modify conceptual elements whenever they are found to interfere with progress, and we should invent new constructs that are capable of enhancing yet further development.

In this respect it is important to consider the historical, social-cultural dimension. Theories of the human situation must adapt to meet the changing conditions and new challenges that inevitably result from developments within society. For example, MacIntyre (1981) has shown how the continuing thread of the classical tradition of teleology may be traced, 'in essence', from Homeric Greece to the Europe of the Middle Ages.[1] He notes, however, that *specific* conceptions of personal virtue and of the form and function of a whole human life changed and developed in important respects as the Western experience evolved from a heroic society, through the democracy of the Athenian city-state, to the diversity and conflict of medieval Europe. If we are now to attempt to resurrect the classical teleological tradition, it is imperative that the new formulation reflects our modern understanding and experience. Furthermore, in this historical process we must recognize that only to the extent that human society is stagnant should we expect to obtain complete and *final* answers to questions of what constitutes personal virtue and the *good life*.

---

1 The teleological tradition, it should therefore be noted, is essentially a post-axial innovation.

Equally important, as MacIntyre points out, it is an implicit assumption of teleological conceptions of human existence that although we must have *some* prior interpretation of the goal if we are to make any progress toward it, during our search we discover more and more what that goal is. A theory of self-actualization, in this view, can therefore only ever be partially accurate — it is always to some extent vague and incomplete. The most we should hope for is that our theory provides a useful stopgap position and a signpost to the next way station.

Self-Actualization as Myth

The human mind is a strange and wonderful device that is able, given an appropriate symbolic 'language' (painting, poetry, music, myth, etc.) to think meaningfully and productively in ways that cannot be reduced to the manipulation of verbal or mathematical propositions. In this way, a theory of self-actualization should, I believe, be understood as providing a *myth* of human development, a meaningful narrative that enables people to make sense of their existence, to plan their route through life, to conjure elusive experiences and events, and to facilitate subtle transformations (cf. Feinstein & Krippner, 1997; Larsen, 1996). It is a mistake, therefore, to consider research into self-actualization only as a philosophical or scientific enterprise. More fundamentally, it is a personal and mythical quest.

The concept of the mythical quest is central to the classical teleological tradition, where it articulates the underlying assumption that the unity of a human life is best understood as a *narrative* unity (MacIntyre, 1981). Within this common narrative structure (cf. Campbell's, 1975, account of the heroic adventure) human beings set out on a quest to achieve the human good. On their journeys through life they meet with various perils and evils that are to be overcome or defeated by the exercise of personal virtues. Only by surmounting all obstacles and meeting all challenges is the goal of the quest finally to be understood.

The proper function of a theory of self-actualization is, I believe, to reinforce this narrative structure and to encourage and assist individuals and groups in their quests for the human good. To this end, an adequate theory would provide a myth that provisionally outlines the goal, points the way forward, anticipates the pitfalls and dangers, and describes the virtues necessary to overcome adversity.

In referring to theories of self-actualization as 'mythical', I do not wish to imply that they are meaningless fictions that defy the facts and bear no relation to reality. On the contrary, I am using the term *myth* in its original, allegorical sense, to indicate the expression of higher or deeper realities via the medium of symbol. This is, of course, not an entirely new point and, from their various perspectives, many writers have recognized the vital functions that myths fulfil, including Nietzsche, William James, Freud, Jung, Mircea Eliade and Joseph Campbell (see also Feinstein & Krippner, 1997; Holt, 2005; Larsen, 1996).

In the wake of the undermining of purely local, culture-bound myths that has been the inevitable result of global exploration and communication, technological advance, and our modern cosmopolitan sophistication, humanistic and transpersonal psychologists have, in effect, attempted to invent, self-consciously and *de novo*, a universal mythology that was more suited to twentieth century understanding and taste, yet is aimed at providing the same sense of meaning, direction, and conceptual support that other cultures found in their own mythical systems. This is in many ways a laudable project that, if recognized as such, might lead to fruitful developments. Campbell (1976), for example, clearly indicates such a need: 'Evidently some mythology of a broader, deeper kind than anything envisioned anywhere in the past is now required: some *arcanum arcanorum* far more fluid, more sophisticated, than the separate visions of the local traditions' (p. 18). At the same time, there are certain hazards in this project that must be faced. Perhaps the most important of these is the danger of 'mythmongering' (Friedman, 1967, 1974). In our search for the essence of all myths, or the 'perennial philosophy' we run the risk of deriving a minimalist artefact that lacks the impact and immediacy of older myths that were themselves authentic responses to the exigencies of existence.

> We extract a perennial myth and feel we are very close to the heart of reality when in fact we are freezing on the doorstep. No myth catches us up as it did ancient men … The mythmonger asks us to accept a rich sense of everything having significant relation to everything else in place of any immediate insight into any particular event or reality (Friedman, 1974, p. 95).

A second, related danger is that of psychologism. I mean by this a form of reductionism that limits our understanding of the nature and function of myth to the purely psychological dimension (see Friedman, 1976). As examples of the psychologizing of myth I would cite Jung's attempts to explain the content of myths in terms of the dynamics of the collective unconscious, and Campbell's (e.g., 1976) claim that mythological symbols may act as sign stimuli in certain innate releasing mechanisms. In contrast, I prefer to follow the example of Mircea Eliade (1968) in arguing that myths can be understood only as expressions of a 'mode of being in the world' (p. 24) or as representing the expression of an authentic cocreative participation in the Mystery of being (Ferrer, 2002). As a consequence, we should ideally approach all myth from a perspective that is simultaneously psychological, sociological, historical, existential, and spiritual.

There is a further and perhaps insoluble difficulty with the attempt to establish a teleological myth of human development that is suited to the modern condition. I have suggested that our traditional understanding must be willing to adapt to meet changing conditions within society. But the problem we now face, as MacIntyre (1981) has shown, is that our modern emotivist culture has lost all sense of continuity with an evolving, living tradition of thought and, in particular, with the concept of the narrative unity of a human life. Within the context of most contemporary Western societies, teleological accounts are simply irrelevant because these societies do not support teleological modes of being. Thus 'to think of a human life as a narrative unity is to think in a way alien to the dominant individualist and bureaucratic modes of modern culture' (*ibid.* p. 211). If we seek to restate the classical tradition of teleology in some form that is appropriate to the modern condition, we cannot therefore simply adapt the tradition to our prevailing culture. Society itself will have to change in fundamental ways. Our new mythology can no longer afford merely to respond to changes in the human situation; it must stimulate transformation, both personal and social. In our society, a teleological myth is politically revolutionary.

Mythical Thinking

The psychological approach to self-actualization *might*, I believe, be capable of providing insights for a new teleological mythology. Unfortunately, most psychologists have failed to recognize explicitly the mythical nature of self-actualization theories. The project has often been confused instead with naturalistic science, with the consequence that the metaphors chosen are limited and perhaps inappropriate. Furthermore, because these metaphors are not generally appreciated as such, there has resulted the advocation of a concrete, literal interpretation by protagonist and critic alike. Such an approach is well exemplified in the concept of an innate, biological 'real self' (e.g., Horney, 1950; Maslow, 1968, chap. 14) and also in Geller's (1982, 1984) rejection of any such concept (after Mead, 1934) on the grounds that the term *self* implies the ability to understand one's own behaviour in terms of shared linguistic meanings and therefore the concept of an innate (i.e., presocial) self is contradictory and nonsensical.

It is precisely this kind of concrete literal view and clever semantic analysis that is antithetical to mythical understanding and therefore destructive of any power that a myth might be capable of generating. Campbell (1976) has argued that the basis of mythical thinking is *make-believe* — the ability to play with and react to symbols or words *as if* they were what they represented — and that, for the make-believe to work, literal objections and concrete thinking must be suspended. Unfortunately it is easy to overstate such arguments and to conclude that myth is simply a form of wishful thinking in which mushiness is king and rational considerations are irrelevant. This is not my intention. The point I wish to make is simply that the *function* of mythical thinking must take priority over its inherent logical precision. For example, I find the *concept* of a personal God nonsensical. What I cannot deny, however, is that *belief* in some such God is highly functional for many people (although not for me). For these people, the *meaning* of God is more extensive that its dictionary definition and may transcend verbal-analytical contradictions. Furthermore, a rational case may be made for suggesting that it may be better to live *as if* a personal God existed rather than *as if* the world is a Godless wilderness[2] (I do recognize, however, that there are other alternatives to this apparently stark contrast).

---

2   In this context we may note, for example, the considerable evidence that religious belief is associated with psychological health and well-being (Fontana, 2003).

In arguing this way, I closely follow William James. In *The Will to Believe*, James (1897/1979) attempts to justify belief in situations where the evidence is insufficient to decide the matter (e.g., the existence of God or the freedom of the will). His case has both a weaker and a stronger form. In the weak version, James argues that having consulted the objective evidence, and having found it inconclusive, we have a right to believe whatever is most *useful* to us (at our own personal risk). In the strong form of the argument, James makes the point that there is a class of truths (e.g., that the world is good, that life is worth living) for which belief itself is a necessary condition for obtaining proof: 'The truths cannot become true till our faith has made them so' (1979, p. 80). Furthermore, the essence of such faith is to live *as if* the object of our belief were true — to act on the assumption of its truth. Thus he argues that 'to trust our religious demands means first of all to live in the light of them, and to act as if the invisible world they suggest were real' (*ibid.* p. 52).

In the strong version of the will-to-believe argument, James clarifies an important aspect of the 'make-believe' quality of myth. The purpose and power of mythical thinking is that in taking the myth seriously, in assuming it is true, and in acting on that assumption, then the myth may become true *in its consequences*. Myths in this sense can become self-fulfilling prophecies.

The relevance of James' arguments to self-actualization is, I hope, apparent. It may be impossible to decide objectively whether or not the notion of self-actualization is 'true'. Yet to assume that it is possible, and to act accordingly, may be better than to deny it. More importantly, living as if self-actualization were possible may itself be a necessary condition for achieving it. The myth of self-actualization may indeed constitute a self-fulfilling prophecy as, conversely, may beliefs that limit the self (cf. Larsen, 1996; Smith, 1973; Vaughan, 1985).

A related interpretation has been made in an interesting paper by Frick (1982). In a consideration of Maslow's need hierarchy, Frick argues that the failure of many people to progress to the level of self-actualization, even though they may be sufficiently gratified at the lower need levels, is due to the lack of a conceptual language of personal growth that includes terms such as potentiality, uniqueness, responsibility, and autonomy. Such concepts, he suggests, have 'an evocative and transformative power' (p. 41) that structures experience, expands awareness, and may release unconscious energies. Conceptual support is therefore a crucial factor in the achievement of self-actualization. In the absence of this support, self-actualization will not occur because people fail to realize it is a possibility, and because they lack the vocabulary to express their experiences and to guide progress.

I agree with Frick's emphasis on the need for a conceptual language of personal development (or *myth* as I would prefer to call it). I cannot, however, accept his attempt to psychologize the 'power' of words. It is naive and wrong, I believe, to suggest that concepts such as 'potentiality' and 'autonomy' have any inherent evocative, transformative, or integrative capacity. Much more important is the *meaning* that these concepts have, *in practice*, for the person who believes in them.

The Evaluation of Myth

In stressing the practical meaning and mythical function of self-actualization theories, we must learn to evaluate them using quite different criteria from those we might normally apply within psychology. It is no longer appropriate to insist that a theory forms a tight and logically consistent conceptual framework from which empirically testable hypotheses may be derived. This is not to say that it becomes impossible to judge or criticize a theory of self-actualization, but only that it is inappropriate to evaluate it according to the tenets of modern analytical philosophy or positivistic science. Instead we must consider the extent to which a theory provides an effective myth.

For a theory of self-actualization to function as a meaningful, useful, and self-fulfilling myth it is essential that the myth is both *believable* and *consequential*. It has become almost a commonplace that the mythologies that once supported the moral order have now been effectively debunked (see Campbell, 1985). Very few people find it possible, for example, to believe any longer in the Biblical creation story as an actual historical event. For a myth to be believable, therefore, any claims or assumptions that are made of a concrete (i.e., non-metaphorical) and evidential nature must not contradict our modern factual understanding. We should remember that it is an important condition of James' will-to-believe arguments that such belief is justified only when objective evidence is absent, equivocal, or irrelevant. Mythical thinking is willful (intentional), not wishful (blind, credulous). A myth must also (and crucially) have consequences for living, or else it becomes idle sophistry. William James' (e.g., 1960) version of functional pragmatism suggests, for example, that the whole purpose of thought is to promote action, and that the significance of a belief is fully expressed in its practical consequences. The central question that should be posed of any myth is therefore not: Is the myth true? We should instead ask: What are the practical implications of living *as if* the myth were true? In the absence of any such implications, a theory of self-actualization cannot provide conceptual support or guidance for personal development (cf. Frick, 1982). Only to the extent that the theory is consequential may it function as a meaningful myth.

In emphasizing the practical implications of self-actualization theory we are, moreover, forced to reintroduce the moral dimension into our considerations. It is not enough to demonstrate that a myth has consequences; we must ask whether these consequences are morally beneficial or ethically defensible. Is self-actualization a good myth or a bad myth? (see Larsen, 1996; O'Hara, 1985). Our answer will, of course, depend upon the fundamental moral position that we adopt. If, as I do, we accept MacIntyre's (1981) historical analysis and share his commitment to a general teleological perspective, then self-actualization is a good myth to the extent that it provides a narrative account of human development, uniquely suited to modern experience and needs, that is capable of supporting and guiding people in their quests for greater realization of the human good. Self-actualization is a bad myth to the extent that it may be shown to fail in this respect or to lead positively away from the good. Part of our task in attempting to decide this issue must be to make explicit our own values as well as those implicit within self-actualization theory (see Smith, 1973).

In summary, in order to evaluate a theory of self-actualization as a myth of human development, we must consider its believability, its consequentiality, and its morality. At the same time, we must be alert to the dangers of mythmongering and psychologism, and we must recognize not only the personal dimension but also the social and political implications of the myth. Using this general evaluative framework, I shall now briefly examine the mythical validity of the psychological approach to self-actualization. Because of the importance and influence of Maslow's contributions, this analysis will concentrate upon the major conceptual elements within his theory.

Maslow's Theory as Myth

Self-Actualization

The concept of self-actualization is, apparently, one of the most optimistic and life-affirming ever proposed within psychology. It extends human horizons, promises ultimate personal fulfilment, and urges each one of us to move toward this ideal state of being. Such idealism is a ready target for cynical dismissal, and it may easily be criticized on purely logical grounds (e.g., Geller, 1982, 1984). From a mythical standpoint, however, our concern is with personal and social import or the message behind the concept. The question, as William James might argue, is whether life becomes more (or less) meaningful if we live *as if* some kind of ideal personal fulfilment is possible. This cannot be answered through a rational demonstration and, in the absence of a 'traditional' solution (see MacIntyre, 1981), requires an existential response from each person. I find it significant, however, that throughout post-axial history and in almost every culture (at least until the advent of post-Enlightenment emotivism and post-modern deconstructionism), humankind seems consistently to have favoured teleological myths that affirm such an ideal process or end-state (entelechy, enlightenment, salvation, apotheosis, existential authenticity, individuation, etc.).

As mentioned earlier, there is one feature, in particular, of Maslow's concept of self-actualization that has been criticized frequently and that clearly detracts from its mythical validity. This is that self-actualization has often been described in a manner that could easily appear to advocate or condone an individualistic, self-seeking approach to life and a concern with purely personal gratification (e.g., Ansbacher, 1971; Aron, 1977; Ellis, nd; Ferrer, 2002; Frankl, 1966; Friedman, 1976; Geller, 1982; Smith, 1973). With such an interpretation, the concept becomes not only ethically dubious, but also restrictive and misleading in that it directs attention away from our responsibilities to other people and away from communal endeavour.

Although a careful reading of Maslow's writings should leave
no doubt that he did not wish to foster this interpretation (e.g.,
Maslow, 1966), the fact remains that much of his theory does
little to undermine it. Even the term itself suggests and reinforces belief in the pre-eminence of self. In contrast, human
development, as Vaughan (1985) suggests, seems to proceed
'from dependence, through independence, to interdependence'
(p. 20). An effective myth of development must therefore guide
the individual beyond ego, toward community. In this respect,
Maslow's myth of self-actualization may be seriously deficient.

A related and, in practice, an important danger is that the goal
of self-actualization may be seen as an 'external' good (MacIntyre, 1981) in which the end is quite distinct from the means to its
achievement. In this way, self-actualization becomes a commodity to be purchased at any cost or sought using whatever means
may seem effective. Such a conception reinforces a manipulative
and driven attitude toward the 'quest' and, it may be said, a state
of permanent dissatisfaction, even desperation. Thus we are
encouraged always to focus upon the fact that we haven't 'made
it' yet. In our consequent desperation, therefore, we may be
tempted to try any and every path that promises 'success' (see
Friedman, 1976; Hendlin, 1983; Koch, 1971). Maslow anticipated
this problem in his discussion of self-transcendence and of the
difference between state and process conceptions of self-actualization (e.g., Maslow, 1966, 1968, chap. 3) yet, as we have seen,
his writings remain equivocal and he fails to offer a satisfactory
resolution.

Perhaps the central issue here is whether self-actualization is a
goal to be sought directly, or whether it emerges as an unsought
'by-product' of living (see Frankl, 1966; Friedman, 1976; Maslow,
1966; Smith, 1973). Friedman (1976) has exposed skilfully the
paradox and dangers involved in attempts to achieve self-actualization by directly 'aiming at the self'.

> We are called up to realize ourselves. Yet to aim directly at so
> doing is always self-defeating ... Once we make ourselves the
> goal ... we embark on a path that is not likely to lead us
> beyond ourselves to genuine dialogue with others. Instead,
> we are more and more apt to view our relations with others
> in terms of our own progress toward becoming whatever we
> feel we should become (Friedman, 1976, p. 7–8).

An approach to the resolution of this paradox is, I believe, to recognize that with self-actualization the relationship between means and ends is *internal*. Thus the means are themselves an indispensable part of the end, in the same way that the exercise of the virtues is not simply a method for achieving the good life, but is itself central to what we mean by the good life (see MacIntyre, 1981). In practice, therefore, the forms of 'planned spontaneity' that Friedman (1976) criticizes are inherently self-defeating. As Friedman recognizes, 'the means must be like the end if the end is to be reached' (*ibid.* p. 9).

Such a conception encourages us to focus upon the *way* of living rather than upon its supposed rewards. Rewards, if they come at all, do so as an internal by-product. We should bear in mind that in the traditional mythical quest, not only is the goal of the quest imperfectly understood at the outset, but the interesting part of the story is what happens *in via* — the challenges and temptations of the path and the manner in which the hero overcomes obstacles and defeats all foes. The denouement is not just a climax but perhaps often an anticlimax. It is also the end of the story. As long as life continues, we are on our Way.

There is another feature of Maslow's approach that I find distasteful and unsound as the basis of a myth of personal development. This is the assumption behind his empirical researches into the attributes of self-actualizing people (Maslow, 1970, chap. 11) that such individuals form a rare and characterologically elite group. This can easily foster the belief that self-actualization is an all-or-none affair and that the achievement of this exalted state is the prerogative of 'Great Men' (Maslow's sample is predominantly male). This interpretation destroys the impact of the myth for the majority of people who rightly conclude that such a concept is irrelevant to their own lives and experience. Maslow's 'aristocratic premise' (Aron, 1977) therefore tends to reinforce an unfortunate feature of Platonic and Aristotelian thought which suggests that certain classes of people are, by nature, incapable of the supposed 'higher' forms of existence (see MacIntyre, 1981). Such an 'aristocratic premise' may be considered to be a general feature of all hierarchical models of spiritual development (such as Wilber's) even if a more politically correct reason may be advanced for some people's apparent inability to achieve higher modes of consciousness (such as lack of education or social disadvantage). This is an important reason, I suspect, why many people choose to reject such hierarchical theories.

Hierarchy of Needs

The 'hierarchy of needs' (Figure 3) has been the most influential of Maslow's ideas, probably because it is a relatively simple concept that has certain face validity. At its crudest, it suggests that there are a small number of basic, universal, 'instinctoid' needs that are organized hierarchically such that the 'lower' needs take priority (both developmentally and in their immediate experienced urgency) over the 'higher' needs. The higher needs (including self-actualization) are believed to emerge only if the lower needs (e.g., physiological, safety, belongingness) are at least partially gratified (e.g., Maslow, 1970, chaps. 4, 5).

I do not wish to dwell on the evidence (largely anecdotal) for and against any such hierarchy, nor to review its applications within organizational psychology (e.g., Herzberg, Mausner & Snyderman, 1993). I should like instead to consider the mythical implications of this theory. Although the concept undoubtedly performs a useful social and welfare function in emphasizing the importance of physical health, material necessities, meaningful employment, and caring relationships, as a myth of personal development I find it generally pessimistic, incompatible with other mythical elements of the theory, and possibly inhibiting. The lower needs are 'deficiency' needs, which require gratification from the physical or social environments. Thus self-actualization becomes, within the theory, effectively impossible for a lonely or materially deprived person who is, moreover, permitted to blame circumstance, and to abdicate existential responsibility for his or her own progress.

The model of development implied by the hierarchy of needs is also essentially mechanistic and, if taken as a basis for living, would promote a unidimensional outlook on life that encouraged focusing upon one need at a time. Furthermore, in postulating that the needs are hierarchically organized, Maslow is effectively devaluing certain fundamental human experience as, for example, in his statement that 'the perfectly healthy, normal, fortunate man has no sex needs or hunger needs, or needs for safety, or for love, or for prestige, or self-esteem, except in stray moments of quickly passing threat' (1970, p. 57).

In this context it is also worth noting that in Maslow's concept of the need hierarchy there is no real understanding of tragedy, understood as an inescapable choice between rival and equally valid goods (see MacIntyre, 1981). In Maslow's theory there are no equally valid, tragic alternatives. Choices, both within and between levels of the hierarchy, may be made simply by deciding which alternative promises greater 'subjective delight' (e.g., Maslow, 1968, chap. 4).

Maslow's discussions of the need hierarchy show that he was aware of some of the difficulties with the theory (cf., Frick, 1982), and on several occasions he attempted to moderate its apparently mechanistic features by emphasizing the importance of will and active decision, particularly in making the transition to the level of self-actualization. Thus he argues, for example, that growth 'requires courage, will, choice, and strength in the individual, as well as protection, permission and encouragement from the environment' (Maslow, 1968, p. 204). He was, however, unwilling or unable to make major revisions of the overall structure and dynamics of the need hierarchy, and in important respects, the model has continued to remain much as originally proposed.

Real Self

The concept of the 'real self' is, I believe, the most elusive with which we shall deal. If interpreted broadly and loosely, the concept implies that each person houses (actually or potentially) an alternative 'Being', or mode of being, that is in some way better (e.g., more mature, more authentic) than the ordinary self of everyday existence. Variations on this general theme may, of course, be found in the myths of many religions (soul, spirit, guardian angel, *Atman*, enlightenment, etc.). Whatever form the belief takes, the message is the same. It implies that each person has depths that are rarely fathomed, and that these depths are the source and centre of our individual identity. It is, moreover, possible to contact or access this source, leading to greater self-awareness and true fulfilment. Most important is the implication in all such beliefs that we already possess everything we need. In a metaphorical sense at least, this higher or deeper Being is, and always has been, *with* (or within) us. It is already *there* if we would but recognize it.[3] At each and every moment a break-through is possible. Self-realization is therefore fundamentally independent of maturation, socialization, permission, or favours, although it may be facilitated by a certain form of education or by a particular way of life.

The heuristic guidance implicit in this concept is clear. To discover the real self we are urged to study *ourselves*, to look within, to dig beneath superficial and changeable appearances. We need not wait for circumstances to improve before we begin (e.g., for gratification of 'lower' needs) nor rely necessarily upon external guidance and support. We should simply get on with it. Such study is not a form of narcissistic self-preoccupation but, on the contrary, involves a critical, objective, and perhaps painful self-examination. To a large extent, the discovery of our 'true identity' involves the parallel realization of who we are not (cf. Vaughan, 1985).

This general concept may, I believe, provide a useful, even profound myth (notwithstanding what I have said about direct aiming at the self). The particular interpretation placed upon it within Maslow's theory is, however, crude, limited, and potentially misguided. In this theory (as in Aristotelian entelechy) the real self is identified with a biological essence, or seed, that presses to unfold according to some predetermined genetic blueprint (see Geller, 1982; MacIntyre, 1981; Smith, 1973). The voice of this real self, moreover, may be heard as inner organismic experience, i.e., feelings of desire and disgust, pleasure and pain.

> We have, each one of us, an essential inner nature that is instinctoid, intrinsic, given, 'natural,' i.e., with an apprecia-ble hereditary determinant ... This inner core, even though it is biologically based and 'instinctoid,' is weak ... All that we have left are instinct-remnants ... Authentic selfhood can be defined in part as being able to hear these impulse-voices within oneself, i.e., to know what one really wants or doesn't want, what one is fit for and what one is not fit for (Maslow, 1968, pp. 190–191).

Although such a concept may be useful in sensitizing people to their own experience, and alerting them to latent talents and capacities, it may easily encourage hedonism, crude physicality,

---

3   In Rawlinson's terms, such an approach represents a 'cool' soteriological tradition (see Chapter 11.)

and a preoccupation with the self. To the extent that the biological core is believed to be hereditary and preformed, the concept
may also promote a fatalistic attitude toward personal growth in
which the (ideal) course of development is seen to be already
mapped out for each individual. This view is deeply pessimistic
and places severe constraints on the role that may be played in
human affairs by choice and decision in a world that is
multivalent and also tragic (see Smith, 1973). By emphasizing
biology, the possibility that the real self might be understood
more adequately by employing existential or transpersonal concepts is also apparently discounted. From the biological point of
view, human will is easily equated with instinctual drive, love
may be confused with desire, joy may be seen as physical pleasure, choice becomes essentially determined, and the 'inner
voice' is that of organismic need.

Another problem with Maslow's purely biological interpretation of selfhood is that it provides a restricted view of the function of social interaction and cultural expression in human
development. According to Maslow's theory, the social and cultural environments may facilitate or inhibit, but do not *contribute*
to, what is essentially a maturational process of development. As
an academic theory, such a view is has been recognized for many
years as clearly inadequate (see, for example, Geller, 1982, 1984;
Ginsburg, 1984; Smith, 1973; Vaughan, 1985). As a myth of personal development, it reinforces individualism, and might easily
be used to support Machiavellian assumptions in which other
people, and society in general, are to be exploited for personal
ends, in this case in the interests of self-actualization (see
Friedman, 1976).

As we have seen, Maslow was aware of some of the problems
of a concrete, biological interpretation of the real self and he
concedes that the real self is, at least partly, self-constructed. He
fails, however, to clearly reconcile this suggestion with his belief
in a biological core and instead gives the impression of *ad hoc* tin-
kering with the theory. In his later years, Maslow also sought to
extend the concept of the real self by including metamotivation,
mystical experience, and moral values within its definition. In
this view, the moral and spiritual life is believed to be 'an aspect
of human biology ... on the same continuum with the "lower"
animal life ... It is part of the Real Self' (Maslow, 1973, p. 341).

This is, I believe, a seriously misguided suggestion. It involves a category mistake, it is reductionistic, and it again ignores the social-cultural-historical dimension of moral and spiritual experience (cf. Smith, 1973).

The biological interpretation has been reconsidered by Ginsburg (1984), who has elaborated the concept of a 'somatic self'. Ginsburg's biological understanding is more sophisticated that Maslow's and he recognizes the dangers, for example, of reducing organism to mechanism. Ginsburg also seeks to explain how 'higher' human capacities such as love, creativity, and self-hood may *emerge* through the dynamic interaction between the organism and its (social) environment, rather than pre-existing in some latent form within each person (cf. Vaughan, 1985). Such a sociobiological approach is, I believe, potentially important, both scientifically and mythically, although there remains the practical danger of confusing people by attempting to mix biological with existential, moral, and spiritual concepts.

Pseudo-Self

Although not an explicit feature of Maslow's theory, the concept of the 'pseudo-self' is crucial to an understanding of his approach. If people do not normally express or actualize their real selves, the implication is that the manifest 'self' is in some way unreal or false. This belief is very ancient and its origin is probably simply the realization that people are capable of lying and pretending. Variations may be recognized in concepts of false witness, temptation, *maya*, mask, persona, 'act', and existential inauthenticity or bad faith. Such myths point to the dangers of rejecting truth and inner wisdom, of responding to flattery and appeals to personal weakness or our 'lower' nature, and of concealing one's real thoughts and feelings behind a socially acceptable facade. Here is a clear message that each one of us must surely recognize from personal experience.

Within humanistic theory (see Horney, 1950; Maslow, 1968, chap. 4; Rogers, 1961), the pseudo-self has generally been equated with the social self, contrasted with the real, biological self. Thus Horney (1950) describes how, in neurotic persons, an 'idealized self' is built up through the influence of other people's reactions and opinions (cf. Mead's, 1934, account of the development of the self through social interaction). This idealized pseudo-self of implanted dreams, artificial cravings, roles and performances is at variance with the biological real self which, being relatively weak, is easily masked and suppressed (see Maslow, 1968, chaps. 4, 14).

There is a clear problem with an interpretation that, if taken literally, identifies the pseudo-self with the social self and, *ipso facto*, the real self with a biological core. In this view, social self is not simply *potentially* false, but *necessarily* so, because it is social rather than 'instinctoid'. Such a view leads to the denial of constructive social involvement, to existential isolation, and to individualistic conceptions of identity.

One important implication of Geller's (1982, 1984) attacks on self-actualization theory is that selfhood can be achieved only in interaction with others. The 'real self' (however conceived) can express itself only through the social self. This means, among other things, that we cannot reveal a person's real self by undermining or destroying the social self (as, for example, seems to be attempted in many modern cults and some so-called 'therapies'). Social self and real self are interwoven and, in unravelling the one, we lose both. Instead, self-actualization must involve the gradual modification of the social self in the direction of greater congruence with whatever it is that we refer to, *metaphorically*, as 'real self'. In this respect, because the transformation that takes place involves the social self, the process of personal development, though the existential responsibility of each person and requiring individual vigilance and effort, may be greatly facilitated by living in genuine dialogue and community with others (cf. Ferrer, 2002; Friedman, 1976).

Peak Experiences and B-Cognition

Maslow's interest in peak experiences derives from his belief that they constitute a means whereby real self may be contacted directly. Similar beliefs are common to most religious systems and, in many religions, psychophysical or psychospiritual exercises have been developed in the attempt to facilitate ecstatic or other kinds of 'mystical' experiences (e.g., fasting, dance, meditation, or devotional prayer).

For the theory of self-actualization, the implication of these beliefs is that the real self manifests most clearly in an altered state of consciousness and, by deliberately manipulating consciousness, such manifestations may be encouraged. This is an important suggestion that is, however, open to misunderstanding and abuse. There is the paradox involved in aiming at the self and in planned spontaneity that Friedman (1976) has described so well. Furthermore, unless the characteristic features of the required alterations in consciousness are well established, and unless perfectly safe methods are used, there is the danger of confusing quite different states and of producing undesired or pathological effects. In practice, such a myth can easily encourage the kind of naive, desperate, and indiscriminate experimentation that we witnessed in the era of 'flower power' and that still attracts those seeking easy answers and instant enlightenment (see Aron, 1977; Hendlin, 1983; Joy, 1985; Marien, 1983; Michael, 1985).

Maslow believed that 'Cognition of Being' (B-Cognition) was the common denominator in all mystical experiences, as well as in forms of awareness such as B-love (love for the 'Being' of another) and artistic appreciation. Maslow's (1968, chap. 6; 1973, chaps. 19, 20) description of B-Cognition undoubtedly provides useful guidelines for distinguishing certain states of consciousness. What it fails to establish, however, are distinctions among quite different transcendent experiences (see Rowan, 1983). Rowan's analysis suggests, for example, that the ecstatic peak experience is but one of several varieties and, more importantly, is not equivalent to the experience of either what he terms 'real self' (existential authenticity) or 'higher self' (inner teacher). If this is the case, then Maslow's emphasis upon B-Cognition and the peak experience may prove misleading. It may, for example, cause people to dismiss perfectly valid transformational experiences simply because they are less spectacular than Maslow's own accounts or fail to match the specific criteria he established.

In this context, Smith (1973) has suggested that Maslow's preoccupation with mystical experience reflects a general 'Dionysian' (nonrational, impulsive, romantic) bias that may actively encourage the kind of emotional excess and anti-intellectualism that characterizes much of the encounter movement and the counterculture. I agree with this analysis of Maslow's work and, in noting its 'mythical' consequences, would support Smith's attempt to provide a counterbalance by reemphasizing the 'Apollonian' (rational, orderly) aspects of self-actualization.[4]

---

4   It is important, of course, not to go to the opposite extreme of excluding the Dionysian approach.

Metamotivation and Self-Transcendence

Maslow's theory of metamotivation (e.g., Maslow, 1973, chaps. 9, 23) suggests that self-actualizing people tend to be motivated by nonpersonal, objective and universal 'Values of Being' (B-Values) that may be apprehended directly in B-Cognition. These 'metamotivations' include truth, beauty, justice, perfection, and aliveness. Thus a person who is metamotivated transcends personal and subjective concerns by identifying with some important task, work, or mission that embodies the B-Values and that benefits other people or humanity as a whole. Within this theoretical approach, self-actualization is effectively equivalent to self-transcendence (see Frankl, 1966; Maslow, 1966).

In the concepts of metamotivation and self-transcendence, Maslow has rediscovered the *bodhisattva* ideal and has attempted to psychologize notions of the religious call or vocation (see Friedman, 1976; Smith, 1973). In this formulation, altruism and selfless effort become the central themes, while the actualization of personal talents and capacities is always 'for the *sake* of the call, vocation, or work' (Maslow, 1966, p. 109). Maslow's research into metamotivation may, I believe, provide his most important contribution to a mythical interpretation of self-actualization (particularly if allied to the notion of B-Love). Such a myth encourages a suspension of selfish concern (e.g., for personal enlightenment or private salvation) and emphasizes the individual's commitment and responsibility to other people and to the whole of life.

In theoretical terms, the concept of self-transcendence through metamotivation apparently seems to contradict, or demote in importance, the actualization of the biological real self. As mentioned earlier, Maslow attempted to resolve this theoretical difficulty by arguing that the B-Values that metamotivate the self-actualizer are aspects of the real self and may therefore be introspected. I have argued that this suggestion is misguided, both conceptually and mythically. However, it might be countered that, whatever the conceptual problems, such a myth may be useful to the extent that it encourages contemplative practice or suggests criteria for identifying the voice of the 'real self' in the impulse toward love, altruism, truth, beauty, perfection, etc. In this way, Maslow's integration may fulfil a pragmatic function in helping to reorientate people whose major current concern is with the actualization of *self*. Vaughan (1985) has suggested, for example, that the concept of a transpersonal self 'is useful in advanced stages of psychological growth to facilitate the shift from personal egocentric goals and ambitions to more altruistic socially conscious values' (p. 25). I accept this possibility, although against this must be weighed another potential scenario — that contemplation, altruism, social consciousness, compassion, even love, may perhaps come to be seen as mere tools to be used for the achievement of *personal* fulfilment (cf. Friedman, 1976).

As discussed earlier, Maslow never managed finally to resolve the question of the relationship between self-actualization and self-transcendence. At various times he considered the possibilities that (a) self-actualization and self-transcendence are simultaneous and equivalent, (b) self-transcendence is the next level in the hierarchy above self-actualization, (c) self-actualization is a by-product of self-transcendence, and (d) there are two different forms of self-actualization, i.e., transcending and nontranscending (see Maslow, 1966, 1973, chaps. 21, 22). One reason for Maslow's difficulty in relating self-actualization and self-transcendence was evidence that certain of his original sample of self-actualizing people appeared not to have peak experiences and were less clearly metamotivated, while other, non-self-actualizing people often reported transcendent experiences (Maslow, 1973, chap. 22). This evidence demonstrates, I believe, the inappropriateness, both empirical and mythical, of Maslow's attempts to identify a criterion group of 'self-actualizers,' and to demonstrate that such people exhibit a common set of characteristics that distinguishes them from ordinary people (see also Smith, 1973).

Conclusions

A conceptually and mythically valid approach to the relationship between self-actualization and self-transcendence must recognize, I suggest, that actualization of self (e.g., the development of personal talents and capacities) may be functional in a life orientated genuinely and non-manipulatively toward a socially and culturally defined human good. Personal fulfilment, if achieved at all, is a by-product, gift, or unsought reward of living the good life (see Frankl, 1966; Friedman, 1976; MacIntyre, 1981; Smith, 1973).

Maslow's theory of self-actualization is undoubtedly an important attempt to characterize a process of personal development that has been recognized in various forms throughout recorded history. Although the diversity of these conceptions has led certain writers (e.g., Geller, 1984) to question the universality and objectivity of any such process, I am inclined to the view that the variety of myths reflects different cultural expressions or manifestations of what is a universal post-axial tendency to structure human existence in narrative, *teleological* form (see MacIntyre, 1981).[5] Maslow's own project, it seems, had two related purposes. First, Maslow attempted to describe, using biological and psychological metaphors, what he considered to be the 'essential,' supracultural, universal features of this teleological structure. Second, having established a generally applicable conceptual framework, he assumed that this would provide an *effective* myth for all time, i.e., a perennial philosophy that will give universally valid practical support and normative guidance.

The analysis I have presented suggests that Maslow's theory fails in important respects, both as a conceptual account and as an effective myth. The conceptual framework of the theory contains ambiguities, contradictions, and distortions that, far from providing stimulating paradoxes, serve only to confuse and frustrate. In particular, I would point to Maslow's suggestions that (a) self-actualization is available to all, yet is found most commonly among American presidents and great musicians, poets, artists, or scientists (usually male), (b) the 'real self' is both hereditary and self-constructed, (c) moral values and spirituality may be reduced to biological instincts, (d) social self and real self are necessarily distinct and independent, (e) the cultural and historical context in which self-actualization occurs is largely irrelevant, (f) true fulfilment involves either the actualization of self, or self-transcendence (or both).

---

5   Although a common narrative structure also characterises the pre-axial version of the perennial philosophy, the pre-axial narrative is not teleological (goal-directed) in the *progressive* sense as understood in post-axial narratives. Thus in the pre-axial narrative, the goal is not evolution or progress but rather healthy maintenance and the re-establishing of harmony.

With respect to the mythical and normative function of the theory, certain conceptual elements may actually inhibit or corrupt the process of self-actualization. Here I would emphasize the following implications that may easily, if mistakenly and unintentionally, be derived from features of Maslow's approach:

- Self-actualization may be sought directly and personally.

- Personal development may be achieved, in mechanistic fashion, through the gratification of deficiency needs.

- Frustration of the deficiency needs prevents self-actualization.

- Self-actualizing people have transcended the needs for sex, love, belongingness, or esteem.

- Self-actualization involves surrender to the pleasure principle, egocentrism, individualism, contempt for the opinions of other people, and the Machiavellian exploitation of social relationships for purely personal ends.

- The form that self-actualization takes is largely predetermined for each person, such that the only choice we may effectively make is to cooperate or not with our *instinctoid* capacities.

- The effect of social interaction is generally to inhibit self-actualization.

- Self-actualization may occur through ecstatic experience, achieved using whatever means may be considered effective (including psychoactive drugs).

- All forms of transcendent experience are equivalent and equally valid.

Although I have great respect for Maslow's contributions to humanistic and transpersonal psychology, I find in his theory only one concept that is unequivocally liberating as a myth of personal development. This is the suggestion that ultimate fulfilment may be achieved (indirectly) by transcending selfish concern through B-Love, metamotivation, and commitment to a nonpersonal task or work that contributes to the human good. This is not to say that such a concept is *sufficient* to provide an effective myth. I believe, for example, that the notions of a 'real self' and 'pseudo-self' are important elements in any mythical interpretation of personal development, provided they are understood to indicate modes of being that are authentic and inauthentic (or, in the case of the real self, of modes that express love, compassion, wisdom, peace, etc.). Specifically, these *modes of being* should not be tied to a theoretical framework that identifies and reifies them in terms, respectively, of biological essence and social process.

The failure of self-actualization theory to provide a coherent myth with clear and effective normative guidance is due, I suggest, to the nature of Maslow's project and consequently to his inappropriate research strategy. In an attempt to establish an objective basis for a myth of human development, and to provide a convincing account within the context of a discipline that defined itself as a biological science, Maslow felt obliged to adopt the metaphors and mimic the methods that were fashionable at the time he was working (1940–1970). Thus the project was confused with naturalistic science, the metaphors chosen were those of a functional biology, and the methods utilized were quasi-empirical. I have argued in this chapter that such an approach is fundamentally inappropriate and misguided.

If the mythical function of self-actualization theories is accepted, it might be suggested by some that an alternative, more fruitful approach may be found in the attempt to extract common features (a perennial philosophy) from a study of comparative religion and mythology — as seems to be occurring, for example, with much of the current psychological interest in spiritual traditions and transpersonal methods. This suggestion fails to recognize, however, that even if we are able to demonstrate parallels and common themes, provide appropriate translations, or develop a universal lexicon, our conceptual understanding may not be capable of serving as an *effective* myth. This, indeed, is the error that Maslow made in assuming that an abstract psychological framework would necessarily provide concrete practical support and guidance. A conceptual skeleton may satisfy our intellect, but it generally fails to speak to the whole person in her or his unique life-situation. Here is the dilemma and the danger of psychologism and mythmongering (Friedman, 1974, 1976).

There is also a danger, in looking to the past or to other cultures for truth's perennial essence, that we fail to appreciate the demands of our own particular historical and cultural situation. As MacIntyre (1981) has shown, a living tradition adapts to social and cultural change. The differences among the variety of myths are therefore as important as the similarities. It is a mistake, then, to think that a mythical solution to all our problems already exists, to be unearthed using the methods of comparative religion and mythology (or through a purely psychological analysis). No quest is as straightforward as that.

The way forward for self-actualization theory is, I believe, to recognize that human life may *become* a mythical quest, and that all such quests take place within a particular social, cultural and historical context. As Smith (1973, p. 30) puts it: '"Becoming fully human" is a personal-cultural-historical adventure.' We can find fulfilment only by 'taking part' in our life's adventure. This adventure is uniquely our own, yet we are also characters in the adventures of others, and we may travel with them for at least part of our journeys (see MacIntyre, 1981). As for practical guidance in the concrete situation, MacIntyre points out that 'I can only answer the question "What am I to do?" if I can answer the prior question "Of what story or stories do I find myself a part?"' (*ibid.* p. 201).

The narrative account that seems to begin to emerge from the analysis of Maslow's work is also the one I find most meaningful. This myth proposes that the true quest is a shared (cocreated) adventure to realize the human good[6] (*shared* because the quest can take place only in the context of a living tradition or community that is itself a social-cultural-historical phenomenon). In this quest, self-interest is transcended in communal endeavour and in aiming toward *the human good* (rather than personal or parochial gain), yet we may be called upon to develop our own individual capacities *for the sake of the quest*. Participation in such a quest is, of course, contingent upon forms of community in which there exists this kind of shared narrative perspective. This, as MacIntyre (1981) recognizes, is in practice the critical problem that faces modern humanity; a problem that, at present, may be capable of being solved only on a local scale.

---

6   By the 'human good' I mean the good that can be expressed through our humanity. This should not be taken to imply an anthropocentric viewpoint that prioritizes human welfare over that of other species or the planet as a whole.

Chapter 8

A Psychohistory and Phenomenology of the Soul

'I cannot understand what *mind* is, or how it differs
from *soul* or *spirit*. They all seem one to me.'
(Saint Teresa of Avila, from *The Book of Her Life*,
cited in Happold, 1970, p. 352.)

Some concept of a transpersonal self appears in most of the major
theories in transpersonal psychology. William James (1902/
1960, p. 490) refers to a 'wider self' — a higher or spiritual self
which is the source of religious experience. Abraham Maslow
talks about a person's 'highest self' which to a large degree overlaps with the highest selves of others (1973, p. 327). Carl Jung
(e.g., 1991) emphasizes the integration of the whole Self, often
represented using spiritual images. The Higher Self (true, spiritual or transpersonal Self) features prominently in the psychosynthesis model developed by Roberto Assagioli (1991, 1993).
John Rowan (1993) refers to the transpersonal self, or Deep Self,
while Michael Washburn (e.g., 1994, 1995) reports the existence
of a higher self at the centre of the repressed unconscious. Stan
Grof (e.g., 1993, 1998, 2000) describes various experiences of the
transpersonal self reported by people in non-ordinary states of

This chapter is a revised and updated version of Daniels (2002a) consciousness. John Heron (1988) distinguishes between the transpersonal self and the cosmic self. Frances Vaughan (1985, 1986) discusses the nature and limitations of the experience of transpersonal identity, while Ken Wilber's integral psychology (e.g., 2000a) describes two independent self-streams that operate at different transpersonal levels.

In this chapter and the next, I examine the concept of the transpersonal self in order to assess and clarify its meaning and value within a psychological approach to the transpersonal. There are several important questions that I shall address:

1. **Do we need a concept of the transpersonal self at all?** This is not at all a frivolous question. On one hand the idea of a 'transpersonal self' may strike some as a contradiction in terms. On the other hand, we have many of the world's developed religious traditions arguing that spiritual development involves a loss of self, while Buddhism radically denies the existence of any permanent self, whether mundane or 'transpersonal'.

2. **What kind of concept is the transpersonal self?** Is the transpersonal self most adequately understood as, for example, a metaphor or symbol, an objective reality, an experience, the subject of experience, a psychological structure, or a developmental process?

3. **Is the transpersonal self a unitary concept or do we need to distinguish between different transpersonal selves?** A related question concerns the extent to which different theorists may articulate very different concepts of the transpersonal self.

4. **What role is played by the *self* in transpersonal experiences and in the process of transpersonal development?**

5. **How do psychological concepts of the transpersonal self compare and relate to religious-metaphysical notions such as the existence of the soul or spirit?**

6. **Can we understand the transpersonal self in purely psychological terms, without assuming a particular metaphysical position?**

In this chapter, I shall consider first the religious-metaphysical questions. I do so because it is very difficult to avoid these questions when discussing the transpersonal self and because, in practice, the psychological theories I shall be discussing in the next chapter are often strongly coloured by their metaphysical assumptions. Religious and philosophical ideas have so subtly and profoundly influenced everyone's thinking in these areas that it is often difficult to appreciate just how much we have been conditioned to understand spiritual concepts in particular ways. For this reason it is useful, I believe, to make explicit some of these influences.

The belief that there is a spiritual aspect or dimension to human personality is one that is shared by most of the world's religions as well as by quasi-religious philosophical systems such as Neoplatonism. This commonly held notion has, however, been understood and expressed in a variety of ways by the different traditions. Some of the most important concepts and terms are presented in Table 10.

Table 10. Concepts of the soul and spirit in religion and philosophy

Religion / Philosophy	Concepts
Shamanism	Soul-Spirit, Spirit helpers (guides, companions, friends, ancestors, power animals, teachers, gods, goddesses)
Egyptian religion	*Khaibit* (shade), *Ka* (double), *Ba* (soul), *Akh* or *Khu* (spirit), *Sahu* (spiritual body)
Zoroastrianism	Individual judged soul, Guardian Spirit / Guardian Angel, evil spirits
Homer	*Thymos* (arousal), *Nous* (thought), *Psyche* (shade-soul)
Pythagoras	Self-moving, immortal, transmigrating, perfectable soul (*psyche*)
Plato	Immortal *psyche*. Tripartite *psyche*: *epithymia* (appetite), *thymos* ('spirited'), *nous / logos* (reason)
Hebrew Bible	Soul (*nefesh*), Spirit (*ruach*)
New Testament	Soul (*psyche*), Spirit (*pneuma*)

Religion / Philosophy	Concepts
Gnosticism	Mind *(nous)*, Soul *(psyche)*, Animal soul, Human soul, Divine soul, Divine spark, Divine light, Spirit *(pneuma)*, Good and evil 'companions,' Original Man
Islam	Perfectable soul, 'Heart'
Jewish mysticism	*Nefesh* (animal soul), *Neshamah* (human soul), *Ruach* (spirit), Ten *Sephiroth* (emanations), *Yechidah* (divine spark), *Adam Kadmon* (heavenly man)
Sufism	Empirical self, Union or extinction *(fana)* of soul with God
Middle Platonism	*Nous* (intellect), *Ego* ('I'), *Daemon* (semi-divine guide)
Neoplatonism (Plotinus)	Soul, World-Soul, *Nous* (higher intelligence), the One (Godhead)
Jainism	*Jiva* (life-monad)
Vedanta	*Atman, Atman-Brahman* (non-dualist), Three bodies (gross, subtle, causal), Five sheaths (physical, vital, mental, intellectual, blissful)
Samkhya, Yoga	*Purusha* (consciousness / spirit), Supreme Self
Taoism	*Kuei* (shade / ghost), *Po* (earthly yin soul), *Hun* (heavenly yang soul), *Shen* (spirit)
Buddhism	5 *skandhas* (aggregates), *Dharma samtana*, (karmic stream), *Pratityasamutpada* (dependent arising), *Anatta* (no-self)
Zen	Original Self, Formless Self
Kant	Noumenal self, Phenomenal (empirical) self
Theosophy	Etheric body, Astral body, Mental body, Causal body, *Atman*
Aurobindo	Psychic being, Higher Mind, Illumined Mind, Intuition, Overmind, Supermind, Sachchidananda, *Atman, Jivatman*, Spark-soul

While there appear to be close similarities between many of these concepts, there are also important distinctions to be made among them. We cannot simply conclude that they are all referring to the same thing — i.e., to commonly shared ideas of the soul or spirit. Most obviously, within most of these traditions it has been found necessary to make specific distinctions between different aspects (or levels) of the human constitution, such as the mind, soul and spirit. Secondly, there appear to be substantial differences of meaning between the sets of concepts found across, or even within, several religions. Thus the Original Self or Formless Self of Zen appears to represent a very different idea from that of the soul/spirit in shamanism. In turn, both of these are quite distinct from the Jain concept of *jiva* (life-monad).

We also need to recognize that the common usage of a particular term such as mind or soul or spirit does not necessarily imply that it always carries the same meaning. To a large extent this may be attributed to problems of translation and the relative paucity and lack of sophistication of the English language in the areas of spiritual experience (in comparison, say, with Sanskrit or even ancient Egyptian). However, the problem is not entirely one of vocabulary. Thus Egyptian scholars have observed that words such as *ka*, *ba* and *khu* themselves changed in meaning and application over the centuries. The Sanskrit *Atman* may also be used in very different senses, ranging from the self of ordinary experience to the divine immortal soul. Similarly, in the Hebrew Bible, the meanings attributed to *nefesh* (soul) or to *ruach* (spirit) are not always constant or consistent.

It seems very likely that many of the historical changes in the meaning of words such as soul and spirit reflect actual developments in human consciousness and our awareness of ourselves (i.e., of our *selves*). Julian Jaynes (1993) has argued, for example, that when the Iliad and the early books of the Hebrew Bible were written (c. 1000–800 BCE) people were not fully self- conscious or self-reflective. They functioned largely on autopilot. If a choice had to be made, they did not think, plan or decide what to do. Rather they were 'told' what to do by the voices they hallucinated from another 'chamber' of the mind (hence Jaynes' description of the human mind at this time as 'bicameral,' i.e., having two chambers).

> Iliadic man did not have subjectivity as do we; he had no awareness of his awareness of the world, no internal mind-space to introspect upon. In distinction to our own subjective conscious minds, we can call the mentality of the Myceneans a bicameral mind. Volition, planning, initiative is organized

with no consciousness whatever and then 'told' to the individual in his familiar language, sometimes with the visual aura of a familiar friend or authority figure or 'god,' sometimes as a voice alone. The individual obeyed these hallucinated voices because he could not 'see' what to do by himself (Jaynes, 1993, p. 75).

According to Jaynes, humankind did not develop self-consciousness (including intellectual and moral consciousness) until around the period when the Odyssey was written (c. 750 BCE), as may be shown by a critical psychological comparison between this text and the Iliad.[1]

Wilber (1996d) has developed an even more controversial thesis that attempts to trace evolutionary changes in consciousness from the mystical participation in nature experienced by the earliest humans, through a series of 'eras' involving magical, mythical, and mental-egoic consciousness, up to our present-day capacity for existential authenticity and transpersonal identity.

Whether or not we agree with the precise formulations of Jaynes or Wilber, there seems little doubt from the historical data that the earliest conceptions of the human soul saw it as some kind of *quasi-physical* reality. This might be a 'spiritual' substance, such as a vapour, perfume, fire, or the breath, or an actual body of some kind (a shade, or double). It seems to be very recent — perhaps only within the last 3000 years — that the soul came to be associated with *psychological* capacities of any kind. When this occurred, the emphasis appears to have focussed originally on desire and 'spiritedness' (the kinds of qualities shared with animals such as pigs or horses). Only later were what seemed to be strictly human capacities for thinking and self-reflection added to the equation. As our self-experience evolved further, concepts of the soul began to incorporate the more sophisticated psychological capacities of free will and 'higher' modes of thought and consciousness such as logic and reason, contemplation, intuition and mystical experience. It was, I believe, as a direct result of recognizing our own capacity for such 'higher' consciousness, that the soul came to be understood as itself participating in the nature of divinity.

---

1   This, of course, is precisely the period when the change occurred from pre-axial to post-axial religions.

In order to understand the historical changes and variations in views of the soul and spirit, it is useful to consider in more detail the phenomenological bases of these concepts. My assumption here is that if these concepts mean anything at all, they must refer to important common human experiences. One reason, therefore, why we have different terms and concepts is that different experiences have given rise to them. A quite secondary consideration is that the various religious, philosophical and psychological schools have engaged in their own (although, as history shows, often mutually influenced) forms of phenomenological analysis, philosophizing and exegesis.

Experiences of the Soul

What experiences, then, could have given rise to the various notions of a soul, spirit or transpersonal self? In my view, we must include at least the following:

1. **Life and death.** The precise difference between a living, breathing person and a corpse remains a profound mystery to this day. Little wonder, perhaps, that our early ancestors attributed the difference to an *animating spirit* that left the body at death, a spirit often identified with the life-giving breath, the beating heart, or physical warmth. Such an interpretation leads almost inevitably to the animistic belief that all living things possess a spirit of their own. Because the animating spirit is the principle of life whereas death is the loss of spirit, it would seem to follow that the spirit itself cannot die, but must be immortal. This argument is, indeed, the basis of one of the Socratic 'proofs' of the soul's immortality (Plato, *Phaedrus* 6, 245c–246a).

2. **Sleep and dreaming.** In dreamless sleep, 'I' seem to disappear. Where have I gone during this time? I cannot have been annihilated because I return in the morning — so it would seem that I must have been somewhere all the time, even though I cannot recall any experience. However I do remember dreams. In these I appear to travel (in my own shape) to other times and places. Although normal dreams may be confused and hazy, in lucid dreams I am fully conscious, can think rationally, act upon intention, and 'return' to the waking body with complete recollection. The simplest explana-

tion for these experiences is that each person can continue to exist in an independent 'dream body' that is an exact double or replica of the physical body.

3. **Out-of-body experiences.** Dramatic experiences that seem to offer further experiential confirmation of the reality of the dream or imaginal body.

4. **Hauntings and apparitions.** Experiences that suggest that a person can survive death in some quasi-physical form. However, the ghost or apparition may appear to be just a shade or shadowy presence that lacks the intelligence, vitality, warmth or 'spark' of a real living person. For this reason it makes sense to distinguish between the animating soul, spark or personality, and the shade or ghost, although both may be immortal. In Homer, for example, the souls (*psyche*) of the dead experience eternal life in the Underworld, but as mere pale shadows of their former selves.

5. **Loss of Soul.** Our ordinary experience of ourselves is that we possess will, vitality and a sense of personal control. However, there are unusual trance or dissociative states (such as of *latah / olon*, and *amok / berserk*), experienced in shamanistic societies, where these personal functions seem to be temporarily lost (see, for example, de Martino, 1988). In these states, the person's behaviour seems to be completely controlled by external events or by some invading outer force. These occurrences are generally interpreted as a 'loss of soul' and are states to be feared. Such states imply that a person can temporarily lose their own will and identity while the body lives on, animated or 'possessed' by some outside power.

6. **Spirit possession.** In cases of spirit possession (which can often result from an experience of soul-loss), the person's body seems to be taken over involuntarily by another *personality* rather than simply by an alien force or power. The possessed person may therefore speak and act with intelligence and purpose.

7. **Mediumistic trance.** Experiences in which the shaman or medium *invites* another spirit or entity to take full control of their body in order to communicate or perform some other

valuable function (such as healing). This is similar to modern-day channelling, although the latter does not always involve the complete dissociation of the ordinary personality in the way that is typical of trance mediumship.

8. **Shamanic journeying.** Ecstatic trance experiences in which the shaman's soul or spirit (dream body) seems to travel to another world, where it communicates with spirit helpers or friends.

9. **Invocation and evocation.** Magical practices that (a) invite or invoke a 'divine spirit' to manifest within consciousness, or (b) summon or evoke a 'spirit' to manifest itself to the senses.

10. **Energetic and 'subtle body' experiences.** Experiences such as *kundalini* awakenings, subtle sounds (*nada*) and lights, and psychic powers (*siddhis*) in which the self seems to be plugged into a powerful source of psychic or spiritual energy. This source may be experienced as a vital or 'subtle' inner body that is somehow intimately connected with the physical body. The energy itself may vary in its form or quality, and these variations are often experienced as correlated with different psychic centres (*chakras*) within the subtle body.

11. **The mental life (Idealism).** Withdrawing into an inner mental world. This may take various forms — introspection, day-dreaming, contemplation, meditation, mental play, mathematical or philosophical reasoning. The implication of such experience is that 'I' (the conscious thinking self) can exist as a purely mental being in a world of ideas that transcends and has, at best, only an indirect relationship to the body or emotions. For Plato, the mental contemplation of ideal Forms represents the highest activity of the human soul. In some philosophies, mental purity is sharply contrasted with a sense of the inadequacy or corruption of the physical world. The pure eternal mental being may then be viewed as somehow weighed down or imprisoned by physical existence, from which it seeks liberation. In extreme cases, this may lead to the belief (e.g., in Gnosticism) that the entire material universe is evil.

12. **Subjectivity and self-reflexive consciousness.** This *mental-intellectual* realization of our own subjectivity occurs at the moment when I have the *thought* that I as exist as an experiencing and active centre. It is therefore based on the simple ideas that '*I* experience *this*' and '*I* do *this*'. Such thinking immediately sets up the Cartesian dualism between subject and object. Since I also realize that any *ideas* about myself are themselves *objects* of experience then 'I' cannot be any *thing* I think I am. The real 'I' must therefore be the *subject* — the witness or agent who is distinct from any mental contents such as perceptions, thoughts, intentions or self-concepts. The Catch-22 in this realization, however, is that once we recognize or identify with (i.e., *think about*) our own subjectivity, we have thereby turned the subject into an object. The eye, therefore, cannot see itself, and any attempt to do so involves us in the hall of mirrors of an infinite regression. Yet we are still left with what seems to be a valid conceptual distinction between subject and object and, on this basis, we may readily erect a philosophy that identifies the pure subject as the 'true', noumenal, transcendent or transpersonal self. Wilber, for example, makes this very point:

> But what could an actual 'transpersonal' experience really mean? It's not nearly as mysterious as it sounds ... You yourself can, right now, be aware of your objective self, you can observe your individual ego or person, you are aware of yourself generally.
>
> But who, then, is doing the observing? What is it that is observing or witnessing your individual self? That therefore transcends your individual self in some important ways? Who or what is that? ... The observer in you, the Witness in you, transcends the isolated person in you (Wilber, 1995a, pp. 280–281).

13. **Intuition and inspiration.** There are times when we are surprised by insights and knowledge whose source is unknown, but appears to come from some deep place within the self. It thus appears that we have access to a larger or higher wisdom that is not directly accessible to the conscious mind. Such experiences may be experienced as a sense of a relationship with an inner Muse or Guide.

14. **Guiding Impulse.** This refers to experiences that seem to indicate a sense of direction, purpose or inevitability to our individual lives that we cannot consciously fathom. It is as if an unseen force is driving and directing our lives according to some prior agenda. Such experiences may be variously attributed to fate, divine prompting, or karmic fulfilment.

15. **Groundedness.** The sense of connection to a deeper, more authentic self. This is typically associated with an experience of clarity, wholeness, 'rightness' and harmony.

16. **Embodiment.** A form of groundedness in which the person experiences profound mind-body integration and physical presence.

17. **Reincarnation experiences.** Memories, desires, phobias, behaviours or physical characteristics apparently associated with a previous personal existence. Such experiences seem to carry the implication that *co-ordinated aspects of human personality* (rather than simply the animating soul, shade, spark, or subject of experience) can survive death and return to another body.

18. **Near-death experiences.** Typically characterized by an out-of-body experience followed by moving towards a loving spiritual light or presence. The NDE offers convincing experiential confirmation of some form of personal survival and also of the reality of our connection with the Divine.

19. **Revelations.** New knowledge that appears to be revealed or communicated by a higher or divine intelligence, often associated with ecstatic visions. Generally the source is experienced as an 'other' being (e.g., an angel or God) although there is usually a sense that I (or my group) have been specially 'chosen' or share a privileged relationship with this being.

20. **Conversion / rebirth.** Experiences, often triggered by a personal crisis, in which consciousness and personality undergo a profound spiritual transformation.

21. **Longbody experiences**. A term used by Aanstoos (1986) and Roll (e.g., 1997) to refer to our experience of a larger soul that extends beyond individual identity to include our deep connection to significant others, the land and possessions.

22. **Species consciousness**. Memories and other experiences of humankind's morphic field, 'akashic records', or repository of collective karmic experience (see Bache, 2000). This is similar to Jung's notion of archetypal experience but, according to Bache, such 'memories' reflect the actual experiences of specific persons and groups (i.e., they have definite *content*) rather than being of the general collective structuring *forms* that are the archetypes.

23. **Cosmic consciousness**. Richard Bucke's (1901) term for a sudden, exalted and joyous experience of the whole universe as a living, ordered and loving Presence, or expression of the Divine. At the same time there is a *direct realization* of (rather than simply an intellectual belief in) the self's immortality (see Chapter 1).

24. **Unitive experience (spiritual marriage)**. Ecstatic, loving surrender and embrace with the divine. A kind of abiding with or union of the soul with the Divine (God). This union may be variously described as one of *identity* (One-*as*-God) or of *communion* (One-*with*-God).

> [T]his secret union takes place in the deepest centre of the soul, which must be where God Himself dwells, and I do not think there is any need of a door by which to enter it. I say there is no need of a door because all that has so far been described seems to have come through the medium of the senses and faculties ... But what passes in the union of the Spiritual Marriage is very different. The Lord appears in the centre of the soul ... This instantaneous communication of God to the soul is so great a secret and so sublime a favour, and such delight is felt by the soul, that I do not know with what to compare it, beyond saying that the Lord is pleased to manifest to the soul at that moment the glory that is in Heaven, in a sublimer manner than is possible through any vision or spiritual consolation. It is impossible to say more than that, as far as one can understand, the soul (I mean the spirit of this soul)[2] is made one with God, Who, being likewise a Spirit, has been pleased to reveal the love that He has for us by

---

2 In making this distinction, St Teresa is making clear that it is not the personality (soul) that is united with God, but rather the person's spiritual essence.

showing to certain persons the extent of that love, so that we may praise His greatness. For He has been pleased to unite Himself with His creature in such a way that they have become like two who cannot be separated from one another: even so He will not separate Himself from her (St Teresa of Avila, *The Interior Castle*, Seventh Mansions, chap. 2, 224–226).

As a result of this participation in or with God, the person is generally reborn or spiritually transformed, becoming a more or less perfect vehicle for the Divine. The temporary ecstatic experience of union thus leads to a permanent sense of living the divine or *unitive life* (Underhill, 1911/1995). On the other hand, if not permanently integrated into the life, unitive experience can also lead to a sense of spiritual loss and to the *Dark Night of the Spirit* (St. John of the Cross, 1991).

25. **Formless consciousness.** Abiding in stillness as the Transcendent Witness — in pure, formless Peace, Being, Ground, Consciousness, Heart, or 'Godhead'. Here the experience is of existing as a Void or silent centre, lacking all distinctions or manifestations, but containing all as dynamic potentiality. In Buddhism this is referred to as *sunyata* (emptiness, voidness). In Vedanta it is called *nirvikalpa samadhi* (i.e., Yogic trance without qualities or forms).

> [Silence] is in the purest part of the soul, in the noblest, in her ground, aye in the very essence of the soul. That is mid-silence, for thereinto no creature did ever get, nor any image, nor has the soul there either activity or understanding, therefore she is not aware of any image either of herself or any creature … there is no activity in the essence of the soul; the faculties she works with emanate from the ground of the essence, but in her actual ground there is mid-stillness; here alone is rest … Call it, if thou wilt, an ignorance, an unknowing, yet there is in it more than in all knowing and understanding without it (Meister Eckhart, from *Sermon I*, cited in Happold, 1970, pp. 276–278).

> To abide as the Self is the thing. Never mind the mind. If the mind's source is sought, the mind will vanish leaving the Self unaffected … Tracing the source of 'I,' the primal I-I [the pure Witness] alone remains over, and it is inex-

pressible. The seat of that awareness is within and the
seeker cannot find it as an object outside him. That seat is
bliss and is the core of all beings. Hence it is called the
Heart ... If the diversity [of the mind] is not manifest it
remains in its own essence, its original state, and that is
the Heart ... To remain as one's Self is to enter the Heart
... Find the source of thoughts. Then you will abide in the
ever-present inmost Self (Sri Ramana Maharshi, from
Talks with Ramana Maharshi, cited in Wilber, 1995a,
p. 307).

It is important to realize that this *direct mystical experience* of
the Transcendent Witness is very different from the simple
intellectual realization of the subjective self previously discussed (No. 12).

26. **Nondual or ultimate consciousness ('One Taste').** In nondual consciousness, the world of form (sensations, perceptions, mental objects, etc.) is experienced in all its fullness
and glory. However there is a fundamental difference
between this ultimate nondual consciousness and our ordinary dualistic (subject-object) awareness. In nondual consciousness, the whole world of form is directly experienced
as the immediate, unconditional, liberated play or expression of Mind, Spirit, Self, or God. This means that there is no
sense of a *separate* Witness or observer, nor any *separate*
world. There is no inside or outside. The Witness just *IS*
everything, and everything just *IS* as it is. In Tibetan
Buddhism, this state is called *Rigpa* — an intelligent, self-
luminous, radiant, pure, ever-present awareness that is the
goal of *Dzogchen* and *Mahamudra* meditation. It is also the
Original Self of Zen.

> Recognize beyond any doubt that this sky-like nature of
> your mind is the absolute master. Where else would all
> the enlightened beings be but in the Rigpa, in the nature
> of your mind? Secure in that realization, in a state of spa-
> cious and carefree ease, you rest in the warmth, glory,
> and blessing of your absolute nature. You have arrived at
> the original ground: the primordial purity of natural sim-
> plicity. As you rest in this state of Rigpa, you recognize
> the truth of Padmasambhava's words: 'Mind itself is

Padmasambhava; there is no practice or meditation apart
from that' (Sogyal Rinpoche, 1992, p. 148–149).

Like the empty sky it has no boundaries,
Yet it is right in this place, ever profound and clear.
When you seek to know it, you cannot see it.
You cannot take hold of it,
But you cannot lose it.
In not being able to get it, you get it.
When you are silent, it speaks;
When you speak, it is silent.
The great gate is wide open to bestow alms,
And no crowd is blocking the way
(Cheng-tao Ke [cited in Watts, 1957, p. 145]).

Experience and Concept

This list is not intended to be an exhaustive catalogue of 'spiritual,' transpersonal or mystical experiences (cf. Chapter 11). It is, however, sufficient for the arguments that I wish to develop in relation to the concept of the transpersonal self. The most obvious point, perhaps, concerns the extraordinary diversity and complexity of these areas of experience. If we were hoping to find *the* soul, or *the* transpersonal self, then we shall need to think again. Little wonder, therefore, that our ancestors found it necessary to make fundamental distinctions between different aspects or levels of the 'soul'. Recognizing the differences between these experiences helps to explain why, for example, the Egyptians distinguished between the *Khaibit, Ka, Ba, Khu, Sahu,* why St. Paul refers to *psyche* (soul) and *pneuma* (spirit), or why Plotinus makes a distinction between soul, *nous* and the One. Here, then, we find the experiential bases of many of the psychological and metaphysical concepts that humankind has invented in order to try to make sense of its own self-experience. Here are the animating spirit, double, shade, astral-dream body, etheric body, subtle-energetic body, Cartesian mind, immortal soul, personality, psyche, consciousness, unconscious, ego, existential self, 'real self', divine spark, divine soul, Oversoul, guardian angel, higher self, witness, Original Self, and no-self. Here also, I believe, are the *experiential foundations* of the world's major religions (cf. Grof, 1998). But this is where the problem strikes home — even though each of these concepts and religious perspectives is based on *experience*, on the face of it they appear to imply multiple, incompatible or contradictory realities. How can we begin to make sense of all these different views of the soul or self? How, for example, can we reconcile *shades* with *guardian angels* or the *original self*? How can we reconcile the seeming nature mysticism of cosmic consciousness with the deity mysticism of St Teresa, or the mind-mysticism of *Dzogchen*?

At this juncture, I should make the point that *experiences* cannot establish the truth (or falsity) of any metaphysical doctrine. In other words, seeing a ghost does not necessarily imply that the ghost exists as an actual entity in itself (as distinct from our perception of it, which may simply be hallucinatory). Similarly an experience of union with God is not a proof of His existence. Phenomenology and ontology (metaphysics) are more or less separate activities although, in my opinion, if metaphysics is to mean anything at all, it must be based on sound phenomenology (cf. Ferrer, 2002). My agenda in this chapter and the next is not primarily with the ontological, metaphysical or theological questions (e.g., the immortality of the soul, the reality of reincarnation, or the divinity of the soul), but rather with a conceptual analysis of the phenomenological data and with their implications for psychological theory and practice. A complication that we shall find, however, is that metaphysical doctrines or assumptions have themselves influenced these psychological theories, such that it will be impossible entirely to ignore these questions.

If, as transpersonal psychologists, we wish to do more than provide a phenomenological description and categorization of these experiences, we are inevitably forced into the attempt to understand and explain them in some way, using some system of constructs that we can reasonably assume, demonstrate, or justify. In this way, we should seek to adopt or create an explanatory framework that is comprehensive, believable, and that can provide effective practical guidance and support for those seeking to explore the transpersonal. In its *purpose*, this is no different from the agenda of myth or religion, i.e., it is *mythical* in the sense discussed in the previous chapter. However, in my view, transpersonal psychology differs fundamentally in its *approach* and *methods*, which are essentially scientific and philosophical. This does not mean that we cannot learn from mythological, religious or metaphysical systems, but that transpersonal psychology should avoid turning itself into a religion, cult or system of belief. In order to do this, it is necessary always to ground our discipline in direct experience (including observation and experiment) and in the rigorous and rational justification of ideas (rather than mere assertion). Because of the nature of our subject-matter it may be impossible entirely to avoid metaphysical assumptions or hypotheses, but these should, I suggest, be kept to a minimum and made explicit (cf. Chapter 10).

Of course a transpersonal psychology cannot be entirely materialist in its outlook. But, as *psychologists*, there is much that we can do, I think, while still remaining true to the data of experience, at the level of psychological explanation. This, perhaps, is the main reason why many transpersonal psychologists prefer to talk about the transpersonal *self*, or transpersonal *identity*, rather than the *soul*. Unlike the term 'soul' which carries all sorts of religious-metaphysical connotations, 'self' and 'identity' are essentially psychological-experiential constructs that make no particular metaphysical assumptions.

Conclusions

The concept of the soul is complex and multifaceted because it is based on a variety of human capacities and experiences. Ideas about the soul have also evolved over the centuries, reflecting developments in human beings' experience of themselves. Since we must expect evolution of human consciousness to continue, the soul is essentially an open-ended construct that is likely to show further refinements and modifications in the future.

At its simplest, the evolution of ideas about the soul seems to involve three major stages. In the first stage, the soul is conceived as a *quasi-physical* reality of some kind, such as a vapour, body or fire. Later ideas about the soul incorporated what we would now describe as *psychological* qualities such as desire, thought, will, self-consciousness and personality. Only relatively recently, it seems, did concepts of the soul begin to include the idea of our human connection with a *divine* reality. Given these very different levels of explanation, confusion can arise, I suggest, when these levels are confounded — for example in the belief that our divine soul (or transpersonal self) has an individual personality, or that human personality has a continuing (immortal) physical substrate. This is, however, a much larger and more complex discussion that I cannot enter into here.

Being an aspect of human *experience*, the soul is something that can be investigated by psychologists, who may prefer to use psychological terms such as 'transpersonal self' or 'transpersonal identity' in preference to the religious terminology. Whatever terminology we decide to use, it is vital that our psychological concepts honour and do justice to the richness and variety of human experience.

Chapter 9

The Transpersonal Self

In the last chapter I considered the historical development and experiential foundations of religious and metaphysical ideas about the soul. In this chapter I shall examine the ways in which nine major theoretical approaches in transpersonal psychology have addressed the question of the transpersonal self. In particular, I shall question how comprehensive and useful these theories are, and what can we learn from the differences among them. The nine theories are:

1. The Metamotivational Theory of Abraham Maslow

2. The Analytical Psychology of C.G. Jung

3. Roberto Assagioli's Psychosynthesis

4. The Holotropic Model of Stan Grof

5. The Integral Psychology of Sri Aurobindo

6. The Structural-Hierarchical Model of Ken Wilber

7. The Spiral-Dynamic Model of Michael Washburn

8. The Feminist Theory of Peggy Wright

9. The Participatory Vision of Jorge Ferrer

Before discussing each of these theories in turn, it perhaps useful to point out that they all share certain common assumptions

This chapter is a revised and updated version of Daniels (2002b)

about the nature of the transpersonal and transpersonal identity. These assumptions are:

- Transpersonal identity involves a *developmental achievement.*

- This achievement entails going *beyond* the experience of both *egoic* and *existential* (authentic) identity.

- Transpersonal identity is associated with the realization of modes of functioning and experience that have distinctly *'spiritual'* qualities.

The different theories are also in basic accord on the *particular* spiritual qualities that we can recognize as characterizing transpersonal identity. Frances Vaughan (1985, p. 28) identifies these as: compassionate, loving, wise, receptive, allowing, unlimited, intuitive, spontaneous, creative, inspired, peaceful, awake, open, and connected.

Where the theories fail to agree is in their *conceptual understanding* of the transpersonal self, and in their *developmental psychology* or explanations of how transpersonal identity may be achieved.

The Metamotivational Theory of Abraham Maslow

As we have seen, Maslow's own interest in the transpersonal derives from his investigations into the experiential and motivational characteristics of exceptional, 'self-actualizing' people. In particular, Maslow became interested in the nature and consequences of mystical-type 'peak experiences', or moments of highest happiness and fulfilment, that were reported by many (but not all) self-actualizers. According to Maslow, these peak experiences involved a special mode of transcendent cognition (Cognition of Being, or B-Cognition) that exhibits qualities of, for example, exclusive attention, holistic perception, self-forgetfulness, and receptivity. Maslow also noted that in B-Cognition, the world was perceived in terms of universal values (B-Values) such as truth, goodness, beauty, unity, aliveness, perfection, justice, order and meaningfulness. As a result of these experiences, the person's values and goals were often transformed — they were now *metamotivated* by the universal B-Values rather than by self-interest. Moreover, so passionate was the commitment to the B-Values that these became *defining qualities of the self.* In this way the person identifies the 'highest self with the highest values of the world' (Maslow, 1973, p. 327) and thereby begins to lose the distinction between self and non-self.

In arguing that the B-Values were genuinely universal, rather than simply cultural, this implied to Maslow that they must be a *biological* potentiality and therefore part of what he termed our organismic 'inner core' or 'Real Self'.

> The spiritual life is then part of the human essence. It is a defining characteristic of human nature ... It is part of the Real Self ... The spiritual life (the contemplative, 'religious,' philosophical or value life) is within the jurisdiction of human thought and is attainable in principle by man's own efforts (Maslow, 1973, p. 341).

Although this may be dismissed as a crude form of biological reductionism, Maslow himself believes that nothing of the actual range, quality or human meaning of spiritual or religious experience is lost in this 'humanistic' identification with the biological. All that is lost, he suggests, is the unnecessary belief in unprovable transcendent metaphysical realities such as the immortal soul, or God.

Maslow's theory can undoubtedly account for many types of transpersonal experience. However, his own emphasis is on the personal and transpersonal 'heights' and as a result he tends to ignore the role of the unconscious and of spiritual crises such as the Dark Night of the Soul.

The Analytical Psychology of C.G. Jung

Like Maslow, Jung's approach to the transpersonal is deliberately and consistently *psychological* rather than metaphysical. In some ways this is paradoxical because Jung was profoundly interested in the spiritual questions and immersed himself throughout his life in the religious and metaphysical literature of the world, especially that of Hermeticism and Gnosticism. He also had a life-long interest in the occult and experienced many events of a paranormal kind, including a profound near-death experience and encounters with 'spirit guides' such as Elijah, Salome, and another that he named Philemon.

Jung's theory is based on the concepts of *archetypes* and the *collective unconscious*. Archetypes are universal patterns of experience, predisposing us to think and feel towards certain objects or events in particular ways. The archetypes exist in the collective unconscious — a universal level of the mind that is a kind of psychological storehouse of shared memory-patterns. The collective unconscious is 'überpersonlich', or 'above the person', existing as a reality that is beyond the individual level of mind and to that extent may be considered to be transpersonal (or at least trans-individual). For Jung, therefore, transpersonal experiences (including the experience of God) are essentially those of the collective archetypes.

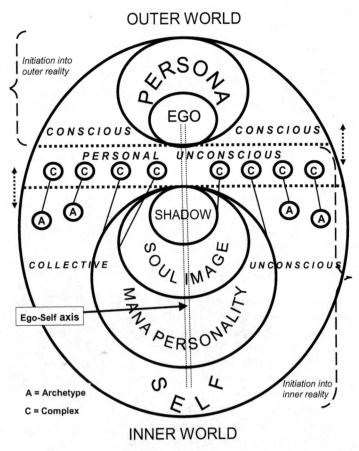

Figure 4. Jung's model of the psyche (after Jacobi, 1968)

Jung's theory of psychological development proposes that human life falls (archetypally) into two main stages. In the first half of life, we undergo an *initiation into outer reality* (see Figure 4). In this, the aim is to adapt to the outer world, through physical, intellectual and social development, and through the creation of the *ego*[1] (the centre of the self-sense, consciousness and agency) and *persona* (our patterns of adaptive behaviour). In the second half of life (often after a mid-life crisis) we turn our attention inwards, towards the larger reality of the whole Self. In this way we undergo an *initiation into inner reality* in which we must learn to acknowledge and adapt to certain major archetypal realities on our psychological journey towards individuation, or the full realization of the archetype of the Self. In Jung's theory, these major archetypal realities are (a) *shadow*, (b) *soul-image* (*anima / animus*), (c) *mana personalities*, and (d) the *Self*.

The archetype of the *shadow* represents our own unacceptable, antisocial, frightening, irrational, or evil characteristics. These are a direct challenge to our conscious self-image and to our sense of rationality and mental control. This so disturbs the conscious mind that it attempts to dissociate from the shadow by repressing these tendencies into the unconscious. The shadow is also projected unconsciously onto other individuals and groups who thereby become the objects of our prejudice, hatred and scapegoating. In dreams and fantasies, the shadow is often experienced in the form of frightening, tormenting figures. For Jung, it was important to learn to *own* our shadow, thereby beginning the important psychological work of integrating the conscious and unconscious within the larger totality of the Self.

The *soul-image* is a complex set of ideas about a person's general relationship to the unconscious mind (which includes much more than the shadow). Essentially the soul-image is an *archetypal personification* of the unconscious, which is therefore experienced as having a distinct personality of its own (Jung believed that this personality was generally contrasexual). The soul-image thus portrays a hidden, mysterious and fascinating part of the self that is experienced by the conscious mind as a semi-autonomous 'other' with whom a relationship is possible.

---

1   According to Jung, it is important that the ego is always connected to the larger reality of the Self (via the ego-self axis) otherwise there is psychological disturbance.

The soul-image appears in multiple guises and has both a positive and negative aspect. In practice, the soul-image is typically projected onto persons of the opposite sex. It also appears in our dreams, fantasies or visions in various opposite-sex personifications. A man's *anima* may be experienced or projected as, for example, a maiden, witch, whore, or mother. For Jung the *anima* or *animus* is also a source of inspiration, vitality and creativity — a person's inner Muse. Jung interpreted his own encounters with Salome as an example of *anima* experience.

Mana is a Polynesian and Melanesian word referring to the essential force or power that resides in objects, plants, animals, and people. For Jung, the *mana personality* represents the archetypal personification of the extraordinary inner power found deep within the unconscious. In contrast to the soul-image, the mana personality is generally experienced as (or projected onto) same-sex figures. For men, it may appear as the *puer aeternus* (eternal boy), Hero, Father, or Wise Old Man, whereas, for women, it may manifest as the *puella aeterna* (eternal girl), Amazon, Great Mother, or Sibyl. Jung's experiences with Elijah were understood as a manifestation of the mana personality.

In Jung's psychology, the *Self* is an archetypal image representing the primal ground and totality of the psyche (conscious and unconscious). More specifically, it refers to the psychological goal of union between consciousness and the unconscious. In this sense, the Self is something to be *realized*. However, this is a theoretical goal that can never be fully attained in practice because, for Jung, the totality of the Self can *never* be fully known (the unconscious will always remain and is always *really* unconscious). The Self is also experienced as an inner guiding and organizing principle that seeks union and balance within the psyche. The Self appears in dreams, fantasies and myths in forms that symbolize wholeness, balance, harmony and perfection — for example, as Christ, Krishna, Buddha, Sun, Circle, Wheel, Square, or Mandala.

Jung's theory is extraordinarily full and rich and provides a framework within which we may interpret very many of the experiences that suggest a transpersonal aspect to the self which I identified in the previous chapter. These include shamanic journeying, encounters with spirit guides, near-death experiences, mediumistic experience, reincarnation experiences, intuition and inspiration, conversion and rebirth, revelations, guiding impulses, species consciousness, cosmic consciousness, and unitive experience (spiritual marriage). Furthermore the theory is metaphysically extremely parsimonious — everything hinges on the single assumption of the reality of the collective unconscious.

Where Jung has particular difficulty, however, is in accounting for the experiences of formless and nondual consciousness. In 1958 the Zen scholar Shin'ichi Hisamatsu visited Jung's home at Küsnacht in Switzerland. Their discussion focussed on the relationship between Jung's concept of Self and the Zen notion of 'No Mind' or 'Original Self'. Hisamatsu was very surprised by Jung's insistence that the Self could not be fully known, because there would always be an unconscious stratum.

> **Hisamatsu:** Now then, which is our True Self, the unconscious or consciousness? Which one is called 'True Self' or 'Self'?

> **Jung:** Consciousness calls itself 'I' (*ich*), while the Self (*Selbst*) is not 'I' at all. The Self is the whole, because personality — you as a whole — consists of consciousness and the unconscious. It is the whole or, in other words, the 'Self'. But I know only consciousness; the unconscious remains unknown to me.

> **Hisamatsu:** According to your view, the 'Self' is the whole. From this the question follows: Is 'I-consciousness' different from 'Self-consciousness' or not?

> **Jung:** In ordinary usage, people say 'self-consciousness,' but psychologically this is only 'I-consciousness'. The Self is unknown, for it indicates the whole, that is, consciousness and the unconscious ...

> **Hisamatsu:** What? The self cannot be known?

> **Jung:** Perhaps only one half of it is known, and that is the *ego*. The *ego* is half of the Self ...

> **Hisamatsu:** The essential point of ... liberation is how we can be awakened to our Original Self. The Original Self is the self which is no longer bound by a myriad of things. To attain this self is the essential point of freedom. It is necessary, therefore, to release oneself even from the collective unconscious and the bondage which derives from it ... What we generally

call 'self' is the same as the self [*Selbst*] characterized by you, Professor Jung. But it is only after the emancipation of this self that the 'Original Self' of Zen emerges. It is the True Self described in Zen as the Self which is realized in absolute emancipation and is without dependence on anything ... The True Self has no form or substance, whatsoever ... It is quite different from the ordinary *Atman*. Zen's True Self has neither spiritual form nor physical shape ... Therefore the True Self can never be bound by a myriad of things. Liberation, the essence of religious freedom, rests on this point ... Ultimately, to become 'The Formless Self' is the essence of Zen (Meckel & Moore, 1992, pp. 106–113).

This fascinating exchange encapsulates the critical difference between Jung's concept of the Self and that of Zen. Thus for Zen, the Original Self is fully known and awakened unto itself. In Hisamatsu's commentary on their conversation, he writes:

'No Mind' of Zen is ... not only known, but most clearly known, as it is called '*Kaku*' (awakening) or '*ryoryo jochi*' (always clearly comprehending). But this is not a state in which something is merely known. Rather, it is a clear 'self-awakening in and to itself' that is without a separation between knower and known. 'No Mind' is a state in which self is most clearly awakened to itself, such as when we are utterly absorbed in our work ... the 'Self' of Zen is not concerned with anything internal or external ... Rather, it is unbounded self-awakening. Therefore the 'Self' of Zen is neither the *ego* of psychoanalysis, which is excited and disturbed by the *unconscious*, nor is it the self, which is composed of *ego* and unconscious (*ibid.*, p. 117, italics in original).

Jung himself was clearly very dissatisfied with their conversation, and he wrote to the translator:

I am sorry to say that your plan of publishing Dr. Hisamatsu's interview with me ... is a most delicate and correspondingly dangerous procedure, with which I can hardly consent ... You would be astonished at how little our knowledge and understanding of Zen is, which I gathered from my talk with Dr. Hisamatsu. That is not his fault, but my incompetence. Yet this is equally true as regards our European psychology of the Unconscious in Dr. Hisamatsu's case (*ibid.*, pp. 114–115).

As well as Jung's apparent failure to grasp the nature of formless or nondual consciousness, there is another problem that some commentators (e.g., Assagioli, 1993; Wilber, 1995a) have identified in his whole approach to the transpersonal. This is that the concept of the collective unconscious fails to make any clear or adequate distinction between genuinely transpersonal ('higher' or spiritual) archetypes and those that are non-transpersonal or 'lower'. For these commentators, archetypes such as the *shadow, anima* or *mana personality* may indeed be universal-collective, but there may not be anything specifically or necessarily *transpersonal* about them. Although the mana personality often takes the form of numinous figures such as the Wise Old Man or Priestess, it may also manifest as the eternal boy or girl. Assagioli (1993, p. 19) thus observes that 'what Jung has called the "collective unconscious" ... includes elements of different, even opposite natures, namely primitive, archaic structures and higher, forward-directed activities of a superconscious character'. Wilber argues more forcefully that Jung is guilty of 'elevationism,' i.e., reading 'a deeply transpersonal and spiritual status into experiences that are merely indissociated and undifferentiated and actually lacking any sort of integration at all' (1995a, p. 206).

Now this leads us once again directly back to one of the key issues in transpersonal psychology — what do we really understand by the term *transpersonal*? For Jung, the collective unconscious is itself a transpersonal ('überpersonlich') reality precisely because it is *universal* — transcending both individual and social-cultural experience. According to this view, *any* archetypal experience is a transpersonal experience. But what, then, are we to make of the specifically *spiritual* archetypes such as the Sage, God or Goddess? What is unique or special about these? Jung's answer, and it may indeed be adequate, is that the spiritual archetypes are those of *mana personality* and *Self* — archetypes that represent 'spiritual power' or the realization of wholeness, balance and perfection. For his critics, however, the concepts of archetypes and collective unconscious are simply too neutral and too inclusive to qualify as a full and satisfactory psychological account of transpersonal experience.

Roberto Assagioli's Psychosynthesis

It is precisely the need to distinguish between the 'higher' and 'lower' levels of the unconscious that is emphasized in Assagioli's psychosynthesis theory. As we have seen, Assagioli was a practitioner of Patanjali's Raja Yoga and student of the esotericist Alice Bailey and in many ways his theories represent an attempt to psychologize these spiritual teachings. In particular, Assagioli was concerned to reintroduce the concept of the personal *soul* or *Atman* into psychology.

Assagioli's theory of the transpersonal (a term that he adopted in his later writings) is summarized well in his famous 'egg diagram' (Figure 5).

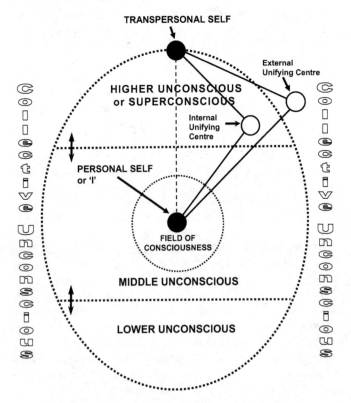

Figure 5. Assagioli's Model of the Psyche
(after Assagioli, 1965; Firman & Gila, 1997).

The first thing to note about this diagram is that the personal egg contains *both* the higher and lower unconscious. In Assagioli's model, therefore, the higher unconscious (or 'superconscious') is distinguished clearly from the collective unconscious. The collective unconscious represents the individual's relationship with 'other human beings and with the general psychic environment' (Assagioli, 1993, p. 19). In contrast, the higher unconscious is the source of 'higher intuitions and inspirations ... higher feelings ... states of contemplation, illumination, and ecstasy ... higher psychic functions and spiritual energies' (*ibid.*, p. 17–18). It is also the source of higher values. The higher unconscious, then, is essentially the realm of spiritual *content* (images, energies, etc.). Experience in this realm, according to Assagioli, generally *precedes* consciousness of the Higher Self.

Assagioli's equivalent to the personal soul appears at the apex of the higher unconscious. Assagioli variously refers to this as the Self, Higher Self, Spiritual Self, True Self, Real Self, Noumenal Self, or Transpersonal Self. The Higher Self is different from the conscious self, or I, which itself is the 'point of pure self-awareness ... the center of our consciousness' (*ibid.* p. 18) and which is merely the reflection or projection of the Higher Self. However, such *reflection* or *projection* means that there are not really *two* separate selves in us, but that this is simply a relative appearance:

> Indeed, it is *as if* there were two selves, because the personal self is generally unaware of the other, even to the point of denying its existence; whereas the other, the true Self, is latent and does not reveal itself directly to our consciousness ... There are not really two selves, two independent and separate entities. The Self is one; it manifests in different degrees of awareness and self-realization. The reflection appears to be self-existent but has, in reality, no autonomous substantiality. It is, in other words, not a new and different light but a projection of its luminous source (*ibid.* p. 20, italics in original).

The Higher Self is therefore the 'permanent center ... situated beyond or "above" [the conscious self]' (*ibid.* p. 18). The Higher Self can, however, be *consciously realized* in states of cosmic consciousness or by using psychological methods such as Raja Yoga.

The real distinguishing factor between the little self and the higher Self is that the little self is acutely aware of itself as a distinct separate individual, and a sense of solitude or of separation sometimes comes in the existential experience. In contrast, the experience of the spiritual Self is a sense of freedom, of expansion, of communication with other Selves and with reality, and there is a sense of Universality. It feels itself at the same time individual and universal (*ibid.*, p. 87).

Such realization — i.e., the expansion of personal consciousness into that of the Higher Self — makes possible the transformation of the whole personality around this new centre. This, for Assagioli, is the goal of *spiritual or transpersonal psychosynthesis* (which he distinguishes from *personal psychosynthesis*, or the development of a well-integrated personality).

However, spiritual psychosynthesis cannot generally be achieved immediately or directly (even temporary states of cosmic consciousness or *samadhi* do not fully or permanently transform the personality). Instead, the spiritual ascent or growth is long and difficult, involving a series of intermediate stages and plateaux, perhaps including some form of explicit psycho-spiritual practice. More generally, it entails developing relationships with dynamic 'unifying centres' (representations or ideal models of the Higher Self) that serve to create a link between the conscious self and Higher Self. Such unifying centres may be external (e.g., a Guru, spiritual ideology or good cause), or internal (e.g., an inner teacher or inner Christ).

Assagioli also mentions two wider forms of psychosynthesis. *Interindividual psychosynthesis* involves the recognition of our interconnectedness and interdependence and the development of harmonious interpersonal and inter-group relationships. Beyond this, there is *cosmic synthesis* or 'the Supreme Synthesis'. This is the individual expression of a larger or wider 'spiritual, super-individual Reality ... a divine being or ... cosmic energy — the Spirit working upon and within all creation ... shaping it into order, harmony and beauty, uniting all beings ... with each other through links of love' (*ibid.* p. 31).

Assagioli's theory accounts effectively for the vast majority of transpersonal experiences. What Jung understands as the expressions of spiritual archetypes (experiences of spirit guides, near-death experiences, intuition and inspiration, etc.) Assagioli sees as manifestations of the higher unconscious, or supercon-scious. Assagioli's theory provides, however, a more convincing account of cosmic consciousness, which is understood as the conscious realization of the Higher Self. Where Assagioli seems to have some difficulty is in explaining the differences between cosmic consciousness and the other major types of mystical experiences such as formless Witnessing, theistic unitive experi-ence, and non-dual consciousness. Unitive and nondual experi-ence could both be considered as experiences of the supreme reality (divine being or *Brahman*), but that begs the question why, then, are these experiences so different?

However, there is perhaps a price to pay for the seemingly greater scope and precision of Assagioli's model. This is the increase in the number of metaphysical assumptions made. Assagioli himself is quite clear about this when appealing to a cosmic 'spiritual, super-individual Reality'. Where he is less clear is in relation to the Higher Self. It is quite difficult to read Assagioli without drawing the conclusion that he views the Self as an actual ontological reality (the Soul, or *Atman*). However, like Jung, he also claims to be concerned essentially with the undeniable *psychological* reality of spiritual Self, rather than with the question of its ontological or metaphysical status.

> We would therefore emphasize our neutrality towards those 'ultimate' problems, for our concern is to focus on living psy-chological experience and psychological facts ... We are not attempting to force upon psychology a philosophical, theo-logical or metaphysical position (*ibid.*, p. 193).

In Jung's case, this type of explanation may satisfy the reader, simply because it is unclear exactly what Jung's own religious beliefs were. With Assagioli, however, it is much less convincing because of his known allegiance to particular spiritual and eso-teric doctrines such as those of Yoga and Alice Bailey.

The Holotropic Model of Stan Grof

Stan Grof's approach to the transpersonal is perhaps the most comprehensive of all the major theorists. This is because it incor-porates, and provides explicit accounts of, a remarkably wide range and diversity of transpersonal experiences. As previously discussed, the origins of Grof's theory lie in his extensive investi-gations of the therapeutic potential of psychedelic drugs and of

Holotropic Breathwork™. Grof found that the types of extraordinary experience reported using LSD and Holotropic Breathwork were remarkably similar and included sensory alterations, emotional reliving of past events and traumas, death and rebirth episodes, and a wide variety of psychic, archetypal and mystical experiences.

In order to account for these experiences, Grof suggests that we have access to three domains of the psyche. In addition to the personal or biographical unconscious of psychoanalysis, there are the *perinatal* (literally 'around birth') and *transpersonal* domains. He suggests that, in practice, experiences of a spiritual and transformational nature can represent both perinatal and transpersonal influences and may result from the mediation of the transpersonal by the perinatal.

The perinatal domain represents the effect of intrauterine and birth experiences, which can be understood in terms of four common (archetypal) patterns. These patterns, known as Basic Perinatal Matrices, continue to affect us throughout our lives — an influence that includes the modification or colouring of transpersonal experience. For example, the symbiotic union and security of intrauterine existence (BPMI) is connected with blissful 'oceanic' experiences of oneness with the universe, or encounters with blissful deities. BPMII (associated with uterine contractions) may lead to experiences of being caught hopelessly in a dangerous and grotesque world of nightmare creatures and images, or to the Dark Night of the Soul. BPMIII (represented by the opening of the cervix and the movement down the birth canal) is a time of optimism, excitement and struggle. BPMIII experiences may take the form of titanic death-rebirth struggles, apocalytpic visions, or wild, sexual ecstasies. BPMIV represents the moment of birth. It is typically associated with experiences of ego death and rebirth, sacrifice, visions of brilliant light, or ecstatic union with specific deities, God or the Divine Self.

Grof does not attempt, however, to fully *explain* all spiritual-archetypal experiences in terms of perinatal influences. Thus he also postulates the existence of a 'genuinely' transpersonal (universal), ontological level of reality. The fundamental difference, then, between the perinatal and the transpersonal domains is that the perinatal is essentially an aspect of *personal* or *collective* psychology (a consequence of individual and collective human-personal experience), whereas the transpersonal represents a level of *universal* (absolute) mind or consciousness.

> To understand the transpersonal realm we must begin thinking of consciousness in an entirely new way ... as something that exists outside and independent of us, something that in its essence is not bound by matter ... Transpersonal consciousness is infinite, rather than finite, stretching beyond the limits of time and space (Grof, 1993, p. 83).

In this way, Grof's understanding of the transpersonal domain differs from both the collective unconscious of Jung and the higher unconscious of Assagioli. Jung's collective unconscious thus partly overlaps with both perinatal and transpersonal, whereas Assagioli's Higher Unconscious is essentially a subset of Grof's transpersonal.

As we saw earlier, Grof suggests that it is useful to divide the transpersonal domain into three major regions of experience:

(a) The extension of consciousness *within* ordinary space-time reality. This includes experiences such as identification with other people or groups, union with the physical world, clairvoyance, and memories of past lives.

(b) The extension of consciousness *beyond* ordinary space-time reality. This includes shamanic journeying, channelling, encounters with mythical-archetypal figures, and formless consciousness (Void).

(c) 'Psychoid' experiences. These are experiences that are neither clearly mental nor physical, such as UFO encounters, synchronicities, psychokinesis, poltergeists and magic.

Grof's account of transpersonal experiences is remarkable for its originality and scope, and for the challenge that it offers to our traditional understanding of spiritual experience. His daring suggestion that spiritual experience reflects or is modified by intrauterine and childbirth events is, of course, highly controversial (see, for example, Wilber, 1997, chap. 7) as is his willingness to include paranormal experiences within the realm of the transpersonal (cf. Chapter 2).

In relation to the transpersonal *self*, Grof recognizes a variety of such *experiences* (e.g., of the inner core, divine Self, Oversoul, universal self, etc.) but, unlike Assagioli, he does not prioritize or explicitly reify the concept of Self. Grof's metaphysical position emphasizes the fundamental realities of the *psyche* and of a *universal (non-individual) consciousness* which overlaps, and gives birth to, but is not identical with the material world (Grof, 1998, 2000). This universal consciousness itself contains many levels or regions of experience. These include not only the personal, archetypal and spiritual, but also other universes and other dimensions.

The Integral Psychology of Sri Aurobindo

Sri Aurobindo Ghose is one of the most important Indian spiritual philosophers of the twentieth century and a major influence on transpersonal psychology through the related work of Ken Wilber.

Born in Calcutta in 1872, Aurobindo came to England aged seven to receive a British education, mainly in the Classics. He obtained a scholarship to Cambridge University and after distinguishing himself in his studies he returned to India in 1893. In the early 1900s he became involved in the Bengali Nationalist movement and also took up the practice of Yoga. In 1908 he was arrested and imprisoned by the British authorites on a charge of belonging to a terrorist organization. During the year he then spent in jail, Aurobindo studied the Hindu scriptures, continued to meditate and practice Yoga, and had a number of profound spiritual experiences, including cosmic consciousness and Nirvana. After his acquittal in 1909 he moved to Pondicherry, renounced violent protest, and dedicated the remainder of his life to spiritual writing and teaching. At Pondicherry, in 1914, he first met Mirra Alfassa / Mirra Richard. Born in 1878 in Paris of Turkish and Egyptian parents, Mirra had a history of mystical, psychical and visionary experiences, was a student of occultism, and had founded a group of spiritual seekers in Paris. On meeting each other, Aurobindo and Mirra recognized their strong spiritual and psychic connection which led to Mirra becoming Aurbindo's chief spiritual collaborator. Known as The Mother, she took charge of the organization of Aurobindo's ashram (spiritual community) at Pondicherry and continued this work after Aurobindo's death in 1950 until her own in 1973. In the 1960s The Mother's vision led to the founding and construction (which is still ongoing) of a spiritual township called Auroville, near Pondicherry (www.auroville.org), which aims to create a model for universal harmony and union.

Aurobindo's philosophy and psychological system is articulated in his main writings (*The Life Divine*, 1939–40/1970; *The Synthesis of Yoga*, 1948–55/1990; see also Dalal, 2001). A major feature of Aurobindo's approach is an idealistic vision of human and cosmic perfectability, based on the notion of spiritual culture and the refining of human nature. In many ways, this is like the classical Greek (Platonic) ideal of the refined intellectual life but, for Aurobindo, life must be based on a spiritual rather than purely intellectual or rational foundation. Because of Aurobindo's idealism, his philosophy is strongly soteriological. He links this salvational agenda, however, into a metaphysical and cosmological scheme in which human beings play a fundamental role in the spiritual unfolding of the universe.

As a religious-metaphysical system, Aurobindo's philosophy is fundamentally Vedantic but he introduces into Vedanta a strong evolutionary perspective. In this model, although the Absolute (Divine, Supreme Being) is originally above all manifestation it may be said to have a threefold aspect as existence-consciousness-bliss (Sachchidananda). In order to manifest, the Absolute becomes folded in, or *involved*, in matter. For Aurobindo, this involutionary process means that all matter contains consciousness, albeit in a concealed *inconscient* form (see Figure 6). This initial involution of the Divine then turns into an evolutionary process in order that the Divine may become fully realized in the world of form. Evolution itself has brought about the successive emergence of complex material forms, life, mind and (at least potentially) spirit. This, of course, is essentially the perennialist idea of the Great Chain of Being and, as a theory of spiritual evolution, it bears close comparison with the process philosophies and theologies of Teilhard de Chardin (1959), Alfred North Whitehead (1929) and Charles Hartshorne (e.g., 1964).

Because, for Aurobindo, the evolution of mind and spirit expresses itself most directly in the human realm, his philosophy focuses strongly on the human condition and human psychology. Humankind, he argues, is essentially at the leading edge of evolution and therefore, as a species, we have a major role to play in the process of cosmic and spiritual advance. This, then, is

Aurobindo's version of an *anthropic principle* (see Barrow & Tipler, 1988), or the notion that cosmological evolution requires, or is preprogrammed for, the evolution of life, human intelligence and, in Aurobindo's view, *spirituality*.

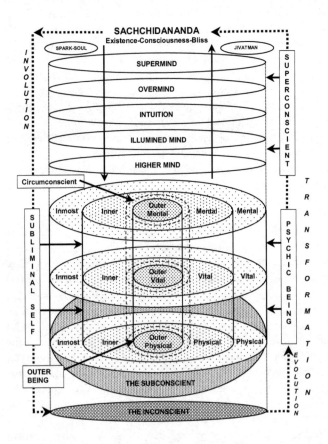

Figure 6. The psychological-philosophical model of Sri Aurobindo (after Aurobindo, 1970; Dalal, 2001).

Aurobindo begins his exploration of human nature with the *inconscient* realm of matter, as expressed in the form of the body. Because the inconscient contains Sachchidananda in concealed form, this means that the body itself has a kind of consciousness and knowledge (i.e., the 'wisdom of the body') which is, however, generally outside our own conscious awareness.

Midway between the inconscient body and conscious awareness is the realm of the *subconscient*. This represents lower, inferior, and (in psychodynamic terms) *unconscious* aspects of our being. Aurobindo was familiar with psychoanalytic thought and his notion of the subconscient is more or less equivalent to the Freudian unconscious, Assagioli's lower unconscious, or the personal unconscious of Jung.

The next constituent factor in human psychology is the *outer or surface being*, which forms the basis of our ego structure and which expresses itself in our ordinary relations to the outer world. Aurobindo suggests that it is useful to recognize three aspects of our outer being: (1) *physical* (sensory, perceptual), (2) *vital* (emotional, motivational) and (3) *mental* (thinking, intelligence).

For Aurobindo, our outer being is only a small part or expression of a larger self that he calls the *inner being*, or *subliminal self*. This represents a much wider (though generally hidden) consciousness which is more aware, more intelligent, and more knowledgeable than the outer self, or ego (which the inner being supports). The subliminal self processes and remembers all the information that we are exposed to (even that which we did not consciously acknowledge)[2] and it is also open to other realms and other realities. It is the subliminal self that is active in dreams, and that can explain psychic awareness and other extraordinary abilities such as those of the autistic savants (cf. Treffert, 2000). Like the outer being, the subliminal self has physical, vital and mental components.

Existing as a kind of antechamber between the inner and outer beings is the *circumconscient*. The circumconscient is analogous to an 'aura' of awareness that surrounds us and through which we may access the greater knowledge of the inner being and of other realities.

---

2   In this sense, the outer being represents a filtered (and often distorted) version of the consciousness of the subliminal self.

Supporting both our inner and outer beings is the inmost being, or *psychic being*.[3] The psychic being, for Aurobindo, is the evolving soul-personality which transmigrates from life to life, becoming spiritually transformed on its journey.[4] According to Aurobindo, we do not start out with a fully formed psychic being (other than in the sense of a nascent divine spark-soul). Rather we *create* a psychic being as the result of the spiritual achievements of our various lives. Moreover, through spiritual practice (e.g., Aurobindo's own approach of *Integral Yoga*), the psychic being can become an instrument of higher, spiritual consciousness. This can then result in the transformation of the inner and outer beings (physical, vital, and mental) and, consequently, of the world.

The spiritual impulse to transform comes from the realm of the *superconscient* (cf. Assagioli's higher unconscious). It is from here that spiritual awareness descends to the psychic, subliminal and surface beings, giving the opportunity for individual transformation and for the expression of spirituality in the real world.

Aurobindo's model recognizes five different modes of higher, spiritual consciousness:[5]

1. *Higher mind* refers to forms of higher wisdom and spiritual clarity.

2. *Illumined mind* is the mind of the seer — a level of consciousness beyond higher mind that involves the experience of spiritual light and inner vision. It may be associated with rapture and ecstasy.

3. *Intuition* is an immediate revelatory truth or knowledge, based on intimate contact and union with the object of

---

3   I have chosen to represent the outer-inner-inmost beings with the outer at the centre in Figure 6 in order to emphasize the point that the inmost being includes and supports (in Wilber's terminology: 'transcends and includes') the inner being which, in turn, includes and supports the outer being.

4   Above the psychic being and outside of the evolutionary process is the central eternal, unchanging Spirit (Atman, Jivatman) which, however, is *represented* by the psychic self.

5   Aurobindo's descriptions of these different levels of superconscient experience are not always easy to follow, nor straightforward to summarize in a few words.

knowledge. With intuition, the person becomes immediately aware of the significance of a truth.

4. *Overmind* is a kind of global, boundless or universal consciousness that is comparable to cosmic consciousness.

5. *Supermind* refers to a state which is supramental and above all categories of thought. It is an absolute truth-consciousness that is not concerned with appearances or phenomenal experience, that arises as knowledge by identity, and that realizes the unity of all things.

It is most important to realize that the purpose of spiritual development, for Aurobindo, is not the achievement of these higher modes of consciousness *for their own sake*, nor for a liberation or escape from the world of ordinary experience. Rather the purpose of higher consciousness is to *transform* ordinary experience, the person and the world in a spiritual direction. Ultimately, the aim is to be able to fully express and actualize the Divine (Sachchidananda) in the realm of manifest reality by leading the fully spiritual life.

Aurobindo's elaborate and powerful theory provides a way of describing and explaining many of the experiences identified in the previous chapter. These include dream experience, subtle body experience, intuition, reincarnation experiences, revelations, species and cosmic consciousness, unitive experience, formless consciousness and One Taste. Clearly Aurobindo is able to do this only by a certain proliferation of metaphysical concepts that represent different aspects of the transpersonal self (the subliminal self, psychic being, spark-soul, Jivatman, superconscient, Sachchidananda). Given that Aurobindo was writing as a spiritual teacher rather than as a psychologist, this is, of course, both understandable and acceptable. It is legitimate to question, however, whether such avowedly metaphysical doctrines are appropriate for a scientific transpersonal psychology (see Chapter 10).

The Structural-Hierarchical Model of Ken Wilber

Ken Wilber provides an approach to the transpersonal based on the (post-axial) 'perennial philosophy' that he suggests may be found among all sophisticated spiritual traditions. The perennial philosophy, he argues, recognizes an ultimate Ground (e.g., Consciousness, Spirit, or God) that manifests in time as the Great Chain of Being. For Wilber (after Aurobindo) the Great Chain begins when the Ultimate Reality first becomes *involved* in Matter, and then *evolves* in progressively higher forms (Life and Mind), before it eventually *realizes itself* as Spirit. In this way the evolutionary process manifests as a 'spectrum of consciousness' (Wilber, 1993).

In terms of psychological development, the spectrum of consciousness manifests through a sequence of 'fulcrums' or milestones of development in the sense of self, each of which is associated with its own potential pathologies and treatments[6] (see Table 11).

Following development through various prepersonal and personal fulcrums, culminating in the achievement of existential (*Centaur*) identity, the sense of self continues to evolve through three fulcrums of transpersonal experience — *subtle*, *causal* and *ultimate*. Students of Vedanta will immediately recognize Wilber's adoption here of terms from the teaching of the 'three bodies' (gross, subtle and causal).

The *subtle* level refers to all transpersonal experiences that operate at the level of *thought* or imagination. These include, for example, psychic perceptions, cosmic consciousness, visions, hypnotic states, illuminations, encounters with spirit guides, subtle-body awareness, past-life memories, archetypal experiences, and unitive experiences. Wilber sometimes distinguishes between low-subtle (psychic-astral) and high-subtle (archetypal-divine) experiences (e.g., Wilber, 1996b, chap. 8). At the low subtle or psychic level, experiences are still closely tied to the gross physical realm (Wilber, 1995a, pp. 607–608). Such experiences include nature mysticism, cosmic consciousness, clairvoyance, *siddhis*, ghosts, and Grof's 'psychoid' experiences. The high subtle (or truly subtle), on the other hand, represents experiences that are entirely at the level of mind or thought, with little reference to the gross realm. These include deity mysticism, visions, illuminations, and experiences of archetypes.

In contrast to the subtle, the *causal* level operates not with thought, but with the *root of attention*. Causal experiences, therefore, are those that are based on our capacity for Witnessing.

---

6   For an interesting discussion of these transpersonal pathologies and treatments, see Wilber, 1986a, 1986b.

Table 11. Wilber's structural-hierarchical model of self development (after Visser, 2003; Wilber 1986a, 2000a)

Major Level	Fulcrum	Self-Stage	Pathology	Treatment	Lines of the Self		
					Ego	Soul	Spirit
Transpersonal		Ultimate Ground (Nondual / One Taste)	None	Nondual mysticism			
	F-9	Causal self (Pure Witness)	Dissociation of subject from world	Formless mysticism			
	F-8	Subtle self (Archetypal)	Archetypal fragmentation	Theistic mysticism			
	F-7	Psychic self	Psychic inflation	Nature mysticism			
	F-6	Centaur (Integrated self)	Existential crisis	Existential therapy (e.g., Logotherapy)			
Personal	F-5	Mature Ego	Identity crisis	Introspection / Counselling			
	F-4	Role self	Script pathology	Script analysis			
	F-3	Self-concept	Neuroses	Uncovering therapies			
	F-2	Emotional self	Borderline disorders	Structure-building therapies			
Prepersonal	F-1	Physical self	Psychosis	Physical therapies			
	F-0	Basic Perinatal Matrices	Birth traumas	Intense regressive therapies (e.g., Holotropic Breathwork)			

Such experiences include soul mysticism (Happold, 1970; Zaehner, 1961), silent awareness, *sunyata* or emptiness, formless radiant bliss, the 'No Mind' of Zen, and of identity with Eckhart's abstract Godhead (rather, than with a personal God). Wilber sometimes distinguishes between the 'low causal' and 'high causal' (see, for example, Wilber, 1996b, chap. 9). In the low causal, there is still some sense of self or identity (e.g., as the Godhead, Brahman, or 'final God'), whereas at the high causal, the sense of self is entirely transcended in the experience of pure formlessness or Void.

According to Wilber, *beyond* the causal, there is the possibility of 'Ultimate' nondual consciousness, *Rigpa*, or 'One Taste'. He describes nondual consciousness as follows:

> When one breaks through the causal absorption in pure unmanifest and unborn Spirit, the entire manifest world (or worlds) arises once again, but this time as a perfect expression of Spirit and as Spirit. The Formless and the entire world of manifest Form — pure emptiness and the whole Kosmos — are seen to be not-two (or nondual). The Witness is seen to be everything that is witnessed, so that, as Ramana puts it, 'The object to be witnessed and the Witness finally merge together ... and Absolute consciousness alone reigns supreme.' But this nondual consciousness is not other to the world: 'Brahman is the World ... the whole cosmos [Kosmos] is contained in the Heart ... All this world is Brahman.' ... No objects, no subjects, only this ... ever-present as pure Presence, the simple feeling of being: empty awareness as the opening or clearing in which all worlds arise, ceaselessly: I-I is the box the universe comes in. ... the world arises as before, but now there is no one to witness it ... In that pure empty awareness, I-I am the rise and fall of all worlds, ceaselessly, endlessly. I-I swallow the Kosmos and span the centuries ... It is as it is, self-liberated at the moment of its very arising. And it is only *this* (Wilber, 1995a, pp. 308–310).

This description of nondual experience is very clear. However, it begs the question: How exactly is nondual One Taste different from the cosmic consciousness that Wilber has also attributed to the low-subtle (psychic)? Compare the description above with, for example, Wilber's own discussion of cosmic consciousness as exemplified by Emerson's experience and account of the Over-Soul:

[In] direct Kosmic consciousness ... the Over-Soul becomes, or is *directly one with* [italics in original] the physiosphere and biosphere and noosphere ... And Emerson means this literally! According to Emerson, this Kosmic consciousness is not poetry ... rather, it is a direct realization ...With the Over-Soul, the World Soul, it is not that individuality disappears, but that ... it is negated and preserved in a deeper and wider ground, a ground that conspicuously includes all of nature and its glories ... since the Over-Soul is an experienced identity with all manifestation, it is an identity that most definitely and exuberantly embraces nature, and, to that degree, it begins to undercut the subject/object dualism. Emerson explains:

We see the world piece by piece, as the sun, the moon, the animal, the tree; but the whole, of which these are the shining parts, is the soul [the Over-Soul, the World-Soul]. And this deep power in which we exist and whose beatitude is all accessible to us, is not only self-sufficing and perfect in every hour, *but the act of seeing and the thing seen, the seer and the spectacle, the subject and the object, are one.* [italics added] (Wilber, 1995a, p. 284–285).

In some endnotes, Wilber (1995a) attempts to explain why this does not count as a genuinely nondual or ultimate experience. Thus he writes:

[Psychic mysticism] is mysticism, but mysticism with one foot still in the gross. It is gross-oriented mysticism (and that is what *all* of these wildly different phenomena have in common, from paranormal to kundalini to nature mysticism to cosmic consciousness ... the psychic is, and can be, the home of anything from initial meditation experiences to paranormal phenomena, from out-of-the-body experiences to kundalini awakenings, from a simple state of equanimity to full-blown cosmic consciousness: they are *all* the subtle realm breaking into the gross realm at the common border: the psychic ...) Emerson's own insights and awakenings often pass into the causal and the nondual, but it is a matter of degree, and his paradigmatic presentation is of the psychic-level Over-Soul ... nation-nature mysticism does not generally recognize the subtle or causal dimensions ... It is an identity with all of the waking-state (gross) Kosmos (*ibid.* p. 609, italics in original).

Now this *might* be a satisfactory explanation, although it seems to promote an unfortunate devaluation of the physical world and essentially depends upon our acceptance of Wilber's ideas about the spectrum of consciousness and of the chain of the three bodies of Vedanta. Also to most people, I think, there is a vast difference in the apparent spiritual quality and value of an OBE and cosmic consciousness (which, to Wilber, are both psychic, or low subtle, level experiences). More problematic, however, is the fact that Wilber's later and more informal accounts of nondual One Taste (1999a) seem clearly to contradict the view that it is fundamentally different from cosmic consciousness:

> You simply *are* everything that is arising moment to moment. You do not see the sky, you are the sky. You do not touch the earth, you are the earth. You do not hear the rain, you are the rain. You and the universe are what the mystics call 'One Taste' ... subject and object become One Taste and infinity happily surrenders its secrets ... *One Taste or 'cosmic consciousness'* − the sense of oneness with the Ground of all creation − is the deepest core of the nearly universal consensus of the world's great wisdom traditions ... It is very simple, very obvious, very clear − concrete, palpable, unmistakable (Wilber, 1999a, p. 56–57, italics added).

In my view (and Wilber seems here to imply the same), there may be no fundamental conceptual or experiential difference between cosmic consciousness and nondual One Taste. It is true that the *focus* of cosmic consciousness may be with the natural world, whereas One Taste also includes mental and 'spiritual' forms (i.e., the larger Kosmos, not just the physical Cosmos). Yet, for me, both experiences imply a nondual union of subject and object. The same can also be said for the deity mysticism of the unitive spiritual marriage, so that there may, in fact, be no essential *psychological* distinction between any of these experiences. Cosmic consciousness, spiritual marriage and One Taste may thus differ psychologically only in the particular *object* or *focus* of their union. Of course this leaves open the question of whether there is an important *religious, theological* or *moral* distinction between the experiences, but that is another, larger matter.

This aside, Wilber's distinction between psychic, (high) subtle, causal and nondual consciousness provides a useful means of *classifying* transpersonal experiences (although, of course, it is not entirely original). It is comprehensive in its coverage and clearly articulates the different qualities associated with various experiences. However, the question of whether Wilber is right to propose a *developmental or evolutionary sequence* through these 'levels' of experience is more problematic since, for example, it implies that soul mysticism (e.g., formless consciousness) is a 'higher' form of experience than God mysticism (e.g., spiritual marriage). For a fuller discussion of this important question here see Chapter 11 and also Ferrer's (2002) intelligent discussion of the problem of ranking spiritual traditions.

What, then, does Wilber have to say about the transpersonal *Self*? In this, I shall attempt to follow his most recent psychological formulations (Wilber, 2000a). Wilber (*ibid.*, p. 125) argues that the three 'great realms — gross, subtle, and causal — are home to three different lines of self' (see Table 11). These are *ego, soul,* and *spirit* (or witness).

The *ego* (or frontal self) includes all those self-structures or self-stages that serve to orient us to the gross (physical) world. The *soul* (or deeper psychic) is the self-system that operates at the level of subtle reality (pure thought). Finally the *Witness* (Spirit or Self) is adapted to the causal realm (root attention). According to Wilber, these lines or streams of the self are more or less independent. They are always simultaneously present, although to varying degrees, and each *develops* alongside the others.

The Self (Spirit or Witness) is also charged with the role of attempting to integrate the various self-streams, along with other aspects of our experience (such as our cognitive development, world view, moral values, or sexual identity). In general terms, psychological development can be understood as a process whereby the 'center of gravity of consciousness increasingly shifts from ego to soul to Self' (*ibid.*, p. 127). Although arguing for the importance of integrating the different self-streams, Wilber also emphasizes that integration should not be seen as an entirely interior and individual endeavour. In contrast, the truly integrated life must involve a *simultaneous* development in the collective and exterior domains (or 'quadrants'). In this way we should engage in a truly 'integral therapy' or 'integral practice' that includes, for example, physical training, relationship work, community service and political action (see, for example, Wilber, 1999a, 129-131; Wilber 2000a, 112-114).

As a *psychological* account of the transpersonal self, Wilber's theory is neat, internally consistent and in accord with much of the experiential and developmental data. However, Wilber does not intend his analysis to be merely psychological and, as a consequence, it merges almost seamlessly with a particular metaphysical perspective. Thus the soul and Witness are not understood simply as *psychological structures* that emerge during the lifetime of the individual, but rather they exist as immortal or timeless *metaphysical realities*.

As well as Vedanta, Wilber's metaphysics is based closely on that of the *Tibetan Book of the Dead* (Fremantle & Trungpa, 1992) and on the metaphysical perspective of Sri Aurobindo. According to this view, the soul (deeper psychic being) evolves from one life to the next, descending into the present body from the *bardo* realms in which it continues to exist between death and rebirth. Wilber argues that only such a view logically and convincingly explains the fact that young children can have genuinely *transpersonal* experiences, even before the frontal egoic (*personal*) identity has developed. Such experiences, he considers, represent those 'trailing clouds of glory' (after Wordsworth) of the continuing awareness and memory of the deeper psychic being (see, for example, Wilber, 1996b, chap. 18; 1997, pp. 179–184; 2000a, pp. 141–142). This is, of course, an intriguing and exciting possibility. Unfortunately, however, the *logical necessity* of such an interpretation requires an acceptance of Wilber's own theoretical assumptions (i.e., that the transpersonal cannot *precede* the personal). Grof's theory, for example, provides a powerful alternative interpretation of infants' transpersonal experiences.

As well as the arguing for the pre-existence of the soul, Wilber suggests that the experience of *timelessness* associated with cosmic consciousness, formless awareness and One Taste provides direct confirmation of the eternal existence of the Transcendent Witness or Self.

> The pure Witness, itself being timeless or prior to time, is equally present at all points of time. So of course this is the Self you had before your parents were born; it is the Self you had before the Big Bang, too. And it is the Self you will have after your body — and the entire universe — dissolves ... because it exists prior to time, period (Wilber, 1999a, p. 366).

However, Wilber seems to be confusing here two quite separate meanings of 'timeless'. I do not doubt that we can have experiences in which there is no associated sense of time and, *in that sense*, they are timeless, taking place 'outside of' or with no reference to time. But that kind of *momentary timelessness* is not the same thing as being *eternal* in the sense of lasting forever or *throughout all time*. In fact, the two conceptions totally contradict each other since the latter implies experience *in time*. Better evidence that the Witness is eternal (existing through time) would be a *memory* of existing in a previous life, although again that is problematic for a variety of logical, psychological and evidential reasons.

Without doubt, Wilber's sophisticated theory represents a major achievement to which all transpersonal psychologists are indebted. For me, however, Wilber tends to be inconsistent and prejudicial in his analysis of mystical experience. As well as being highly metaphysical in its outlook and assumptions, Wilber's theory also relies perhaps too heavily upon the *particular* religious and metaphysical perspectives of Vedanta and Buddhism. For this reason it may not be as universally valid, or applicable, as Wilber would have us believe.[7]

The Spiral-Dynamic Model of Michael Washburn

Michael Washburn (e.g., 1994, 1995) has developed a transpersonal psychology based on psychoanalytic, ego-developmental and Jungian perspectives. As we saw in Chapter 1, his theory focuses on the changing developmental relationship between two fundamental systems: (a) the *Dynamic Ground* or *nonegoic core* and (b) the *ego*. According to Washburn the psyche originally exists as a dynamic, nonegoic core or ground of potentials (both *preegoic* and *transegoic*). With the emergence of the ego, the non-egoic core becomes repressed, leading to a fundamental separation between ego and Dynamic Ground. Transpersonal development involves the reconnection and integration of the

---

7   Rowan (2004) has taken me to task for failing to appreciate that Wilber's sources include many examples that are not VBA (Rowan's acronym for my 'narrow selection' of Vedanta, Buddhism and Aurobindo when characterizing Wilber's influences). In my opinion, however, this does not alter the fact that the scheme to which they are being incorporated is fundamentally based on VBA structures.

Preegoic Phase

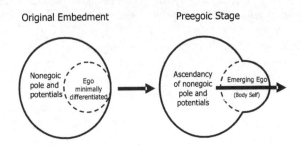

Egoic Phase

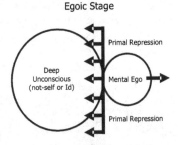

Transegoic Phase

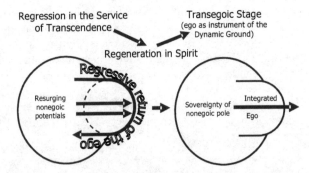

Figure 7. Washburn's model of psychological development
(After Washburn, 1994, 1995)

ego with the nonegoic core, leading to a psycho-spiritual regeneration and redemption (Figure 7).

For Washburn (as for Jung), transpersonal development generally begins around midlife when the mature ego has completed its own developmental tasks. At this time, in order to fulfil the larger agenda of integrating the whole psyche, the ego withdraws from the world, turns inward and begins to open up to the dynamic ground. The pull to withdraw from the world often leads to an experience of alienation and aridity — i.e., to the *Dark Night of the Senses* described by St John of the Cross (1991). Following this, the ego approaches the threshold of the unconscious nonegoic core. It does this with some ambivalence since the nonegoic core is experienced as primitive, dark and dangerous, but also as exciting and fascinating. If the ego is ready to undergo its 'night sea journey' into the realm of the unconscious it begins to make contact with the deeper, numinous, *transegoic* potentials of the dynamic ground. This may result in ecstasies, illuminations, visions and experiences of subtle energies. However, according to Washburn, such experiences are, at this stage, of an immature variety and this false dawn soon gives way the *Dark Night of the Spirit* described by St John of the Cross (1991). Thus the ego is thrust into an abyss of darker, frightening, negative experiences such as guilt, worthlessness, dread, cynicism, paranoia, intimations of evil, strangeness, visions of wrathful deities and devouring demons.

> The ego struggles against these forces with all its strength but finally succumbs and is taken captive by them. It is swallowed up in the 'belly of the beast'(Washburn, 1994, p. 238).

For Washburn (cf. Grof), this voyage into the depths of the unconscious is not a psychotic breakdown, but represents a *regression in the service of transcendence*. Eventually, as the ego learns to endure these experiences and to recognize them as expressions of the self's own nonegoic core, it ceases to struggle against them. This change of attitude results in the ego becoming increasingly open to the *positive, transegoic,* potentialities of the nonegoic core. These include a sense of enchantment, spiritual intoxication, rejoicing, religious ecstasy, love, rebirth, integration, guiding or angelic visions, and a sense of greater connection with other people, the body, and nature. As these positive experiences gradually come to predominate over negative experiences, the ego moves from the stage of *regression in the service of transcendence* to that of *regeneration in spirit*. Washburn argues that the ultimate goal and purpose of such transpersonal regeneration is 'postdualistic integration' (*ibid.*, p. 27) or the integrative life. This represents the ego's stabilization on the plane of transpersonal experience and the integration of such experience in the personality, in relationships, and in engagement with the world. Thus 'in achieving integration, we finally become complete human beings' (*ibid.*, p. 293). The integrated life, Washburn suggests, is characterized by transparency and I-Thou intimacy, the feeling of blessedness, 'hallowed resplendence' (the equivalent of One Taste or cosmic consciousness), mature contemplation (enstatic absorption, with or without form), 'tertiary cognition' (creative thinking), and the physical embodiment of spiritual qualities.

As we have seen, there are just two main components to the self in Washburn's theory — the nonegoic core and the ego. Transegoic experience does not represent a *third* component, but is rather the consequence of the change in the ego's *attitude* towards the nonegoic core, which has always contained both preegoic and transegoic potentials. However, Washburn does also talk about a 'higher self' or 'transpersonal self' at the centre of the nonegoic core. Thus in the process of regeneration in spirit:

> The ego now sees that behind the surface of ego identity and at the center of the repressed depths of the soul there lies a redeemable core, a higher self — a self of spontaneity and generosity, outgoingness and outreachingness — that needs to be elicited into activity and induced to grow (*ibid.*, p. 258).

It is unclear from Washburn's account exactly how he conceives the higher self — whether as an experience, as a metaphor, symbol or archetypal personification of human perfection, as a psychological structure, as a potentiality, or as an actual metaphysical entity. Wilber (e.g., 1997, chap 6) has criticized Washburn's theory more generally for what he sees as its reductionistic metaphysical assumptions and its failure to distinguish adequately between the preegoic and transegoic potentialities of the nonegoic core. According to Wilber, Washburn's model simply confuses the great 'domains' of body and spirit. Washburn responds to this criticism by arguing that Wilber's own theory is unparsimonious and is based on the fallacy of concluding that what is a real difference between preegoic and transegoic *stages of development* (or *experiences*) necessarily implies the existence of different prepersonal and transpersonal *structures* (Washburn, 1998).

Washburn's (1994) discussion of the phenomenology of transpersonal experiences is both rich and comprehensive, and he provides a convincing analytic-developmental explanation of many of these experiences. His suggestion that transpersonal development represents a *spiralling* process in which the ego must return to the depths of the unconscious before it becomes regenerated in spirit contrasts starkly with the essentially *linear* ascent from prepersonal, to personal, to transpersonal proposed by Wilber. Washburn's theory is consistent with much of the clinical data and undoubtedly represents many people's experience of transpersonal development especially, perhaps, those who do not follow a structured path of meditation (for whom Wilber's theory may have greater appeal). Washburn (e.g., 1994, pp. xiii-xiv) also points to important cultural differences, and he suggests that the spiral paradigm (shared by Jung and Grof) is closer to Western experience of spiritual development, whereas the ladder paradigm is more consistent with Eastern spirituality (especially Buddhism and Vedanta). We are not yet in a position, he argues, where a truly cross-cultural transpersonal perspective has been achieved.

The Feminist Theory of Peggy Wright

Peggy Wright (1998a) criticizes much of the theorizing in transpersonal psychology, especially that of Wilber, for being androcentric and patriarchal in its assumptions and therefore for ignoring or devaluing women's experience of spirituality (cf. Heron, 1998). She argues that these theories also pay insufficient attention to the spiritual experiences of indigenous peoples, which are often simply dismissed as 'primitive'.

Wright's own transpersonal approach is based on her experience with indigenous ways of knowing (including shamanic journeying) and on feminist theories of the self, especially the work of Nancy Chodorow (1978) Jean Baker Miller (1991) and Carol Gilligan (1993). These emphasize the concept of a 'connected self' or self-in-relationship. As well as recognizing our relationship and interconnectedness with other people, Wright also argues for the importance of establishing healthy relationships with our body and emotions, and with the natural world. To encourage this, we should pay much more attention to experiences of Goddess-focussed and indigenous spirituality (cf. Christ, 2004; Starhawk, 1999). This immanent, descending and feminine approach to the transpersonal is contrasted with what she sees as the dominant transcendent, ascending and masculine approach of Wilber.

According to Wright, the connected self is one that is open, empathic and responsive to others. In particular, to exist as a self-in-relationship requires us to have 'permeable' boundaries. This permeability allows self and other to be simultaneously experienced in a form of nondual awareness. Wright sees permeability as a central feature of women's experience, including their experience of the transpersonal. Unfortunately, she argues, this experience is misunderstood and misrepresented by Wilber, for whom permeability represents the primitive absence of clear boundaries between the self and the world. For Wilber, the claim that permeability is the essential feature of women's transpersonal experience is therefore an example of what he calls the *pre/trans fallacy* (Wilber, 1980), i.e., the failure to recognize the difference between prepersonal and transpersonal levels. Wright responds by arguing that Wilber is himself guilty of what she calls the *pre/perm* fallacy, i.e., the failure to distinguish between the prepersonal *lack* of boundaries with the mature *permeable* boundaries of the connected self. In an important reply to Wright's critique, Wilber (1998) argues that his own view is that permeability may express itself at various levels, for example as prepersonal permeable (selfish), sociocentric permeable (care), worldcentric permeable (universal care) or spiritual permeable (universal union). In simply proposing the fact of permeability as the key to women's experience of the transpersonal, Wilber argues that Wright fails to acknowledge important developmental (hierarchical, structural) changes that occur in the permeable self. Wilber characterizes his own approach, therefore, as one which can readily incorporate women's (permeable) experience of the transpersonal without itself falling into what he sees as the feminist trap of totally denying any hierarchical-structural development.

Wright's own response to this (1998b) is to welcome Wilber's new recognition of permeability and to acknowledge her own acceptance of prepersonal, personal and transpersonal stages of the permeable self. Thus although it may seem to Wilber that

Wright is advocating the ideas of immanence, permeability and interconnectedness as *alternatives* to those of transcendence and individual achievement, Wright also recognizes the importance of a healthy integration of these different perspectives. This, she argues, will require new models of transpersonal development that are capable of incorporating both the feminine and masculine value-spheres, and also the spiritual experiences of indigenous peoples. Clearly, however, she does not see Wilber's current formulations as capable of providing this more integral perspective.

The Participatory Vision of Jorge Ferrer

Ferrer's (e.g., 2000, 2002, 2005) participatory and pluralistic approach understands transpersonal development (spiritual liberation) as essentially involving a radical movement away from self-centredness, and towards the realization of special states of discernment.

> I propose that most traditions do lead to the same ocean, but not the one portrayed on the perennialist canvas. The ocean shared by most traditions does not correspond to a single spiritual referent or to 'things as they really are,' but, perhaps more humbly, to *the overcoming of self-centredness*, and thus a liberation from correspondingly limiting perspectives and understandings ... most genuine spiritual paths involve a gradual transformation from narrow self-centredness towards a fuller participation in the Mystery of existence (Ferrer, 2002, p. 144–145, italics in original).

This 'Ocean of Emancipation' (involving the liberation from self-centredness) is, for Ferrer, the *only* essential common factor that may be identified across spiritual traditions. In rejecting all other absolutist conceptions of the goal of spiritual development (including the perennialist ones), Ferrer instead argues that different spiritual paths cocreatively enact different transpersonal realities — that the 'transconceptual disclosures of reality' or special states of discernment that are achieved may be specific to particular traditions and methods.

> *the various traditions lead to the enactment of different spiritual ultimates and/or transconceptual disclosures of reality*. Although these spiritual ultimates may apparently share some qualities ... they constitute independent religious aims whose conflation may prove to be a serious mistake ... the view I am

advancing here is that *no pregiven reality exists, and that differ-ent spiritual ultimates can be enacted through intentional or spon-taneous creative participation in an indeterminate spiritual power or Mystery (ibid.,* pp. 147, 151, italics in original).

Moreover, because there is no absolute spiritual ultimate, it is not possible to evaluate objectively the validity of spiritual enactments (other than in terms of their capacity to foster selfless awareness), nor to place spiritual traditions, ontologies or expe-riences into any kind of hierarchy. Rather we must recognize the existence of multiple spiritual truths, many of which may appar-ently contradict each other — as shown, for example, in the debates between the Advaita and theistic schools of Sankara and Ramanuja (Ferrer, 2005, p. 117).

The implications of Ferrer's approach for theories of the transpersonal self are that there may be expected to be many different expressions of the transpersonal self (or many transper-sonal selves) which may be specific to particular paths, tradi-tions, or spontaneous enactments of cocreative participation in the Mystery of being. All they may finally have in common is a quality of selfless awareness. In this respect, Ferrer's perspective can readily accommodate many, if not all, of the different types of experience of the transpersonal self identified in the previous chapter which may be understood as different spiritual enactments.

Ferrer is critical, however, of transpersonal conceptions that may serve to sustain or promote self-centredness and spiritual narcissism. This is essentially the basis for his objections to experientialist and individualistic agendas within transpersonal psychology which, he argues, foster the Cartesian dualisms between self and world, mind and body, or subject and object. From this perspective, therefore, we would expect Ferrer to be generally critical of transpersonal experiences that imply and may reinforce a *subtle Cartesian* split (e.g., out-of-body experi-ences, states of possession, introvertive absorption) at least to the extent that these experiences might encourage a self-centred, spiritually materialistic or narcissistic concern with our own individual mind, soul or spiritual development. Ferrer does con-cede, however, (after Wade, 1996; Washburn, 1995; Wilber, 1996a) that such Cartesian experiences may be valuable in the early stages of transpersonal development:

Cartesian consciousness may be the necessary starting point of spiritual inquiry (in the modern West, I would qualify). From this viewpoint, the descriptive value of the experiential vision — geared to a Cartesian model of cognition — may be limited to the first stages of the spiritual path, in which the spiritual seeker undergoes temporary openings which are typically interpreted in Cartesian terms as transient experiences, being more prone to fall into spiritual narcissism and integrative arrestment (sic) (Ferrer, 2002, pp. 186–187).

For Ferrer, deeper realization of the transpersonal self must be understood and experienced as a fully embodied, integrated, multidimensional *enactment* that emerges in our cocreative transformational participation with our physical bodies, vital energies, emotions, relationships, social and political involvements, cosmos and the divine.

> [T]ranspersonal events engage human beings in a participatory, connected, and often passionate knowing that can involve not only the opening of the mind, but also of the body, the heart, and the soul ... participatory knowing refers to a multidimensional access to reality that includes not only the intellectual knowing of the mind, but also the emotional and empathic knowing of the heart, the sensual and somatic knowing of the body, the visionary and intuitive knowing of the soul, as well as any other way of knowing available to human beings (Ferrer, 2002, p. 121, italics in original).

Summary and Conclusions

We have covered some difficult and complicated territory. Let me try to summarize the various conceptions of the transpersonal self that these theories suggest or imply. According to these different conceptions, aspects of the transpersonal self, or transpersonal identity, may be understood as:

1. The organismic 'inner core' or Real Self.

2. Self-identification with highest values.

3. The whole psyche — conscious and unconscious.

4. The higher unconscious.

5. An archetype (inspiring, powerful, integrating, spiritual).

6. The extension or 'raising' of consciousness.

7. The integration of conscious and unconscious.

8. A guiding force or organizing principle.

9. An inner unifying centre.

10. A permanent centre of Being.

11. The reincarnating psychic being.

12. A subtle self-stream.

13. The individualized divine soul (Atman).

14. The Universal Self (Atman-Brahman).

15. The Transcendent Witness (possibly eternal).

16. No Self or One Taste (anatta).

17. The spiritual transformation of the personality.

18. The connected / permeable self.

19. The worldcentric-permeable or spiritual-permeable self.

20. The integrated, embodied spiritual life.

In listing these various concepts, several of which show some overlap in meaning, I am seeking to do justice to their richness and diversity, and to recognize the importance of each for any attempt to understand fully the nature of transpersonal experience. I am not suggesting at all that we must choose between them, although I note that several imply metaphysical assumptions or conclusions. That may indeed be unavoidable if we are fully to make sense of people's experience of the transpersonal and I do not entirely rule out such ideas. As long as they are made explicit, and as long as they do not violate reason, or the facts, or morality, then fair enough. Neither am I arguing, *a priori*, in favour of any particular conception, although my own clear preference is with Aurobindo, Washburn and Ferrer's notions of the integrated, embodied, spiritual life (No. 20). Having argued the need for transpersonal psychologists to be explicit about their metaphysical assumptions I should perhaps add that my own metaphysical views are not fully formed and I remain open to various hypotheses (see my discussion on metaphysics in the next chapter).

I have tried to give a fair and accurate account of all nine theories, while pointing out what others, and I, see as some of their failings and limitations. As with the various conceptions of the transpersonal self, I do not think that it is possible at this stage in the development of transpersonal psychology to select any one theory as being the most adequate. On the contrary, I think that we can all learn much from each of these interesting and very different perspectives.

In relation specifically to the concept of the transpersonal Self, I can think of no better words to conclude this chapter than those of Frances Vaughan.

> The concept of a transpersonal Self, like any theoretical construct, is … considered an expedient or transitional teaching rather than a final teaching … To pursue this dimension of identity is to embark on the spiritual path. But the person who sets out on the spiritual path never arrives at the destination, because who one thinks one is turns out to be only an illusion of a separate self that ultimately dissolves into the deity, or larger whole.
>
> Once the illusory nature of all self-concept is perceived in the context of absolute subjectivity, the transpersonal Self can be perceived as an image of qualities one chooses to value, rather than a separate identity to be constructed. It may be considered as existing *a priori* as an embodiment of abstract ideals such as truth, goodness, and beauty … or it may be considered to have no existence apart from concrete expressions and manifestations … Either way, identification with and expression of a transpersonal Self is an alternative to choose, an identity to seek, a value to create, and a reality to be experienced as long as one feels that one exists as a subject, separate from the world of objects (Vaughan, 1986, p. 54).

Chapter 10

On Transcendence in Transpersonal Psychology

The 'trans' in transpersonal is often taken to mean 'transcendence'. Yet the more I think about this, the more I realize that the concept of transcendence is a rather difficult and slippery one and one that can imply very different things to different people. My unease in relation to transpersonal psychology is the sense I have that many people use this notion of transcendence to smuggle into this field all sorts of questionable but generally unquestioned metaphysical and ontological assumptions. I notice such smuggling whenever I have a conversation with someone, or read a book, where certain words are introduced without caution, comment or explanation. Words such as 'Divine', 'God', 'Goddess', 'spirit', 'soul', 'reincarnation', 'karma', 'auras', 'energies', 'chakras', 'third eye', 'akashic records', 'angels', or 'demons'. I often find myself very uncomfortable in these situations. My unease is mainly that in being drawn into this dialogue I am being asked to accept and collude with metaphysical assumptions that I simply do not share, or that I know are not shared by large numbers of other people. If these words were being used phenomenologically — as short hand descriptions of people's

This chapter is a revised and updated version of Daniels (2001b)

actual experience, then that would be quite another matter. My sense, however, is that they are very rarely used in this way. Rather they seem to be used as a way of implying and asserting a particular metaphysical reality that is often beyond question.

The point I am making has very real implications for transpersonal psychology. This relatively new area of interest has had (and is still having) a very hard time convincing sceptics both within and outside the psychological profession that it represents a valid area of scientific concern. One of the main reasons for this, I think, is that it is seen by these people as implying and based on a metaphysics that is antiquated, false, dubious or incapable of demonstration. For these reasons, therefore, transpersonal psychology cannot be considered to be a science. It is at best a comforting and therapeutic system of quasi-religious belief and practice. At worst, it is mumbo-jumbo, mythmongering, humbug and New-Age fluff.

The answer to these concerns, I believe, is for transpersonal psychology to be very cautious and self-critical in its concepts, definitions and theories. In particular, it is vital that we question very carefully the metaphysical beliefs behind our statements and either take pains to eliminate what may often be unnecessary assumptions, or else be quite clear and explicit about the metaphysical bases of our research, theory and practice. In other words, we need to adopt the phenomenological rule of *époche* and learn to bracket or put to one side, wherever possible, our preconceptions and beliefs.

An interesting example of this is shown in the debate that took place in the *Journal of Transpersonal Psychology* several years ago, on the definition of transpersonal psychology. From a survey, review and summary of 40 definitions published from 1968–1991, Lajoie & Shapiro (1992, p. 91) proposed that transpersonal psychology is:

> concerned with the study of humanity's highest potential,
> and with the recognition, understanding, and realization of
> unitive, spiritual, and transcendent states of consciousness.

However, as we saw in Chapter 2, Walsh & Vaughan (1993a) have argued that there are various problems with this definition. I will leave aside for the moment the point that there is more to the transpersonal than achieving states of consciousness. More immediately relevant is that Lajoie & Shapiro include in their definition several terms that, even if they do not clearly or explicitly say so, at least imply a particular set of metaphysical beliefs. Thus the assumption seems to be that there is a 'spiritual' reality that 'transcends' our ordinary consciousness and that humanity's 'highest potential' is to achieve an experience of 'unity' with this transcendental reality.

We can demonstrate that this implies a system of religious or metaphysical belief simply by pointing out that other belief systems do not agree with these assumptions. For example a materialist would have difficulty accepting the reality of the 'spiritual', whereas certain theologians and religious fundamentalists, while accepting the reality of the spiritual, would reject the implied notion of 'union' with the Divine. What Lajoie & Shapiro are presenting here, under the guise of an objective, scientific definition, is a particular version of mystical ontology.

To circumvent these difficulties, Walsh & Vaughan (1993a) present their own definition of transpersonal experiences which is deliberately constructed in such a way as to make as few disputable metaphysical assumptions as possible. As quoted earlier, their definition is:

> *Transpersonal experiences* may be defined as experiences in which the sense of identity or self extends beyond (trans.) the individual or personal to encompass wider aspects of humankind, life, psyche or cosmos (*ibid.*, p. 103).

The only ontological realities implied by this definition are human beings, life, psyche and cosmos. Furthermore the only other assumption is that it is possible to have experiences in which the sense of self can extend beyond the individual or personal realm — again a non-controversial assumption that is justified and very easily demonstrated from empirical evidence and, often, personal experience.

In my view, Walsh & Vaughan's definition provides an excellent starting point for our investigations into the transpersonal.[1] The concepts of 'psyche' and 'cosmos' are sufficiently clear and

---

1   My own, rather simpler, version of this definition, presented in Chapter 1, is that the transpersonal 'refers to experiences, processes and events in which our normal limiting sense of self is transcended and in which there is a feeling of connection to a larger, more meaningful reality'. In using the term 'transcended' in this definition, I mean simply 'going beyond' ordinary personal selfhood. This should not be taken to imply a belief in an ontological transcendental or metaphysical realm. I use 'transcend,'

uncontroversial, yet they are also broad enough to encompass the widest possible range of human experiences, from those of simple rapture and flow, to love and merging with another person or group, to full-blown mystical unitive experience and cosmic consciousness.

However, while one of the virtues of Walsh & Vaughan's definition is that it is all-encompassing, the question still begs to be asked: how does this precisely relate to the concept of transcendence? Does the transpersonal imply a belief in transcendence or the transcendental and, if so, how are transcendence and transcendental best understood?

Abraham Maslow (1973) lists 35 meanings of 'transcendence'. These include loss of self-consciousness, mystical fusion, letting be, letting things happen, unselfish love, getting off the merry-go-round, enjoying the cosmos, being self-determined, surpassing one's limitations, being independent of culture, being fully accepting of the self, doing one's duty, accepting death, having intrinsic conscience, being absorbed in what one is doing, integrating dichotomies, and being metamotivated. None of these meanings is in any way controversial, although we need to note that Maslow understands the notion of 'mystical fusion' phenomenologically, as a psychological experience. This does not, therefore, necessarily imply or require the existence of a metaphysically transcendent reality to which we actually become fused. Maslow is himself very clear to distinguish between this phenomenological approach and the metaphysical one. Thus in discussing another meaning of transcendence he notes:

> Transcendence also means to become divine or godlike, to go beyond the merely human. But one must be careful here not to make anything extrahuman or supernatural out of this kind of statement. I am thinking of using the word 'metahuman' or 'B-human' in order to stress that this becoming very high or divine or godlike is part of human nature even though it is not often seen in fact (sic). It is still a potentiality of human nature (Maslow, 1973, pp. 286–287)

Maslow is here adopting a view that is very reminiscent of Carl Jung's approach to the question of metaphysical realities.

---

therefore, simply to paraphrase Walsh & Vaughan's (1993a) own 'extends beyond (trans.)'

Thus, for Jung, the spiritual realm is very real, and includes God, the Goddess and other divine archetypes. However, for Jung, these archetypes exist as undeniable *psychological* or experiential realities — they are a basic constituent of the *human* condition. The implication of Jung's analysis is that these spiritual archetypes do not, and indeed *cannot*, exist in a fundamentally transcendental sense — if we mean by this that they have a separate reality beyond the realm of human experience. In other words, the 'transcendental' is only *experienced* as being transcendent. It is in fact an essential, perhaps the most intimate, part of our collective human nature, a view that is also echoed in Christian humanism (e.g., Freeman, 2001).

The question that needs to be addressed here, I think, is whether the spiritual or divine realm is an actual Other. Now 'Otherness' can be understood in two main ways. Firstly, otherness implies separateness and ontological independence in the sense that the Other could exist without us. From this point of view the flowers in the field, the mountains and stars are genuinely Other. They would exist even if humankind had never evolved, and will continue to exist long after our species has become extinct. From the perspective of the individual human being, another person is also fundamentally Other in having a separate and independent existence. It is important to note, however, that the 'Otherness' of persons is also characterized by a recognition of their subjectivity. This is the second meaning of Otherness. Another person is therefore another *Being*, not merely a separate *object*. He or she is therefore someone with whom we can genuinely enter into what Martin Buber (e.g., 1970) calls an I-Thou relationship, based on an acceptance and respect of the Other's subjectivity and essential Otherness. But what of God? What of the Goddess?

Maslow and Jung both seem to be arguing that the Divine is an aspect of our common or collective *human* experience. As Maslow puts it, we must not make of the divine 'anything extrahuman or supernatural'. Or as Jung argues:

> It should not be overlooked that I deal with those psychic phenomena which prove empirically to be the bases of metaphysical concepts, and that when I say 'God,' I can refer to nothing other than demonstrable psychic patterns which are indeed shockingly real (Jung, cited in Wehr, 1988, p. 472).

> Today, probably the only way to an understanding of reli-
> gious matters is the psychological approach, and this is why I
> endeavour to melt down historically solidified ways of
> thinking again and recast them in the light of immediate
> experience (Jung, cited in Wehr, 1988, p. 299).

> It would be a regrettable mistake if anybody should under-
> stand my observations to be a kind of proof of the existence
> of God. They prove only the existence of an archetypal image
> of the deity, which to my mind is the most we can assert psy-
> chologically about God (Jung, 1958b, p. 73).

The paradox, some would say contradiction, in Jung's position
is that he often writes (especially in *Answer to Job*, Jung, 1969)
seemingly from the viewpoint of a theologian rather than a psychologist. In this way he discusses God as if He was an actual
subjective Other with whom one could have a real conversation
and a genuine I-Thou relationship. For Maslow, the problem is
less acute because he advocates a form of mystical atheism that
does not fully acknowledge the kind of personalized religious
experience reported by Jung.

This highlights, I believe, an interesting problem for Jung and
for transpersonal psychology in general. Many people, although
I am not one of them, claim that their understanding of the
transpersonal derives from their experience of a very personal
relationship with God. I note here that it usually is God rather
than the Goddess — a fact that may be of more than passing significance and to which I shall briefly return later. Furthermore,
and essentially, in these people's experience God is apprehended as a genuine Other — as an actual Transcendental Subject or Thou. How do we make sense of this metaphysically and
psychologically? It seems to me that there are only two possibilities. Either God actually exists as a Thou — as an independent
quasi-personal Being, or else these people are experiencing a
kind of illusion, albeit one that may be, for many, a source of joy
and comfort. According to the second interpretation, God only
appears to be Other, perhaps because of a projected religious
phantasy, or because of our failure to move beyond what Wilber
would call subtle levels of consciousness.

If a projected phantasy, then, of course, God does not really
exist at all as an actual Being — as a Thou — he is simply an
image conjured up from the personal or collective unconscious,

an image that in practice is likely to be strongly influenced by cultural myths and beliefs. We therefore never really had a genuine I-Thou relationship with God — the apparently personal relationship was rather one of I-It — based upon our projected collective fantasies of what God must be like.

This, I think, is also the contradiction in Jung's whole approach to the religious questions. He writes as if he is in an I-Thou relationship with God, but essentially he considers God to be an archetypal *It,* existing within or perhaps containing the entire collective unconscious (cf. Buber's, 1988, important critique of Jung's 'psychic immanence'). For Jung, therefore, God is the archetypal product of humankind's millions of years of psychological evolution and, as such, is fundamentally dependent upon humankind for His very existence. Humankind has created God, not the other way round.[2] For Jung, God may be real, but He is a real *thing,* an archetypal 'psychic pattern', not a real person. Furthermore, because God exists as a pattern within the human psyche, He is not even a truly separate *object* (in the way that flowers, mountains or stars are). The implication therefore seems to be that when humankind becomes extinct, so shall God.

According to this way of thinking it is possible to have a 'conversation' with God in the same way that we can query our computer's vast database. The Voice of God therefore speaks to us simply as a manifestation and constellation of the collective experience and wisdom of human beings throughout the ages, not as the utterances of an actual transcendent Other. This, indeed, is very much the way that I read and understand the alleged *Conversations with God* reported by Neale Donald Walsch (e.g., 1997) in his series of bestselling books.

Wilber takes a rather different position, but one that has, I think, rather similar implications. According to Wilber, what we experience as 'God' is simply a limited manifestation of the larger reality of Spirit as seen through the particular lens of subtle or archetypal awareness. If we develop to the supposed 'higher' realms of causal and ultimate consciousness we will firstly realize our essential Identity with God and finally transcend entirely all such archetypal forms in our experience of boundless awareness and One Taste. In this way, our experience

---

2   Of course, this begs the important question of why humankind should have created an archetype of God in the first place.

of God is seen as a kind of stepping stone to the nondual absolute. From this point of view, Spirit was just masquerading as God. Thus Spirit appears, in subtle awareness, as a transcendent Thou, but really Spirit is our own face all along. In nondual awareness, therefore, we transcend entirely the distinction between Self and Other that is implied in the I-Thou relationship.

One of the major difficulties with both Jung's and Wilber's interpretations is that they do not accord with most religious people's own interpretations of their relationship with God. In the first place, these people would be offended by and would strongly deny the suggestion that their religious experience is based on any form of projection, whether personal or archetypal-collective. As Lancaster (2002) puts it: 'Ultimately, the victim of Jung's approach to religion is *faith*, and Buber castigates the great betrayal which is thereby perpetrated' (italics in original). This is the danger of psychologism, which Jung himself recognized and that he attempted to deny was a feature of his own position. Thus he writes:

> I have been asked so often whether I believe in the existence of God or not that I am somewhat concerned lest I be taken for an adherent of 'psychologism' ... What most people overlook or seem unable to understand is the fact that I regard the psyche as *real* ... God is an obvious psychic and non-physical fact, i.e., a fact that can be established psychically but not physically (Jung, 1969, p. 463–464, emphasis in original).

But this is a very weak defence. What Jung seems to fail to recognize is that he *is* advocating a form of psychologism, that he is doing it in this statement, and that this is the fundamental problem that religious people have with his work. Thus, for Jung, God is a psychic fact, not a transcendent Thou (Buber, 1988).

Wilber does not fall into the trap of psychologism, because he bases his theories on an understanding of the metaphysical reality of Spirit, not of psyche. However, a problem with Wilber's position is that he clearly advocates a *particular* metaphysical and religious doctrine, and one that has the effect of devaluing (relatively speaking) theistic religious experience, even if it does not deliberately seek to do so (cf. Ferrer, 2002). I find it very hard not to draw the conclusion from Wilber's work that Buddhism and certain forms of Hinduism, particularly the *Dzogchen*, *Zen* and *Advaita Vedanta* traditions, tend to represent structurally *higher* forms of religion than the monotheistic faith traditions of Christianity, Judaism and Islam.

In my view Wilber should be more explicit or at least more cautious about the metaphysical assumptions behind his work, as indeed should all people working in this area. Wilber does address this question in various places and his answer has consistently been that his theories are based upon a *universal* metaphysics — in other words that they simply represent the perennial philosophy,[3] which all intelligent people in all times and cultures have agreed upon.

In my opinion this will not do. For a start the idea of the perennial philosophy seems to me to offer the potential for gross exaggeration and over-simplification, and in practice can often represent a failure and refusal to examine fully important differences among the world's religions (cf. Ferrer's, 2002, powerful critique of perennialism and his own advocacy of a pluralistic ontology and soteriology). Secondly, while there may indeed be some kind of common denominator among many of the great religious traditions, such as the belief in a Divine reality, or the idea of the Great Chain of Being, these perennial features appear rather minimalist and anaemic when compared to the highly developed philosophies and soteriological practices of any of the World's major religions. Certainly these common denominators fail to capture the sense of richness, depth and authority found within real living traditions. More importantly, however, Wilber's metaphysics are *not* universal or perennial, even in the general and minimalist sense proposed by Huxley. Rather, Wilber's whole approach is avowedly and specifically Buddhist and Vedantist. Moreover, it represents a particular form of Buddhism and Vedanta (i.e., the nondual schools) — closely associated with the Vajrayana and Zen traditions, which Wilber has personally engaged with.

Let me make it clear that I have no personal axe to grind here. I do not follow any religion but am interested in, and respect, all traditions. Rather I am trying to say that Wilber is, I believe, smuggling in a particular form of Buddhist and Advaita Vedantist metaphysics, theory and practice under the glib and appealing cloak of the 'perennial philosophy'. Nor is it accept-

---

3   As we have seen, in Wilber's approach, the perennial philosophy is essentially that expressed in its *post-axial* version.

able, I would argue, for Wilber to use his idea of the perennial *psychology* to present disguised metaphysical beliefs. There may indeed be very strong parallels and complementary relations between different psychological approaches, as Wilber's brilliant analyses have shown (e.g., Wilber 2000a). But we need to be very cautious in drawing *metaphysical* conclusions from these *psychological* data. In this sense there is perhaps some redeeming virtue in Jung's clearly professed psychological approach, and his consistent refusal to get drawn into metaphysical speculation.

Let me return to the question of transcendence. Of the 35 meanings of transcendence listed by Maslow (1973) it is interesting that only *three* of these make any specific reference to the spiritual or transcendental realm and then, as we have seen, somewhat ambiguously or reluctantly. These three are:

- 'mystical experience. Mystic fusion' (No. 7).
- 'to be divine or godlike, to go beyond the merely human' (No. 23).
- 'Bucke's ... cosmic consciousness' (No. 31).

Furthermore, when Maslow condenses all the meanings of transcendence into an overall summary definition, he ends up with this:

> Transcendence refers to the very highest and most inclusive or holistic levels of human consciousness, behaving and relating, as ends rather than as means, to oneself, to significant others, to human beings in general, to other species, to nature and to the cosmos (Maslow, 1973, p. 292).

What is notable here is how *humanistic* this definition is and how, like Walsh & Vaughan's (1993a) rather similar definition, it makes no reference whatsoever to spiritual, religious or metaphysical dimensions. For Maslow, it seems, transcendence is essentially a very human phenomenon, clearly this-worldly rather than other-worldly.

In my opinion, this is a very significant observation, especially when we consider how, by way of contrast, certain of the dominant theoretical paradigms in transpersonal psychology tend to promote a quasi-religious perspective on the transpersonal (especially those of Assagioli and Wilber). Thus transcendence is largely seen within these paradigms as equivalent to the achieve-

ment of psychic, spiritual or mystical states and structures, a process that can be very much facilitated, it is claimed, through
various forms of psycho-spiritual practice such as meditation.
For example, Wilber's model essentially equates transpersonal
development with the movement from grounded personal
authenticity and individuation (the 'Centaur' stage) to the higher
levels of psychic, subtle, causal and nondual consciousness.
Moreover, in order to bring about such transpersonal development, Wilber advocates some form of explicit, structured spiritual practice.

> [A]uthentic spirituality does involve practice ... such as
> active ritual, contemplative prayer, shamanic voyage, inten-
> sive meditation, and so forth. All of those open one to a direct
> experience of Spirit, and not merely beliefs or ideas about
> Spirit ... A qualified teacher with whom you feel comfort-
> able, is a must. One might start by consulting the works of
> Father Thomas Keating, Rabbi Zalman Schachter-Shalomi,
> the Dalai Lama, Sri Ramana Maharshi, Bawa Muhaiyadeen,
> or any of the many widely acknowledged teachers in any of
> the great lineages (Wilber, 1999c, p. 568).

Again, I don't think that we can let this go unchallenged. For a
start, of course, Wilber is making metaphysical assumptions
about the reality of Spirit (note the big 'S') and is also essentially
equating the transpersonal life with the religious or quasi-
religious life. Although Wilber (e.g., 1999c) also argues for the
importance an integral approach to practice, which attempts to
work simultaneously on all the levels and quadrants of our
Being, he is still committed to the notion that the 'higher'
transpersonal levels involve explicit spiritual practice. Furthermore, as John Heron (1998) has powerfully argued, Wilber is
advocating a very patriarchal approach to spirituality, based on
what Heron considers to be projected authority onto spiritual
teachers (mostly men) rather than a faith in one's own inner
authority.

James Horne (1978) has suggested an interesting and, I
believe, important distinction between 'serious mysticism',
based on intentional practice, and 'casual mysticism' which represents a more relaxed, open attitude in which mystical experiences are acknowledged and welcomed when they come but are
not explicitly sought. Andrew Rawlinson (1997) also makes a

similar distinction between 'structured' and 'unstructured' traditions in his wonderful and extraordinary encyclopaedia, *The Book of Enlightened Masters*. Although Wilber is clearly an advocate of a serious, disciplined, structured soteriology, the point is that *both* serious or structured and casual or unstructured approaches are possible and perhaps both are equally valid.

In my youth I was very much a believer in serious mysticism, whereas in the last 15 years I have become much more casual, some might say lazy in my approach. Not only has my attitude changed, but I now also question the dominance of the mystical or, as I called it earlier, the *exotic* agenda within transpersonal psychology. As we have seen, one of the major unresolved debates in this area is that between Wilber and his feminist critics. From the feminist point of view (for example Heron, 1998; Wright, 1998a), Wilber's whole notion of transcendence is flawed by the patriarchal, androcentric, authoritarian, and hierarchical assumptions upon which it is based. According to Wright, transpersonal development does not necessarily represent an instrumental, agentic ascent to higher modes of mystical consciousness. From a feminine perspective, the transpersonal is more about achieving wholeness and integration, about learning to become open or more permeable to one's body, to others and the environment, and about love, communion, relationship and interconnectedness.

One thing that I particularly note here is the relative absence of any *metaphysics* of the spiritual realm in this approach. It seems to me that the feminine approach to the spiritual is very much of spiritual with a small 's'. It is about transcendence, but not about the Transcendental. Although the feminine approach sometimes promotes the image of the Goddess or Great Mother rather than of God, this is generally done, it seems to me, in a more or less casual, symbolic or *mythical* fashion (cf. Christ, 2004). Thus the Goddess is seen as an archetypal image that represents the principles of communion, oneness with nature, ecological harmony, nurturing and benevolence rather than being seen as an actual transcendental Other with whom one has a personal spiritual relationship. Actually I wonder sometimes whether it is mainly the *men* who relate to the Goddess as a transcendent Other — but that is a different and rather larger matter.

This feminine perspective seems much more compatible with the general humanistic agenda and also with many of the meanings of transcendence compiled by Maslow (1973). For example, Maslow includes among his list:

- 'To accept the natural world ... to let *it* be *itself*' (No. 9).
- 'Transcendence of the We-They polarity' (No. 10).
- 'Identification love' (No. 12).
- 'Transcendence of non-involved, neutral, non-caring, spectator-type objectivity' (No. 25).
- 'Fusion of facts and values' (No. 26).
- 'The recognition of (the) value, and wonder of individual differences' (No. 33).

The distinction made by Peggy Wright and others between the male and female value spheres echoes other differentiations that are often made in this area. These include the classical theological distinction between transcendence and immanence, Wilber's (e.g., 1996a) description of ascending (other-worldly) and descending (this worldly) spirituality and the related principles of Eros and Agape, and also the distinction made by Warwick Fox (e.g., 1993) between vertical and horizontal transcendence. Fox is especially relevant in the present context because he recognizes that *both* of these are forms of transcendence in the sense that both vertical and horizontal development involve an extending or expanding of our sense of self beyond its ordinary egoic boundary. Furthermore, Fox asks some very pertinent questions.

> Transpersonal ecologists ask transpersonal psychologists: Does a focus on consciousness per se put us in touch with genuinely 'higher' — more real or more evolved — states of being and forms of reality or is consciousness more like a hall of mirrors in which we can 'lose ourselves' in endless fascination but to no inherently 'higher' end? This question is highly relevant to the question of whether we attempt to transcend our duly limited (and often painfully defensive) egoic sense of self by 'vertical' means (e.g., by attempting to experience 'higher' states of being and forms of reality) or by 'horizontal' means (i.e., by attempting to experience ourselves as intimately bound up with the world around us; as leaves, as it were, on a single evolutionary Tree of Life) (Fox, 1993, p. 241).

Fox's conclusion, as also of most others who have looked at these questions, including Wilber and Ferrer, is that both approaches are important and both should be acknowledged and honoured. It is in this spirit that I earlier presented a taxonomy that seeks to acknowledge the value and significance of both 'mundane' and 'exotic' experiences and practices (Chapter 4).

For me, the transpersonal is precisely about the expansion and extension of our sense of self — about the transformation of the self beyond its relatively enclosed and impermeable egoic boundary. Such transformation constitutes transcendence in the broad, Maslowian sense. It may involve any of the various types of transformative experience and practice — both mundane and exotic, positive and negative — that I identified in Chapter 4. Importantly, as we have seen, this notion of transformation, or of transcendence in the broad sense, makes no assumptions whatsoever about the metaphysical existence of a spiritual or transcendental reality. As far as I am concerned there may be no such thing as Spirit with a big 'S,' of Spirit-as-transcendental-reality. I say this even if certain transpersonal experiences, on the face of it, do seem to suggest such a reality. But this does not therefore mean that I do not recognize or believe in the experiential reality of the human spirit or of the value of spiritual development (both with a small 's'), nor that I am therefore not really a transpersonalist.

If we are to succeed as transpersonal psychologists, we should, I believe, take an intelligent interest in and always be open to the possible metaphysical interpretations of our researches into religious experiences and states of consciousness. But it is equally important to make explicit and to question these metaphysical interpretations. This is particularly true when *particular* metaphysical assumptions come to dominate a field in the way that those of Ken Wilber have done.

Jung claimed that he was essentially a phenomenologist who, rather like William James, was principally concerned with describing and interpreting the facts of religious experience, quite apart from their metaphysical implications (although James himself clearly believed in a metaphysical transcendent reality). Unfortunately Jung's writings do not always confirm this impression. In contrast, Ken Wilber is not primarily a phenomenologist, but rather a theoretician and metaphysician.

Shadow, Self, Spirit

As I have tried to show, Wilber's theories and metaphysics, while claiming to be 'perennial', are essentially Buddhist, Advaita Vedantist and non-theistic. Given that this is the case, it begs the question: to what extent is Wilber in a position to recognize and discuss adequately the significance of theistic religious experience, which is easily dismissed within his scheme as 'merely' subtle? (Cf. Ferrer, 2002; Schlamm, 2001).

I am not suggesting at all that we should adopt a theistic metaphysics, but rather that, as transpersonal psychologists, we should aim to bracket as far as possible ALL metaphysical assumptions in what should essentially become a phenomenological examination of experiences of transformation, or of transcendence in the broad sense. This, it seems to me, is a reasonable and legitimate agenda for transpersonal psychology, at least in the short and medium term. Furthermore we can do this, I believe, even while ourselves following our own individual or collective spiritual paths, whether exotic or mundane, structured or unstructured. Indeed, being a good phenomenologist — being able to examine experience as it is, prior to its possible distortion and contamination by beliefs and interpretations — is one of the essential features of meditation practice as I understand it. Also it is perhaps important for anyone, but particularly those who would follow a religious or spiritual path, and especially if they are also transpersonal psychologists, to constantly acknowledge and to question the often unspoken assumptions upon which their practice is based. Otherwise we indeed risk becoming ideologues and mythmongers.

In suggesting that transpersonal psychology should aim to bracket metaphysical assumptions about the transcendental realm, I follow closely Friedman's (2002) *agnostic* position. Friedman argues a Kantian view that transpersonal psychology cannot engage in direct speculation about the Transcendent because the noumenal is outside the remit of science (i.e., it is beyond the phenomenal or observable). This does not mean, of course, that we must necessarily *deny* the reality of the Transcendent, but only that, as transpersonal psychologists, we are limited to exploring the ways in which the Transcendent is experienced phenomenally or, as Ferrer (2002) would put it, the ways in which we cocreatively participate in what is an indeterminate and inexhaustible Mystery of being (as opposed to a determined Given).

For Ferrer, however, our cocreative participation in the Mystery of being inevitably *creates its own ontology*. Because of the many forms in which this participation may be expressed, many different ontologies (and spiritual ultimates) may be cocreated. In this sense therefore, for Ferrer, there is a 'fundamental interrelationship, and even identity, between phenomenology and ontology' (*ibid.*, p. 177).

The implication of Ferrer's position for transpersonal psychology is that, to the extent that the discipline represents a *unified*, cocreative participation in the Mystery of being, then transpersonal psychology will inevitably create its own unique ontology (note that it is important to realize that this ontology must *emerge* in the process of cocreation, not be imported or bought off the shelf as a pre-existing truth). However, to the extent that transpersonal psychology is a fragmented discipline, involving many different forms of cocreative participation, then very different ontologies may be expected to emerge. In my opinion, this latter situation prevails, which explains the fundamental differences between the ontological positions adopted by, for example, Jung, Maslow, Grof, Assagioli, Washburn, Wilber, transpersonal ecologists and feminists.

In the light of these *de facto* differences in the ontological assumptions made by different transpersonal approaches, and the absence of any fully accepted unified paradigm within transpersonal psychology, we can do little more, as a discipline, than recognize (and value) these differences. In particular, it is vital that we remain pluralistic at this time and do not fall into the trap of committing the discipline as a whole to any *particular* ontology. This is another reason, I believe, why transpersonal psychologists must be careful to be explicit about, and for the discipline *as a whole* to bracket, any metaphysical or transcendentalist assumptions that may be made (which themselves represent only one of many possible ontologies).

Lancaster (2002, 2004) has argued that such a bracketing is not possible within transpersonal psychology because the very nature and efficacy of the discipline depends upon acceptance of the metaphysical realities of consciousness, Spirit, the divine, and the Transcendent. Thus transpersonal psychology cannot, he suggests, adopt Flournoy's (1903) 'famous *principle of the exclusion of the transcendent* – that psychologists should neither reject nor affirm the independent existence of realms postulated in religion' (Lancaster, 2002, p. 50, italics in original).

In my opinion, Lancaster confuses the meanings of (1) the *transpersonal* and (2) the metaphysical *transcendent* (cf. Friedman, 2002). As we have seen, much that is transpersonal (extending the sense of self beyond the limited horizons of the ordinary self) does not involve religious or transcendental experience in the metaphysical sense, nor even an emphasis on *consciousness* as such. Also many of the major theorists in transpersonal psychology do not find it necessary to utilize metaphysical concepts[4] even when talking about transcendence (e.g., Jung, Maslow, transpersonal ecologists and transpersonal feminists). Lancaster refers to such non-metaphysical conceptions of transcendence as 'mealy-mouthed' (*ibid.*, p. 43) but, in this dismissal, he is, I believe, effectively denying or devaluing the significance of a vast range of non-Transcendental, mundane experiences of the transpersonal.

I am, of course, not arguing that metaphysical concepts are meaningless or without value in our attempts to understand certain aspects of the transpersonal. Rather I am simply pointing out that the transpersonal does not *depend upon* a conception of the metaphysical Transcendent and that, as a science, transpersonal psychology cannot be *based upon* such metaphysical assumptions. Lancaster himself concedes this latter point, arguing that '[m]y major premise is not that transpersonal psychology should necessarily embrace a metaphysic of transcendence, but that where such a metaphysic is embraced ... those involved have not breached the boundaries of our discipline' (*ibid.*, p. 43). I agree with this, although I would add that the onus is on those within the discipline who do embrace such a transcendental metaphysic to be explicit about their metaphysical assumptions, not to impose these on others, and to recognize the validity of other, non-metaphysical transpersonal ontologies. In fact, my main objection to the incorporation of metaphysical assumptions in transpersonal psychology is less with the *general* (unspecified and indeterminate) notion of a Transcendent Reality (or 'Mystery') to which Lancaster refers, but rather with the smuggling in of *specific* (and often dubious) metaphysical con-

---

4   By 'metaphysical' I mean concepts that imply the existence of an ontological reality beyond the physical and psychological realms.

cepts such as the reincarnating individual soul, chakras, God, or Absolute Consciousness, unless this is done explicitly and also tentatively (i.e., as a *hypothesis*, not as a given). Finally, I would point out that it remains possible for transpersonal psychologists to investigate people's experiences and metaphysical interpretations of the Transcendent, without themselves 'buying into' any particular metaphysical belief system. Those transpersonal psychologists who can remain agnostic in this way are also, I believe, in a better position to undertake such investigations since they will be less likely to allow their own views to bias their research.

Chapter 11

Contexts and Modes of Mystical Experience

What is Mysticism?

The word 'mysticism' (*mystica*) was first used by the 5th or 6th century Neoplatonist monk known as Pseudo-Dionysius the Areopagite. The word has the same etymology as 'mystery' which itself derives from the mystery cults of ancient Greece and Rome (from the Gk. *mystes*, initiate, and *mystos*, keeping silence). Of course ideas and experiences that we now associate with mysticism predate Neoplatonism and may be identified in religious traditions and cultures throughout the world. In the West, the old word used to refer to these areas of experience and practice was 'contemplation,' a term that held sway for many years, such that the widespread use of 'mystical' and especially 'mysticism' is relatively modern (Butler, 1922).

What then is mysticism? In contemporary usage, the term is often used loosely to refer to a range of phenomena and beliefs including the paranormal, occultism, magic, spiritualism, and Eastern or new age philosophies, as well as to the sublime experiences of saints and spiritual geniuses. More generally the word may also be applied pejoratively to point towards any tendency to woolly, wishful and unsubstantiated thinking, or to idle metaphysical speculation. Most scholars, however, are more focussed in their definition. There is a general consensus that mysticism

---

This chapter is a revised and updated version of Daniels (2003)

involves states of *noesis* (i.e., of knowledge and insight). Mystical knowledge, however, is based on the *individual's direct experience* rather than upon adopting systems of belief, attitude or conduct that derive from established teaching, theory or dogma (whether traditional or 'new age'). Moreover, this experience is understood, at least by the experiencer, to be that of a *fundamental Reality* (rather than of the 'ordinary reality' — or unreality — that we usually experience). In this sense mystical experience differs from normal perception and cognition which are directed to the familiar worlds of sensory experiences and ideas. For the same reason, although mysticism is *empirical* in the sense that it is based on direct experience, it differs from traditional scientific empiricism in the objects of its enquiry and in its epistemology and methods. In particular, mystical knowledge implies the possibility of direct intuitive access to knowledge in a way that transcends sensation and cognition. Being essentially empirical, however, Wilber (1979) argues that the mystical 'eye of contemplation' may provide the basis for a 'higher' and more encompassing vision of science than one constrained to use only the eyes of sensory observation and reason.

Most writers on mysticism go further than merely identifying mystical experience with direct knowledge of a fundamental Reality. Additionally, they generally aim to specify either (a) the kind of direct experience that mysticism involves (most typically one of union), and/or (b) the kind of fundamental Reality that is experienced (e.g., a theistic God or some other spiritual 'ultimate' or transcendent reality). In my opinion, however, these identifications jump ahead of the data in a way that may artificially exclude certain sorts of experiences and may therefore prejudice and limit research and theory in this area. In contrast, I shall define mysticism more generally as *the individual's direct experience of a relationship to a fundamental Reality*. Hick (1989) usefully characterizes such Reality ('the Real') in a way that is neutral as regards different religious conceptions of the 'transcendent'. However, Hick's analysis focuses specifically on some sort of religious or transcendent conception of a single 'ultimate' Reality (an example of what Ferrer, e.g., 2002, has called the 'Myth of the Given'). Consistent with my argument in the previous chapter, I shall define the Real in more general terms that do not presuppose a metaphysical conception of the

Real, that encompass a pluralism of religious and non-religious interpretations, and that allow for experiences that may be of a 'fundamental' but not necessarily 'ultimate' Reality. In this sense, my understanding of the Real is closer to what Ferrer (e.g., 2002) refers to as the 'Mystery'.

The idea of a fundamental Reality implies, I suggest, three basic characteristics:

1. **Absolute existence** (i.e., it is understood to be self-existent and not merely a temporary or relative appearance).

2. **Absolute value** (its value is experienced as self-evidential, not a matter of opinion or fashion).

3. **Fundamental human meaning** (it has a profound effect on human life, imbuing it with a sense of purpose and significance).

According to these criteria, such a fundamental Reality is distinguishable from particular subjective states, such as pleasure, since these are temporary and relative (i.e., pleasure is not understood as existing *in itself*, separate from our experience of it). Fundamental Reality is also not the same as the physical world of matter (which has no self-evidential value or meaning).

Defining mystical experience as the direct experience of a relationship to a fundamental Reality allows different types of relationships to be acknowledged and investigated. It also usefully leaves open the question of exactly how this Reality is to be experienced and conceived (whether, for example, as God, Nature, Spirit, Mind, Self, Void, the Mystery of being, or some other concept).

Mystical, Religious and Transpersonal Experience

Mystical experience, as I have defined it, is not necessarily the same as religious experience (cf. Fontana, 2003; Wainwright, 1981). Religious experience includes many phenomena that are not direct personal experiences of a relationship to a fundamental Reality. Most obvious is the fact that much, perhaps most, religious experience reflects an *indirect* relationship to the Real (which is approached through intermediary representatives or representations such as priests, scriptures, moral precepts, rites and rituals, symbols, or works of art). Also religious experience often expresses relative personal needs (e.g., for forgiveness or a sense of control) or relative social demands and expectations (e.g., feelings of duty or obligation) rather than representing any fundamental, self-evident Reality. In the same way that religious experiences are not always mystical, so mystical experiences are not always religious, at least in the generally accepted sense of this word. For example, some forms of introspective absorption and nature mysticism do not involve the experience of a *divine* Reality that is, for many, the hallmark of true religion (cf. Hick, 1989). This distinction between mystical and religious experience is also supported empirically in the structure of Hood's Mysticism Scale (e.g., Hood, Morris & Watson, 1993) which identifies separate factors of mystical experience and religious interpretation.

Mystical experience is also not precisely coterminous with transpersonal experience although there is much experiential overlap between them. Walsh & Vaughan's (1993a, p. 103) very broad definition of transpersonal experiences as those 'in which the sense of identity or self extends beyond (trans.) the individual or personal to encompass wider aspects of humankind, life, psyche or cosmos' allows for the inclusion of a range of phenomena (e.g., fetal or past-life memories) that do not necessarily involve experiencing a relationship to a 'fundamental Reality' (cf. also Grof's, 1988, 2000 extensive and varied list of transpersonal experiences). More importantly, while many mystical experiences are indeed transpersonal because they involve an extension of the sense of identity or self beyond the individual or personal, some mystical experiences are not. For example, the direct experience of God's overpowering presence is sometimes associated with the feeling of personal insignificance, weakness or sin, i.e., to an emphasis or fixation on the boundaries of individual or personal identity rather than their extension. Such an experience is *mystical* in the sense defined above (i.e., it is a direct experience of relationship to a fundamental Reality, but is not *transpersonal* since it does not expansively *transform* or extend the sense of self.

Essentialists vs. Constructivists

All investigators recognize that there are many varieties of mystical experience. The major debate centres on whether these many forms represent different *interpretations* or *accounts* of what is essentially the same *experience* (or a few basic types of experience) or whether, on the other hand, the experiences themselves are fundamentally different. According to the first, perennialist, view (e.g., Forman, 1998; Huxley, 1947; Smith, 1976; Stace, 1960; Underhill, 1911/1995) people everywhere have the same basic experience(s) but they may interpret and describe them rather differently depending upon the personal, social, cultural and linguistic context. If this view is correct, it makes sense, as Wainwright (1981) has argued, to try to identify the essential cross-cultural characteristics and types of mystical experience (i.e., the characteristics and types that exist *prior* to any secondary interpretative differences).

At the other extreme are the constructivists (e.g., Gimello, 1978, 1983; Katz, 1978) who argue that the experiences themselves (rather than simply their post-hoc interpretations) are profoundly and irrevocably determined by predisposing personal, social, and cultural factors, including religious doctrines and particular forms of spiritual practice. Thus there are, according to Katz (1978), no pure or unmediated experiences. For this reason there can be no true common experiential denominators in mysticism. The implication of this second view is that there is, in principle, an indefinite number of different mystical experiences, each one potentially unique to the individual experiencer, although there may be identifiable commonalities of experience within particular mystical traditions. It is not possible, however, to identify meaningfully the essential (cross-cultural) qualities and types of mystical experience — we can only attempt to understand how the many contextual factors combine together to produce particular experiences in particular people(s).

A third, middle, position (e.g., Hick, 1989; Smart, 1973; Zaehner, 1961) argues that while mystical experiences themselves (rather than just their interpretations) are strongly influenced by their personal, social and cultural contexts, it is possible to recognize certain cross-cultural 'family resemblances' among them (Hick, 1989). For Hick, these family resemblances result because the experiences represent various encounters with 'the Real' (which Hick believes is an actual onto-logical reality). For this reason, mystical experiences must reflect in an important way the qualities that are manifested in human consciousness by the Real (e.g., they express selflessness, love, knowledge, and understanding rather than narcissism, hatred, ignorance, or bigotry). A similar argument is made by Ferrer (e.g., 2002) who, while denying that reality has any fixed essence, acknowledges that 'it presents us with identifiable qualities, ten-dencies and restrictions ... that impose limitations on the human creative participation and expression of spiritual truths' (*ibid.,* p. 167).

In my view Hick is right to recognize the family resemblances that exist between different mystical experiences, although I do not necessarily share his transcendental explanation for these. Whatever the explanation, there are, without doubt, discernible and often striking similarities to be observed between the accounts of mystical experiences found in the literature of quite different times and cultures. These similarities can, in principle, be fully accounted for by constructivist arguments, but some form of *interaction* between the essentialist and constructivist views would seem to me to provide the simplest and most con-vincing means of explanation. From this interactionist point of view, the research agenda involves the following tasks:

- identifying the essential characteristics of the major types of mystical experience;
- accounting intelligibly for the differences between these types;
- understanding the ways in which the various 'prototypical' experiences may be conditioned or modified by contextual factors.

Characteristics and Types of Mystical Experience

All writers on mysticism have found it necessary first to address the problem of what is to *count* as a mystical experience and what is to be considered non-mystical (including states that may be con-fused with or masquerade as mystical ones). One solution has involved the attempt to identify the phenomenological character-istics that distinguish between mystical and non-mystical states.

William James

William James (1902/1960) proposes two characteristics that together 'entitle any state to be called mystical' (p. 367):

1. Ineffability — the experience cannot be expressed in words.

2. Noetic quality — mystical states are states of knowledge and deep insight.

James also observes that mystical states are typically (3) transient (lasting two hours at most) and (4) passive (the will is in abeyance). Despite their ineffability, transiency and passivity, mystical states are recollected with a profound sense of their importance and they produce a lasting modification of the person's inner life (i.e., mystical experiences are not just transportative but also transformative).

Evelyn Underhill

In contrast with James' phenomenological-psychological approach to mysticism, Evelyn Underhill (1911/1995) bases her classic study on a spiritual-transcendental view. For Underhill, the essence of mysticism is the direct awareness of, and ultimately *union with*, the Absolute (or Divine Reality).

> Mysticism, in its pure form, is the science of ultimates, the science of union with the Absolute, and nothing else ... the mystic is the person who attains to this union (*ibid.*, p. 72).

Underhill dismisses James' four marks of the mystic state and in their place proposes her own four 'rules' or 'tests' of mystical experience (*ibid.*, pp. 81-94).

1. **Mysticism is practical, not theoretical**. Direct experience and action mark the true mystic, not speculation or passivity.

2. **Mysticism is an entirely spiritual activity**. Its aims are wholly transcendental and spiritual — always set upon the 'changeless One'.

3. **The business and method of mysticism is love**. The One is a personal Object of Love that 'draws [the mystic's] whole being homeward, but always under the guidance of the heart' (*ibid.*, p. 81).

4. **Mysticism entails a definite psychological experience**.

> Living union with the One [the Unitive Life] is arrived at by
> an arduous psychological and spiritual process — the
> so-called Mystic Way — entailing the complete remaking of
> character and the liberation of a new, or rather latent, form of
> consciousness ... which is sometimes inaccurately called
> 'ecstasy' but is better named the Unitive State (*ibid.* p. 81).

Underhill further argues (*ibid.*, pp. 167ff.) that this process of
psychological and spiritual transformation involves the five
'great stages' identified by the Neoplatonists and medieval
(Christian) mystics: (a) awakening or conversion, (b) self-knowledge or purgation, (c) illumination, (d) surrender, or the Dark
Night, and (e) Union or the active Unitive Life.[1] She also notes
that the principal method or art employed by the mystic on this
path towards Union is that of *introversion* (recollection, quiet,
and contemplation).

As a corollary to these four rules, Underhill adds that:

5. **True mysticism is never self-seeking**.

R.C. Zaehner

Like Underhill, R.C. Zaehner (1961) bases his analysis of mysticism on a religious-transcendental (specifically Christian) interpretation. Unlike Underhill, however, Zaehner is more informed
about Eastern and non-religious forms of mystical experience.
On the basis of a cross-cultural comparison, Zaehner identifies
three distinct categories of mysticism:

1. **Nature mysticism**, based on all-in-one (or *panenhenic*) experience, such as the experience of cosmic consciousness (Bucke,
   1901/2001). For Zaehner, nature mysticism is essentially
   non-religious.

2. **Monistic mysticism**, based on the absorptive experience of
   one's own self or spirit as the Absolute (e.g., Advaita
   Vedanta).

3. **Theistic mysticism**, based on the experience of loving communion or union with a personal God.

---

1   Note that these do not appear to correspond in any obvious way to
     Wilber's transpersonal stages, despite Wilber's own claim that Underhill's
     developmental model is 'virtually identical to my scheme' (Wilber, 2000c,
     p. 76). Underhill's model is, in fact, much more consistent with
     Washburn's spiral-dynamic theory. See also Collins (nd.)

In my opinion, these are valid and useful *descriptive* categories. Zaehner, however, unfortunately insists on *ranking* them hierarchically in terms of their moral value and significance. For Zaehner (a Roman Catholic), theistic mysticism is the highest or best, followed by monistic mysticism, with nature mysticism trailing a poor third.

F.C. Happold

Happold (1970) makes identical distinctions to Zaehner, but refers to these as (1) **nature-mysticism**, (2) **soul-mysticism**, and (3) **God-mysticism**. Unlike Zaehner, however, Happold considers these three categories to be of equal status. Happold also makes a useful distinction between:

- **Mysticism of love and union** — based on the urge to escape from the sense of isolated selfhood and the achievement of peace through a closer participation with Nature or God.

- **Mysticism of knowledge and understanding** — based on the urge to find the secret of the Universe, to understand it in its wholeness.

In characterizing the experiential qualities of mystical experience, Happold follows William James closely. To James' four 'marks' of (1) ineffability, (2) noetic quality, (3) transiency and (4) passivity, Happold adds:

5. **Consciousness of the Oneness of everything** — the experience of unity, as All in One and One in All. For Happold, this panenhenic experience is not (as for Zaehner) a distinguishing feature of nature mysticism or cosmic consciousness because, in theistic mysticism also, 'God is felt to be in everything and everything to exist in God' (Happold, 1970, p. 46). Happold also suggests that the same panenhenic experience may be found in soul mysticism.

6. **Sense of timelessness** — mystic experiences cannot be described in terms of normal clock time, or past, present and future. They have a timeless quality in which 'all is always now' (*ibid.*, p. 48).

7. **Conviction that the familiar phenomenal *ego* is not the real I** — that within us there is another, True Self (variously described by different mystical traditions as, for example, the *Atman*, spark, centre, apex of the soul, or ground of the spirit).

Walter Stace

For Walter Stace (1960), the core or hallmark of the fully developed mystical experience is the sense of ultimate, non-sensuous, non-intellectual *unity*. This means that sensuous phenomena such as paranormal experiences, visions and voices, and hyper-emotionalism are not themselves mystical, although they may accompany unitive experience. Stace argues that mystical experiences must be identified on purely phenomenological grounds. If two experiences are phenomenologically identical, they are the same experience, no matter how different their causes might have been (the principle of *causal indifference*) or how they might be interpreted. In practice this leaves open the possibility, for example, that genuine mystical experiences may result from the use of mind-altering substances. In this respect Stace is in complete disagreement with Zaehner (1961) who argues that such a view is profoundly misguided.

In identifying the phenomenological characteristics of mystical (as *unitive*) experience, Stace makes a fundamental distinction between *extravertive* and *introvertive* mysticism. Extravertive mysticism looks outward and perceives the Unity of the World. Introvertive mysticism looks inward and finds the One at the centre of the self, in the Heart, or in the experience of oneness with God. Extravertive mysticism is more or less equivalent to Zaehner's panenhenic nature mysticism. Introvertive mysticism is comparable with monistic or soul mysticism, although theistic mysticism is also generally introvertive (cf. Underhill, *op. cit.*). In this way, Stace points out that introvertive mysticism is historically and culturally the more important. More contentiously, like Zaehner, he also argues that it represents a higher, more developed, form of experience.

Stace describes seven characteristics of extravertive and introvertive mystical experience, of which the final five are identical in the two types. These are:

1. **Unity**. Either (a) the extravertive Unifying Vision that All is One (as in cosmic consciousness), or (b) the introvertive Unitary Consciousness in which all sensory and conceptual content has disappeared so that only a void or empty unity remains.

2. **Subjectivity**. Either (a) the extravertive apprehension of a subjectivity (life, consciousness, presence) in all things, or (b) the introvertive sense of non-spatial and non-temporal Being or Consciousness.

3. **Reality**. The sense of objectivity and realness to the experience.

4. **Positive affect**. The feeling of blessedness, joy, happiness, satisfaction, etc.

5. **Sacredness**. The feeling that what is apprehended is holy, sacred, or divine (for Stace, this is the quality that leads to the experience often being *interpreted* theistically).

6. **Paradoxicality** or logical inconsistency (e.g., the experience is both empty and full).

7. **Ineffability** — the experience cannot be put fully into words.

Of all the phenomenologists of mystical experience, Stace has been the most influential, especially in psychology. Stace's seven features of mystical experience were used as assessment criteria in Walter Pahnke's (1963, 1966) famous 'Good Friday Experiment' into the effects of the psychedelic drug psilocybin on the experiences of trainee ministers during a religious service[2] (Pahnke also added criteria of *transiency*, and *persisting positive changes in attitude and behaviour*). Stace's seven characteristics (together with the distinction between extravertive and introvertive mysticism and the factor of religious interpretation) also provide the basis for Ralph Hood's widely used psychometric instrument, the Mysticism Scale or M Scale (Hood, 1975; Hood, Morris & Watson, 1993).

William Wainwright

Wainwright (1981) follows Stace's general outline of mystical experience which he defines as unitary states which are noetic, but which lack any *specific* empirical content. By this, Wainwright means that the knowledge gained in mystical states is not of *anything* in particular. This absence of empirical content accounts for the often claimed ineffability of mystical experience. On the basis of this definition, like Stace, Wainwright seeks to distinguish mystical experience from the sense of sacredness,

---

2   See also Doblin's (1991) long-term follow-up of this study.

visions and voices, occult and paranormal experience, and religious feeling and sentiments, since, unlike mystical experience, these all have specific content.

Wainwright also follows Stace in distinguishing between extravertive and introvertive mysticism, but he suggests that we need to recognize different varieties of each of these.

Extravertive mysticism, he suggests, comes in four distinct types:

1. The experience of the unity of and with nature.

2. The sense of nature as a living presence.

3. The sense that everything is occurring in an eternal present.

4. The experience of the emptiness of the phenomenal world.

Introvertive mysticism, Wainwright argues, comes in two main types, although he also recognizes that other types may be possible:

1. The monistic experience of pure, empty consciousness (formless Witnessing).

2. The theistic (dualistic) experience of the 'naked', loving awareness of God.

Rudolf Otto

The sense of *sacredness* is central to the theologian Rudolf Otto's analysis of religious experience. In *The Idea of the Holy* (1917/1950), Otto argues for the importance of the non-rational (non-conceptual) in religious experience. The core of religious experience, he argues, is the sense of the *numinous*. This term, coined by Otto from the Latin *numen* (God), refers to a direct experience of the holy or sacred, stripped of its ethical and rational aspects. The numinous is basically ineffable and cannot be explained in terms of other categories — it is a primary feeling-response that may be pointed to using analogies, but must be directly experienced to be understood fully. For many people, he suggests, the numinous may be found in prayer and meditation, in solemn rituals or liturgies, or as a response to the atmosphere invoked by religious monuments and buildings, including ruins.

Such experience may come in various forms: as a tranquil mood of worship, a strange thrill and excitement, a sense of

beauty and glory, a violent, intoxicated frenzy, or even as something demonic and barbaric (note the ethical neutrality of the
concept). At its core, numinous experience is a response to a
'wholly other' object of profound mystery (the *mysterium*). This
mysterium manifests in two ways. One the one hand, it is the
overpowering mystery (*mysterium tremendum*) — experienced as
awesome, majestic and dynamic. On the other hand, it is also an
object of fascination and attraction (*mysterium fascinans*) that
captivates, possesses, or ravishes us and to which we turn for
mercy, love and salvation.

Although Otto includes so-called 'primitive' experiences (e.g.,
animism, magic and shamanism) within his account of the
numinous, together with devotional and more 'everyday' feeling-
responses, such as those invoked by religious ceremonies or the
atmosphere of religious places, his discussion often focuses
specifically on *mystical* experience as traditionally understood.
For Otto, mystical experience is essentially a particular intensi-
fied or pure form of numinous experience (Schlamm, 1991).
Some writers on mysticism, however, in focussing upon the
introvertive or unitive qualities of mystical experience, attempt
to distinguish mystical from numinous experience, including the
related phenomena of prophecy and devotionalism, since the latter are all based on the experience of an external 'wholly other'
(e.g., Smart, 1964; Wainwright, 1981). Otto, in contrast, sees the
concept of numinous experience as establishing an inclusive
category of religious experience in which the introvertive and
unitive experiences are particular varieties.

According to the definition of mystical experience I have
offered, the relationship between numinous and mystical experience is understood rather differently. Because numinous experience represents the individual's direct experience of a
relationship to a fundamental Reality (the *mysterium*) it is clearly
mystical. However, for me, mystical experience is the broader
category, in which numinous experience (in the sense of the
experience of a wholly Other) represents one particular variety.

Andrew Rawlinson

This interpretation is also basically consistent with Andrew
Rawlinson's model of experiential comparative religion (1997,
2000). Rawlinson views the numinous and introvertive as exam-

ples of two basic forms of mystical experience (the 'hot' and the 'cool'). According to Rawlinson:

- **Hot** is that which is other than oneself, and which has a life of its own. Hot experiences are thus similar to those of the numinous, as characterized by Otto. Hot mysticism, Rawlinson argues, is typically associated with the ideas of revelation and grace and includes elements found in both theistic and magical traditions.

- **Cool** is based on experiences of the essence of the self. It is quiet and still. Cool mysticism is therefore similar, if not precisely identical, to the monistic, soul and introvertive mysticism of, respectively, Zaehner, Happold and Stace. In cool mystical traditions, salvation or spiritual transformation does not depend on any Other, but rather is a matter of self-realization.

Rawlinson's distinction has the particular advantage of recognizing both numinous and introvertive forms of mystical experience without prioritizing either one on intellectual, developmental, moral, or spiritual grounds. To underscore this, the terms 'hot' and 'cool' are sufficiently value-neutral to provide useful reference points for discussion. Furthermore, Rawlinson emphasizes that hot and cool do not represent two exclusive categories of experience, but should rather be viewed as defining a bipolar dimension. This means that, in practice, the two forms of experience may overlap to some degree, leaving open the possibility of recognizing a range of mixed or 'warm' experiences in which the Real is neither wholly Other, nor wholly Self.

Ken Wilber

In contrast to Rawlinson's even-handed approach, Ken Wilber presents an essentially hierarchical view of the various types of mystical experience. Wilber does not derive his model directly from the phenomenological data but rather attempts to fit these data into an *a priori* theoretical model of spiritual evolution. As we have seen, Wilber's model is based closely on the Vedantic doctrine of the 'three bodies' (gross, subtle and causal) and on the nondual (*Advaita*) Vedanta of Sankara.

Wilber (e.g., 1995a, 1996b, 1999a, 2000a) recognizes four main levels of mystical consciousness (although some variations to this basic model have appeared over the years). These four levels are:

1. **Psychic mysticism** (sometimes referred to as 'low subtle'). For Wilber, this term covers all mystical experiences that are tied closely to the 'gross' (physical) realm. This includes extrasensory perception and other paranormal powers such as the Yogic *siddhis*, as well as all forms of nature and extravertive mysticism, including cosmic consciousness.

2. **Subtle mysticism** (sometimes 'high subtle'). In Vedanta, the 'subtle' refers to the level of pure thought or Mind. Subtle mysticism thus covers all forms of purely mental or imagistic experience. These include visions, voices, inspiration, ecstasies, feelings of love, radiance or gratefulness, sense of 'higher' presences, encounters with archetypes, angels or deities, *savikalpa samadhi* (meditative absorption with mental content), and most experiences of union with God. Subtle mysticism therefore incoroprates Otto's numinous and much of theistic mysticism, especially that known classically as *kataphatic* (based on positive affirmation, sensory and imagistic experience).

3. **Causal mysticism**. In Vedanta, the 'causal' level refers not to any mental activity, but to the formless Spirit, Transcendent Witness, or root of attention. Causal mysticism is more or less equivalent to monistic or soul mysticism. More specifically, it is *apophatic* in the classical sense — i.e., it represents the culmination of the *via negativa* or the path of denying all manifestation (Smart, 1983). The causal involves the cessation of all sensory experience and mental activity, resulting in what has been called a 'pure consciousness event' (e.g., Forman, 1998). Thus in the absence of all mental content, pure, formless awareness is reported to remain. This is a kind of 'unknowing' or ignorance — 'yet there is in it more than in all knowing and understanding without it' (from Sermon I by Meister Eckhart, cited in Happold, 1970, p. 278). Such formless consciousness is most generally associated with the Void or *sunyata* (emptiness) of Buddhism and the *nirvikalpa samadhi* (formless meditative state) of Yoga.

4. **Nondual mysticism**. For Wilber (e.g., 1999a, 2000a), nondual mysticism is based on the experience of 'One Taste'. Wilber describes this as an *'ever-present* consciousness' (1999a, p. 137), or the simple experience of *'just this'* (*ibid.*, p. 97,

emphasis in original). According to Wilber, this awareness arises *out of* the emptiness of causal consciousness:

> in that pure emptiness, which you are, the entire manifest world arises ... Resting in that empty, free, easy, effortless witnessing, notice that the clouds are arising in the vast space of your awareness. The clouds are arising within you — so much so, you can taste the clouds, you are one with the clouds, it is as if they are on this side of your skin, they are so close. The sky and your awareness have become one, and all things in the sky are floating effortlessly through your own awareness. You can kiss the sun, swallow the mountain, they are that close ... and that's the easiest thing in the world, when inside and outside are no longer two, when subject and object are nondual, when the looker and looked at are One Taste (*ibid.*, p. 88).

In nondual consciousness or One Taste, therefore, the ordinary world of form (including sensations, perceptions, mental images, emotions, etc.) is *fully present* and is directly experienced as the immediate, unconditional, liberated play or expression of the Self or Witness. The Witness is not separate from the world, but rather everything arises *as the Self.*

Wilber's taxonomy of mystical experiences has become widely influential, at least within transpersonal psychology (less so within religious studies). As a *descriptive* account, the causal and nondual levels are well articulated. The psychic and subtle levels, however, appear very mixed bags. Wilber's inclusion of cosmic consciousness within the category of psychic mysticism seems particularly odd. As we have seen, his argument for doing this is based on the purely ontological grounds that cosmic consciousness is an experience of the 'gross' physical realm (Wilber, 1995a, pp. 608-609). Phenomenologically, however, as I argued in Chapter 9, cosmic consciousness would seem to have much in common with One Taste, as Wilber himself has acknowledged when writing of 'One Taste or "cosmic consciousness" — the sense of oneness with the Ground of all creation' (*ibid.*, p. 57).

In Wilber's accounts, the subtle level also has extremely wide coverage, including experiences as seemingly diverse as visions and voices, experiences of love and radiance, and union with the Deity. Wilber may here be contrasted with most other writers on mysticism, who have generally found it necessary to make fundamental distinctions between these phenomena (e.g., James, 1902/1960; Smart, 1964; Underhill, 1911/1995; Wainwright, 1981).

Most problematic of all, however, is Wilber's *hierarchical arrangement* of the four levels, which he bases on his 'perennialist' assumptions about the evolutionary Great Chain or Nest of Being (Matter-Life-Mind-Soul-Spirit). Wilber (e.g., 2000a) interprets Soul as corresponding to subtle experience, and Spirit as causal-nondual. Accordingly he suggests that causal and nondual mysticism are the 'highest' and developmentally final forms. I do not doubt that, within certain traditions, the sequence from psychic to nondual characterizes the meditative paths they espouse (most notably Advaita Vedanta and Buddhism, which have most influenced Wilber's thinking). But, in my opinion, Wilber has yet to demonstrate convincingly that this sequence applies universally across mystical traditions (cf. Ferrer, 2002; Heron, 1998; Schlamm, 2001).[3] For example, Wilber's prioritizing of causal (monistic) over most forms of theistic (subtle) mysticism directly contradicts Zaehner's (1961) interpretation of the mystical literature (although this also seems biased).

Wilber (2000a) identifies parallels between his scheme and that of several other traditional and more modern accounts of mystical progress, both East and West. These include those of Pseudo-Dionysius, Plotinus, St. Gregory, St. Teresa of Avila, Hazrat Inayat Khan, Kabbalah, Sri Aurobindo, Evelyn Underhill and the theosophist C.W. Leadbeater. Some of the examples in Wilber's tables of correspondences may appear rather strained or contrived even though Wilber is rather selective in his choice of traditions and exemplars (for example he generally ignores indigenous perspectives). It also needs to be recognized that many of the apparently independent traditions he includes (e.g., Neoplatonism, Christianity, Kabbalah, Sufism, Vedanta, and Theosophy) have, in fact, often close historical and cultural links. Similarities among them may therefore represent a *common intellectual and doctrinal heritage* rather than any universal truth about the path of spiritual progress.

---

3   Visser (2003) also criticizes the placement of the astral-psychic as the first *stage* within the transpersonal. Astral-psychic experience, he argues, involves more the expansion of the *senses* rather than the expansion of the *Self*, so that spiritual development can occur without any necessary development of paranormal capacities.

As we have also seen, Wilber's hierarchy seems to downplay the significance of the mystical experiences of women and of indigenous peoples, which themselves emphasize a sense of connection to nature, to the body and emotions, and to other people. Female mysticism is also strongly associated (at least within Christianity) with voices and visionary experience, pain and suffering, ecstasies, creative expression, spiritual longing and devotion, love, friendship and compassion (Wiethaus, 1993). To the extent that such experiences are understood as either subtle or gross/psychic, they do not, in Wilber's scheme, achieve the spiritual maturity that he associates with formless causal absorption or nondual One Taste. It is therefore unsurprising that Wright (1998a) and Heron (1998) among others have concluded that Wilber's model is fundamentally androcentric, patriarchal and misogynist.

It is perhaps unfair to single out Wilber for such criticism. The history of both Western and Eastern mysticism is dominated by hierarchical and patriarchal assumptions and practices. For this reason, it is important that future research should, as Wright (1998a) argues, examine the mystical experiences and interpretations of women. A problem with the historical evidence, however, is that the major women mystics (e.g., St Teresa, Julian of Norwich) have themselves lived and operated within a culture and ecclesiastical context that was itself strongly patriarchal. For this reason their accounts are likely to be biased, if only because they were the subject of close scrutiny and censorship by the Church (McNamara, 1993).

Social Mysticism

Although more evident in the experiences of women mystics, the social-interpersonal dimension of mysticism has been generally neglected in mystical scholarship. Of course, ideas of interpersonal connectedness or *inter-being* (Thich Nhat Hanh, 1996; Walley, 2002) and of love, compassion and spiritual friendship are central to many mystical traditions (e.g., Sufism, Christianity, Buddhism, Tantra, Guru and Karma Yoga). It is perhaps surprising, therefore, that none of the mystical typologies we have examined adequately recognizes what may be called 'social mysticism' (i.e., experiences of the Real in relationships with other people). The explanation, I believe, is that most mystical traditions, even those that emphasize love, compassion and the

Heart, have themselves tended to focus on the introverted, contemplative or meditative path. While these traditions often recognize the importance of *expressing* or *translating* socially the mystical insights that are first experienced in contemplation, they generally give little consideration to mystical experiences that are themselves directly social-interpersonal in origin (e.g., experiences of deep empathy or communion with other people). While nature mysticism made a strong claim for recognition in the 19th century, through the writings of the romantic poets and American transcendentalists, social mysticism has yet to find widely influential champions and advocates.

One writer who has examined the potential of intimate relationships for generating spiritual experience and transformation is John Welwood (e.g., 1991). Welwood discusses six different levels of connection that may form between intimate partners:

1. **Symbiotic fusion** (the failure to establish a separate identity).

2. **Companionship** (sharing activities and each other's company).

3. **Community** (sharing common interests, goals or values).

4. **Communication** (sharing of thoughts, feelings and other experiences).

5. **Communion** (deep recognition of another person's Being). This relationship, for Welwood, clearly expresses a kind of mystical experience. Thus he notes that:

   > This often takes place in silence — perhaps while looking into our partner's eyes, making love, walking in the woods, or listening to music together. Suddenly we feel touched and seen, not as a personality, but in the depth of our being. We are fully ourselves and fully in touch with our partner at the same time. This kind of connection is so rare and striking that it is usually unmistakable when it comes along. While two people can work on communication, communion is more spontaneous, beyond the will. Communication and communion are deeper, more subtle forms of intimacy than companionship and community, taking place at the level of mind and heart (Welwood, 1991, p. 203).

6. **Union**. Beyond communion, Welwood suggests there can be 'a longing to overcome our separateness altogether, a longing for total *union* with someone we love' (*ibid.*, p. 203). However, he also argues that this longing 'is more appropriately directed to the divine, the absolute, the infinite. When attached to an intimate relationship, it often creates problems' (*ibid.*, p. 203).

Another researcher who strongly emphasizes the mystical potential to be found within interpersonal relationships is Jenny Wade (1998, 2000). Specifically, Wade has investigated unitive and other mystical experiences that arise spontaneously through ordinary people's sexual activity (she is less interested in the transcendental sexual disciplines of Tantra and Taoism). In these experiences, she reports, people describe all of the major characteristics of mystical states, including ecstatic unity, bliss, no separation between self and other, transcendence of time and space, paradoxicality, sense of the numinous, the oneness of all phenomena, realness and ineffability. In some cases advanced meditators reported that the loss of self during sex matched or even exceeded that which was achieved through meditation practice.

Putting the Pieces Together —
The '5 x 5 Model' of Mysticism

Although not exhaustive, the above discussion provides, I believe, the raw material necessary to attempt a broader and more coherent understanding of mystical experience. Any such attempt will need to find a way of incorporating not simply the extraordinary range of phenomena that form the basic research data, but also be able to accommodate or reasonably challenge the different views and interpretations proposed by other investigators.

The model I shall propose is based on the assumption that there are (a) important universal experiences at the core of mysticism, and (b) fundamental differences in the ways that these experiences are modified by context and interpretation. In this way, I am attempting to bridge both perennialist and contextualist arguments. Like Hick (1989) my own position is rather more on the side of the contextualists, i.e., that mystical experiences are not simply *interpreted* differently after they occur, but are actually *experienced* in different ways depending

Table 12. Categories of mystical experience –

THE REAL AS (or IN)				MODE	
				HOT	
				NUMINOUS	**DIALOGIC**
			Experience of the Real	Presence	Communication
			Relationship of the Real	Wholly Other	Other as Initiator
			Sense or feeling	Numinosity	Voices / Visions
C O N T E X T O F E X P E R I E N C E	**H O T** **T H O U**	**GOD(S) or DIVINE BEING(S)**	View	Sacredness and Reality of the Divine	Divine intervention in human affairs
			Typical statement	"I felt overwhelmed by God's Majesty"	"God spoke to me"
			Examples	Sense of Divine presence	Divine visions and voices; Prophecy
	A L L	**NATURE or COSMOS**	View	The natural world as frightening or wondrous	Nature as revelatory
			Typical statement	"I experienced a mysterious presence in the woods"	"The babbling stream talks to me of hidden things"
			Examples	Seeing nature spirits and fairies; Enchantment; *Mana*	Communication with nature spirits, animals, plants, etc.
	W A R M **W E**	**SOCIAL BEING or COMM-UNITY**	View	Group or person(s) as object(s) of special power	Group or person(s) as initiatory
			Typical statement	"I felt the seething energy of the crowd"	"I was suddenly swept up and transformed"
			Examples	Nuremberg Rallies; Charismatic leaders	Revivalism; Direct transmission from guru
	I T	**PSYCHE or MIND**	View	Psyche as wondrous, dynamic and powerful	Psyche (the unconscious) as revelatory
			Typical statement	"I felt an extraordinary surge of energy"	"I saw mysterious signs and portents"
			Examples	Kundalini awakenings; Ecstatic states; Lights; Apparitions	Illuminations; Vision quest; Oracular knowledge
	C O O L **I**	**SELF / SOUL or MONAD**	View	The self has a powerful Guardian Spirit	Deeper Self as source of wisdom and guidance
			Typical statement	"I was aware of someone watching over me"	"I was warned by an inner sense"
			Examples	Guardian Angel; Daemon; Ancestors	Inner voice; Insight; Intuition; Sixth sense

– *The '5 x 5' model*

O F   **E X P E R I E N C E**

WARM		COOL
SYNERGIC	**UNITIVE**	**NONDUAL**
Co-operation	Communion / Union	Identity
Other as Friend	Other as One with self	Not Other
Touch / Taste / Sharing	Oneness together	Pure Being
Personal relationship with the Divine	Oneness with the Divine	"Godhead"; Ultimate Absolute Divine Being
"I was filled with God's love"	"I was united with God"	"I am That I am"
Divine Father & Mother; Julian of Norwich, *bhakti*	Spiritual marriage; St Teresa of Avila	Meister Eckhart; Sankara
Personal relationship with Nature	Oneness of and with Nature	Nature as manifestation or outpouring of Self / Spirit
"I felt I was a child of Nature"	"I saw that the world was one life and meaning"	"I am all the World"
Romantic poets	Cosmic consciousness; Panenhenic (Zaehner)	One Taste (Wilber); *Upanishads*
Close bond between people(s)	Intimate connection with the Being of another person	There is no distinction between self and other
"I felt a sense of kinship with all people"	"I felt that our souls touched in that moment"	"I AM you and you ARE me — we arise as One"
Empathy; Fellow-feeling; Emotional connection	Communion (Welwood); Inter-being; *maithuna*	One Taste (Wilber); Not recommended (Welwood)
Self in touch with larger creative potentials of Mind	Oneness with Mind	Mind as clear, self-luminous reality
"The solution suddenly came to me"	"I was totally absorbed in the focus of my meditation"	"All is enlightenment mind"
Creative inspiration; Muse; Imagination; Rich fantasy	Flow; Contemplation; *savikalpa samadhi*	*Rigpa*; One Taste (Wilber)
"Heart" or "Soul" as spiritual ground	Oneness with Heart or Soul	The Transcendent Witness
"I felt in touch with my Heart (Soul)"	"I was united with mine own Heart (Soul)"	"A blissful, silent, empty unknowing"
Inner spirit; Emotional and spiritual richness	Boundless compassion and loving-kindness; *metta*	Void, *sunyata*, Causal (Wilber), PCE (Forman)

on their context. This context includes not only the *focus* or *object* of the experience (e.g., whether nature, or self, or social experience, or God), but also on the person's prior beliefs and expectations, and on the prevailing social and cultural environment. Where I agree with the perennialists is that there are certain fundamental aspects of mystical experiences that are cross-contextual and cross-cultural.

I have defined mysticism as *the direct experience of a relationship to a fundamental Reality*. The first important consideration in any mystical experience, therefore, is what the Real is understood to be or, perhaps more accurately, where it is to be found — whether, for example, it is in Nature, Self or God. This defines the *context*, *focus*, or *object* of the experience. My reading of the evidence is that we need, in fact, to recognize at least *five* distinct contexts for mystical experience. These are:

1. **Gods(s) or Divine Being(s)**. This entails a transcendental, theistic, supernatural or 'hot' view of the Real.

2. **Nature or Cosmos**. This sees the Real as manifest in the physical and living world. This may also be taken to include the physical body.

3. **Social Being or Community**. This sees the Real in the 'warm' realm of human relationships, sexuality, society or inter-being.

4. **Psyche or Mind**. This refers not to the monistic experience of Self or Soul, but to the experience of the Real in the realm of mental phenomena (archetypes, symbols, images, thoughts, feelings, etc.). This is also the realm, I believe, of language mysticism (cf. Lancaster, 2004).

5. **Self / Soul or Monad**. Here the Real is at the centre or core of one's own self (Soul or Spirit), root of attention, or the seat of consciousness. This corresponds to Rawlinson's (1997, 2000) understanding of 'cool'.

According to these distinctions, when considering the object, focus or context of mystical experience, we may talk about five basic types of mysticism (i.e., theistic, nature, social, mental, and monistic). Of course an objection that may be voiced is that, in many cases, one context is interpreted in terms of another. For example, the experience of the Real in Nature may be later *inter-*

preted as the manifestation of God (as, for example, in pantheistic belief). For the purposes of the present model, however, it is the *primary object, focus or context of experience* that is the crucial consideration, not any secondary interpretation (i.e., the post hoc *interpretation* of God *experienced* in Nature is counted as nature mysticism, not theistic mysticism). A more basic objection might be that experiences themselves may simultaneously span more than one context. For example, a person may directly experience a sense of union with God, and Self, and another person. I accept this possibility but it is not, in my opinion, a critical objection to the model I am proposing. The possibility of mixed experiences does not mean that the identification of basic contexts is invalid any more than the existence of brown or purple invalidates the usefulness of distinctions between the primary colours. It is, of course, a matter for empirical research to what extent mystical experiences are contextually pure or mixed. I also accept that there may be other contexts that some people might wish to identify as basic (e.g., the Arts, the body, physical activity). The five contexts I have identified seem to me, however, to be capable of incorporating these and other suggested contexts.

While these categories define *what* is experienced as Real, or rather *where* the Real is to be found, a second consideration is the manner in which the mystic experiences her or his *relationship* to the Real. On the basis of the previous discussions, I propose five basic modes of experiencing this relationship. These are:

1. **Numinous**. Here the Real is encountered as a 'wholly Other' presence. Such experience is 'hot' in Rawlinson's sense. The main characteristics of such numinous mystical experience are feelings of awe, fear, wonderment or fascination (cf. Otto, 1917/1950). I should make clear at this point that in focusing only on the experience of *presence*, I am using the term 'numinous' in a much more precise and limited sense than that proposed by Otto, for whom the numinous extends to all forms of mystical experience, including the unitive.

2. **Dialogic**. In this mode, the Real is no longer the 'wholly other' of numinous experience (i.e., simply *there* as an object of awe, fear or worship). Instead, a channel of direct contact and communication between the Other and the self is experienced, so that dialogue becomes possible. Such communication generally uses the distant senses (sight and hearing) —

hence mystical experiences in this mode tend to take the form of visions or voices.

3. **Synergic**. Here the Other is experienced as very close to the self, so that it can be known using the near senses (touch and taste). There is also a basic similarity between self and Other, a shared nature, that brings a sense of co-operation, mutual understanding and emotional support. Fundamentally the relationship is experienced as warm, friendly and familial.

4. **Unitive**. In unitive experience the self and Other become *One together*, resulting in the experience of a mystical communion or total intimate knowledge of and participation in each Other's Being. This is different from nondual experience because, in unitive experience, the Reality of the Other (as Other) is implicitly recognized — indeed it is honoured and celebrated. The imagery of sexual union is an often-used and helpful analogy or metaphor for the unitive relationship (e.g., the 'spiritual marriage' of St Teresa of Avila). As Wade (1998, 2000) reminds us, actual sexual congress may also induce such unitive experiences (i.e., the spiritual marriage is not always merely symbolic or metaphorical).

5. **Nondual**. This is based on the experience of *identity* rather than of communion or union (cf. Stace, 1960; Wainwright, 1981). Here the distinction between subject and object breaks down totally, so that there is no experience of anything 'Other' from the self. Instead, everything arises as the self, resulting in a simple but powerful awareness of Being, or the experience of just THIS. In Rawlinson's model, this corresponds to 'cool'.

The major implication of distinguishing between (a) *contexts of experience* and (b) *modes of experience* is that the same modes may express themselves in more than one context, so that we can, for example, recognize both unitive-theistic and unitive-nature mysticism. In fact it is useful and meaningful, I suggest, to fully cross-tabulate the five contexts and five modes, resulting in the identification of *twenty five* distinct varieties of mystical experience. This cross-tabulation is presented in Table 12 as the '5 x 5 model'. To aid understanding and comparison, I have distinguished each type in terms of its view of Reality, and have coupled this with a sample statement that reflects this view and experience. Some examples of each type are also given.

It is important to examine some of the assumptions and implications of this model. Firstly, although the five *contexts of experience* are effectively ranked on the dimension of hot–warm–cool, I see no clear grounds for imputing here any moral, spiritual or developmental hierarchy. There is, in my opinion, no rational basis for assuming, for example, that god-focused (theistic) mysticism *generally* represents a higher (lower), better (worse), or more mature (immature) form than that represented in any of the other contexts.

However, when it comes to a consideration of the *modes of experience* (also ranked on hot–warm–cool), an implicit developmental sequence or hierarchy may be discerned. This sequence is basically one of *increasing involvement with the Real* (from merely apprehending a presence, through stages of communication and co-operation, to full communion, union or even identity). From this point of view, it seems reasonable to argue, for example, that unitive mysticism is more advanced than numinous mysticism. Thus the spiritual marriage of St Teresa is a more sublime experience than that of the presence of the *mysterium* because the implied relationship with the Real is closer.

The internal logic of the hierarchy from numinous to unitive or nondual seems to hold up reasonably well *within* each of the five mystical contexts, although the question of whether nondual experience is necessarily higher than unitive is more problematic. Also problematic are attempts to evaluate the various types of experience *across* contexts. It is unclear, for example, whether a mental-synergic experience (such as creative inspiration) has the same *value* as one that is theistic-synergic (such as the experience of Divine Love) since one of the possible grounds for evaluation (the context) is different in the two cases. Of course this raises the more general question of how mystical experiences are to be evaluated, but this is beyond the scope of the present discussion (see, Hick, 1989; Swinburne, 1979; Wainwright, 1981, for an introduction to some of the issues involved).

It also needs to be acknowledged that while a developmental sequence from numinous to unitive or nondual experience is implied by the logical structure of these ideas, the question of whether individuals actually move through this sequence stage by stage is essentially a matter for empirical research. On the face of it, however, such an invariant sequence seems unlikely. For example a personal relationship with God would not seem *always* to develop from previous experience of divine communications such as visions and voices, although this may well occur in certain cases (e.g., St Teresa). Nor does the experience of flow or contemplation seem necessarily dependent upon previous creative inspiration. Of course it is necessary to distinguish between the underlying *form* of the various types of mysticism proposed and their particular *contents* or *exemplars*. Thus a basic dialogic-social experience of a group or other person as initiatory does not necessarily imply that the individual concerned has frequented revivalist gatherings. Furthermore, it is always possible (likely in my opinion) that a person may develop a particular mode of experience in one context (e.g., social synergy) and another mode in a quite different context (e.g., unity with nature). Such are some of the complexities involved in this model. Above all, it is important to realize that this model is presented primarily as a *typology* rather than as an attempt to establish the reality of specific developmental pathways.

Another issue raised by the model concerns the important question of what experience that is *not* mystical is like. Following the definition of mystical experience I have been using, nonmystical experience may be understood as occurring when there is *no direct experience of a relationship to a fundamental Reality*. This can arise, I suggest, in two main ways: The first is through *inattention and forgetfulness*. Much of our ordinary life is taken up with activities (often interesting and enjoyable enough) that we allow to distract us from an experience of the Real. Put simply, we do not experience the Real because we are not looking for it. This inattentiveness in turn causes us to forget that the Real is, in fact, all around us, so that we become effectively blinkered to it. One solution to this problem is to engage in activities where the Real may, as it were, more easily force itself on our attention (e.g., retreats, walks in the mountains, exposure to great literature and art, meetings with spiritual teachers, falling in love, or becoming meaningfully involved in the suffering of others). For some people, this strategy may also include the use of mind-altering drugs such as LSD, psilocybin, or MDMA.

Another more fundamental but rather less easy solution is to *train our attention* so that we may more readily experience the Real. This, indeed, is the primary purpose of meditation practice as I understand it. This is not to say that meditation in the formal sense is the only way to train the attention towards a realization of the Real. Such attentional training may also include, for example, more 'mundane' activities such as painting, crafts, writing, musical practice, dance or sport. It is therefore not surprising to discover that such activities have been identified by Csikszent-mihalyi (e.g. 1990) as ones that can lead to the experience of 'flow'.

The second type of non-mystical experience occurs when the Real is directly experienced as *absent from life*. Appropriating and extending the Rawlinson metaphor, this is the area of 'cold' experience. Its main characteristic is the sense that there is nothing in life that has any real significance or meaning. There is no fundamental Reality or else the relationship to this appears irre-vocably severed. As a result the world and the self seem quite 'dead'. Such experience includes loss of faith, the Dark Night of the Soul, serious depression, and a powerful sense of existential alienation from nature, the world, other people and the self. In Christian mysticism, the Dark Night is generally seen as occur-ring *after* the illuminations, visions and ecstatic raptures, but before the final union or full spiritual transformation of the per-sonality (e.g., Underhill, 1911/1995; Washburn, 1994). This is an important observation that may well extend to other contexts than the religious.

In this way, I am arguing that such cold, dark experiences may result from an experience of *loss* of the Real (e.g., disappointment in love, disenchantment with the natural world, disillusionment with the self or society), rather than from the failure ever to expe-rience it. It should not be forgotten, for example, that mystical experiences are very common in childhood and adolescence (e.g., Hardy, 1979) but may not always continue into adulthood.[4] Furthermore, this identification of 'cold' non-mystical experi-ence is not intended to deny the point made earlier, that these affectively negative experiences can represent spiritual emer-gencies that themselves may have a profound transformational effect on the person.

---

4   This in itself may be a factor contributing to a nostalgic, romantic view of childhood.

Conclusions

Perhaps the main value of the 5 x 5 model is that it is capable of incorporating an extremely wide range of mystical experiences. Some, of course, would say that it is too wide in including, for example, kundalini awakenings, experiences of crowds, the sixth sense, or awareness of nature spirits. To a large extent these objections may reflect underlying moral concerns or personal and metaphysical biases of one kind or another. The 5 x 5 model is an attempt to describe the richness and variety of mystical experiences without introducing morality or specific biases into the debate as well as to accommodate different metaphysical perspectives. I have included experiences not because I necessarily endorse their spiritual validity or value in all cases, but because they fall within the remit of mysticism as I have defined it.

Furthermore the model is not simply a *list* of experiences, but rather a structured framework within which mystical experiences may be understood and investigated. I find this framework to be intelligible, and generally consistent with previous research and theory. It implies that mysticism (as defined) expresses itself in a variety of forms, many of which can be recognized and understood by ordinary people when they are encouraged to reflect upon their own experiences of life. Mystical experience is not the exclusive preserve of meditators, hermits, saints or sages. It may be found among poets, artists, lovers, and athletes, in the special bond between parent and child, in our appreciation of nature, in our fears, and in our response to the pain and suffering of others. Mysticism is, I believe, our common heritage and birthright. We ignore it at our own loss, which is the loss of the Real.

Chapter 12

Whither Transpersonal Psychology?

In this final chapter, I shall reflect on the current status and possible future directions of transpersonal psychology. In particular, I want (a) to identify the main 'live issues' that face the discipline at this time and (b) to offer some suggested ways forward that may encourage a more integrative perspective on the transpersonal.

As an academic field, transpersonal psychology seems to be slowly but steadily growing in recognition and influence, as evidenced, for example, by the increasing number of universities around the world that now offer courses or modules in the subject at undergraduate and postgraduate level. At a wider level, however, transpersonal psychology is becoming more known to the general public from a range of popular writings and websites and, particularly, through the prolific work of Ken Wilber. Wilber is the author of more than 25 books in the areas of transpersonal and integral psychology and philosophy, and his works have been translated into around 30 languages — making him 'the most widely translated academic writer in America' (www.integralnaked.org). Almost single-handedly, he has raised the profile of transpersonal studies to that of a major cultural phenomenon.

Yet Wilber (2000b) reports that he stopped referring to himself as a transpersonal psychologist in 1983 and that:

> Psychology as we have known it, I believe, is basically dead.
> In its place will be more integral approaches. Put differently,
> my belief is that psychology as a discipline — referring to any
> of the four traditional major forces (behavioristic, psychoan-
> alytic, humanistic/existential, and transpersonal) — is
> slowly decaying and will never again, in any of its four major
> forms, be a dominant influence in culture or academia.

In its place Wilber advocates an 'integral psychology' that is
not really a psychology at all because it incorporates an all-
quadrant, all-level (AQAL) approach that requires a perspective
that moves beyond the limitations of psychology to include
'higher and wider dimensions of reality' (*ibid.*). For this reason,
he refuses to endorse the term 'fifth force' as a characterization of
his approach because he views the integral approach as existing
outside the restricted frame of psychological understanding.

As will be apparent from much that I have written, I generally
endorse Wilber's integral AQAL approach, although I have
much more sympathy with the AQ than with the AL (cf.
Washburn, 2003a). In other words, I believe that it is vital that we
expand our understanding to incorporate both inner and outer,
and individual and collective perspectives on transpersonal
knowing. I do not, however, accept Wilber's own formulation of
the transpersonal 'levels'. Put yet another way, I accept the
'wider' in Wilber's framework but not his own characterization
of the 'higher'. Unfortunately, Wilber seems committed to
restricting the term 'integral psychology' to an approach which
explicitly accepts his own Spectrum model of transpersonal
development. Because my own perspective does not fit precisely
within the terms of his model, I cannot, therefore, comfortably
adopt the designation 'integral psychology' to refer to my
approach, no matter how much I might otherwise prefer to.
Furthermore, I believe that I am not alone in taking this view. To
the extent that 'integral psychology' requires the adoption of a
specifically Wilberian paradigm, it essentially precludes alternative perspectives and, consequently, open, critical debate and it
will, therefore, alienate many people. Integral psychology, then,
is in danger of becoming a dogma and most independent
thinkers in the field will, I predict, refuse to have anything much
to do with it.

In the absence of any better term, my guess is that the term and discipline of *transpersonal psychology* will survive Wilber's defection relatively intact, as will the general area of *transpersonal studies* and the other specific transpersonal disciplines such as transpersonal psychiatry, transpersonal anthropology, transpersonal sociology and transpersonal ecology. As Oscar Wilde is famously reported to have said: 'Rumours of my death have been greatly exaggerated'.

Transpersonal psychology has always included and been comfortable with a variety of different, often conflicting, perspectives on the transpersonal, and has always encouraged lively debate (witness the pages of any of the major transpersonal journals). This is both refreshing and vital to creativity and progress in our collective attempts to understand the Mystery at the heart of the transpersonal. While some people may clamour for the certainty that a closed perspective offers, this is not only inimical to an academic and scientific endeavour but, perhaps more importantly, it may be profoundly unhelpful to people seeking spiritual fulfilment. Maps can be useful, but as Wilber himself regularly acknowledges, they are not the territory. Also, of course, it is vital that any map is both accurate and usable.

In my opinion, Wilber's map of *transpersonal* development (the hierarchy from psychic, to subtle, to causal, to nondual) is probably *not accurate* in certain fundamental respects, except perhaps to describe the path of transpersonal development within particular meditation traditions. This does not mean that I reject out of hand Wilber's entire spectrum or the holarchical approach in general. For example, I think that his characterization of the stages of development from the *prepersonal to personal* levels is broadly correct (Washburn, 2003a, also agrees on this). However, I believe that his placement of the Centaur stage (personal integration, self-realization, existential authenticity, individuation) *before* the transpersonal level is fundamentally mistaken. Rather I suggest, after Jung, that the process of individuation is a life-long process that involves the integration not only of personal realities (e.g., body and mind, consciousness and the personal unconscious) but also of collective and transpersonal experience. The realization of the Self is therefore simultaneously the ongoing achievement of an integrated, embodied, spiritual life in which we fully participate in the world (cf.

Washburn's 'regeneration in spirit', or Underhill's 'unitive life', or Ferrer's notion of cocreative participation). Of course, Wilber does suggest that the higher, transpersonal stages *transcend and include* the Centaur stage, rather than *replacing* it, but in my opinion it is more accurate to conceive it the other way round — the Centaur stage of individuation transcends and includes the transpersonal.[1]

In contrast to Wilber, I find Ferrer's (e.g., 2002) vision of a future for transpersonal psychology based on the notion of *participatory spirituality* much more true to my own experience, and much more valuable.

> In a nutshell, the participatory turn conceives transpersonal and spiritual phenomena, not as individual inner experiences, but as participatory events that can occur in different loci, such as an individual, a relationship, a community, a larger collective identity or a place ... the emergence of a transpersonal event can potentially engage the creative participation of all dimensions of human nature, from somatic transfiguration to the awakening of the heart, from erotic communion to visionary cocreation, and from contemplative knowing to moral insight (*ibid.*, p. 184).

This participatory approach embraces a *pluralistic* perspective that recognizes and honours the many ways in which the Mystery of being may be approached, and that spirituality is cocreated in transpersonal events, as well as the various ways in which this Mystery can be represented by different systems of thought, belief and practice.[2] These systems may be religious,

---

1   Visser (2003) also criticizes Wilber's placement of the Centaur level. He points out that placing the Centaur between the personal and transpersonal levels made sense within Wilber's early model of development, which was based on the idea that later stages involve reintegration of aspects of our being that had earlier been differentiated. According to this early model, therefore, the Centaur involves the reintegration of mind and body that had been split with the emergence of the mental-egoic stage (cf. Washburn's model, e.g., 1994, 1995). However Visser argues that such placement is illogical within Wilber's later 'transcend and include' scheme because, according to this, the emergence of the mental level should itself *include* the body, making the concept of a separate, later, Centaur stage redundant.

2   In my opinion, a genuinely pluralistic recognition and honouring of different perspectives is *not* the same as the recognition but *incorporation* of multiple approaches within any rigid structural scheme, no matter how

mythical, philosophical, psychological, sociological, political, ecological, etc.

Such a pluralism is not, however, purely relativistic because not only does the Mystery itself constrain our experience and limit the ways in which this Reality may be adequately expressed and symbolized, but also it is possible to evaluate different experiences and systems in terms of their emancipatory function — i.e., in terms of whether they encourage a move towards selfless awareness (Ferrer, 2002). This view is entirely consistent with that which I argued in relation to mythical thinking — that our narratives must be evaluated in terms of whether they are capable of supporting and guiding people in their quests for greater realization of the human good. Ferrer and I also agree that, because transpersonal events are essentially *cocreated*, the development of *forms of relationship and community* in which transpersonal events may emerge may be central to the soteriological, emancipatory agenda.

In my opinion, the discipline of transpersonal psychology itself represents a form of community in which transpersonal events may arise. This may happen not only in our practical activities, such as workshops and training events, but also through the progress of our scientific investigations, and in the context of the (often heated) debate and dialogue that can occur in our journals, books and conferences.

An important implication of a pluralistic approach is that there can never be one final, ultimately valid perspective on the transpersonal. As Ferrer (2002) recognizes, this also applies to his own participatory and pluralistic perspective, which he does not claim to be true 'in an absolute or objective way' (*ibid.*, p. 188) but is simply, he believes, 'more consistent with the goals of world spiritual traditions, and a more fruitful way to think and live spiritual and transpersonal phenomena today' (*ibid.*, p. 188). Ferrer also recognizes that there is an ongoing and creative tension that exists in transpersonal studies between universalism and pluralism, or the One and the Many. We are not, as a disci-

---

universal or 'perennial' this may be claimed to be. In this respect, I reject Wilber's attempts (e.g., 2000a) to impose his general schematic structure on the world's rich variety of spiritual perspectives. Although my own '5 x 5' model of mysticism is itself a schematic framework, this is offered as a tentative broad *typology* to aid thinking and research in this area, rather than as a fixed and narrow stage-structural hierarchy.

pline, confronted with making a *choice* between universalism and pluralism (for example, as may be represented in the different approaches of Wilber and Ferrer), but rather with the need to make progress on the basis of a *creative dialectic* between the two perspectives. An example of such a creative response to the apparently conflicting demands of universalism and pluralism is to be found, I believe, in the various interactionist positions taken in relation to the perennialist-constructivist debate on mystical experience, including that represented by my own '5 x 5' model of mysticism.

There are also, I believe, other dialectics that exist in transpersonal psychology that we shall need to find creative ways of engaging with in the coming years. The most important of these, I think, is that between *descending* and *ascending* currents (cf. Chapter 1). This dialectic itself expresses itself in many forms or variants (e.g., immanence and transcendence, wider/deeper and higher, eco and ego, mundane and exotic). In the context of transpersonal theory, it is found particularly in debates that focus upon:

- Pre-axial (maintaining) and post-axial (progressive) agendas.
- Religious and non-religious perspectives on the transpersonal.
- Indigenous spirituality and the established world religions.
- Feminine and masculine forms of transpersonal experience and development.
- Spiral-dynamic and structural-hierarchical (ladder) models of transpersonal development.

As with the universalism-pluralism dialectic, our task is not, I suggest, to choose between what may be seen as conflicting approaches, but rather to find creative responses that enable us to see the spiritual truth that is expressed in both perspectives. In other words we need to adopt Both-And, rather than Either-Or, thinking and practice.[3]

In terms of the pre-axial/post-axial dialectic, we must cocreatively develop a post-post-axial vision in which psycho-

---

3   Both-and thinking is an essential feature of Wilber's concept of an integral-aperspectival *vision-logic* (e.g., Wilber 2000a) which, he argues first emerges at the Centaur stage.

logical, social and spiritual *progress* is sought alongside and in support of a focus on healthy *maintenance* of our physical and psychological being, our relationships, human society, and the planet. It is not a question of *either* progress *or* maintenance, but of maintenance-in-progress. In other words, we need a spiritual model that adopts the principle of *sustainable development*.

An important debate that I have focussed upon throughout this book is that between those who understand the transpersonal primarily in religious or quasi-religious terms and those who see the transpersonal and spirituality from a more psychological or humanistic perspective that is essentially agnostic or atheistic regarding the religious questions. Although it is not always easy to categorize certain individuals or movements (e.g., Ferrer, Grof, James, the Christian humanists, and some feminist writers), in the former camp I would place Wilber, Assagioli, Lancaster, Chittister, and most of the scholars of mysticism, whereas the latter group would include Maslow, Jung, Washburn, Wright, the transpersonal ecologists, and myself.

In terms of a way forward in this debate I believe that a first step would be for both camps to acknowledge the importance of the other. This means that those who advocate a religious viewpoint should explicitly recognize the many *non-religious* ways in which spirituality may be enacted by human beings. In return, those favouring a more psychological-humanistic approach should appreciate (a) that, historically, the religious impulse has been one of the most important expressions of human spirituality and, for many people, it remains so, and (b) that much of the important thinking on spirituality and the transpersonal has taken place in the context of theology, the religious traditions, and religious studies. Another way forward is for both sides of the debate to move beyond a view that polarizes those who have 'faith' and those who don't (cf. Lancaster, 2002). In fact, in my opinion, it has never been a matter of transpersonal psychologists either having or denying faith — it has always been a question of 'faith in what?' Maslow, for example, is a most passionate advocate of faith in the human spirit, while Jung has complete faith in the spiritual wisdom of the psyche. In this way, I think it is important for those who have *different* faiths (religious and non-religious) to realize that, as human beings and as explorers of the transpersonal, we share a common *orientation towards faith in spirit* that is, perhaps, much more profound than the different ways that, as individuals and groups, we may understand and express this faith. Of course, as will be clear from my earlier discussions, I am *not* suggesting that this common *orientation* should lead us to presume that we should aim to extract a common, perennial *philosophy*,[4] but rather that we should respect and honour the variety and richness found among the family of our different enactments of spirit (cf. Ferrer, 2002).

For those who would emphasize the role of religious experience and practice, it is becoming increasingly important, however, not only to recognize and respect the differences between the indigenous and 'major' established traditions, but also to find ways in which each may learn from and incorporate important lessons from the other. Within some groups and communities it may indeed become possible to cocreate a 'new religious movement' that itself integrates the vision and insight of both indigenous and established spiritualities. As transpersonal psychologists, we should, I believe, take particular interest in studying such transpersonal events (see, for example, Partridge's, 2004, excellent survey of new religions). It seems to me very unlikely, however, at least in the short term, that a large-scale religious movement will emerge that is capable of representing both indigenous and established perspectives.

The feminine-masculine dialectic is perhaps more difficult to *integrate* because humankind comes in a least two distinct genders. But we can at least, as transpersonal psychologists, acknowledge and investigate the differences between feminine and masculine perspectives on the transpersonal, including the possibility of differences in both experience and development. We will also need to recognize, however, that these investigations may be profoundly influenced by our own gender. In other words, a man investigating women's experience of the transpersonal may come up with quite different results from those obtained by a woman (and vice versa). I am not suggesting, as do some feminists, that only women can study women, or men study men. Rather I am proposing that a more integrative perspective may be obtained when we try, collectively, to step back and consider both men and women's investigations of, and

---

4   Perhaps the only common philosophical position that we share as transpersonalists is the rejection of an entirely *materialistic* worldview.

perspectives on, each gender. Despite our gender differences, as Jung has argued, we each have access to both masculine and feminine qualities in our psychological being (our contrasexual *anima* or *animus*). More importantly, perhaps, we also have access to these in our *relationships* (which themselves, according to Jung, are an important source of the *anima* and *animus*). Sexual relationships (platonic friendship as well as sexually intimacy) may therefore provide a fundamental opportunity not only for our own psychological integration, but also for interpersonal, social, spiritual and, perhaps, even cosmic integration (cf. the perspective of Tantra).[5]

The spiral-dynamic models of Jung, Grof and Washburn seem to contrast strongly with the structural-hierarchical (ladder) model of Wilber. For many years it has seemed impossible to find a way of bridging or integrating these two approaches.[6] Recently, however, Washburn (2003a) has suggested a possible way forward in attempting to open up dialogue between the two perspectives that have, unfortunately, polarized about a 'fault line ... leaving transpersonal psychologists divided into pro- and anti-Wilber groups, thus obscuring the rich diversity of views in the field' (*ibid.*, p. 6). Washburn's basic position is that these perspectives 'are not incompatible as general developmental points of view, that is, if neither one is forced to do all of the work' (*ibid.*, p. 5). By this he means that the structural-hierarchical model may be better at describing the development from prepersonal to personal levels, whereas the spiral-dynamic model may be more appropriate for describing transpersonal

---

5   Wilber presents a different perspective on the relationship between the sexes. He argues (e.g., 1997, 1998) that both men and women exist as 'agency-in-communion' but that men emphasize agency (and ascending), whereas women emphasize communion (and descending) — itself the combined result, Wilber believes, of biological, cultural and social factors. Both men and women, however, have 'profound similarities' (1998, p. 353) and progress, he suggests, through the same basic waves or levels of the spectrum, ending at the ultimate nondual stage at which all polarities (e.g., between male and female) are transcended. Only then, it seems, is agency-in-communion fully and equally realized by both sexes.

6   The psychosynthesis approach of Roberto Assagioli has both spiral-dynamic and hierarchical features, and might provide the basis for a more integrative perspective on transpersonal development, as represented, for example, in the work of Firman & Gila (1997). However, this approach has not been widely influential in transpersonal psychology.

development. This is because the dynamic potentials of the nonegoic core (including transpersonal potentials) are not, Washburn suggests, readily amenable to a structural-hierarchical analysis, but are better characterized and understood from a spiral-dynamic perspective. I have some sympathy with Washburn's view and agree with him that the two perspectives may be better suited to explaining different stages of development. However, his suggestion that the two schools of transpersonal psychologists should carve up the area between them is not, I would argue, particularly helpful as a recipe for integration. It is also unlikely, I believe, to be accepted by the structural-hierarchical camp, which would seem to be being asked to renounce its overall holarchical position and to keep its hands off the transpersonal. Only time will tell whether a new paradigm may be developed that may be truly capable of integrating the spiral-dynamic and structural-hierarchical positions. In the meantime, it is important, I suggest, to learn to live with and learn from the theoretical tensions between the two approaches, as well as to recognize the contribution that may be made by other approaches that cannot be readily fitted within the spiral-dynamic or structural-hierarchical frameworks (e.g., Ferrer's participatory spirituality, transpersonal ecology).

Another important dialectical tension within transpersonal psychology, not directly related to that between the descending and ascending currents, is shown in the ongoing debate within the field concerning the best way to designate our approach or approaches to study. Because, historically, interest in the transpersonal arose from the discipline of *psychology*, and because many of the important figures in the field were (and continue to be) psychologists, psychiatrists and psychotherapists, the term *transpersonal psychology* was coined early on, and has largely stuck. Yet this should not mask the fact that certain key players in transpersonal psychology are not themselves psychologists in the formal sense and may not fall within related disciplines such as psychiatry and psychotherapy. These figures include Aldous Huxley (essayist and novelist), Andrew Rawlinson (religious studies), Huston Smith (religious studies and philosophy), Michael Washburn (philosophy), and Ken Wilber (whose original training was in biochemistry). It is now almost universally accepted within the discipline that much of what takes place under the umbrella term *transpersonal psychology* is perhaps better understood as a broader *transpersonal studies*, or *transpersonal theory*, or as reflecting a multidisciplinary *transpersonal movement* or *transpersonal orientation* (cf. Boucouvalas, 1999). This is because transpersonal psychology does not solely address psychological issues or utilize only psychological methods and models, but rather incorporates contributions from many other approaches such as religious studies, theology, spiritual traditions, philosophy, anthropology, pharmacology, sociology, history, cultural studies and literature. Although I have subtitled this book 'Essays in Transpersonal Psychology' the subject matter that I have included goes well beyond a purely psychological perspective and therefore it might have been more accurately titled 'Essays in Transpersonal Studies,' or 'Essays in Transpersonal Theory'. My choice of subtitle was governed by two considerations: (1) the general currency of the term *transpersonal psychology*, and (2) the fact that I am a psychologist.

In general I very much support this multidisciplinary and multiperspectival agenda which, I believe, provides an excellent model of a truly integral (AQ) approach to knowledge. However, this does beg the important questions of what exactly *psychology* can offer to the study of the transpersonal, and whether, as transpersonal *psychologists*, we should aim to clarify the unique contribution that our discipline might bring to the transpersonal? Walsh & Vaughan (1993a) argue that transpersonal psychology should be understood as one of many (relatively specific) transpersonal disciplines that exist within the larger, multidisciplinary transpersonal movement. Transpersonal *psychology*, they suggest,

> is the area of psychology that focuses on the study of transpersonal experiences and related phenomena. These phenomena include the causes, effects and correlates of transpersonal experiences and development, as well as the practices and disciplines inspired by them (*ibid.* p. 103).

According to this view, transpersonal psychology should primarily concern itself with psychological questions and psychological methods of investigation. Friedman (2002) similarly argues the case for restricting the term transpersonal psychology to a strictly *scientific* approach to investigating the transpersonal.

According to Friedman, this distinguishes the particular perspective of *transpersonal psychology* from the more general approach of *transpersonal studies*, as well as from other specific transpersonal disciplines such as religious studies and philosophy.

What we have here, therefore, are two quite distinct applications of the term *transpersonal psychology*: (1) a convenient umbrella term for what, in practice, may be better characterized as *transpersonal studies*, and (2) the area of *scientific psychology* which investigates the transpersonal. My own view differs slightly from that of Friedman because I do not think that, in practice, we need to *choose* between these two definitions. I am more than happy to call myself a transpersonal psychologist in *both* senses. I recognize, however, that allowing both uses of the term can lead to confusion and may cause particular problems, politically, when transpersonal psychologists attempt to establish the scientific credentials of the discipline within the larger field of mainstream psychology, or when they seek research funding. My own preference (see Chapter 1) would be to restrict the term transpersonal psychology to the *broadly scientific* approach to psychological understanding of the transpersonal. However that does not mean that transpersonal psychologists cannot themselves also contribute to the larger debates within transpersonal studies (as, indeed, I hope I have done in this book). In practice, it is almost certainly too late to change the rather confused status quo, and it seems highly likely that the term transpersonal psychology will continue to be widely used as a synonym for transpersonal studies.

Friedman's (2002) discussion carries, however, a most important implication for transpersonal psychology. This is the imperative to carry out proper scientific investigations into transpersonal phenomena. The majority of journal articles and books in transpersonal psychology are theoretical, conceptual, historical, or comprise reviews of the literature rather than empirically based studies.[7] Yet many of the questions and debates that we have considered in this book are, at least in principle, capable of empirical investigation. These include:

7　Although it is not always easy to distinguish empirical studies, my own analysis of the first 36 volumes of the *Journal of Transpersonal Psychology* (1969–2004) suggests that less than one third of the more than 300 articles published during this period has any empirical content, in the sense of reporting first-hand research data obtained from participants.

- Are there universal sequential stages of transpersonal development?
- How may transpersonal experience and development differ between men and women?
- What are the major types of mystical experiences and how do they correlate with each other?
- What are the transpersonal experiences of children?
- How do people understand the relationship between paranormal and spiritual experience?
- What is the role of spiritual experiences in transpersonal development?
- What is the relationship between transportative and transformative experiences?
- What is the role of regressive experience in transpersonal development?
- What is the influence of perinatal experience on people's approach to the transpersonal?
- How do people become capable of evil, and how may evil be minimized?
- How can we develop beyond self-centredness, towards empathy, compassion and altruism?
- What is the relationship between self-actualization (the actualization of personal talents and capacities) and self-transcendence (metamotivation)?
- Are there different types of self-actualization?
- Are there different types of self-transcendence?
- Do different spiritual paths produce different types of transpersonal experiences, or different modes of transpersonal development?
- Are there gender, age or personality differences between people who follow hot or cool, structured or unstructured paths?
- What other factors might influence people's choice of spiritual path?
- What forms of relationship or community lead to the cocreation of transpersonal events?

We do not, currently, have full or clear answers to any of these questions. We can speculate as much as we like, but perhaps we should bracket or curtail further speculation until we have more informative research data. Of course, as I argued in Chapter 1, empirical research itself depends upon, and arises out, of theoretical and conceptual understanding, and I am not suggesting for one moment that we should abandon transpersonal theory or hermeneutics. Rather I am suggesting that the *balance* between theory and empirical research may need to be tipped in favour of the latter in order to achieve a more integrated approach to transpersonal knowledge. One rather crude but at least practical way that this may be enacted may be to aim for a more equal proportion of empirical and non-empirical papers in our academic journals. Another possible way forward may be for transpersonal psychology (which emphasizes hermeneutics) to engage in a more constructive dialogue with positive psychology (which emphasizes empiricism). Perhaps most importantly, however, we need to find ways of encouraging research in transpersonal psychology, whether this is by attempting to increase the number of funding opportunities in this area for PhD students or for post-doctoral research (which is currently woefully low) or by generally promoting a stronger research culture in the discipline, especially, perhaps, within the universities.

Finally I wish to draw attention to the dialectic in transpersonal psychology between academics and practitioners. Transpersonal psychology (in both senses) is an activity carried out individually and collectively by human beings who are, or should be, fully engaged, at all levels of their being, with the transpersonal quest. Having said that, some people and groups emphasize an intellectual, theoretical, research-based approach to transpersonal knowing. For convenience, I shall call these the *academics*. Other people place more emphasis on experience and practice (for example, meditators, members of spiritual communities, workshop leaders, spiritual teachers, users of psychoactive drugs, psychiatrists, therapists and counsellors, educators, managers, entrepreneurs, medics, or hospice workers). Again, simply for convenience, I shall call these the *practitioners*. Clearly, if I was forced to choose between the two, I would currently have to call myself an academic rather than a practitioner.

Sometimes there can develop a kind of antagonism or mutual mistrust between these two factions. Academics may be tempted to dismiss people's practice on the grounds that it is being undertaken with insufficient attention paid to its conceptual and theoretical assumptions and underpinnings. Practitioners may sometimes criticize academics for over-intellectualizing the field and for failing to appreciate the value of practices and experiences that cannot be tied neatly into any particular conceptual framework.

A basic assumption of the transpersonal approach is that research into the transpersonal cannot be divorced from a commitment to personal and social transformation, so that academics must themselves be practitioners *in some sense*. This does not mean, of course, that they must necessarily follow any structured system of spiritual discipline or only engage in action research. All it implies is that transpersonal academics will need to find some means to experience and express their developing spirituality. The basic model of the transpersonal researcher, therefore, is of the *practitioner-researcher*. In my experience, without exception, all of the academics I have known in the area of transpersonal psychology can be so designated. Interestingly, however, this may not always be the case in other, related, disciplines such as parapsychology or religious studies because, in these, the normative emphasis on *transformation* is generally less apparent.

In my opinion, we need also to recognize a corresponding model for those who might term themselves practitioners, who should therefore aim to become *researcher-practitioners*. In effect, this means that practitioners have an obligation to be informed about the practices they engage in, to study and learn from relevant theory and research, and, perhaps more importantly, to utilize their experience and knowledge to further their own and other people's understanding.

In the MSc in Consciousness and Transpersonal Psychology that we teach at LJMU, the emphasis is on an academic, scholarly approach to understanding the field. The programme is not a practitioner training, and there is comparatively little time that is dedicated specifically to experiential or practical work. This isn't because we value the academic approach above the experiential-practical, but simply because this is what we feel qualified to offer within the context of a Masters degree. However we make it explicit that students are expected to find ways of integrating their academic studies with their own spiritual development, and we have aimed to develop various ways in which the programme may encourage this. Our approach has been vindicated, I feel, in the creative and often moving ways that our students have taken on and often excelled at this challenge.

In terms of the wider community of transpersonal psychologists, I am making a plea not only for the academics and practitioners to engage in more regular and constructive dialogue, but also for each of us, and for all of us collectively, to aim to achieve a harmonious balance between conceptual and practical knowing in these areas. Head, Heart, and Hands are all needed in our shared quest for the human good and for the achievement of spiritual transformation in ourselves, our relationships, our groups and societies, our planet, and, ultimately perhaps, the cosmos as a whole.

Glossary

Absorption — A state of complete mental attention. See also contemplation, flow experience, introvertive mysticism, meditation, samadhi.

Advaita — A nondual school of Vedanta most associated with Sankara which argues for the identity of Brahman and Atman.

Agape — The principle of unconditional or spiritual love. See also Eros, Thanatos, unconditional positive regard.

Agency-in-communion — Wilber's term representing the need to integrate both masculine (instrumental) and feminine (relational) perspectives on development. See also feminist spirituality.

Agnosticism — The position that the truth of religious claims cannot be proven and which maintains the need either for faith or for the suspension of belief.

Akashic records — In Theosophy, a permanent memory of every event that has ever occurred, stored in the 'akasha' or ether. See also morphic field, species consciousness.

Altered state of consciousness — A state of consciousness different from the 'ordinary' states of wakefulness, dreaming, and dreamless sleep.

American Transcendentalism — A nineteenth century philosophical and literary movement that emphasized the union between the individual soul and the world soul or life force. Expressed in the writings of Ralph Waldo Emerson, Henry Thoreau, Margaret Fuller and Walt Whitman. See also romanticism.

Amok — A term used in Malaysia for a dissociative state involving violent outbursts. See also berserk.

Analytical Psychology — Jung's psychological and therapeutic approach. See also anima, animus, archetype, big dreams, collective shadow, collective unconscious, complex, ego, ego-self axis, god-image, individuation, initiation into inner reality, initiation into outer reality, mana personality, night sea journey, persona, psyche, quaternity, self, shadow, soul-image, synchronicity, transcendent function, unconscious, wounded healer.

Anatman — Sanskrit term for the Buddhist doctrine that there is no permanent individual soul. See also Atman, anatta, no-self.

Anatta — Pali term for the Buddhist doctrine that there is no permanent individual soul. See also Atman, anatman, no-self.

Androcentrism — A perspective that prioritizes male experience.

Anima — Jung's term for the unconscious feminine element within a man's psyche. See also animus, soul image.

Animism — The belief that a spirit or divinity resides within every object, controlling its existence and influencing human life and events in the natural world.

Animus — Jung's term for the unconscious masculine element within a woman's psyche. See also anima, soul image.

Anomalous experience — Unusual experiences and events that appear to defy known scientific laws. See also paranormal.

Anthropic principle — The suggestion that the Universe originated in such a way as to allow the emergence of life and mind.

Anthropocentrism — A perspective that prioritizes human experience and human needs.

Apollonian — A perspective that emphasizes rationality and order. See also Dionysian.

Apophatic — A theological perspective that denies that God can be known using categories of thought. It advocates a mystical 'way of negation' (via negativa) which involves knowing God through emptying the mind. See also kataphatic, sunyata, void.

Apotheosis — The elevation of a human being to the level of God or the gods.

AQAL — Wilber's acronym for his all quadrant, all level (also all lines, all states, all types) approach to knowledge and practice.

Archetype — Jung's term for collective structuring patterns of experience within the collective unconscious.

Aristotle (384–322 BCE) — Greek philosopher, scientist and pupil of Plato. Emphasized the importance of sensory observation of the material world. See also empiricism, entelechy, final cause, teleology.

ASC — See altered state of consciousness.

Ascending current — Wilber's term for an approach to transpersonal development that emphasizes transcendence and the elevation of human consciousness to higher, more refined levels. See also descending current, horizontal path, ladder model, vertical path.

Asceticism — A soteriological path of self-denial or self-mortification.

Assagioli, Roberto (1888-1974) — Italian psychiatrist and founder of psychosynthesis.

Astral body — In Theosophy, a subtle body that is the substrate for feelings and desires. The astral body is believed to be capable of separating from the physical body in out-of-body experiences or astral projection, when it is experienced as a replica of the physical body. See also causal body, etheric body, mental body.

Astral projection — The separation of the astral body from the physical body and its travelling to other places. Also refers to techniques for inducing such out-of-body experiences.

Atheism — The theoretical or practical denial of the existence of a deity.

Atman — Sanskrit term generally referring to the immortal divine Soul or true self. See also anatman, anatta, Atman-Brahman, no-self.

Atman-Brahman — Vedantic doctrine of the identity of the true self (Atman) and the Absolute or God (Brahman).

Aurobindo, Sri (1872–1950) — A Western educated Indian spiritual philosopher and teacher. His teachings emphasize the original involution of the Supreme Being in the material world and the subsequent process of material, biological, psychological and spiritual evolution which is directed towards the full realization of the Divine in the world. See also Auroville, circumconscient, higher mind, illumined mind, inconscient, inner being, integral psychology, intuition, Mother, outer being, overmind, psychic being, spark-soul, subconscient, supermind, integral yoga.

Auroville — A model township based on spiritual principles, near Pondicherry, India, founded by The Mother in the 1960s.

Authenticity — Term used in existentialism for living in a way that is honest to the self and that recognizes one's freedom and responsibility. See also good faith.

Autistic savant — A person who, despite severe developmental disabilities demonstrates extraordinary mental skills in a specific area such as mathematical computation, music or art.

Autosymbolic process — Natural tendency of the psyche to produce symbols.

Axial period — The period from around 800 BCE to 200 BCE which Karl Jaspers argues involved a major cultural and psychological paradigm shift in which there developed a focus on the individual and self-consciousness. See also bicameral mind, pre-axial, post-axial.

Bailey, Alice (1880–1949) — The founder of a neo-Theosophical esoteric movement based on a series of writings that she channelled from a spirit entity known as the Tibetan.

Bardo — Tibetan word for the intermediate state between one life and the next. See also rebirth, reincarnation.

Basic Perinatal Matrices — Grof's term for common patterns of psychological experience that have their origins in particular stages of the birth process. See also perinatal.

B-cognition — See: cognition of being.

Behaviour therapy — A therapeutic approach, based on learning theory, which focuses on bringing about adaptive changes in behaviour.

Behaviourism — A perspective in psychology that suggests that the discipline should restrict itself to examining observable behaviours. See also cognitivism.

Berserk — Norse word for a dissociative state in which the person becomes frenzied and violent. See also amok.

Bhakti — In Hinduism, an approach that emphasizes worship and devotion. See also Bhakti Yoga.

Bhakti Yoga — A path of Yoga that focuses on devotion and worship as means of achieving spiritual liberation.

Bicameral mind — Lit. 'two chambered mind'. Julian Jaynes' term for the mind of peoples in early civilizations whom, he claims, were not self-conscious or capable of true volition, but rather hallucinated directions for living from an 'unconscious' chamber of the mind.

Big dreams — Jung's term for powerfully remembered dreams that have significant archetypal or spiritual import.

Bioenergetics — A therapeutic approach that uses body work (e.g., breathing, movement) to encourage the expression of feelings and to relieve emotional and physical blockages. See also Holotropic Breathwork.

Biosphere — The sphere of living organisms. See also Kosmos, noosphere, physiosphere.

Bodhisattva — In Mahayana Buddhism, a being who holds back from final enlightenment in order to help others.

BPM — See Basic Perinatal Matrices.

Brahman — In Hinduism, the Absolute Supreme Reality, or God.

Buddha — (1) A South Asian spiritual teacher, Siddhartha Gautama, c. 564–483 BCE who was the founder of Buddhism. (2) The enlightened One. (3) In Mahayana Buddhism, any fully enlightened being. See also bodhisattva.

Buddhism — Religion based on the teaching of the Buddha. Denies the existence of a Supreme Being and emphasizes the achievement of enlightenment and liberation from suffering. See also anatman, anatta, bodhisattva, dharma samtana, dream Yoga, Dzogchen, eternal indestructible drop, inter-being, lifetime indestructible drop, Mahamudra, Mahayana, mandala, mantra, metta, nirvana, no-self, pratityasamutpada, rebirth, samatha, sunyata, Tantra, Theosophy, Theravada, Vajrayana, vipassana, Zen.

B-values — See values of being.

Cartesianism — A philosophical perspective that is based on René Descartes' dualisms between mind and body, or subject and object. See also Samkhya, subtle Cartesianism.

Catharsis — The release of powerful emotions.

Causal — In Wilber's model, the causal level refers to formless experience in which there is just the transcendent witness or the root of attention. See also causal body, causal self.

Causal body — In Vedanta and Theosophy the 'sheath' or subtle body that persists in dreamless sleep. The causal body does not experience mental forms but exists in a state of bliss. See also astral body, etheric body, mental body.

Causal indifference — Stace's proposition that mystical experiences should be judged in terms of their phenomenological characteristics, not in terms of what caused them.

Causal self — A term used by Wilber for the formless transcendent witness. See also frontal self, subtle self.

Centaur stage — Wilber's term for a stage between personal and transpersonal development involving the achievement of self-actualization, existential authenticity, groundedness, and mind-body integration.

Chakra — Sanskrit word for wheel. Chakras are believed to be centres of energy within the subtle body that are associated with different levels of consciousness. See also kundalini.

Channelling — A process in which knowledge (often of a spiritual nature) is communicated from some other being or entity. See also mediumship.

Charismatic movement — A movement in Christianity that emphasizes personal experience of the Holy Spirit, which is often expressed through healing, prophecy or speaking in tongues.

Chi — In Chinese philosophy, a vital force that is believed to be present in all things.

Christian humanism — A philosophy that promotes Christian values but sees these as expressions of our human nature and a process of self-realization rather than deriving from a transcendent God.

Christianity — Religion based on the life and teachings of Jesus, who is understood to be the Son of God.

Circumconscient — In Aurobindo's system, an antechamber between the outer being and inner being through which the greater knowledge of the inner being and of other realities may be accessed.

Cocreation — Ferrer's term for the act of creating spiritual realities through individual or collective participation in transpersonal events. See also participatory spirituality.

Cognition of Being — Maslow's term for a mode of cognition found in peak experiences that exhibits qualities of, for example, exclusive attention to and holistic perception of an object, self-forgetfulness, passive or 'Taoistic' receptivity, and resolution of dichotomies and conflicts.

Cognitivism — The currently dominant theoretical approach in academic psychology. Cognitivism adopts a positivistic approach to research and attempts to understand mental functioning in terms of information processing models. See also behaviourism.

Collective shadow — Jung's terms for the dark, inferior tendencies within the collective unconscious. See also shadow.

Collective unconscious — Jung's term for a non-personal, shared level of the unconscious which contains various universal archetypes. See also personal unconscious.

Communion — The mystical experience of loving union with God.

Comparative religion — An area within religious studies that examines the similarities and differences among different religions. See also psychology of religion.

Complex — Term coined by Jung to refer to a pattern of unconscious feeling and thinking that is focussed upon a particular object or theme.

Conditions of worth — Carl Rogers' term for the personal characteristics that we learn to express in order to be approved of by others. See also unconditional positive regard.

Connected self — Term used by feminist writers to refer to the self-in-relationship, in contrast to the sense of a separate self.

Consciousness studies — An area of academic research that focuses on understanding the nature of mind and consciousness.

Constructivism — The belief that all experiences are mediated and constructed through the influence of personal, social, linguistic, and cultural factors. For this reason, constructivism denies that there can be any genuinely universal experiences. See also universalism, essentialism.

Contemplation — (1) Early theological term for mystical experience. (2) introspective states of absorption.

Conversion — A profound change in religious beliefs.

Cool traditions — Rawlinson's term for spiritual traditions that emphasize that salvation is to be found through realizing the essence of the self. See also hot traditions.

Cosmic consciousness — A term coined by Bucke to refer to exalted and joyous experiences of our own deep connection to the whole universe, felt as a living and ordered Presence.

Cosmic synthesis — Assagioli's term for the individual expression of a larger or wider spiritual Reality. See also inter-individual psychosynthesis, personal psychosynthesis, transpersonal psychosynthesis.

Cult — A pejorative term for a new religious movement, particularly one that appears to be based on the manipulation and indoctrination of members.

Daemon — (1) In Greek mythology, both good and bad supernatural beings, intermediary between the realm of humans and that of the Gods. (2) A semi-divine guide. See also demon. spirit guide.

Daimon — See daemon.

Dark night of the senses — Term used by St John of the Cross for a process in which the senses are purified and less pleasure is taken in sensory experience. Often accompanied by feelings of fatigue, depression, aridity and alienation. See also Dark night of the soul, Dark night of the spirit.

Dark night of the soul — General term used by St John of the Cross to refer to the dark night of the senses and the dark night of the spirit.

Dark night of the spirit — Term used by St John of the Cross for a profound experience of darkness in which the very foundations of our being are shaken and we are subjected to various spiritual trials. By undergoing this experience, St John believes, God purifies the soul by fire. See also dark night of the senses, dark night of the soul.

D-cognition — See deficiency cognition.

Deep ecology — Term coined by Arne Naess to refer to the promotion of a deep sense of our connection to and responsibility towards all life on the planet. See also transpersonal ecology.

Deep unconscious — Washburn's term for the repressed dynamic ground. This repression occurs at the egoic phase of development. See also primal repression.

Defence mechanism — In psychodynamic theory, a psychological means by which the ego is protected from threats from the unconscious.

Deficiency cognition — Maslow's term for normal cognition, organized by the deficiency needs of the individual, which is characterized by diffused attention, partial awareness, egocentrism, active organization by the perceiver, contradiction and dissociation. See also cognition of being.

Deficiency needs — Maslow's term for lower needs that require satisfaction from the external world. These include physiological, safety, love and belongingness, and esteem needs. See also hierarchy of needs.

Deity — (1) A supernatural entity worshipped in religion. (2) A God or Goddess.

Deity mysticism — Mystical experience of a relationship to a Divine Being or Beings.

Deliverance ministry — Term used in charismatic Christianity to refer to activities aimed at releasing people from possession by demons. See also exorcism, possession, spirit attachment, spirit release therapy.

Demon — An evil supernatural being. See also daemon.

Dependent arising — See Pratityasamutpada.

Dependent origination — See Pratityasamutpada.

Descartes, René (1596–1650) — French philosopher, mathematician and scientist. Argued for the fundamental separation of mind and matter, or body and soul. See also Cartesianism, Samkhya, subtle Cartesianism.

Descending current — Wilber's term for an approach to transpersonal development that emphasizes immanence and the achievement of salvation through a relationship to the body, the natural world, and the unconscious.

Dharma — Sanskrit term used in Indian religions to refer to the divine way, divine Will, or spiritual teachings. See also Tao.

Dharma samtana — Term used in Buddhism to refer to the stream of mind-moments.

Dialogic — Term used in the '5 x 5' model of mysticism to refer to mystical experiences that involve a channel of direct contact and communication between the Other and the self.

Dionysian — A perspective that emphasizes the nonrational, impulsive and romantic. See also Apollonian.

Dissociation — A condition in which different psychological functions become split off from one another or from consciousness.

Divination — Obtaining knowledge using signs, omens or oracles.

Divine, the — General term for an ultimate sacred reality or Supreme Being.

Dream Yoga — A Tibetan Buddhist lucid dream practice that is believed to prepare the practitioner for the process of dying and the entry into the bardo realms. See also Yoga.

Dualism — (1) The Platonic or Cartesian doctrine that mind/spirit and matter/body are fundamentally separate realities. See also subtle Cartesianism, Samkhya. (2) The religious belief in separate and antagonistic forces of good and evil. See also Gnosticism, Zoroastrianism.

Dynamic Ground — In Washburn's theory, the fundamental source of psychic energy, instincts, and creative imagination. Also known as the nonegoic core.

Dzogchen — In Tibetan Buddhism, a meditation practice that focuses on the nondual realization of the emptiness (of self) and of all phenomena. See also Mahamudra, Rigpa.

Eckhart, Johannes (c. 1260–c.1328) — Also known as 'Meister Eckhart'. German mystic and theologian denounced by Pope John XXII as a heretic in 1329.

Ecofeminism — A movement that emphasizes the ways in which both women and nature have been dominated by men and which promotes the values of women, the body, and nature. See also feminism, feminist spirituality, Gaia, Great Web of Being.

Ecstasy — (1) An experience of intense delight and rapture. (2) a popular term for the psychoactive drug MDMA.

Ego — (1) The conscious, rational self, orientated towards the ordinary world of experience. (2) Used popularly to refer to a strong egoic personality.

Egocentrism — Focussing on egoic experience and the needs of the ordinary self.

Egoic — (1) Focussing on the needs and experience of the ego. (2) A stage of development between the preegoic and transegoic.

Ego-self axis — In Jung's psychology, a maintained connection between the ego and the larger reality of the Self.

EHE — Acronym for exceptional human experiences.

Elevationism — Wilber's term for one type of pre/trans fallacy in which primitive, prepersonal experience is elevated to the status of the transpersonal. See also reductionism.

Emancipation — Ferrer's term for the overcoming of self-centredness.

Embodiment — The full physical enactment and expression of spiritual knowledge and consciousness.

Emotivism — Term used by MacIntyre to refer to philosophical positions that are based on an assertion of personal preferences.

Empathy — Understanding the experience of another from the other's perspective.

Empiricism — An approach to knowledge that is founded on direct experience. See also positivism.

Encounter groups — Group activities in which people openly share their emotional experience with the aim of achieving psychological healing or self-realization.

Enlightenment — (1) An eighteenth century philosophical movement that emphasized rationality and humanitarian values. (2) In Indian religions, a sublime state of blissful spiritual realization and knowledge.

Enstasy. An absorptive state in which consciousness is withdrawn into the self. See also samadhi.

Entelechy — The actualization of a goal. See also self-actualization.

Epiphany — A sudden spiritual realization, insight or illumination.

Epistemology — The study of the ways in which we can obtain knowledge.

Époche — See rule of époche.

Eros — In Freudian theory, the life or sex instinct. See also Agape, Thanatos.

Esotericism — An approach to spiritual knowledge based on the study of secret teachings. See also exotericism.

Essentialism — The belief that there are basic universal features to certain experiences. See also constructivism, perennial philosophy, universalism.

Eternal indestructible drop — Buddhist concept (appropriated by Wilber) of a personal essence or karmic stream that continues from one life to the next until enlightenment is achieved. See also lifetime indestructible drop, rebirth, reincarnation.

Etheric body — In Theosophy, a subtle body that houses the vital life-force. See also astral body, causal body, mental body.

Evangelism — Zealous preaching of a religious gospel.

Evocation — In magic, the summoning of a spirit to appear to the senses. See also invocation.

Evolution — (1) The notion of progressive change in nature and/or consciousness. (2) In Aurobindo's philosophy the process by which matter evolves through stages of life, mind and spirit in order to fully realize the Absolute. See also Great Chain of Being, involution.

Exceptional human experience — Term coined by Rhea White to refer to a broad range of psychic, mystical, peak, and anomalous experiences.

Exegesis — The exploration, critical analysis and interpretation of meanings in a religious text.

Existential crisis — A profound crisis in which the person questions the meaning of their life or identity. See also noogenic neurosis.

Existentialism — A nineteenth and twentieth century philosophical movement that emphasizes the implications of human freedom and responsibility and our capacity for self-knowledge.

Exorcism — Religious activities designed to banish demonic forces. See also deliverance ministry, possession, spirit attachment, spirit release therapy.

Exotericism — An approach to spirituality that focuses on outer expressions such as religious observance, rituals and law. See also esotericism.

Exotic approach — Term used in this book to refer to an emphasis on exciting transcendental experiences and practices.

Experientialism — Ferrer's term for a general emphasis in transpersonal studies on inner subjective experiences.

Exteriorization — The external (physical) manifestation of an inner (psychological) process. See also psychoid.

Extrapersonal — Experiences and activities that involve a relation to something *outside* the ordinary self but not genuinely beyond, higher or transpersonal.

Extravertive mysticism — Term coined by Stace to refer to experiences of unity with the external world. See also introvertive mysticism.

Fakirism — The demonstration of supernormal physical or magical feats by so-called 'holy men,' especially in India.

Fana — Sufi term for the extinction of the self and the ecstatic union with the Divine.

Fascinans — Rudolf Otto's term for the fascinating and attractive qualities of the mysterium to which we turn for love, mercy and salvation.

Feminism — A cultural movement that emphasizes the ways in which women are dominated in society and which promotes women's experience and values.

Feminist spirituality — An approach which focuses on women's experience and understanding of spirituality. See also agency-in-communion, androcentrism, connected self, ecofeminism, feminism, Goddess, Julian of Norwich, neopaganism, permeability, pre/perm fallacy, Teresa of Avila.

Ferrer, Jorge — Spanish psychologist now living and teaching in America. See also cocreation, emancipation, experientialism, inner empiricism, mystery of being, myth of the given, ocean of emancipation, participatory spirituality, spiritual narcissism, subtle Cartesianism.

Fifth force — Term sometimes suggested for Wilber's integral psychology (but rejected by him). See also first force, second force, third force, fourth force.

Final cause — In Aristotelian thought, the end towards which things strive.

First Force — Maslow's term for behaviourism. See also second force, third force, fourth force, fifth force.

Flatland — Wilber's term for a mono-dimensional perspective that fails to acknowledge other perspectives or other quadrants.

Flow experience — Term used by Csikszentmihalyi to refer to experiences in which there is total involvement in an activity. See also absorption.

Focussing — Paying close attention to an object.

Formless consciousness — A mystical state in which one is aware, but there are no contents of consciousness such as sensations, perceptions, thoughts or feelings. See also causal, pure consciousness event, transcendent witness.

Fourth Force — Term used by Maslow and others to refer to transpersonal psychology. See also first force, second force, third force, fifth force.

Freud, Sigmund (1856–1939) — Austrian physician and the founder of psychoanalysis. See also primary process, psyche, psychodynamic, secondary process, unconscious.

Freudianism — Psychological theories and practices based on the work of Sigmund Freud. See also psychoanalysis, psychodynamic.

Frontal self — Wilber's term for the egoic self-stream, orientated towards the physical world. See also outer being, subtle self, causal self.

Fulcrum — Wilber's term for the major milestones of self development in the spectrum model.

Functionalism — A school of thought in psychology that emphasizes the behavioural functions of thinking and consciousness.

Fundamentalism – A philosophical or (more usually) religious perspective which advocates a rigid adherence to certain fundamental beliefs or principles, and is generally associated with intolerance of alternative views.

Gaia — A term used to refer to planet Earth as a living being.

Gestalt therapy — A psychotherapeutic system developed by Fritz Perls that focuses on developing the client's awareness of 'here and now' sensations, feelings and behaviours.

Glimpse experience — An experience in which the person has a sense of glimpsing some deeper reality that is normally hidden from awareness. Sometimes known as a 'peek experience'.

Gnosticism — A religious-philosophical tradition, originating in the period before Christianity, that emphasizes salvation through higher knowledge. A central theme in Gnosticism is the evil that is manifest in the material world and the need to escape this through magical or mystical practices. See also Zoroastrianism.

God — (1) The Divine, Supreme Being. (2) A deity, often male. See also Goddess, Horned God.

God mysticism — Another term for deity mysticism.

Goddess — (1) a female deity. (2) The archetypal female nature deity worshipped in neopaganism. See also feminist spirituality.

Godhead — Term used in Christian theology to refer to the ultimate abstract nature of the Divine, existing beyond God's personality.

God-image — Term used by Jung to refer to the archetypal image and experience of God.

Good faith — Term used by Sartre to refer to acting from an honest position that recognizes our individual freedom and responsibility. See also authenticity, existentialism.

Grace — The free bestowing by the Divine or a supernatural being of love, protection or other favours.

Great Chain of Being — The belief in a sequence of evolutionary development from Matter, to Mind, to Soul (and or Spirit). See also Great Web of Being, perennial philosophy.

Great Web of Being — The belief in the fundamental interconnectedness and inter-dependence of all aspects of creation. See also ecofeminism, Gaia, Great Chain of Being.

Grof, Stanislav (b. 1930) — Czech psychiatrist who pioneered psycholytic therapy and developed Holotropic Breathwork™. See also basic perinatal matrices, holotropic, perinatal, psychoid, spiral-dynamic, spiritual emergency.

Gross — In Wilber's philosophy (after Vedanta), the material, physical world. See also biosphere, physiosphere.

Groundedness — A sense of being fully embodied, whole, centred and balanced in ourselves and in relationships.

Growth needs — In Maslow's model, the needs for self-actualization and creativity. See also deficiency needs, hierarchy of needs.

Guardian angel — A spiritual being that is believed in Zoroastrianism, and also some Christian and new age philosophies, to watch over and protect a person.

Guided fantasy — A visualization technique in which the person is led on an imaginary journey, usually by verbal instruction. See also shamanic journey, vision quest.

Gurdjieff, George (d. 1949) — A Greek-Armenian mystic who taught that human beings are normally in a condition of 'sleep' and that we need to wake up to higher modes of consciousness.

Guru — Sanskrit term for a spiritual teacher.

Guru Yoga — A system of Yoga practice based on working with the dynamics of the guru-disciple relationship.

Hatha Yoga — Yogic practice that focuses on physical activities for promoting well-being such as posture, hygiene, diet, and breathing.

Heart — (1) The fundamental essence of the self. (2) the transcendent witness. (3) Qualities within the self that express love and compassion.

Hedonism — An emphasis on living a life devoted to pleasure.

Hermeneutic — Emphasizing the importance of interpretation, meaning and explanation.

Hermeticism — An adherence to occult philosophies and the occult sciences such as alchemy, astrology and magic.

Heterarchy — As used in transpersonal studies, this generally refers to the egalitarian sharing of power and authority, as opposed to hierarchical authority.

Hexing — Putting a curse on someone.

Hierarchy — (1) A sequence of progressively higher forms. (2) Authority based on position within a system of ranks or grades.

Hierarchy of needs — A theory proposed by Maslow which postulates a hierarchical sequence of human needs and motivations. See also deficiency needs, growth needs.

High causal — Wilber's term for a level associated with formless consciousness. See also causal.

High subtle — Wilber's term for a level associated with the experience of archetypal forms. See also subtle.

Higher mind — Aurobindo's term for the realization of higher wisdom and greater clarity of thought. See also vision-logic.

Higher Self — Term used in psychosynthesis for the true, spiritual or transpersonal self.

Higher unconscious — Assagioli's term for the realm of the unconscious that is the source of spiritual experience. Also called the superconscious. See also lower unconscious, middle unconscious, superconscient.

Hinduism — A diverse Indian religion that believes in a Supreme Being (Brahman) who manifests in many forms. Hinduism teaches the doctrines of karma and reincarnation. See also bhakti, mandala, mantra, maya, nirvana, Sachchidananda, Samkhya, Tantra, Theosophy, Upanishads, Vedanta, Vedas.

Holarchy — A sequence of increasing levels of wholeness. See also hierarchy, holon.

Holism — A perspective that views phenomena in terms of their properties as wholes. See also holon, holarchy.

Holon — A term coined by Arthur Koestler to refer to wholes which are parts of larger wholes. See also holarchy.

Holotropic — Term coined by Stan Grof meaning 'orientated towards wholeness' that he applies to a range of altered experiences that may, for example, be induced by psychoactive drugs, by Holotropic Breathwork, or other activities.

Holotropic Breathwork™ — A mind-altering technique developed by Stan and Christina Grof that involves lengthy sessions of altered breathing combined with loud evocative music and body work. See also bioenergetics, holotropic.

Homunculus theory — A theory that proposes that the human being is genetically pre-programmed and that development involves the growth and realization of this genetic blueprint.

Horizontal path — A route to transpersonal development that involves an expansion of our sense of self *outwards* into the wider world of other people, society and nature. See also ascending current, descending current, vertical path.

Horned God — Modern term for the archetypal male nature god. See also Goddess, neopaganism.

Hot traditions — Rawlinson's term for spiritual traditions which emphasize that salvation is to be found through a relationship to a wholly Other reality. See also cool traditions.

Human Potential Movement — A term used from the 1960s to refer to a broad range of humanistic methods and therapies which aim to promote self-realization.

Humanism — An educational and philosophical outlook that emphasizes the personal worth of the individual and the central importance of human values as opposed to religious belief.

Humanistic psychology — The third force in psychology that focuses on developing the capacity of human beings for self-realization and other 'positive' qualities such as love, empathy, creativity, and altruism. See also first force, second force, fourth force, fifth force.

Idealism — (1) An approach that promotes an ideal state of being. (2) A philosophical theory that emphasizes the primacy of the mental world. See also dualism, Platonism, utopianism.

Idealized self — A false self-system based on the introjection of other people's views of the self.

Identity — (1) The sense of oneself as a person. (2) The nondual mystical experience of oneness *as* the Real.

I-I — Ramana Maharshi's term for the ultimate Self, or transcendent witness, that exists beyond mental forms.

Illumination — The direct communication of spiritual knowledge to the mind. See also epiphany.

Illumined mind — In Aurobindo's philosophy a level of consciousness beyond higher mind that involves the experience of spiritual light and inner vision.

Immanence — The belief that the Divine is fully present in the natural Universe.

Inconscient — In Aurobindo's philosophy the material world (including the body) that, however, contains Sachchidananda in involved, concealed form.

Indigenous religions — Traditional religious beliefs and practices found among descendants of peoples who originally inhabited a territory prior to any colonization or settlement from outside. Generally used to refer to native religious traditions that are not represented in the major world religions.

Individualism — A perspective that focuses on the independence of the individual person.

Individuation — Jung's term for the process of psychological integration that leads towards realization of the archetype of the Self. See also initiation into inner reality.

Ineffability — The quality of an experience that cannot be expressed in words.

Initiation — In religious, esoteric and magical traditions, a formal introduction to the mysteries, to the hidden powers, or to a select community of practitioners.

Initiation into inner reality — In Jung's psychology, the second of two stages of human life in which the person confronts archetypal realities within the collective unconscious, leading to individuation. See also initiation into outer reality.

Initiation into outer reality — In Jung's psychology, the first of two stages of human life in which the person learns to adapt to the outer world. See also initiation into inner reality.

Inner Being — In Aurobindo's philosophy, a much wider (though generally hidden) consciousness which is more aware, more intelligent, and more knowledgeable than the outer being, or ego (which the inner being supports).

Inner empiricism — Term used by Ferrer for the tendency within transpersonal studies to ground inquiry in disciplined introspection and intersubjective consensus.

Instinctoid — Term used by Maslow to refer to the instinct-like nature of basic needs and tendencies within the self. See also hierarchy of needs.

Integral psychology — (1) The psychological theories of Sri Aurobindo. (2) Wilber's AQAL approach.

Integral Transformative Practice — A long-term programme of disciplined practice developed by George Leonard and Michael Murphy that aims to work on developing positive transformation and integration of body, mind, heart, and soul.

Integral Yoga — A system of Yoga practice that aims to integrate spiritual awareness into ordinary life.

Interactionism — An approach that suggests that there are both universal and contextual aspects to mystical experience.

Inter-being — Term used by the Vietnamese Buddhist monk Thich Nhat Hanh to refer to the interdependence of all phenomena and all life.

Inter-individual psychosynthesis — Assagioli's term for a wider form of psychosynthesis that involves the recognition of our interconnectedness and interdependence and the development of harmonious interpersonal and inter-group relationships.

Introjection — In psychodynamic theory the internalization within the unconscious of aspects of the external environment, including persons.

Introvertive mysticism — Term coined by Stace to refer to mystical experiences of unity at the centre of the self, in the Heart, or in the experience of oneness with God. See also deity mysticism, extravertive mysticism, monistic mysticism, soul mysticism, theistic mysticism.

Intuition — (1) Knowledge that does not result from direct observation or rational analysis. (2) In Aurobindo's philosophy an immediate revelatory truth based on intimate contact and union with the object of knowledge. See also empiricism.

Invocation — In magic, the inviting of a 'divine spirit' to manifest within consciousness. See also evocation.

Involution — In Aurobindo's philosophy, the process of cosmic creation in which Absolute Spirit stepped down and took darkened form in material substance. See also evolution.

Islam — A monotheistic religion based on the writings of the prophet Muhammad which teaches the doctrine of submission to God (Allah).

I-Thou — Buber's term for a relation of true dialogue between whole beings.

Jainism — An Indian religion that emphasizes asceticism and the perfectability of the human soul. Jainism teaches the doctrine of reincarnation and denies the existence of a Supreme Being. See also jiva.

Jiva — In Jainism, the reincarnating individual soul.

Jivatman — Term used in Indian mysticism for the individual soul.

Jnana Yoga — A Yoga practice that focuses on the gaining of spiritual knowledge and liberation through the intensive study of scriptures and the deep contemplation of spiritual ideas.

John of the Cross, St. (1542–1591) — Spanish priest, mystic, poet and friend of St. Teresa of Avila. Author of a mystical treatise on the dark night of the soul.

Judaism — The religion of the Jewish people, based principally on the Torah and the Talmud.

Julian of Norwich (c. 1342–c.1416) — English mystic, anchoress (hermit) and author of *Revelations of Divine Love*. Dame Julian's revelations emphasize the all-encompassing love of God, joy, compassion, spiritual friendship and a faith that 'all shall be well'.

Jung, Carl Gustav (1875–1961) — Swiss psychiatrist and founder of analytical psychology.

Kabbalah — Mystical tradition within Judaism.

Kant, Immanuel (1724–1804) — German philosopher who proposed the unknowability of things in themselves, although we must presume their existence. See also noumenal self, noumenon, phenomenal self, phenomenon.

Karma — The doctrine that a person's actions produce direct personal consequences for good or bad. Often linked to a belief in reincarnation.

Karma Yoga — A Yoga path of liberation through selfless action.

Kataphatic — In theology, an approach to mystical knowing based on positive affirmation, sensory and imagistic experience. See also apophatic.

Kosmos — Term used by Wilber to refer to the All (including the physiosphere, biosphere and noosphere).

Kundalini — In Yoga and Tantra, a vital energy that can be aroused and channelled up through the chakras, leading eventually to spiritual enlightenment or liberation.

Kundalini awakening — An experience of arousal of the kundalini energy, often occurring very powerfully.

Ladder model — A structural-hierarchical model of development that proposes a series of invariant stages or rungs that involve progressively higher modes of being. See also hierarchy, spectrum model.

Language mysticism — A form of mystical practice, especially associated with Kabbalah and Mantra Yoga, that uses language for bringing about spiritual development. This includes exegetical analysis of scriptures as well as contemplation upon and mental permutation of sounds, letters and words. See also exegesis, mantra, Mantra Yoga, speaking in tongues.

Latah — A dissociative state found in Malayan cultures, often caused by shock, in which the person shows heightened suggestibility and may imitate other people, animals, or environmental events. See also olon.

Levels — (1) Hierarchical or holarchical arrangements of psychological, social, cultural or spiritual achievements. (2) Wilber's formulation of a universal structural sequence of development. See also fulcrum, ladder model, lines, spectrum model, structural-hierarchical.

Liberation — In Indian philosophies, achieving spiritual salvation by freeing the self from the suffering and illusion of the world.

Lifetime indestructible drop — Buddhist concept (appropriated by Wilber) referring to the self that develops within a specific lifetime. Essentially equivalent to Wilber's concept of the frontal self. See also eternal indestructible drop.

Lines — In Wilber's model, the different aspects or areas of our psychological and spiritual makeup that each develop through the levels or fulcrums more or less independently. These include intellectual, aesthetic, moral, sexual, emotional and spiritual lines, as well as the different lines of the self. See also self-streams.

Logotherapy — Psychotherapeutic approach developed by Viktor Frankl that emphasizes the achievement of meaning in life. See also noogenic neurosis.

Longbody — A term used by Aanstoos and Roll to refer to our experience of a larger soul that extends beyond individual identity to include our deep connection to significant others, the land and possessions.

Low causal — Term used by Wilber for a level associated with experiences which are almost, but not quite, causal (formless). These include experiences of blissful union with a 'final archetype,' or 'final God'.

Low subtle — Term used by Wilber for a level associated with astral-psychic and paranormal experience.

Lower unconscious — Term used by Assagioli to refer to the Freudian unconscious of primitive impulses and emotionally charged complexes. See also subconscient.

Lucid dream — A dream in which one is aware that one is dreaming. In such dreams the person is fully conscious and often capable of controlling dream events. See also Dream Yoga.

Magic — Activities in which there is an attempt to conjure and utilize unseen forces. See also neopaganism, occultism, theurgy, Wicca, witchcraft.

Magical thinking — As used by Wilber, primitive or prepersonal superstitious thinking in which there is a failure to differentiate fully the self from the natural and social worlds.

Mahamudra — Sanskrit for 'Great Seal'. A method within Tibetan Buddhism involving the direct, nondual experience of the true nature of Mind. See also Dzogchen.

Mahayana — Sanskrit for 'Greater Vehicle'. One of the three major schools of Buddhism which is found mainly in Northern India, China, Tibet and Japan. Mahayana Buddhism emphasizes the universal quest for enlightenment which may be achieved in many ways, including the path of faith. See also Theravada, Vajrayana, Zen.

Maithuna — Tantric sexual congress involving the experience of Union.

Mana — A Polynesian and Melanesian word referring to the essential force or power that resides in objects, plants, animals, and people. See also animism.

Mana Personality — In Jung's psychology, the archetypal personification of the extraordinary inner power found deep within the unconscious.

Mandala — In Hinduism and Buddhism, a geometric design representing the Cosmos, often used a focus for meditation.

Mantra — In Hinduism and Buddhism, a sacred sound, syllable or word, used as a focus for meditation.

Mantra Yoga — Seeking spiritual salvation through the use of speech and sacred sounds. See also language mysticism, mantra.

Maslow, Abraham (1908–1970) — American psychologist and one of the founders of humanistic psychology and transpersonal psychology. See also cognition of being, deficiency cognition, deficiency needs, first force, fourth force, growth needs, hierarchy of needs, instinctoid, metahuman, metamotivation, metaneeds, metapathology, peak experience, plateau experience, prepotency, real self, second force, self-transcendence, third force, values of being.

Materialism — (1) The doctrine that only the physical universe is ontologically real. (2) A way of life that focuses on material gain. See also spiritual materialism, spiritual narcissism.

Maya — In Hinduism, the illusoriness of the phenomenal world.

Meditation — Various techniques of attentional training which aim to be helpful in the spiritual quest. See also absorption, contemplation, focussing, mindfulness, samatha, vipassana, zazen.

Mediumship — In spiritism, the attempt to communicate with deceased persons or discarnate beings using an intermediary individual. See also channelling, mental mediumship, physical mediumship.

Mental body — In Theosophy, a subtle body that is the substrate of thoughts, ideas, intellect and reason.

Mental mediumship — Mediumistic communication that focuses on the receiving of information rather than physical manifestations. See also mediumship, physical mediumship, spiritism, spiritualism.

Mental mysticism — Mystical experience that involves mental phenomena or psychological realities (archetypes, symbols, images, thoughts, feelings, etc.).

Mental-egoic — In Wilber's scheme, a stage of development that involves the development of egoic consciousness, the self-concept and personae.

Mesmerism — An approach to healing developed by the Austrian physician Franz Anton Mesmer (1734–1815) which involved the supposed transmission of 'magnetic' force to the patient, often resulting in the induction of a trance.

Metahuman — Maslow's term for the highest expressions of human nature that are experienced as divine or godlike.

Metamotivation — Maslow's term for a higher form of motivation that aims to actualize the universal values of being.

Metaneeds — Maslow's term for spiritual needs.

Metapathology — Maslow's term for pathological manifestations of the spiritual impulse.

Metaphysical — Existing in a realm that transcends physical or psychological realities.

Metaphysics — A branch of philosophy that considers the reality of invisible forces that may exist beyond the physical and psychological realms. See also ontology.

Metta — A Buddhist practice of loving-kindness.

Middle unconscious — Term used by Assagioli for psychological elements (e.g., memories, thoughts, feelings) that are outside present awareness but available to waking consciousness.

Mindfulness meditation — Meditation techniques that involve observing the activity of the mind. See also vipassana, zazen.

Monistic mysticism — Term used by R.C. Zaehner for the absorptive experience of one's own self or spirit as the Absolute. See also introvertive mysticism, soul mysticism.

Monotheism — The religious conception of a single and transcendent God or ultimate spiritual principle.

Morphic field — Term used by Rupert Sheldrake to refer to a structuring field that exists around and influences all holons.

Mother, The — Name given to Mirra Alfassa/Richard (1878–1973), the spiritual collaborator of Sri Aurobindo and founder of Auroville.

Mundane approach — Finding the transpersonal in the ordinary experience of living. See also Integral Yoga.

Mysterium — Term used by Rudolf Otto to refer to the Divine as a wholly Other object of profound mystery. See also fascinans, Mystery of Being, tremendum.

Mystery of Being — Ferrer's term for the indeterminate and profoundly mysterious nature of Reality. See also mysterium.

Mystic — A person who practices or teaches mysticism or has mystical experiences.

Mystic Way — Term used by Evelyn Underhill for the process of psychological and spiritual transformation and the achievement of the unitive life.

Mystical experience — The individual's direct experience of a relationship to a fundamental Reality.

Mysticism — An approach that seeks direct and immediate knowledge of a spiritual reality.

Myth — (1) A mistaken belief or half-truth, (2) A narrative story that gives meaning to human life.

Myth of the Given — Term from postmodernism used by Ferrer for the mistaken belief in a fixed spiritual reality. See also perennial philosophy, relativism, universalism.

Mythical thinking — (1) Thinking using the concepts and images of myths. (2) Archetypal thinking.

Mythmongering — The promotion of unproven and unhelpful beliefs and myths.

Mythology — (1) The study of myths. (2) A system of myths.

Nada — Inner sounds.

Nada Yoga — Yogic practice that focuses on working with inner sounds.

Narcissistic rage — Term used by Heinz Kohut for a powerful rage occasioned by a perceived threat to the self.

Nature mysticism — Mystical experiences that occur in relation to the natural world.

NDE — See near-death experience.

Near-death experience — A profound pattern of experience that may occur when a person has nearly died or has clinically died and then been resuscitated. Typical features of the NDE include a sense of peace, out-of-body experience, moving through a dark tunnel, the encounter with a loving light, meeting deceased relatives or friends, or spiritual beings, and a life review. See also negative NDE.

Negative NDE — An unpleasant, frightening or hellish near-death experience.

Neopaganism — Term used for a variety of new religious movements that are based on the revival of pre-Christian religion. Neopagan religions often emphasize nature, magic, and the worship of the Goddess and/or Horned God.

Neoplatonism — A philosophical school developed by Plotinus and others from the 3rd century CE which postulates the existence of a single spiritual source of all things (the One) with which the individual soul may be united in mystical experience. See also Platonism.

New Age — An umbrella term for a loose collection of alternative philosophies, religions and practices that emphasize spiritual development and a holistic perspective.

New religious movements — Religious groupings that have developed outside the mainstream traditions or that offer radically different interpretations of traditional religious belief and practice. See also cult.

Night sea journey — Term used by Jung to refer to the disturbing but ultimately transformational process in which the person is forced to confront the depths of the unconscious.

Nirvana — Term used in Hinduism and Buddhism for an ultimate blissful state of spiritual emancipation or liberation from ignorance and attachment.

Nirvikalpa samadhi — Meditative absorption without qualities, forms or mental content. See also causal, formless consciousness, pure consciousness event, samadhi, savikalpa samadhi.

No Mind — Term used in Zen to refer to nondual consciousness. Also known as Original Self.

Noetic — Referring to states of deep knowledge and insight.

Nondual — A state of consciousness or being in which there is no awareness of the distinction between subject and object, or self and other. A condition in which everything is experienced arising as the self. See also Cartesianism, dualism.

Nonegoic core — See dynamic ground.

Non-mystical experience — Experience in which there is no awareness of a relationship to a fundamental Reality.

Noogenic neurosis — Term used by Viktor Frankl to refer to a pathological condition of meaninglessness, inertia and boredom with life. See also existential crisis, logotherapy.

Noosphere — The realm of mind. See also biosphere, Kosmos, physiosphere.

Normative — Proposing a norm or ideal model for behaviour.

No-self — (1) The Buddhist doctrine that there is no permanent human soul or self. See also anatman, anatta. (2) The experience of no-self. See also No Mind, nondual.

Noumenal self — Kant's term for the real, unknowable self. See also phenomenal self.

Noumenon — In Kant's philosophy, the unknowable thing in itself, as distinct from the object of experience. See also noumenal self, phenomenal self, phenomenon.

Numinous — Term coined by Rudolf Otto from the Latin *numen* (God) to refer to a direct ineffable experience of the holy or sacred, stripped of its ethical and rational aspects.

OBE — See out-of-body experience.

Object — In object relations theory, a person or thing with which a person has a significant relationship.

Object relations — A psychodynamic theory of human development and method of psychotherapy which focuses on the ways in which we internalize relationships with significant others (objects) and later enact these relationships, often in conflicted ways.

Occultism — The belief in, study of, and/or manipulation of hidden forces. See also magic, neopaganism, theurgy, Wicca, witchcraft.

Ocean of Emancipation — In Ferrer's approach, the various ways in which self-centredness may be overcome.

Oceanic feeling — Term used by Freud for the experience of blissful, unbounded and timeless oneness with the world.

Olon — A Tungus word for a dissociative state very similar to latah.

One Taste — Term used by Wilber for nondual experience.

One, the — Term used in Neoplatonism for the single Absolute spiritual reality.

Ontology — (1) A branch of philosophy concerned with examining what is real, or what can be said to exist. (2) Beliefs about what is real.

OOBE — See out-of-body experience.

Oracle — Communication from a supernatural source in response to an inquiry. See divination.

Original Self — The nondual self of Zen.

Outer being — In Aurobindo's philosophy, the surface being (ego structures) that express themselves in our ordinary life. See also frontal self, inner being.

Out-of-body experience — An experience in which the location of consciousness and self appears to be outside of the physical body.

Overmind — Aurobindo's terms for universal mind or cosmic consciousness.

Oversoul — The universal soul or spirit of the American Transcendentalists.

Panenhenic — R.C. Zaehner's term for the 'all-in-one' experience of nature mysticism.

Panentheism — The belief that the world is a part of God, but that the wholeness of God also transcends the world. See also process theology.

Pantheism — The belief that everything is divine, that God is not separate from but totally identified with the world, and that God does not possess personality or transcendence.

Paranormal — Phenomena that appear to contradict scientific understanding. See also anomalous experience.

Parapsychology — A research discipline that investigates scientifically evidence of the paranormal, especially in controlled laboratory conditions. See also psychical research.

Participatory spirituality — Ferrer's approach to understanding how spiritual realities are cocreated through our participation in the Mystery of Being.

Patanjali (prob. c. 100–400 CE) — The author of the Yoga Sutras which describe the stages of Raja Yoga.

Patriarchy — A system of rule and authority based on power invested in senior men.

PCE — See pure consciousness event.

Peak experience — Term used by Maslow for moments of highest happiness and fulfilment. See also plateau experience, trough experience.

Peek experience — See glimpse experience.

Perennial philosophy — The belief that all religions share a common doctrinal and experiential core.

Perennialism — See perennial philosophy.

Perinatal — Lit. 'around birth'. Grof's term for patterns of experience associated with various processes occurring in pregnancy and childbirth. See also Basic Perinatal Matrices.

Permeability — The state of being open and penetrable to the world. Argued by Peggy Wright to be the essential feature of women's spiritual experience. See also feminist spirituality, pre/perm fallacy.

Persona — Jung's term for the archetypal mask or set of performances that forms our manifest personality.

Personal — (1) Relating to the individual person. (2) In Wilber's model, a structural level based on mental-egoic consciousness and the development of the individual personality. See also prepersonal, transpersonal.

Personal psychosynthesis — Term used by Assagioli to refer to the achievement of a well-integrated personality, centred on the personal ego. See also cosmic synthesis, inter-individual psychosynthesis, psychosynthesis, transpersonal psychosynthesis.

Personal unconscious — In Jung's psychology, the realm of the unconscious that contains elements deriving from personal experience, such as repressed memories and emotional complexes. See also collective unconscious.

Phantasy — Term used in psychodynamic approaches to refer to unconscious imaginings (as contrasted with *fantasy*, which is generally used to refer to the activity of the *conscious* imagination).

Phenomenal self — In Kant's philosophy, the ordinary, knowable self of experience. See also noumenal self, noumenon, phenomenon.

Phenomenological method — A technical procedure for investigating the essential qualities of an experience. See also phenomenology, rule of époche.

Phenomenology — The 1st-person study of conscious experience. See also phenomenological method.

Phenomenon — In Kant's philosophy, the fully knowable object of experience. See also noumenal self, noumenon, phenomenal self.

Phylogenetic experience — Experiences in which the person becomes aware of the evolution of life forms.

Physical mediumship — Mediumship that expresses itself in paranormal physical phenomena such as materializations, levitation, or discarnate voices.

Physiosphere — The physical, material universe. See also biosphere, Kosmos, noosphere.

Plateau experience — Term used by Maslow for experiences of serenity and peace as opposed to the high-energy peak experiences.

Plato (c. 427–347 BCE) — Greek philosopher and pupil of Socrates. Taught the existence of a non-material realm of perfect Ideas or Forms and a method of inquiry involving the constant questioning of assumptions. See also Aristotle, dualism, idealism, Platonism, soul.

Platonism — The idealistic philosophy of Plato. See also Neoplatonism.

Plotinus (c. 205–c. 270 CE) — An Egyptian-Roman philosopher and founder of Neoplatonism.

Pollyanna paradigm — Term used by Art Levine to caricature the ingenuous tendency in much humanistic psychology to believe that by looking on the bright side, everything can be made OK. See also new age, positive thinking.

Polytheism — The belief in and worship of many gods.

Positive psychology — A research approach promoted by Martin Seligman that focuses on the empirical study and support of positive emotions, traits and institutions.

Positive shadow — Unconscious potentialities for goodness and creativity.

Positive thinking — An approach advocated in much new age literature that emphasizes focussing the mind on positive outcomes and the making of positive affirmations. See also Pollyanna paradigm.

Positivism — A philosophical and scientific approach which argues that knowledge should be based only on direct sensory experience and experimentation. See also empiricism.

Possession — A condition in which the person appears to be controlled or taken over by another force, being or spirit. See also deliverance ministry, exorcism, spirit attachment, spirit release therapy.

Post-axial — Cultures and philosophical or religious traditions that developed after the axial period. See also pre-axial, bicameral mind.

Postmodernism — An approach that emphasizes the ways in which knowledge is constructed by the human mind and which rejects the notion of absolute truth. See also constructivism.

Pragmatism — (1) Looking at problems from a practical perspective. (2) William James' argument that metaphysical questions should be tested through the consideration of their practical consequences.

Prakriti — In Samkhya philosophy, the world of physical and mental substance.

Pratityasamutpada — In Buddhist philosophy, the doctrine of dependent origination in which all events and experience arise from a chain of causation.

Pre/perm fallacy — Peggy Wright's term for the mistaken assumption that permeable experience is necessarily prepersonal. See also connected self, feminist spirituality, pre/trans fallacy.

Pre/trans fallacy — Wilber's suggestion that many approaches to spirituality fail to distinguish correctly between prepersonal and transpersonal structures because both share the property of being *nonpersonal*. The pre/trans fallacy comes in two forms: Ptf-1 (reductionism) and Ptf-2 (elevationism). See also pre/perm fallacy.

Pre-axial — Cultures and religious traditions that existed before the axial period. See also post-axial, bicameral mind.

Preegoic — A level of development before the emergence of mental-egoic consciousness. See also ego, egoic, personal, prepersonal, transegoic, transpersonal.

Prepersonal — A level of development before the emergence of mental-egoic consciousness and the individual personality. See also ego, egoic, personal, preegoic, transegoic, transpersonal.

Prepotency — A term used by Maslow to indicate that the hierarchy of needs represents a sequence of decreasing levels of potency or subjective urgency. The lower needs are therefore *more* potent than the higher needs.

Primal repression — In Washburn's model, the repression of the dynamic ground into the deep unconscious that occurs with the development of mental-egoic consciousness.

Primal wound — Term used by Firman & Gila for the fundamental damage caused to the child's sense of self which results from the failure of adult caretakers to empathize with and mirror accurately the child's experience.

Primary process — Freud's term for thinking that derives from unconscious activity, need gratification and wish fulfilment. See also secondary process, tertiary cognition.

Process theology — A modern theological movement which adopts a panentheistic perspective and argues that God is involved in the cosmic process and in evolution.

Projected authority — Term used by John Heron for the tendency to invest spiritual authority in some external source (e.g., a teacher, book, doctrine, or group).

Projection — An unconscious defence mechanism in which unacknowl-edged threatening aspects of the self are projected onto external objects, especially other people. See also repression.

Pseudo-self — A false self-concept built up through the introjection of others' views of the self. See also idealized self, real self, true self.

Psyche — Term used in psychodynamic theory to refer to the whole of a person's psychological nature and experience, including both con-scious and unconscious layers.

Psychedelic — Lit. 'revealing the psyche'. A term coined by the British psychiatrist Humphrey Osmond to refer to mind-altering drugs such as mescaline and LSD. Also used to refer to the experiences induced by these drugs. See also altered states of consciousness, holotropic, psycholytic therapy.

Psychic — (1) Exhibiting paranormal awareness, (2) In psychodynamic theory, pertaining to the psyche, (3) In Wilber's model, the low subtle level.

Psychic being — In Aurobindo's and Wilber's philosophies, the soul-personality that evolves from one life to the next. See also karma, rebirth, reincarnation, subtle self.

Psychic immanence — Term used by Buber to criticize Jung's belief that God is an aspect of the psyche.

Psychic mysticism — Term used by Wilber to cover all mystical experi-ences that are tied closely to the gross (physical) realm. This includes extrasensory perception and other paranormal powers such as the Yogic siddhis, as well as all forms of nature mysticism and extraver-tive mysticism, including cosmic consciousness.

Psychical research — The scientific investigation of paranormal experi-ences and events, generally not involving laboratory experimenta-tion. See also parapsychology.

Psychoactive — Inducing alterations in consciousness. See also altered states of consciousness, psychedelic.

Psychoanalysis — Psychological theory and psychotherapeutic practice based directly on the approach and methods of Freud. See also psychodynamic.

Psychodrama — A form of group psychotherapy involving the dramatic enactments of emotional conflicts.

Psychodynamic — A psychological and psychotherapeutic approach, originating in Freudianism, that emphasizes the role of unconscious processes. See also object relations, psychoanalysis.

Psychoid — Term used by Stan Grof to refer to events and experiences which involve a mysterious or paranormal connection between mind and matter.

Psychologism — An approach that reduces transcendental or spiritual events and experiences to the level of purely *psychological* explana-tion. See also reductionism.

Psychology of religion — An area of academic psychology which examines religious experiences, beliefs and behaviours and develops psychological explanations for these. See also comparative religion, religion, religious studies.

Psycholytic therapy — Lit. 'mind loosening' psychotherapy which utilizes psychedelic drugs to facilitate the process.

Psychosis — Severe mental disorder involving a breakdown in the integration of the personality and loss of contact with reality.

Psychosurgery — The use of surgical techniques on the brain in an attempt to alleviate mental disorders.

Psychosynthesis — Psychological and psychotherapeutic approach developed by Roberto Assagioli which emphasizes the need to explore and integrate all areas and levels of the psyche. See also cosmic synthesis, higher self, higher unconscious, inter-individual psychosynthesis, lower unconscious, middle unconscious, personal psychosynthesis, superconscious, transpersonal psychosynthesis, unifying centre.

Ptf-1 — See pre/trans fallacy.

Ptf-2 — See pre/trans fallacy.

Puella aeterna — Archetype of the eternal girl.

Puer aeternus — Archetype of the eternal boy.

Pure consciousness event/experience — Term used by Forman to refer to contentless or formless consciousness. See also causal, transcendent witness.

Purusha — In Samkhya philosophy, the conscious being, soul or spiritual self.

Quadrant Model — Wilber's suggestion that a truly integral approach must recognize that all phenomena should be examined from a perspective that considers both (1) insides and outsides, and (2) the singular and the plural. This requires an integration of knowledge in the four quadrants of: interior-individual, exterior-individual, interior-collective and exterior-collective. See also AQAL, integral psychology.

Qualia — The essential uncommunicable qualities of an experience, such as redness.

Quaternity — The archetypal principle of four, which Jung understood to be an expression of wholeness, balance and self-realization.

Quietism — A form of mystical practice involving passivity, stillness and quiet contemplation. See also meditation.

Radical empiricism — William James' proposal that the empirical method can be extended beyond that of sensory observation of the external world, to encompass observation of internal mental states and processes.

Raja Yoga — A system of practice based on the Yoga Sutras of Patanjali which emphasizes control of the body and mind, the practice of meditation and the realization of samadhi.

Ramana Maharshi (1879–1950) — Indian sage and mystic in the tradition of Advaita Vedanta. Taught a method called 'self-inquiry' that involves focusing on the I-thought in order to trace its source to the I-I.

Ramanuja (1017–1137 CE) — An Indian Vedanta philosopher who taught a theistic belief in a personal God.

Real self — (1) Term used by Maslow to refer to the organismic self. (2) Used variously by different writers to refer to the true essence of the self that is distinct from the ordinary ego or personality. See also false self, idealized self, self-actualization, true self.

Real, the — (1) Term used by Hick to refer to the transcendent reality that is understood in different ways by different religions. (2) A fundamental but not necessarily transcendent reality.

Rebirth — Term used in Buddhism to refer to some kind of personal continuation from one life to the next. Since Buddhism does not accept the notion of a permanent self, this is not literally a reincarnation of the same fixed entity. See also anatman, anatta, eternal indestructible drop, karma, no-self.

Reductionism — (1) Reducing phenomena to a lower level of explanation (e.g., using physiological explanations for psychological processes). (2) Wilber's term for one type of pre/trans fallacy in which transpersonal experiences are interpreted in a way that reduces them to the prepersonal. See also elevationism, psychologism.

Regeneration in Spirit — Washburn's term for the process in which, following the regression in the service of transcendence, the person becomes transformed by the transpersonal potentials of the dynamic ground.

Regression in the service of transcendence — Washburn's term for the often disturbing process in which the ego turns back to face and reconnect to the dynamic ground or deep unconscious. See also regeneration in spirit.

Reincarnation — The belief in transmigration, or the progress of the individual soul from life to life. This progress is often seen as serving the purpose of spiritual evolution. See also eternal indestructible drop, karma, rebirth.

Relativism — A feature of postmodern thought which argues that all human activities must be understood as dependent upon context and that no absolute or independent criteria can be used to evaluate different perspectives. See also constructivism.

Religion — A collective system of spiritual beliefs and practices.

Religious studies — An academic discipline that studies religions. See also comparative religion, psychology of religion.

Repression — An unconscious defence mechanism in which threatening aspects of the self are pushed deep down into the unconscious. See also deep unconscious, primal repression, projection.

Retro-romanticism — Wilber's term for an approach to the transpersonal that has a romantic attachment to prepersonal experience. See also descending current, pre/trans fallacy, romanticism.

Revivalism — A group movement within evangelical Christianity that emphasizes religious awakening and conversion.

Rigpa — Term used in Dzogchen for the absolute nondual nature of Mind.

Ritual magic — The use of ceremonial activities for magical purposes.

Romantic poets — Group of poets, including Byron, Keats, Shelley, Coleridge and Wordsworth. See also romanticism.

Romanticism — An intellectual and artistic movement that began in Europe in the late 18th and early 19th centuries, expressed in the works of the Romantic poets. The romantic movement emphasized nature, emotion and imagination and rejected classical ideals and establishment values. An important influence on American Transcendentalism.

Rule of époche — A principle of the phenomenological method in which previous conceptions and beliefs are put to one side (bracketed) before investigating an experience. See also phenomenology.

Sachchidananda — Term used in Hindu philosophy for the unmanifest Absolute in its threefold aspect of existence-consciousness-bliss.

Salvation — (1) In Christianity, the condition of being saved or delivered by Jesus or God, (2) Used more generally to refer to the achievement of spiritual perfection or liberation.

Samadhi — Meditative absorption or Yogic trance. See also nirvikalpa samadhi, savikalpa samadhi.

Samatha — A Buddhist form of meditation involving concentration and tranquility. See also vipassana.

Samkhya — School of Hindu philosophy that forms the basis of Yoga. It argues for the reality of two basic principles: purusha and prakriti. The purpose of spiritual practice is to realize our true nature as purusha.

Sandbox syndrome — Term used by Marien to criticize an immature tendency within humanistic psychology and the human potential movement to focus on utopian ideals without providing a clear programme for their implementation in the real world. See also Pollyanna paradigm.

Sankara (c. 800 CE) — Hindu philosopher and founder of the school of Advaita Vedanta. Sometimes transliterated as Shankara.

Satanism — (1) Used by some Christians to denounce a range of occult and magical philosophies and practices, (2) Used by certain people to characterize their own philosophy and practice. Self-styled Satanists generally reject and react against the Christian God and Christian morality, focus on the fulfilment of egoic desires, and may worship an archetypal principle of evil.

Savikalpa samadhi — Meditative absorption with mental content. See also nirvikalpa samadhi, samadhi.

Schutz encounter — An intensive 'open' encounter group advocated by Will Schutz which emphasizes the body and energy.

Scientific materialism — A perspective that emphasizes the rational, scientific investigation of the material world.

Scientism — A dogmatic perspective that proposes that only the material world is real and that all phenomena can be fully explained using the principles and methods of a materialist science.

Second Force — Maslow's term for Freudianism. See also first force, third force, fourth force, fifth force.

Secondary process — Conscious, rational thinking, based on reality testing. See also primary process, tertiary cognition.

Self — (1) Personal being. (2) The ordinary ego or personality. (3) In Jung's psychology, the Self is an archetypal image representing the primal ground, totality and integration of the psyche (conscious and unconscious). (4) The soul or individual spirit. (5) The real self. See also causal self, conditions of worth, survival personality, false self, frontal self, higher self, idealized self, psychic being, self-actualization, self-realization, self-streams, subtle self, transcendent witness.

Self-actualization — Term used in humanistic psychology to refer to the full realization of a person's potential.

Self-centre — An object (e.g., a person, group, norm, value, role, belief, ideology or worldview) that serves to define and maintain the self-system. See also selfobject, unifying centre.

Self-centredness — See egocentrism.

Selfobject — Term used by Kohut to refer to the role that significant others play in creating and defining the self. See also self-centre, unifying centre.

Self-realization — Term used in different ways to refer to the realization of a better state of being. See also apotheosis, enlightenment, individuation, liberation, psychosynthesis, salvation, self-actualization.

Self-streams — According to Wilber, the self has three different lines or streams: (1) the frontal self, or ego, (2) the deeper psychic being, or soul and (3) the transcendent witness, Self, or Spirit.

Self-transcendence — (1) For Maslow, the transcendence of personal identity in peak experiences or through metamotivation. (2) For Frankl, the actualization of meanings and purposes that go beyond the self.

Sexual mysticism — Mystical experience that occurs in the context of sexual activity.

Shadow — Jung's term for the archetype of darker, sinister, hidden tendencies within the psyche that contrast with the consciously expressed ego or persona. See also collective shadow, positive shadow.

Shamanic journey — A healing practice in which the person undertakes a journey in imagination during which help is sought from spirit helpers or spirit guides who often appear in the form of animals. See also vision quest.

Shamanism — An indigenous spiritual tradition in which the shaman (seer or sorcerer) undergoes, in trance, a journey to the spirit world to bring back knowledge or power to heal the community. See also shamanic journey, vision quest.

Siddhis — Paranormal powers associated with the practice of Yoga.

Social mysticism — Mystical experiences that occur as an aspect of our relationship with other people.

Sociobiology — An approach that seeks a biological and evolutionary basis for social phenomena.

Soteriology — The study or doctrine of salvation.

Soul — Term used in many different senses. See, for example, Atman, causal body, causal self, eternal indestructible drop, jiva, jivatman, longbody, noumenal self, oversoul, psychic being, purusha, soul-image, spark-soul, subtle self, World-Soul.

Soul mysticism — Term used by F.C. Happold for the absorptive mystical experience of the essence of the self. See also enstasy, introvertive mysticism, monistic mysticism.

Soul-image — In Jung's psychology a general term for the anima and animus.

Spark-soul — In Aurobindo's philosophy, the spark of the Divine contained in all beings.

Speaking in tongues — The uttering of words or sounds that appear to represent an unknown language. Also known as glossolalia. See also charismatic movement.

Species consciousness — Memories and other experiences of humankind's morphic field, akashic records, or repository of collective karmic experience.

Spectrum model — Wilber's structural-hierarchical model of development. See also fulcrum, level, spectrum of consciousness.

Spectrum of Consciousness — Wilber's model for the development of consciousness through levels of the spectrum. See also spectrum model.

Spiral Dynamics — A structural-hierarchical approach to understanding the development of value systems within organizations and societies developed by Beck & Cowan.

Spiral-dynamic — An approach, illustrated in the theories of Jung, Grof and Washburn, which argues that transpersonal development involves recontacting the dynamic potentials within the unconscious.

Spirit — A term used in a variety of different senses including: (1) an animating principle; (2) a supernatural being; (3) consciousness; (4) the soul, (5) the transcendent witness, (6) the essence of the Divine. See also spirit attachment, spirit guide, spiritism, spirit release therapy, spirituality, spiritualism.

Spirit attachment — The belief that psychological disturbances can reflect the attachment of a spirit entity to a person. See also deliverance ministry, exorcism, possession, spiritism, spirit release therapy.

Spirit guide — In certain beliefs, a spirit entity or archetypal being that communicates information and guidance.

Spirit helper — See spirit guide.

Spirit release therapy — A therapeutic method that aims to release the person from spirit attachment. See also deliverance ministry, exorcism, possession.

Spiritism — The belief in a realm of discarnate spirit entities (e.g., deceased persons) with whom communication is possible. See also spiritualism.

Spiritual emergency/emergence — Term used by Stan and Christina Grof for disturbing and often overwhelming crises that may be indistinguishable from psychosis, but which represent a process of transformation and spiritual opportunity.

Spiritual marriage — The loving, blissful union of the soul with God. See also Teresa of Avila.

Spiritual materialism — Term used by Chögyam Trungpa for a form of self-deception in which spirituality becomes a subtle means to fulfil egocentric desires.

Spiritual narcissism — Term used by Ferrer for a focus on the achievement of spiritual benefits for the self such as sublime inner experiences.

Spiritual psychosynthesis — See transpersonal psychosynthesis.

Spiritualism — A spiritist movement that originated in America in the 1840s and became fashionable on both sides of the Atlantic in the late 19th and early 20th centuries.

Spirituality — A belief in spirit or a commitment to a spiritual perspective on life. Often used in a non-religious sense.

Structural-hierarchical — Theories such as Wilber's spectrum model and Spiral Dynamics that propose a hierarchical sequence of structural stages of development.

Structured path — Term used by Rawlinson for traditions that emphasize a systematic and disciplined soteriological method. See also unstructured path.

Subconscient — Term used by Aurobindo for the psychodynamic (Freudian) unconscious.

Subliminal self — See inner being.

Subtle — (1) non-physical. (2) In Vedanta and in Wilber's approach, the realm or level of thought and imagination.

Subtle body — In Theosophy and other esoteric traditions, non-physical bodies that human beings are believed to possess. See also astral body, causal body, etheric body, mental body.

Subtle Cartesianism — According to Ferrer, spiritual understanding that is based on a Cartesian split between subject and object.

Subtle self — Wilber's term for the deeper psychic being (soul). See also causal self, frontal self, self-streams.

Sufism — A mystical philosophy within Islam that emphasizes love and the constant remembrance of God.

Sunyata — Buddhist term for the experience of the void, or emptiness.

Superconscious — See higher unconscious.

Supermind — Aurobindo's term for a 'Truth-Consciousness' that is above all mental forms and divisions but arises as knowledge by identity.

Supreme Being — See the Divine.

Surface Being — See outer being.

Survival — The belief that the some aspect of the human being (generally the personality or soul) survives bodily death. See also reincarnation, spiritism.

Survival personality — According to Firman & Gila, a false self that, in the absence of empathic acceptance, is formed by adapting to the non-empathic behaviours, values and opinions of the caretakers.

Swedenborg, Emanuel (1688-1772) — Swedish scientist, philosopher and mystic. As a result of his own visionary experience in which he met and spoke with angels and spirits, Swedenborg developed a philosophy based on a belief in survival of death and the importance of developing spiritual understanding. Swedenborg's writings led to the founding of the Church of the New Jerusalem which survives to this day.

Symbiosis — Living together as one biological or psychological system.

Symbolic interactionism — A sociological perspective that emphasizes the social construction of the self. See also constructivism.

Synchronicity — Jung's term for external events that occur in meaningful coincidence with processes in the psyche. See also psychoid.

Synergy — Acting in harmony and collaboration, to the benefit of all parties.

Tai Chi — A Chinese system of exercise involving smooth movements that aims to produce a healthy flow of chi and a state of physical and mental relaxation.

Talmud — The collection of early Rabbinic writings which form the basis of Orthodox Judaism.

Tantra — An ancient tradition, which is found in both Hinduism and Buddhism, that focuses on awareness and use of the energies of the body, relationships and the cosmos for spiritual purposes. Tantra uses ritual and magic and is often associated in the West with sexual spiritual practice. See also maithuna, sexual mysticism.

Tao — In Taoism, the eternal source of everything and all change. See also Dharma.

Taoism — A Chinese philosophical and religious system which emphasizes living in effortless harmony with the Tao.

Teleology — The belief that everything develops towards the realization of a final cause. See also Aristotle, entelechy.

Teresa of Avila, St. (1515–1582) — Spanish Carmelite nun, mystic, religious reformer, writer and friend of St John of the Cross. Teresa experienced a number of visions, voices and mystical experiences, including those of union. See also spiritual marriage.

Tertiary cognition — Creative and integrative thinking. See also primary process, secondary process, vision-logic.

Thanatos — In Freudian theory, the instinct towards death and stagnation. See also Agape, Eros.

Theistic mysticism — R.C. Zaehner's term for the experience of loving communion or union with a personal God. See also deity mysticism, God mysticism, Ramanuja.

Theology — The study of the Divine or religion.

Theosophy — A philosophical system that derives from the writings of Helena P. Blavatsky who founded the Theosophical Society in 1875. Theosophical teachings are based on an esoteric interpretation of Hinduism and Buddhism and on the belief in the perennial philosophy at the core of all religions.

Theravada — Pali for 'Elder Doctrine'. One of the three major schools of Buddhism, Theravada adheres closely to the original teachings of the Buddha. It proposes that enlightenment is achieved through one's own spiritual effort and, especially, through the monastic life. Found chiefly in Southeast Asia and Sri Lanka. See also Mahayana, Vajrayana.

Theurgy — The use of magic to achieve spiritual salvation.

Third Force — Maslow's term for humanistic psychology. See also first force, second force, fourth force, fifth force.

Three eyes — Wilber (after St. Bonaventure) proposes three 'eyes' by which we may gain knowledge: (1) sensory experience (the eye of flesh), (2) rational analysis (the eye of reason), and (3) direct spiritual insight and illumination (the eye of contemplation). Each eye is a valid source of knowledge in its own right, and the knowledge obtained using one eye cannot be reduced to that of another. See also reductionism.

Token economy — The use of tokens as rewards in an educational or treatment programme that aims to change behaviour.

Tonglen — A Tibetan meditation practice in which the meditator visualizes taking negative and harmful influences into the self and sending out positive and beneficial influences.

Torah — In Judaism, the teachings given by God to Moses.

Trailing clouds of glory — The belief that a child is born not as a blank slate, but with an unconscious memory of its spiritual origins.

Trance — An altered state of consciousness in which the person is relatively unaware of the surroundings. See also dissociation, Mesmerism.

Trance mediumship — Mediumship in which the medium enters a trance state.

Transcendence — Going beyond or above the normal situation.

Transcendent function — Term used by Jung to refer to the natural tendency of the psyche to creatively resolve oppositions and to unify unconscious and conscious contents.

Transcendent witness — The pure subject of experience. See also causal self, I-I, pure consciousness event.

Transcendent, the — Often used to refer to a metaphysical reality beyond the physical and psychological realms.

Transegoic — A level of development after the emergence of mental-egoic consciousness.

Transformation — A profound change from our usual egoic, self-centred existence to some ultimately more satisfying or valuable condition. See also egocentrism, emancipation, transportation.

Transmigration. See reincarnation.

Transpersonal — (1) Beyond the individual or personal. (2) A level of development after the personal. See also prepersonal.

Transpersonal ecology — An approach that emphasizes the importance of expanding our concern and sense of self outwards to achieve a wider and deeper identification with the natural world or Gaia. See also deep ecology, ecofeminism.

Transpersonal psychology — (1) Sometimes used in the general sense of transpersonal studies. (2) Scientific investigation of the psychological aspects of transpersonal events.

Transpersonal psychosynthesis — Assagioli's term for the synthesis of personal ego and the higher self or transpersonal self. Also known as spiritual psychosynthesis.

Transpersonal self — Term used by Assagioli as an alternative to higher self. See also Atman, causal self, real self, spirit, subtle self, true self.

Transpersonal studies — Umbrella term for a general range of approaches and disciplines for investigating the transpersonal.

Transportation — Temporary alterations in consciousness that are not generally transformational.

Tremendum — Rudolf Otto's term for the awesome, majestic and dynamic qualities of the mysterium. See also fascinans.

Trough experience — Term sometimes used for the opposite of a peak experience, involving profound unhappiness, despair or suffering.

True self — Term used in various approaches to refer to the real self, as distinguished from the ordinary ego or false self.

Ultimate consciousness — In Wilber's theory, another term for nondual consciousness, or One Taste.

Unconditional positive regard — Carl Rogers' term for the unconditional giving of love and approval. See also agape.

Unconscious — (1) not conscious. (2) In psychodynamic theory, the realm of the psyche that is not available to consciousness. See also collective unconscious, deep unconscious, higher unconscious, lower unconscious, middle unconscious, personal unconscious.

Unifying centre — In psychosynthesis, representations or ideal models of the higher self that serve to create a link between this and the ego. See also self-centre.

Union — Term often used for a mystical experience of communion or identity. See also spiritual marriage, unitive experience.

Unitive experience — A mystical experience of oneness or union.

Unitive life — Evelyn Underhill's term for a permanent sense of living in union with the Divine.

Universalism — The perspective that there is one truth in all religions. See also perennial philosophy, relativism.

Unstructured path — Rawlinson's term for a soteriological approach that does not follow any particular structured system, method or disciplined practice.

Upanishads — Part of the Hindu scriptures that provide commentaries on the Vedas and which focus mainly on philosophical and soteriological questions.

Utilitarianism — A perspective that emphasizes the practical utility of actions in achieving the greatest happiness for the greatest number of people.

Utopianism — A social, political or religious approach which aims to achieve a state of paradise or perfection. Often used to refer to to the impracticability of such ideas. See also Pollyanna paradigm, sandbox syndrome.

Vajrayana — Sanskrit for 'Diamond Vehicle'. One of the three major schools of Buddhism, Vajrayana is a Tantric form of Mahayana Buddhism found in Tibet and Japan. See also Theravada.

Values of Being — Maslow's term for universal values that are basic in human nature and may be discovered in cognition of being. These B-Values include Truth, Goodness, Beauty, Unity, Aliveness, Perfection, Justice, Order, and Meaningfulness.

Vedanta — Hindu philosophical school that emphasizes the divinity of the soul (Atman) and the achievement of salvation through service, meditation and self-knowledge. See also Advaita, Ramanuja, Sankara.

Vedas — Early Hindu scriptures comprising hymns, incantations, rituals, meditations, mythology, metaphysics and cosmology.

Vertical path — A route to transpersonal development that involves the elevation of human consciousness to higher, more refined levels. See also ascending current, descending current, horizontal path, ladder model.

Via negativa — A theological approach which argues that God cannot be known and can only be understood negatively (i.e., in terms of what He is not). (2) A soteriological approach which aims to realize God though a path of denying all manifestation and of mental emptiness. See also Void.

Vipassana — A Buddhist form of mindfulness meditation which aims at gaining insight into the nature of mind. Vipassana entails witnessing the physical sensations and mental activity as these arise in consciousness. See also samatha, zazen.

Vision quest — In some Native American cultures, the ritual seeking of guidance from the spirit world through visions induced by isolation or fasting. Often undertaken by males as a rite of initiation at puberty. See also shamanic journey, shamanism.

Vision-logic — Wilber's term for a higher mode of systemic thinking that is capable of holding and integrating different perspectives that may formerly have been considered contradictory or incompatible. Wilber argues that vision-logic arises at the Centaur stage of development. See also tertiary cognition.

Visualization — Techniques of meditation or prayer involving the mental imagination of sensory (especially visual) experience. See also guided fantasy, shamanic journey, vision quest.

Void — The experience of ultimate emptiness. See also via negativa, sunyata.

Washburn, Michael — American professor of philosopher. See also deep unconscious, dynamic ground, primal repression, regeneration in spirit, regression in the service of transcendence, spiral-dynamic.

Wicca — A modern neopagan religion which uses witchcraft for benign purposes.

Wilber, Ken (b. 1949) — American writer and philosopher. See also agency-in-communion, AQAL, ascending current, causal, causal self, Centaur stage, descending current, elevationism, eternal indestructible drop, fifth force, flatland, frontal self, fulcrum, gross, high causal, high subtle, holarchy, integral psychology, Kosmos, ladder model, levels, lifetime indestructible drop, lines, low causal, low subtle, magical thinking, mental-egoic, One Taste, perennial philosophy, personal, pre/trans fallacy, prepersonal, psychic, psychic being, psychic mysticism, quadrant model, reductionism, retro-romanticism, self-streams, spectrum model, spectrum of consciousness, structural-hierarchical, subtle, subtle self, three eyes, ultimate consciousness, vision-logic.

Witchcraft — The use of magic, especially as traditionally practiced in rural communities. See also shamanism, Wicca.

Witness — See transcendent witness.

World-Soul — The animating spiritual force of the universe.

Wounded healer — Jung's archetype of the healing power that may be discovered by working through our psychological wounds.

Yoga — An ancient Indian tradition that aims to lead the practitioner towards spiritual consciousness and liberation. See also Bhakti Yoga, Dream Yoga, Guru Yoga, Hatha Yoga, Integral Yoga, jnana Yoga, Karma Yoga, Mantra Yoga, Nada Yoga, Raja Yoga, Samkhya.

Zazen — The Zen practice of mindfulness meditation, traditionally performed while sitting.

Zeitgeist — The 'spirit of the times' or general outlook of a period or movement.

Zen — A school of Mahayana Buddhism, found mainly in China, Japan, Korea and Vietnam, which emphasizes the path of meditation and self-realization.

Zoroastrianism — Religion of Zoroaster, originating in Iran, which is based on the belief in a universal struggle between spiritual principles of light and darkness. See also Gnosticism.

References

Aanstoos, C.M. (1986). Psi and the phenomenology of the long body. *Theta, 13-14*, 49-51.

Allport, G.W. (1955). *Becoming: Basic Considerations for a Psychology of Personality*. New Haven, CT.: Yale University Press.

Anderson, S.R. & Hopkins, P. (1991). *The Feminine Face of God: The Unfolding of the Sacred in Women*. New York: Bantam.

Ansbacher, H.L. (1971). Alfred Adler and humanistic psychology. *Journal of Humanistic Psychology, 11(1)*, 53-63.

Aron, A. (1977). Maslow's other child. *Journal of Humanistic Psychology, 17(2)*, 9-24.

Assagioli, R. (1991). *Transpersonal Development: The Dimension Beyond Psychosynthesis*. London: Thorsons.

Assagioli, R. (1993). *Psychosynthesis: The Definitive Guide to the Principles and Techniques of Psychosynthesis*. London: Thorsons.

Aurobindo, Sri (1970). *The Life Divine*. Pondicherry: Sri Auroindo Ashram. (First published 1939-40).

Aurobindo, Sri (1990). *The Synthesis of Yoga*, 6th Edn. Silver Lake, WI.: Lotus Light Publications. (First edition published 1948-55).

Bache, C.M. (2000). *Dark Night, Early Dawn: Steps to a Deep Ecology of Mind*. Albany: State University of New York Press.

Bair, D. (2003). *Jung: A Biography*. Boston, New York, London: Little, Brown & Co.

Barrow, J.D. & Tipler, F.J. (1988). *The Anthropic Cosmological Principle*, New Edition. Oxford: Oxford University Press.

Beck, D. & Cowan, C. (1996). *Spiral Dynamics: Managing Values, Leadership and Change*. Oxford & Malen, MA.: Blackwell.

Boorstein, S. (Ed.). (1996). *Transpersonal Psychotherapy*, 2nd Edn. Albany: State University of New York Press.

Boucouvalas, M. (1999). Following the movement: From transpersonal psychology to a multi-disciplinary transpersonal orientation. *Journal of Transpersonal Psychology, 31(1)*, 27–39.

Braud, W. (1997). 'Parapsychology and Spirituality: Implications and Intimations'. In C.T. Tart (Ed.). *Body, Mind, Spirit: Exploring the Parapsychology of Spirituality*. Charlottesville, VA.: Hampton Roads. pp. 135-152.

Braud, W.G. & Anderson, R. (1998). *Transpersonal Research Methods for the Social Sciences: Honoring Human Experience*. Thousand Oaks, CA.: Sage.

Broughton, R. (1991). *Parapsychology: The Controversial Science*. London: Rider.

Buber, M. (1970). (trans. W. Kaufmann). *I and Thou*. Edinburgh: T. & T. Clark.

Buber, M. (1988). *Eclipse of God: Studies in the Relation between Religion and Philosophy*. Atlantic Highlands, NJ.: Humanities Press International.

Bucke, R.M. (2001). *Cosmic Consciousness: A Study on the Evolution of the Human Mind*. Bedford, MA.: Applewood Books. (First published 1901).

Butler, C. (1922). *Western Mysticism: The Teaching of SS. Augustine, Gregory and Bernard on Contemplation and the Contemplative Life*. London: Constable.

Campbell, J. (1975). *The Hero with a Thousand Faces*. London: Sphere.

Campbell, J. (1976). *The Masks of God: Primitive Mythology*. Harmondsworth, Middlesex: Penguin.

Campbell, J. (1985). *Myths to Live By*. London: Paladin.

Caplan, M., Hartelius, G. & Rardin, M.A. (2003). Contemporary viewpoints on transpersonal psychology. *Journal of Transpersonal Psychology, 35(2)*, 143-162.

Chittister, J.D. (1998). *Heart of Flesh: A Feminist Spirituality for Women and Men*. Grand Rapids/Cambridge: Eerdmans, & Toronto: Novalis.

Chodorow, N. (1978). *The Reproduction of Mothering*. Berkeley: University of California Press.

Christ, C.P. (2004). *Rebirth of the Goddess: Finding Meaning in Feminist Spirituality*. New York & London: Routledge.

Clarke, I. (Ed.). (2001). *Psychosis and Spirituality: Exploring the New Frontier*. London: Whurr.

Collins, P. (nd.). 'Integral Approach: A Comparison of Underhill and Wilber'. Accessed 18th April 2005 from http://indigo.ie/~peter/underhill.html

Cortright, B. (1997). *Psychotherapy and Spirit: Theory and Practice in Transpersonal Psychotherapy*. Albany: State University of New York Press.

Csikszentmihalyi, M. (1990). *Flow: The Psychology of Optimal Experience*. New York: Harper & Row.

Dalal, A.S. (2001). *A Greater Psychology: An Introduction to Sri Aurobindo's Psychological Thought*. New York: Tarcher/Putnam.

Daniels, M. (1981). *Morality and the Person: An Examination of the Relationship of Moral Development to Self-Actualization, Mental Disorder, and Personality*. Unpublished doctoral dissertation, University of Leeds.

Daniels, M. (1982). The development of the concept of self-actualization in the writings of Abraham Maslow. *Current Psychological Reviews, 2(1)*, 61-76.

Daniels, M. (1988). The myth of self-actualization. *Journal of Humanistic Psychology, 28(1)*, 7-38.

Daniels, M. (1992). *Self-Discovery the Jungian Way: The Watchword Technique.* London & New York: Routledge.

Daniels, M. (1997). Holism, integration and the transpersonal. *Transpersonal Psychology Review, 1(3)*, 12-16.

Daniels, M. (1998). Transpersonal psychology and the paranormal. *Transpersonal Psychology Review, 2(3)*, 17-31.

Daniels, M. (2000). The shadow in transpersonal psychology. *Transpersonal Psychology Review, 4(3)*, 29-43.

Daniels, M. (2001a). Towards a transpersonal psychology of evil. *Transpersonal Psychology Review, 5(1)*, 15-27.

Daniels, M. (2001b). On transcendence in transpersonal psychology. *Transpersonal Psychology Review, 5(2)*, 3-11.

Daniels, M. (2002a). The transpersonal self: 1. A psychohistory and phenomenology of the soul. *Transpersonal Psychology Review, 6(1)*, 17-28.

Daniels, M. (2002b). The transpersonal self: 2. Comparing seven psychological theories. *Transpersonal Psychology Review*, 6(2), 4-21.

Daniels, M. (2003). Making sense of mysticism. *Transpersonal Psychology Review*, 7(1), 39-55.

De Martino, E. (1988). *Primitive Magic: The Psychic Powers of Shamans and Sorcerers.* Bridport, Dorset: Prism Press.

Dennett, D.C. (1991). *Consciousness Explained.* Harmondsworth, Middlesex: Penguin.

Doblin, R. (1991). Pahnke's 'Good Friday' experiment: A long-term follow-up and methodological critique. *Journal of Transpersonal Psychology*, 23(1), 1-28.

Eliade, M. (1968). *Myths, Dreams, and Mysteries: The Encounter between Contemporary Faiths and Archaic Reality.* London: Collins.

Ellenberger, H. (1970). *The Discovery of the Unconscious.* New York: Basic Books.

Ellis, A. (nd). 'Achieving self-actualization'. Accessed 15th April 2005 from http://web.archive.org/web/19980118214914/www.irebt.org/essays/achieve1.html

Feinstein, D. & Krippner, S. (1997). *The Mythic Path: Discovering the Guiding Stories of Your Past – Creating a Vision for Your Future.* New York: Tarcher/Putnam.

Fenwick, P. & Fenwick, E. (1995). *The Truth in the Light: An Investigation of Over 300 Near-Death Experiences.* London: Headline.

Ferguson, M. (1980). *The Aquarian Conspiracy: Personal and Social Transformation in the 1980s.* London: Paladin Books.

Ferrer, J.N. (2000). 'Transpersonal Knowledge: A Participatory Approach to Transpersonal Phenomena'. In T. Hart, P.L. Nelson & K. Puhakka (Eds.). *Transpersonal Knowing: Exploring the Horizon of Consciousness.* Albany: State University of New York Press. pp. 213-252.

Ferrer, J.N. (2002). *Revisioning Transpersonal Theory: A Participatory Vision of Human Spirituality*. Albany: State University of New York Press.

Ferrer, J.N. (2005). 'Spiritual Knowing: A Participatory Understanding'. In C. Clarke (Ed.). *Ways of Knowing: Science and Mysticism Today*. Exeter: Imprint Academic. pp. 107-128.

Firman, J. & Gila, A. (1997). *The Primal Wound: A Transpersonal View of Trauma, Addiction, and Growth*. Albany: State University of New York Press.

Flournoy, T. (1903). Les principes de la psychologie religieuse. *Archives de Psychologie, 2,* 33-57.

Fontana, D. (2003). *Psychology, Religion, and Spirituality*. Leicester: BPS Blackwell.

Forman, R.K.C. (1998). What does mysticism have to teach us about consciousness? *Journal of Consciousness Studies, 5(2),* 185-201.

Fox, W. (1990). Transpersonal ecology: 'Psychologizing' ecophilosophy. *Journal of Transpersonal Psychology, 22(1),* 59-96.

Fox, W. (1993). 'Transpersonal Ecology'. In R. Walsh & F. Vaughan (Eds.). *Paths Beyond Ego: The Transpersonal Vision*. Los Angeles, CA.: Jeremy P. Tarcher / Perigee. pp. 240-241.

Fox, W. (1995). *Toward a Transpersonal Ecology*. Albany: State University of New York Press.

Frankl, V. (1966). Self-transcendence as a human phenomenon. *Journal of Humanistic Psychology, 6(2),* 97-106.

Frankl, V.E. (1967). *Psychotherapy and Existentialism: Selected Papers on Logotherapy*. New York: Simon & Schuster.

Frankl, V.E. (1966). Self-transcendence as a human phenomenon. *Journal of Humanistic Psychology, 6(2),* 97-106.

Freeman, A. (2001). *God in Us: A Case for Christian Humanism*. Exeter: Imprint Academic.

Fremantle, F. & Trungpa, C. (Trans.). (1992). *The Tibetan Book of the Dead : The Great Liberation Through Hearing in the Bardo*. Boston & London: Shambhala.

Freud, S. (1920). 'Beyond the Pleasure Principle'. In J. Strachey (Ed. and Trans.), *The Standard Edition of the Complete Psychological Works of Sigmund Freud (Vol. 18)*. London: Hogarth Press, 1953-1966. (Originally published 1920).

Frick, W.B. (1982). Conceptual foundations of self-actualization: A contribution to motivation theory. *Journal of Humanistic Psychology, 22(4),* 33-52.

Friedman, H. (2002). Transpersonal psychology as a scientific field. *International Journal of Transpersonal Studies, 21,* 175-187.

Friedman, M. (1967). *To Deny our Nothingness: Contemporary Images of Man*. New York: Delacorte.

Friedman, M. (1974). *The Hidden Human Image*. New York: Delacorte.

Friedman, M. (1976). Aiming at the self: The paradox of encounter and the human potential movement. *Journal of Humanistic Psychology, 16(2)*, 5–34.

Fromm, E. (1947). *Man for Himself: An Inquiry into the Psychology of Ethics.* New York: Holt, Rinehart & Winston.

Fromm, E. (1964). *The Heart of Man: Its Genius for Good and Evil.* New York, Evanston & London: Harper & Row.

Fromm, E. (1973). *The Anatomy of Human Destructiveness.* New York: Holt, Rinehart & Winston.

Geller, L. (1982). The failure of self-actualization theory: A critique of Carl Rogers and Abraham Maslow. *Journal of Humanistic Psychology, 22(2)*, 56–73.

Geller, L. (1984). Another look at self-actualization. *Journal of Humanistic Psychology, 24(2)*, 93–106.

Gilligan, C. (1993). *In a Different Voice: Psychological Theory and Women's Development.* Cambridge: Harvard University Press.

Gimello, R.M. (1978). 'Mysticism and Meditation'. In S.T. Katz (Ed.), *Mysticism and Philosophical Analysis.* New York: Oxford University Press. pp. 170–199.

Gimello, R.M. (1983). 'Mysticism in its Contexts'. In S.T. Katz (Ed.), *Mysticism and Religious Traditions.* New York: Oxford University Press. pp. 61–88.

Ginsburg, C. (1984). Toward a somatic understanding of self: A reply to Leonard Geller. *Journal of Humanistic Psychology, 24(2)*, 66–92.

Green, E.E. & Green, A.M. (1986). 'Biofeedback and States of Consciousness'. In B.B. Wolman & M. Ullman (Eds.) *Handbook of States of Consciousness.* New York: Van Nostrand Reinhold.

Grof, C. & Grof, S. (1995). *The Stormy Search for the Self: Understanding and Living with Spiritual Emergency.* London: Thorsons.

Grof, S. (1988). *The Adventure of Self-discovery.* Albany: State University of New York Press.

Grof, S. (1993). *The Holotropic Mind: The Three Levels of Human Consciousness and How They Shape Our Lives.* New York: HarperCollins.

Grof, S. (1998). *The Cosmic Game: Explorations of the Frontiers of Human Consciousness.* Albany: State University of New York Press.

Grof, S. (2000). *Psychology of the Future: Lessons from Modern Consciousness Research.* Albany: State University of New York Press.

Grosso, M. (1997). 'The Parapsychology of God'. In C.T. Tart (Ed.). *Body, Mind, Spirit: Exploring the Parapsychology of Spirituality.* Charlottesville, VA.: Hampton Roads. pp. 101–117.

Grosso, M. (2001). 'Psi Research and Transpersonal Psychology: Some Points of Mutual Support'. In D. Lorimer (Ed.). *Thinking Beyond the Brain: A Wider Science of Consciousness.* Edinburgh: Floris Books. pp. 101–121.

Hackforth, R. (Ed.). (1972). *Plato's Phaedrus.* Cambridge: Cambridge University Press.

Hale, C.S. (1992). Psychocatabolism and the dark night of the self. *Journal of Humanistic Psychology, 32(1)*, 65–89.

Happold, F.C. (1970). *Mysticism: A Study and an Anthology*, Rev. Edn. Harmondsworth, Middlesex: Penguin Books.

Hardy, A. (1979). *The Spiritual Nature of Man: A Study of Contemporary Religious Experience.* Oxford: Clarendon Press.

Harman, W.W. (1993). Towards an adequate epistemology for the scientific exploration of consciousness. *Journal of Scientific Exploration, 7*, 133–143.

Harner, M. (1980). *The Way of the Shaman.* New York: Harper & Row.

Hartshorne, C. (1964). *Man's Vision of God and the Logic of Theism.* Hamden, CN.: Archon Books.

Haynes, R. (1970). *Philosopher King: The Humanist Pope Benedict XIV.* London: Weidenfeld & Nicolson.

Hendlin, S.J. (1983). Pernicious oneness. *Journal of Humanistic Psychology, 23(3)*, 61–81.

Heron, J. (1988). *Cosmic Psychology.* London: Endymion Press.

Heron, J. (1998). *Sacred Science: Person-Centred Inquiry into the Spiritual and the Subtle.* Ross-on-Wye: PCCS Books.

Herzberg, F., Mausner, B. & Snyderman, B.B. (1993). *The Motivation to Work.* Piscataway, NJ.: Transaction.

Hick, J. (1989). *An Interpretation of Religion: Human Responses to the Transcendent.* Basingstoke & New York: Palgrave.

Hillman, J. (1977). *Re-visioning Psychology.* New York: Harper Perennial.

Holt, J. (2005). 'Creativity as the Immune System of the Mind and the Source of the Mythic'. In. C. Clarke (Ed.). *Ways of Knowing: Science and Mysticism Today.* Exeter: Imprint Academic. pp. 34–50.

Hood, R.W., Jr. (1975). The construction and preliminary validation of a measure of reported mystical experience. *Journal for the Scientific Study of Religion, 14*, 29–41.

Hood, RW., Jr., Morris, R.J. & Watson, P.J. (1993). Further factor analysis of Hood's Mysticism Scale. *Psychological Reports, 3*, 1176–1178.

Horne, J. (1978). *Beyond Mysticism.* Waterloo: Wilfrid Laurier University Press.

Horney, K. (1950). *Neurosis and Human Growth: The Struggle Toward Self-Realization.* New York: Norton.

Huxley, A. (1947). *The Perennial Philosophy.* London: Chatto & Windus.

Huxley, A. (1954). *The Doors of Perception.* New York: Harper.

Irwin, H.J. (2004). *An Introduction to Parapsychology*, 4th Edn. Jefferson, North Carolina: McFarland.

Jacobi, J. (1968). *The Psychology of C.G. Jung: An Introduction with Illustrations.* 7th Edn. London & Henley: Routledge & Kegan Paul.

Jaffe, D. T. (1985). Self-renewal: personal transformation following extreme trauma. *Journal of Humanistic Psychology, 25(4)*, 99–124.

James, W. (1960). *The Varieties of Religious Experience: A Study of Human Nature.* London: Fontana. (First published 1902).

James, W. (1979). *The Will to Believe and Other Essays in Popular Philosophy*. Cambridge, MA.: Harvard University Press. (First published 1897).

Jaspers, K. (1977). *The Origin and Goal of History*. Westport CT.: Greenwood Press Reprint. (Originally published in German 1949).

Jaynes, J. (1993). *The Origin of Consciousness in the Breakdown of the Bicameral Mind*. London: Penguin Books.

John of the Cross, Saint (1991). 'The Dark Night'. In *The Collected Works of Saint John of the Cross*. Rev. Edn. Trans. K. Kavanaugh & O. Rodriguez. Washington, DC.: ICS Publications.

Joy, W.B. (1985). The new age, Armageddon, and mythic cycles. *Journal of Humanistic Psychology, 25(1)*, 85–89.

Julian of Norwich (1998). *Revelations of Divine Love*. Trans. E. Spearing. London: Penguin Classics.

Jung, C.G. (1902). *On the Psychology and Pathology of So-called Occult Phenomena*. Leipzig: Mutze. (in German).

Jung, C.G. (1954). *The Practice of Psychotherapy*. London: Routledge. (Collected Works of C.G. Jung, Vol. 16).

Jung, C.G. (1958a). *The Undiscovered Self*. London: Routledge & Kegan Paul.

Jung, C.G. (1958b). *Psychology and Religion*. Yale: Yale University Press.

Jung, C.G. (1966). *Two Essays on Analytical Psychology,* 2nd Edn. London: Routledge. (Collected Works of C.G. Jung, Vol. 7).

Jung, C.G. (1967). *Symbols of Transformation,* 2nd Edn. London: Routledge. (Collected Works of C.G. Jung, Vol. 5).

Jung, C.G. (1969). *Psychology and Religion: West and East*. London: Routledge. (Collected Works of C.G. Jung, Vol. 11).

Jung, C.G. (1983). *Memories, Dreams, Reflections*. London: Fontana.

Jung, C.G. (1991). *Aion: Researches into the Phenomonology of the Self,* 2nd Edn. London: Routledge. (Collected Works of C.G. Jung, Vol. 9, Part 2).

Katz, S.T. (1978). 'Language, Epistemology and Mysticism'. In S.T. Katz (Ed.), *Mysticism and Philosophical Analysis*. New York: Oxford University Press. pp. 22–74.

Kekes, J. (1990). *Facing Evil*. Princeton, New Jersey: Princeton University Press.

Koch, S. (1971). The image of man implicit in encounter group theory. *Journal of Humanistic Psychology, 11(2)*, 109–127.

Koestler, A. (1967). *The Ghost in the Machine*. London: Arkana.

Kohut, H. (1977). *The Restoration of the Self*. Madison, Conn.: International Universities Press.

Kohut, H. (1978). *The Search for the Self: Selected Writings of Heinz Kohut, 1950–1978. Vol. 1*. Madison, Conn.: International Universities Press.

Kremer, J.W. (1998). 'The Shadow of Evolutionary Thinking'. In D. Rothberg & S. Kelly (Eds.). *Ken Wilber in Dialogue: Conversations with Leading Transpersonal Thinkers*. Wheaton, IL.: Quest Books. pp. 239–258.

Lajoie, D.H. & Shapiro, S.I. (1992). Definitions of transpersonal psychology: The first twenty–three years. *Journal of Transpersonal Psychology, 24(1)*, 79–98.

Lancaster, B.L. (2002). In defence of the transcendent. *Transpersonal Psychology Review, 6(1)*, 42–51.

Lancaster, B.L. (2004). *Approaches to Consciousness: The Marriage of Science and Mysticism.* Basingstoke, Hampshire & New York: Palgrave MacMillan.

Langone, M.D. (1995). *Recovery from Cults: Help for Victims of Psychological and Spiritual Abuse.* New York: Norton.

Larsen, S. (1996). *The Mythic Imagination: The Quest for Meaning Through Personal Mythology.* Rochester, Vermont: Inner Traditions.

Laski, M. (1961). *Ecstasy: In Secular and Religious Experience.* London: Cresset Press.

Leonard, G. & Murphy, M. (1995). *The Life We Are Given: A Long-Term Program for Realizing the Potential of Body, Mind, Heart, and Soul.* New York: Tarcher/Putnam.

Levine, A. (1985). The Pollyanna paradigm. *Journal of Humanistic Psychology, 25(1)*, 90–93.

MacIntyre, A. (1981). *After Virtue: A Study in Moral Theory.* London: Duckworth.

Marien, M. (1983). The transformation as sandbox syndrome. *Journal of Humanistic Psychology, 23(1)*, 7–15.

Maslow, A.H. (1943a). Preface to motivation theory. *Psychosomatic Medicine, 5*, 85–92.

Maslow, A.H. (1943b). A theory of human motivation. *Psychological Review, 50*, 370–396.

Maslow, A.H. (1948a). 'Higher' and 'lower' needs. *Journal of Psychology, 25*, 433–436.

Maslow, A.H. (1948b). Some theoretical consequences of basic need-gratification. *Journal of Personality, 16*, 402–416.

Maslow, A.H. (1949). The expressive component of behavior. *Psychological Review, 56*, 261–272.

Maslow, A.H. (1950). Self-actualizing people: A study of psychological health. *Personality, Symposium No. 1*, 11–34.

Maslow, A.H. (1955). 'Deficiency Motivation and Growth Motivation'. In M.R. Jones (Ed.), *Nebraska Symposium on Motivation: 1955.* Lincoln, NB.: University of Nebraska Press. pp. 1–30.

Maslow, A.H. (1956). Defense and growth. *Merrill-Palmer Quarterly, 3*, 36–47.

Maslow, A.H. (1959). Cognition of being in the peak experiences. *Journal of Genetic Psychology, 94*, 43–66.

Maslow, A.H. (1961). Peak experiences as acute identity experiences. *American Journal of Psychoanalysis, 21*, 254–262.

Maslow, A.H. (1965). 'Some Basic Propositions of a Growth and Self-actualization Psychology'. In G. Lindzey & L. Hall (Eds.), *Theories of*

Personality: Primary Sources and Research. New York: Wiley. pp. 307–316.

Maslow, A.H. (1966). Comments on Dr Frankl's paper. *Journal of Humanistic Psychology, 6(2)*, 107–112.

Maslow, A.H. (1967a). Neurosis as a failure of personal growth. *Humanitas, 3*, 153–169.

Maslow, A.H. (1967b). A theory of metamotivation: the biological rooting of the value-life. *Journal of Humanistic Psychology, 7(2)*, 93–127.

Maslow, A.H. (1968). *Toward a Psychology of Being*, 2nd Edn. Princeton, NJ.: Van Nostrand.

Maslow, A.H. (1969a). Theory Z. *Journal of Transpersonal Psychology, 1(2)*, 31–47.

Maslow, A.H. (1969b). Various meanings of transcendence. *Journal of Transpersonal Psychology, 1(1)*, 56–66.

Maslow, A.H. (1970). *Motivation and Personality*, 2nd Edn. New York: Harper & Row.

Maslow, A.H. (1973). *The Farther Reaches of Human Nature*. Harmondsworth, Middlesex: Penguin.

May, R (1982). The problem of evil: An open letter to Carl Rogers. *Journal of Humanistic Psychology, 22(3)*, 10–21.

McLynn, F. (1997). *Carl Gustav Jung*. New York: St. Martin's Press.

McNamara, J.A. (1993). 'The Rhetoric of Orthodoxy: Clerical Authority and Female Innovation in the Struggle with Heresy'. In U. Wiethaus (Ed.). *Maps of Flesh and Light: The Religious Experience of Medieval Women Mystics*. Syracuse, NY.: Syracuse University Press. pp. 9–27.

Mead, G.H. (1934). *Mind, Self, and Society*. Chicago: University of Chicago Press.

Meckel, D.J. & Moore, R.L. (Eds.). (1992). *Self and Liberation: The Jung / Buddhism Dialogue*. New York: Paulist Press.

Metzner, R. (1999). *Green Psychology: Transforming our Relationship to the Earth*. Rochester, VT.: Park Street Press.

Michael, D.N. (1985). Aquarians riding the third wave. *Journal of Humanistic Psychology, 25(1)*, 79–84.

Miller, J. (1991). 'The Development of Women's Sense of Self'. In J. Jordan, A. Kaplan, J. Miller, I Stiver, & J. Surrey. (Eds.). *Women's Growth in Connection: Writings from the Stone Center*. New York: Guilford Press.

Murphy, G. & Ballou, R.O. (Eds.). (1961). *William James on Psychical Research*. London: Chatto & Windus.

Murphy, M. (1992). *The Future of the Body: Explorations into the Further Evolution of Human Nature*. New York: Tarcher/Putnam.

Murphy, M. & Donovan, S. (1997). *The Physical and Psychological Effects of Meditation: A Review of Contemporary Research with a Comprehensive Bibliography, 1931–1996*, 2nd Edn. Petaluma, CA.: Institute of Noetic Sciences.

Naess. A. (1973). The shallow and the deep, long range ecology movement: A summary. *Inquiry, 16*, 95–100.

Neher, A. (1990). *The Psychology of Transcendence*, 2nd Edn. New York: Dover.

Nicol, J. F. (1982). 'Britain'. In I. Grattan-Guinness, *Psychical Research: A Guide to its History, Principles and Practices*. Wellingborough, Northants.: Aquarian Press.

O'Hara, M. (1985). Of myths and monkeys: A critical look at a theory of critical mass. *Journal of Humanistic Psychology, 25(1)*, 61–78.

Otto, H.A. (1968). Motivation and human potentialities. *Humanitas, 3*, 293–306.

Otto, R. (1950). (Trans. J.W. Harvey). *The Idea of the Holy: An Inquiry into the Non-Rational Factor in the Idea of the Divine and Its Relation to the Rational*. 2nd Edn. New York: Oxford University Press. (First German Edition, 1917).

Pahnke, W.N. (1963). *Drugs and Mysticism: An Analysis of the Relationship between Psychedelic Drugs and the Mystical Consciousness*. Unpublished doctoral dissertation, Harvard University.

Pahnke, W.N. (1966). Drugs and mysticism. *International Journal of Parapsychology, 8*, 295–314.

Partridge, C. (Ed.). (2004). *Encyclopaedia of New Religions: New Religious Movements, Sects and Alternative Spiritualities*. Oxford: Lion Publishing.

Peck, M. Scott (1997). *People of the Lie: The Hope for Healing Human Evil*, 2nd Edn. New York: Simon & Schuster.

Perry, J.W. (1974). *The Far Side of Madness*. Englewood Cliffs, NJ.: Prentice-Hall.

Perry, J.W. (1976). *Roots of Renewal in Myth and Madness*. San Francisco: Jossey-Bass.

Peters, R.S. (1960). *The Concept of Motivation*, 2nd Edn. London: Routledge & Kegan Paul.

Phillips, W.M., Watkins, J.T., & Noll, G. (1974). Self-actualization, self-transcendence, and personal philosophy. *Journal of Humanistic Psychology, 14(3)*, 53–73.

Plato. See Hackforth (1972).

Radin, D.I. (1997). *The Conscious Universe: The Scientific Truth of Psychic Phenomena*. New York: HarperEdge.

Ramana Maharshi (1984). *Talks with Sri Ramana Maharshi*. Tiruvannamalai: Sri Ramanasramam.

Rao, K.R. (1997). 'Some Reflections on Religion and Anomalies of Consciousness'. In C.T. Tart (Ed.). *Body, Mind, Spirit: Exploring the Parapsychology of Spirituality*. Charlottesville, VA.: Hampton Roads. pp. 68–82.

Rawlinson, A. (1997). *The Book of Enlightened Masters: Western Teachers in Eastern Traditions*. Chicago & La Salle, IL.: Open Court.

Rawlinson, A. (2000). A model of experiential comparative religion. *International Journal of Transpersonal Studies, 19*, 99–108.

Rogers, C.R. (1959). 'A Theory of Therapy, Personality, and Interpersonal Relationships, as Developed in the Client-centered Framework'. In S. Koch (Ed.), *Psychology, The Study of a Science. Vol. 3: Formulations of the Person and the Social Context*. New York: McGraw-Hill. pp. 184–256.

Rogers, C.R. (1961). *On Becoming a Person*. Boston: Houghton Mifflin.

Roll, W.G. (1997). 'My Search for the Soul'. In C.T. Tart (Ed.). *Body, Mind, Spirit: Exploring the Parapsychology of Spirituality*. Charlottesville, VA.: Hampton Roads. pp. 50–67.

Rothberg, D. & Kelly, S. (Eds.). (1998). *Ken Wilber in Dialogue: Conversations with Leading Transpersonal Thinkers*. Wheaton, IL.: Quest Books.

Rowan, J. (1983). The real self and mystical experiences. *Journal of Humanistic Psychology, 23(2)*, 9–27.

Rowan, J. (1993). *The Transpersonal: Psychotherapy and Counselling*. London & New York: Routledge.

Rowan, J. (2004). Correspondence. *Transpersonal Psychology Review, 8(1)*, 86.

Schechner, R. (1988). *Performance Theory*. New York: Routledge.

Schlamm, L. (1991). Rudolf Otto and mystical experience. *Religious Studies, 27*, 389–398.

Schlamm, L. (2001). Ken Wilber's spectrum model: Identifying alternative soteriological perspectives. *Religion, 31*, 19–39.

Seligman, M. & Csikszentmihalyi, M. (2000). Positive psychology: An introduction. *American Psychologist, 55(1)*, 5–14.

Shotter, J. (1975). *Images of Man in Psychological Research*. London: Methuen.

Smail, D. (1984). *Illusion and Reality: The Meaning of Anxiety*. London: Dent.

Smart, N. (1973). *The Science of Religion and the Sociology of Knowledge*. Princeton: Princeton University Press.

Smart, N. (1983). 'The Purification of Consciousness and the Negative Path'. In S.T. Katz (Ed.), *Mysticism and Religious Traditions*. New York: Oxford University Press, pp. 117–129.

Smart, N. (Ed.). (1964). *Philosophers and Religious Truth*. New York: Macmillan.

Smith, H. (1976). *Forgotten Truth: The Primordial Tradition*. New York: Harper & Row.

Smith, M.B. (1969). *Social Psychology and Human Values*. Chicago: Aldine-Atherton.

Smith, M.B. (1973). On self-actualization: A transambivalent examination of a focal theme in Maslow's psychology. *Journal of Humanistic Psychology, 13(2)*, 17–33.

Sogyal Rinpoche (1992). *The Tibetan Book of Living and Dying*. London: Rider.

Spilka, B., Hood, R.W. Jr., Hunsberger, B. & Gorsuch, R. (2003). *The Psychology of Religion: An Empirical Approach*, 3rd Ed. New York: Guilford Press.

Stace, W.T. (1960). *Mysticism & Philosophy*, Philadelphia: J. B Lippincott.

Starhawk (1999). *The Spiral Dance: A Rebirth of the Ancient Religion of the Great Goddess*, 20th Anniversary Edition. New York: HarperCollins.

Staub, E. (1989). *The Roots of Evil: The Origins of Genocide and Other Group Violence*. Cambridge, New York & Melbourne: Cambridge University Press.

Stavely, H. & McNamara, P. (1992). Warwick Fox's 'transpersonal ecology': A critique and alternative approach. *Journal of Transpersonal Psychology, 24(2),* 201–211.

Steele, S. (1994). The multistate paradigm and the spiritual path of John of the Cross. *Journal of Transpersonal Psychology, 26(1),* 55–80.

Stevens, A. (1990). *On Jung*. London: Penguin Books.

Storr, A. (1997). *Feet of Clay*. New York: HarperCollins.

Sutich, A.J. (1969). Some considerations regarding transpersonal psychology. *Journal of Transpersonal Psychology, 1(1),* 11–20.

Sutich, A.J. (1976). The emergence of the transpersonal orientation. *Journal of Transpersonal Psychology, 8(1),* 5–19.

Swinburne, R. (1979). *The Existence of God*. Oxford: Clarendon Press.

Szasz, T.S. (1972). *The Myth of Mental Illness*. St Albans: Granada.

Szasz, T.S. (1974). *Ideology and Insanity*. Harmondsworth, Middlesex: Penguin.

Tart, C.T. (1975). *States of Consciousness*. New York: Dutton.

Tart, C.T. (2003). Spiritual motivations of parapsychologists? Empirical data. *Journal of Parapsychology, 67,* 181–184.

Tart, C.T. (2004). On the scientific foundations of transpersonal psychology: Contributions from parapsychology. *Journal of Transpersonal Psychology, 36(1),* 66–90.

Tart, C.T. (Ed.). (1997). *Body, Mind, Spirit: Exploring the Parapsychology of Spirituality*. Charlottesville, VA.: Hampton Roads.

Taylor, E. (1996). 'William James and Transpersonal Psychiatry'. In. B.W. Scotton, A.B. Chinen, & J.R. Battista. (Eds.). *Textbook of Transpersonal Psychiatry and Psychology*. New York: Basic Books. pp. 21–28.

Taylor, E. (2001). Positive psychology and humanistic psychology: A reply to Seligman. *Journal of Humanistic Psychology, 41(1),* 13–29.

Teilhard de Chardin, P. (1959). *The Phenomenon of Man*. London: Collins.

Teresa of Avila, Saint (1976). 'The Book of Her Life'. In *The Collected Works of St. Teresa of Avila. Vol. 1.* Trans K. Kavanaugh & O. Rodriguez. Washington, DC.: ICS Publications.

Teresa of Avila, Saint (1980). 'The Interior Castle'. In *The Collected Works of St. Teresa of Avila. Vol. 2.* Trans K. Kavanaugh & O. Rodriguez. Washington, DC.: ICS Publications.

Thich Nhat Hanh (1996). *Cultivating the Mind of Love: The Practice of Looking Deeply in the Mahayana Buddhist Tradition*. Berkeley: Parallax Press.

Treffert, D.A. (2000). *Extraordinary People: Understanding Savant Syndrome*. Backinprint.com: Authors Guild.

Trungpa, C. (1973). *Cutting Through Spiritual Materialism*. Boston & London: Shambhala.

Underhill, E. (1995). *Mysticism: The Development of Humankind's Spiritual Consciousness*, 14th ed. London: Bracken Books. (First published 1911).

Van Lommel, P., van Wees, R., Meyers, V. & Elfferich, I. (2001). Near-death experience in survivors of cardiac arrest: A prospective study in the Netherlands, *The Lancet, Vol. 358, No. 9298*, 2039–45.

Vaughan, F. (1985). Discovering transpersonal identity. *Journal of Humanistic Psychology, 25(3)*, 13–38.

Vaughan, F. (1986). *The Inward Arc: Healing and Wholeness in Psychotherapy and Spirituality*. Boston & London: Shambhala.

Velmans, M. (2000). *Understanding Consciousness*. London: Routledge.

Vich, M.A. (1990). The origins and growth of transpersonal psychology. *Journal of Humanistic Psychology, 30(2)*, 47–50.

Visser, F. (2003). *Ken Wilber: Thought as Passion*. Albany: State University of New York Press.

Wade, J. (1996). *Changes of Mind: A Holonomic Theory of the Evolution of Consciousness*. Albany: State University of New York Press.

Wade, J. (1998). Meeting God in the flesh: Spirituality and sexual intimacy. *ReVision, 21(2)*, 35–41.

Wade, J. (2000). 'The Love that Dares Not Speak Its Name'. In T. Hart, P.L. Nelson, & K. Puhakka (Eds.). *Transpersonal Knowing: Exploring the Horizon of Consciousness*. Albany: State University of New York Press. pp. 271–302.

Wainwright, W.J. (1981). *Mysticism: A Study of Its Nature, Cognitive Value and Moral Implications*. Madison, WI.: University of Wisconsin Press.

Walley, M. (2002). Toward a psychology of inter-being: Putting the heart back into psychology. *Transpersonal Psychology Review, 6(1)*, 3–11.

Walsch, N. D. (1997). *Conversations with God, Book 1: An Uncommon Dialogue*. London: Hodder & Stoughton.

Walsh, R. & Vaughan, F. (1993a). On transpersonal definitions. *Journal of Transpersonal Psychology, 25(2)*, 199–207.

Walsh, R. & Vaughan, F. (Eds.). (1993b). *Paths Beyond Ego: The Transpersonal Vision*. New York: Tarcher/Putnam.

Walsh, R.N. (1993). The transpersonal movement: A history and state of the art. *Journal of Transpersonal Psychology, 25(3)*, 123–139.

Washburn, M. (1990). Two patterns of transcendence. *Journal of Humanistic Psychology, 30(3)*, 84–112.

Washburn, M. (1994). *Transpersonal Psychology in Psychoanalytic Perspective*. Albany: State University of New York Press.

Washburn, M. (1995). *The Ego and the Dynamic Ground*, Rev. Edn. Albany: State University of New York Press.

Washburn, M. (1998). 'The Pre-trans Fallacy Reconsidered'. In D. Rothberg & S. Kelly (Eds.). *Ken Wilber in Dialogue: Conversations with Leading Transpersonal Thinkers*. Wheaton, IL.: Quest Books. pp. 62–83.

Washburn, M. (2003a). Transpersonal dialogue: A new direction. *Journal of Transpersonal Psychology, 35(1)*, 1–19.

Washburn, M. (2003b). *Embodied Spirituality in a Sacred World*. Albany: State University of New York Press.

Watts, A. (1957). *The Way of Zen*. London: Thames & Hudson.

Wehr, G. (1988). *Jung: A Biography*. Boston: Shambhala.

Welwood, J. (1983). On spiritual authority: genuine and counterfeit. *Journal of Humanistic Psychology, 23(3)*, 13–38.

Welwood, J. (1991). *Journey of the Heart: Intimate Relationship and the Path of Love*. London: Mandala.

White, R.A. (1997). 'Exceptional Human Experiences and the Experiential Paradigm'. In C.T. Tart (Ed.). *Body, Mind, Spirit: Exploring the Parapsychology of Spirituality*. Charlottesville, VA.: Hampton Roads. pp. 83–100.

Whitehead, A.N. (1929). *Process and Reality: An Essay in Cosmology*. New York: Macmillan.

Wiethaus, U. (Ed.). (1993). *Maps of Flesh and Light: The Religious Experience of Medieval Women Mystics*. Syracuse, NY.: Syracuse University Press.

Wilber, K. (1977). *The Spectrum of Consciousness*. Wheaton, IL: Quest Books.

Wilber, K. (1979). Eye to eye: Science and transpersonal psychology. *ReVision, 2*, 3–25.

Wilber, K. (1980). The pre/trans fallacy. *ReVision, 3(Fall)*, 51–72. (Reprinted in K. Wilber, *Eye to Eye*, 3rd Edn. Boston: Shambhala, 1996).

Wilber, K. (1986a). 'The Spectrum of Psychopathology'. In K. Wilber, J. Engler & D.P. Brown, *Transformations of Consciousness: Conventional and Contemplative Perspectives on Development*. Boston & London: Shambhala. pp. 107–126.

Wilber, K. (1986b). 'Treatment Modalities'. In K. Wilber, J. Engler & D.P. Brown, *Transformations of Consciousness: Conventional and Contemplative Perspectives on Development*. Boston & London: Shambhala. pp. 127–159.

Wilber, K. (1991). *Grace and Grit: Spirituality and Healing in the Life and Death of Treya Killam Wilber*. Dublin: Gill & MacMillan.

Wilber, K. (1993). *The Spectrum of Consciousness*, 2nd Edn. Wheaton, IL.: Quest Books.

Wilber, K. (1995a). *Sex, Ecology, Spirituality: The Spirit of Evolution*. Boston & London: Shambhala.

Wilber, K. (1995b). An informal overview of transpersonal studies. *Journal of Transpersonal Psychology, 27(2)*, 107–129.

Wilber, K. (1996a). *A Brief History of Everything*. Dublin: Gill & MacMillan.

Wilber, K. (1996b). *The Atman Project: A Transpersonal View of Human Development*, 2nd Edn. Wheaton, IL.: Quest Books.

Wilber, K. (1996c). *Eye to Eye: The Quest for a New Paradigm*, 3rd Edn. Boston & London: Shambhala.

Wilber, K. (1996d). *Up From Eden: A Transpersonal View of Human Evolution*, 2nd Edn. Wheaton, IL.: Quest Books.

Wilber, K. (1997). *The Eye of Spirit: An Integral Vision for a World Gone Slightly Mad*. Boston & London: Shambhala.

Wilber, K. (1998). 'A More Integral Approach'. In D. Rothberg & S. Kelly (Eds.). *Ken Wilber in Dialogue: Conversations with Leading Transpersonal Thinkers*. Wheaton, IL.: Quest Books. pp. 305–367.

Wilber, K. (1999a). *One Taste: The Journals of Ken Wilber*. Boston & London: Shambhala.

Wilber, K. (1999b). 'Two Humanistic Psychologies'. In *The Collected Works of Ken Wilber, Vol. 4*. Boston, Mass.: Shambhala. pp. 218–230.

Wilber, K. (1999c). 'Integral Psychology'. In K. Wilber. *The Collected Works of Ken Wilber, Vol. 4*. Boston, Mass.: Shambhala. pp. 423–717.

Wilber, K. (2000a). *Integral Psychology: Consciousness, Spirit, Psychology, Therapy*. Boston & London: Shambhala.

Wilber, K. (2000b). 'Waves, Streams, States, and Self — A Summary of My Psychological Model (Or, Outline of An Integral Psychology)'. Accessed 29 March 2005 from http://wilber.shambhala.com/html/books/psych_model/psych_model8.cfm/xid,2712128/yid,99 180670

Wilber, K. (2000c). *The Collected Works of Ken Wilber, Volume 8*. Boston, MA.: Shambhala.

Wilber, K. (2002). 'On Critics, Integral Institute, My Recent Writing, and Other Matters of Little Consequence: A Shambhala Interview with Ken Wilber'. Accessed 29 March 2005 from http://wilber.shambhala.com/html/interviews/interview1220.cfm/xid,2932119/yid,35866009

Wilber, K. (2003). 'Foreward'. In F. Visser. *Ken Wilber: Thought as Passion*. Albany: State University of New York Press. pp. xi–xv.

Wilson, C. (1972). *New Pathways in Psychology: Maslow and the Post-Freudian Revolution*. London: Victor Gollancz.

Wright, P. (1995). Bringing women's voices to transpersonal psychology. *ReVision, 17(3)*, 3–10.

Wright, P.A. (1998a). 'Gender Issues in Ken Wilber's Transpersonal Theory'. In D. Rothberg & S. Kelly (Eds.). *Ken Wilber in Dialogue: Conversations with Leading Transpersonal Thinkers*. Wheaton, IL.: Quest Books. pp. 207–236.

Wright, P.A. (1998b). 'Difficulties with Integrating the Feminine'. In D. Rothberg & S. Kelly (Eds.). *Ken Wilber in Dialogue: Conversations with Leading Transpersonal Thinkers*. Wheaton, IL.: Quest Books. pp. 388–391.

Wulff, D.H. (1997). *Psychology of Religion: Classic and Contemporary*, 2nd Edn. New York: Wiley.

Yogananda, P. (1946). *Autobiography of a Yogi*. New York: Philosophical Library.

Zaehner, R.C. (1961). *Mysticism: Sacred and Profane*. New York: Oxford University Press.

Zimmerman, M. E. (1994). *Contesting Earth's Future: Radical Ecology and Postmodernity*. Berkeley and Los Angeles: University of California Press.

Zimmerman, M.E. (1998). 'A Transpersonal Diagnosis of the Ecological Crisis'. In D. Rothberg & S. Kelly (eds.). *Ken Wilber in Dialogue: Conversations with Leading Transpersonal Thinkers*. Wheaton, IL.: Quest Books. pp. 180–206.

Name Index

Aanstoos, C.M., 169, 295
Adler, A., 116
Alfassa, M., 192, 297
Allah, 36, 294
Allport, G.W., 59, 118
Anderson, R., 24
Anderson, S.R., 35
Anne of the Incarnation at Segovia, 40
Ansbacher, H.L., 128, 143
Aristotle, 118, 123, 129, 133, 134, 145, 148, 280, 288, 302, 312
Aron, A., 143, 145, 152
Assagioli, R., 9, 20, 30, 31, 83, 159, 177, 185, 186-89, 191, 195, 196, 225, 231, 269, 271, 280, 284, 291, 293, 295, 297, 301, 305, 313
Aurobindo, Sri, 9, 24, 53, 162, 177, 192-97, 198, 204, 214, 250, 281, 283, 287, 291, 292, 293, 294, 297, 300, 304, 309, 310, 311

Bache, C.M., 170
Bailey, A., 20, 186, 189, 281
Bair, D., 42
Ballou, R.O., 41
Barrow, J.D., 194
Beck, D., 309
Beethoven, L. van, 120
Benedict XIV, see Lambertini, P.
Benedict, R., 116, 119
Blavatsky, H.P., 312
Bonaventure, St., 312
Boorstein, S., 25
Boucouvalas, M., 15, 59, 68, 273
Braud, W., 24, 40
Broughton, R., 40
Buber, M., 102, 220, 222, 223, 294, 304

Bucke, R.M., 17-19, 170, 225, 241, 284
Buddha, 109, 182, 282, 312
Butler, C., 234
Byron, Lord, 307

Campbell, J., 136-39, 141
Caplan, M., 12, 24
Cheng-tao Ke, 173
Chittister, J.D., 35, 269
Chodorow, N., 209
Christ, C.P., 210, 227
Christ, Jesus, 109, 182, 283, 307
Clarke, I., 57
Coleridge, S.T., 307
Collins, P., 241
Cortright, B., 25
Cowan, C., 309
Csikszentmihalyi, M., 26, 75, 261, 288

Dalai Lama, 226
Dalal, A.S., 53, 193, 194
Daniels, M., 39, 63, 71, 94, 115, 130, 159, 177, 216, 234
Dass, R., 24
De Martino, E., 166
Dennett, D.C., 25
Descartes, R., 78, 168, 173, 212, 213, 282, 285, 286, 288, 299, 311
Donovan, S., 24

Eckhart, J. (Meister Eckhart), 171, 200, 248, 255, 286
Einstein, A., 120
Elfferich, I., 54
Eliade, M., 137, 138
Elijah, 179, 182
Ellenberger, H., 83
Ellis, A., 130, 143

Emerson, R.W., 17, 200-01, 279

Feinstein, D., 136, 137
Fenwick, E., 54, 58
Fenwick, P., 54, 58
Ferguson, M., 75
Ferrer, J., 9, 12, 24, 28, 31, 35-37,
    45, 50, 52, 54, 66, 68, 69, 76, 77,
    79, 80, 113, 129, 130, 138, 143,
    151, 174, 177, 203, 211-13, 214,
    223, 224, 229, 230, 231, 235, 236,
    239, 250, 266-68, 269, 270, 272,
    283, 286, 288, 293, 298, 300, 301,
    310, 311
Firman, J., 73, 83, 101, 108, 186,
    271, 303, 311
Flournoy, T., 231
Fontana, D., 12, 13, 43, 50, 139, 236
Forman, R.K.C., 238, 248, 255, 305
Fox, W., 27, 35, 66-68, 79, 228, 229
Frankl, V.E., 83, 125, 127, 128, 130,
    143, 144, 153, 155, 295, 299, 308
Freeman, A., 220
Fremantle, F., 204
Freud, S., 3, 20, 32, 42, 43, 74, 99,
    116, 120, 137, 195, 287, 289, 295,
    300, 303, 304, 308, 310, 312
Frick, W.B., 130, 140-41, 142, 147
Friedman, H., 13, 14, 230, 232,
    273-74
Friedman, M., 77, 118, 128, 130,
    131, 137, 138, 143, 144, 145, 149,
    151, 152, 153, 154, 155, 157
Fromm, E., 101, 116
Fuller, M., 279

Gabriel, 19
Geller, L., 130, 132-34, 135, 139,
    143, 148, 149, 151, 155
Gila, A., 73, 83, 101, 108, 186, 271,
    303, 311
Gilligan, C., 209
Gimello, R.M., 238
Ginsburg, C., 149, 150
Goldstein, K., 116
Gorsuch, R., 13
Green, A.M., 47, 49, 55
Green, E.E., 47, 49, 55
Gregory, St., 250
Grof, C., 22, 46, 56, 57, 83, 291, 310

Grof, S., 9, 12, 21, 22-23, 30, 31, 34,
    40, 43, 46, 47, 48, 54, 56, 57, 74,
    83, 90-92, 159, 173, 177, 189-92,
    198, 204, 207, 209, 231, 237, 269,
    271, 281, 290, 291, 301, 304, 309,
    310
Grosso, M., 40
Gurdjieff, G., 24, 290
Gurney, E., 40

Hale, C.S., 46, 83
Happold, F.C., 9, 159, 171, 200,
    242, 247, 248, 309
Hardy, A., 19, 20, 261
Harlow, H., 116
Harman, W.W., 16, 43
Harner, M., 83
Hartelius, G., 12, 24
Hartshorne, C., 193
Haynes, R., 41
Hendlin, S.J., 131, 144, 152
Heron, J., 28, 35, 76, 77, 79, 90, 93,
    160, 209, 226, 227, 250, 251, 303
Herzberg, F., 146
Hick, J., 27, 36, 235, 237, 238-39,
    253, 259, 306
Hillman, J., 79, 80, 81, 83, 84
Hisamatsu, S., 183-84
Holt, J., 137
Homer, 135, 161, 166
Hood, R.W. Jr., 13, 237, 244
Hopkins, P., 35
Horne, J., 82, 85, 226
Horney, K., 116, 118, 121, 125, 139,
    150
Hunsberger, B., 13
Huxley, A., 19, 22, 28, 120, 224,
    238, 272

Irwin, H.J., 54, 58

Jacobi, J., 180
Jaffe, D.T., 83
James, H., 16
James, W., 9, 16-17, 19, 20, 22, 27,
    40, 41, 42, 70, 120, 137, 140-43,
    159, 226, 229, 240, 242, 250, 269,
    303, 305
Jaspers, K., 27, 281
Jaynes, J., 28, 163, 164, 282
Jehovah, 36

John of the Cross, St., 83, 171, 207, 284, 294, 312
John XXII, 286
Joy, W.B., 152
Julian of Norwich, 163, 251, 255, 288, 294
Jung, C.G., 3, 4, 9, 20, 30, 31, 34, 37, 42, 43, 64, 72-74, 80, 83, 87, 89, 91, 92, 99, 100, 126, 137, 138, 159, 170, 177, 179-85, 188, 189, 191, 195, 205, 207, 209, 219-23, 225, 229, 231, 232, 265, 269, 271, 279, 280, 282, 283, 284, 286, 289, 292, 293, 294, 296, 299, 301, 304, 305, 308, 309, 311, 313, 315

Kant, I., 91, 133, 162, 230, 294, 299, 301, 302
Katz, S.T., 238
Keating, T., 226
Keats, J., 307
Kekes, J., 95-98, 101
Kelly, G., 3
Kelly, S., 79
Khan, H.I., 250
Koch, S., 131, 144
Koestler, A., 32, 291
Kohlberg, L., 3
Kohut, H., 105, 108, 298, 308
Kremer, J.W., 28, 35, 46, 52, 77
Krippner, S., 136, 137
Krishna, 109, 182

Lajoie, D.H., 24, 45, 46, 217, 218
Lambertini, P., 41
Lancaster, B.L., 12, 15, 25, 50, 223, 231-32, 256, 269
Langone, M.D., 93
Larsen, S., 136, 137, 140, 142
Laski, M., 19
Leadbeater, C.W., 250
Leonard, G., 25, 88, 293
Levine, A., 64, 77, 302

Machiavelli, N., 149, 156
MacIntyre, A., 133-36, 138, 142, 143, 144, 145, 147, 148, 155, 157, 158, 286
Maharshi, R., 172, 200, 226, 292, 306
Marien, M., 64, 77, 152, 307

Mary, Virgin, 109
Maslow, A.H., 3, 8, 9, 19, 21, 30, 31, 65, 74, 75, 83, 115-29, 131, 132, 135, 139, 140, 143-58, 159, 177, 178-79, 219, 220, 221, 225, 228, 229, 231, 232, 269, 283, 285, 288, 289, 290, 291, 293, 296, 297, 301, 302, 303, 306, 308, 312, 314
Mausner, B., 146
May, R., 64, 77
McLynn, F., 42
McNamara, J.A., 251
McNamara, P., 67
Mead, G.H., 139, 150
Meckel, D.J., 184
Mesmer, F.A., 41, 297, 313
Metzner, R., 35
Meyers, V., 54
Michael, D.N., 152
Miller, J., 209
Moore, R.L., 184
Morris, R.J., 237, 244
Moses, 312
Mother, the, *see* Alfassa, M.
Muhaiyadeen, B., 226
Muhammad, 294
Murphy, G., 41
Murphy, M., 24, 25, 88, 293

Naess, A., 66, 285
Neher, A., 43
Nicol, J.F., 41
Nietzsche, F., 76, 134, 137
Noll, G., 130, 135

O'Hara, M., 142
Osmond, H., 304
Otto, H.A., 128
Otto, R., 9, 19, 245-47, 248, 257, 288, 298, 300, 313

Padmasambhava, 172-73
Pahnke, W.N., 244
Partridge, C., 270
Patanjali, 186, 301, 305
Paul, St., 173
Peck, M. Scott, 101
Perls, F., 289
Perry, J.W., 83
Peters, R.S., 132
Philemon, 179

Phillips, W.M., 130, 135
Piaget, J., 3
Piper, L., 41
Plato, 28, 145, 161, 162, 165, 167, 193, 280, 286, 292, 299, 302
Plotinus, 28, 162, 173, 250, 299, 302
Preiswerk, H., 42
Pseudo-Dionysius, 234, 250
Pythagoras, 161

Radin, D.I., 60
Ramanuja, 212, 306, 312, 314
Rao, K.R., 40
Rardin, M.A., 12, 24
Rawlinson, A., 9, 85, 148, 226, 246-47, 256, 257, 258, 261, 272, 284, 292, 310, 314
Richard, M., *see* Alfassa, M.
Rilke, R.M., 71
Rogers, C., 3, 75, 102, 113, 132, 150, 284, 314
Roll, W.G., 169, 295
Roosevelt, F.D., 120
Rothberg, D., 79
Rowan, J., 47-49, 50, 51, 55, 56, 79, 82, 152, 159, 205

Salome, 179, 182
Sankara, 212, 247, 255, 279, 307, 314
Sartre, J-P., 123, 290
Schachter-Shalomi, Z., 226
Schechner, R., 54
Schlamm, L., 230, 246, 250
Schutz, W., 87, 308
Schweitzer, A., 120
Seligman, M., 26, 65, 75, 302
Shankara, *see* Sankara
Shapiro, S.I., 24, 45, 46, 217, 218
Sheldrake, R., 297
Shelley, P.B., 307
Shotter, J., 16
Siddhartha Gautama, *see* Buddha
Smail, D., 77
Smart, N., 238, 246, 248, 250
Smith, H., 238, 272
Smith, M.B., 130, 132, 140, 142, 143, 144, 148, 149, 150, 152, 153, 154, 155, 158
Snyderman, B.B., 146
Socrates, 165, 302

Sogyal Rinpoche, 173
Spilka, B., 13
Spinoza, B., 120
Stace, W., 9, 19, 238, 243-44, 245, 247, 258, 282, 288, 293
Starhawk, 210
Staub, E., 106, 108, 112
Stavely, H., 67
Steele, S., 46
Stevens, A., 89
Storr, A., 93
Sutich, A., 21, 74
Suzuki, D.T., 24
Swedenborg, E., 17, 311
Swinburne, R., 259
Szasz, T.S., 132

Tart, C.T., 14, 19, 40, 43, 54, 60, 61
Taylor, E., 17, 26
Teilhard de Chardin, P., 193
Teresa of Avila, St., 40, 159, 170-71, 174, 250, 251, 255, 258, 259, 260, 288, 294, 310, 312
Thich Nhat Hanh, 251, 293
Thoreau, H., 17, 120, 279
Thorndike, E.L, 116
Tibetan, the, 281
Tipler, F.J., 194
Treffert, D.A., 195
Trungpa, C., 24, 68, 76, 204, 310

Underhill, E., 9, 19, 171, 238, 240-41, 243, 250, 261, 266, 298, 314

Van Lommel, P., 54
Van Wees, R., 54
Vaughan, F., 11, 15, 24, 45, 47, 49, 59, 66, 68, 81, 140, 144, 148, 149, 150, 154, 160, 178, 215, 217-19, 225, 237, 273
Velmans, M., 15, 25
Vich, M., 21, 74
Visser, F., 79, 199, 250, 266

Wade, J., 28, 82, 212, 253, 258
Wainwright, W.J., 236, 238, 244-45, 246, 250, 258, 259
Walley, M., 251
Walsch, N.D., 222
Walsh, R., 11, 15, 21, 24, 45, 47, 49, 59, 68, 81, 217-19, 225, 237, 273

Washburn, M., 9, 31, 34-35, 52, 79,
    159, 177, 205-09, 212, 214, 231,
    241, 261, 264, 265, 266, 269, 271,
    272, 285, 286, 303, 306, 309, 315
Watkins, J.T., 130, 135
Watson, J.B., 115
Watson, P.J., 237, 244
Watts, A., 24, 173
Wehr, G., 220, 221
Welwood, J., 9, 82, 93, 131, 252-53,
    255
Wertheimer, M., 116, 119
White, R.A., 40, 43, 287
Whitehead, A.N., 193
Whitman, W., 17, 19, 279
Wiethaus, U., 251
Wilber, K., 6, 8, 9, 19, 27, 28, 30-34,
    46, 48, 49, 51-56, 59, 63, 66-67,
    68, 79, 80, 81, 84, 88, 89, 90, 91,
    92, 110-14, 145, 160, 164, 168,
    172, 177, 185, 191, 192, 196,
    197-205, 208, 209, 210-11, 212,
    221, 222-25, 226, 227, 228,
    229-30, 231, 235, 241, 247-51,
    255, 263-66, 268, 269, 271, 272,
    279, 280, 282, 283, 285, 286, 287,
    288, 289, 290, 291, 293, 294, 295,
    296, 297, 300, 301, 303, 304, 305,
    306, 307, 308, 309, 310, 311, 312,
    313, 315
Wilber, T., 84
Wilde, O., 265
Wilson, C., 115
Wordsworth, W., 52, 204, 307
Wright, P., 9, 35, 79, 177, 209-11,
    227, 228, 251, 269, 301, 303
Wulff, D.H., 13

Yogananda, P., 2

Zaehner, R.C., 9, 19, 200, 238,
    241-42, 243, 247, 250, 255, 297,
    300, 312
Zarathustra, 76
Zimmerman, M.E., 27, 35, 66, 67,
    79
Zoroaster, 161, 286, 289, 290, 316

Subject Index

5 x 5 model of mysticism,
see mysticism

Absolute, the, 287, 294, 300, 307
absolute consciousness,
see consciousness
absolutism, 78, 302
absorption, 12, 23, 184, 200, 208,
212, 219, 237, 241, 248, 251, 255,
279, 284, 287, 288, 297, 299, 307,
308, 309
abuse, 97, 101, 103
in spiritual contexts, 93
academic psychology,
see psychology
academics, 276-78
acting out, 73
Adam Kadmon, 162
advaita, see Vedanta
agape, 228, 279
agency, 29, 168, 181, 271
agency-in-communion, 271, 279
aggression, 99, 111
agnosticism, 230, 233, 269, 279
aiming at the self, see self
akashic records, 170, 216, 279, 309
akh, 161
alien abduction, 23, 40, 44, 83, 86
alienation, 52, 83, 86, 88, 207, 261,
284
Allah, 294
all-quadrant holism, 66-69
altered states of consciousness, see
consciousness
altruism, 20, 21, 153, 154, 275, 292
American Psychological Association, 25
American Transcendentalism, 17,
19, 252, 279, 300, 307
amok, 166, 279

analytical psychology, 4, 20, 30,
42, 72, 80, 87, 177, 179-85, 205,
207, 279, 293, 294, 296, 301, 309
anatman/anatta, 162, 214, 279
ancestral experience, 23, 46
androcentrism, 35, 209, 227, 251,
280
angels, 44, 169, 207, 216, 248, 254,
311, see also guardian angel
anima, 181-82, 185, 271, 280, 309
animism, 27, 53, 165, 246, 280
animus, 181-82, 271, 280, 309
anomalous experience, 41, 280,
287
Answer to Job, 221
anthropic principle, see evolution
anthropocentrism, 66, 68, 158, 280
anthropology,
see transpersonal anthropology
Apollonian approach, 152, 280
apophatic mysticism,
see mysticism
apotheosis, 143, 280
apparitions, 40, 42, 60, 166, 174,
198, see also presence
AQAL, 33, 67-68, 264, 280, 293,
see also quadrant model
Aquarian Conspiracy, 75
archetypes, 20, 47, 80, 86, 170,
180-82, 190, 192, 199, 208,
220-23, 256, 280, 282, 283, 291,
293, 295, 296, 297, 298, 307, 315
archetypal-divine, 49, 53, 198
concept, 126, 179-80, 220-23
experience of, 23, 32, 52, 190,
191, 198, 248
Goddess, 227, 289,
see also Goddess
good and evil, 7, 89-90, 109,

see also evil

Horned God, *see* God

spiritual/transpersonal, 55, 185, 188, 190, 213, 220, 310
see also anima, animus, God, mana personality, persona, puella aeterna, puer aeternus, quaternity, self, shadow, soul-image

aristocratic premise, 145

Aristotelianism, 118, 123, 129, 133, 145, 148, 288

ascending current, 27-32, 34, 37, 67, 69, 78, 89, 210, 228, 268, 271, 272, 280

asceticism, 29, 280, 294

Association for Transpersonal Psychology, 21, 38

astral body, *see* body

astral projection, 280

astral-psychic level, 198, 250, 295

atheism, 269, 280
mystical, 21, 221

atman, 21, 36, 147, 162, 163, 184, 186. 189, 196, 214, 242, 279, 281, 314

Atman-Brahman, 36, 162, 214, 279, 281

attachment, 55, 299

auras, 44, 216

Auroville, 192, 193, 281, 297

authenticity, 49, 101, 102, 143, 157, 164, 169, 178, 226, 265, 281, 283
and self-actualization, 125, 131, 152

authoritarianism, 227

autistic savant, 195, 281

Autobiography of a Yogi, 2

autosymbolic process, 52, 281

axial period, 27, 28, 281, 302, 303

ba, 161, 163, 173

bad faith, 150

bardo, 204, 281, 286

Basic Perinatal Matrices, 190, 199, 281, 282

B-cognition, *see* cognition: of being

Becoming, theory of, 121-23

behaviour therapy, *see* therapy

behaviourism, 3, 16, 21, 74, 115, 116, 264, 281, 288

Being, theory of, 123-27

belief, 140, *see also* will to believe

benevolence, 7, 8, 103-07, 109, 113-14, 227

berserk, 166, 281

bhakti, 255, 281

Bhakti Yoga, *see* Yoga

Bible, 141, 163

bicameral mind, 163, 282

big dreams, *see* dreams

biocentrism, 66

bioenergetics, 87, 282

biosphere, 201, 282, 294

birth process, 22, 199, 281, 301, *see also* perinatal

B-love, *see* love

bodhisattva, 92, 153, 282

body, 28, 29, 207, 208, 210, 213, *see also* embodiment
astral, 162, 173, 280
body self, *see* self
causal, 162, 282
dream, 166, 167, 173
etheric, 162, 173, 287
inconscient, 195
mental, 162, 297
and mind, 195
physical, 166, 167, 213, 280
spiritual, 161
subtle, 23, 48, 162, 167, 173, 197, 198, 280, 282, 283, 287, 297, 310
wisdom of, 195

body-mind-spirit, 65-67, *see also* Great Chain/ Nest/Holarchy of Being

body work, 22, 24, 282, 291, 308

Book of Enlightened Masters, 227

bookcase episode (Freud & Jung), 42

borderline disorders, 199

both-and thinking, 268

BPM, *see* Basic Perinatal Matrices

Brahman, 36, 162, 189, 200, 214, 279, 281, 282, 291

Brahman-Atman, *see* Atman-Brahman

British Psychological Society, 25, 38, 43

Bronze Age, 53

Buddhism, 14, 17, 24, 28, 52, 78-79, 81, 160, 162, 171, 209, 223-24, 230, 248, 250, 251, 279, 282, 285, 287, 295, 296, 297, 299, 303, 306, 307, 311, 312, 315
  Buddhist psychology, 14
  Buddhist psychotherapy, 37
  Mahayana, 282, 296, 314, 316
  Theravada, 312
  Tibetan, 172, 286, 296, 312
  Vajrayana, 224, 314
  Vietnamese, 293
  and Wilber, 204-05, 223-24, 250
  Zen, *see* Zen
B-values, *see* values of being
bystander apathy, 105-06

California Institute of Integral Studies, 37
Cartesianism, 78, 168, 212, 213, 282, 286, 311
casual mysticism, *see* mysticism
catharsis, 83, 84, 86, 282
causal level, 32, 53, 55, 78, 80, 81, 162, 198, 200-03, 222, 226, 247-51, 255, 265, 282
  high, 200, 291
  low, 200, 295
causal body, *see* body
causal indifference, 243, 282
causal mysticism, *see* causal level, mysticism
causal self, *see* self
centaur stage, 49, 198, 199, 226, 265-66, 268, 283, 315
chakras, 47, 48, 167, 216, 233, 283, 294
channelling, 12, 44, 54, 56, 86, 167, 191, 281, 283, 285
character
  development, 110
  evil, *see* evil
charismatic movement, 283, 285
chi, 283, 311
Chinese philosophy, 283, 311, 312
Christianity, 28, 54, 220, 224, 241, 250, 251, 261, 269, 283, 289, 290, 298, 307
  charismatic,
    see charismatic movement
  Christian humanism, 220, 269,

283
  Christian mysticism,
    see mysticism
Church
  censorship, 251
  of England, 1-2
  of the New Jerusalem, 311
  paranormal investigations, 41
circumconscient, 194, 195, 283
clairvoyance,
  see extrasensory perception
cocreation, 36, 80, 138, 158, 211-13, 230, 231, 266-70, 275, 283, 301
cognition
  of being, 123, 127, 152, 178, 283, 314
  deficiency, 124, 285
  innocent, 86
cognitive development, 203
cognitivism, 3, 16, 25, 283
coincidences, *see* synchronicity
cold experience, 261
collective consciousness,
  see consciousness
collective shadow, *see* shadow
collective unconscious, 20, 30,138, 170, 179-83, 185, 186, 280, 283, 293
  and God, 221-22
  Grof on, 191
  higher and lower, 185
  in psychosynthesis, 187
  transpersonal, 20, 180, 185
communication, 252, 254, 257, 259
communion, 29, 170, 227, 241, 252, 253, 255, 258, 259, 266, 271, 283, 312, 314, *see also* union
community, 252, 267, 275
companionship, 252
comparative religion, *see* religion, religious studies
compassion, 12, 20, 21, 29, 75, 86-87, 93, 103, 178, 251-52, 255, 275, 290, 294
  failure of, 94, 104
complexes, 180, 284, 295, 301
conditional love, *see* love
conditions of worth, 102, 284
conformity and evil, 106
connected self, *see* self

consciousness, 16, 17, 29, 78, 164, 167, 169, 173, 180, 191, 232, 249, 287, 302, 304, 305, 308, 309, 313, 314, 315
  absolute, 90, 200, 233
  average and advanced modes, 53
  causal,
    see causal level, mysticism
  collective, 60
  cosmic,
    see cosmic consciousness
  dualistic, 172
  egoic, *see* egoic, self-consciousness
  evolution of, 163-64, 175
  expansion, 22
  field of, 186
  formless,
    see formless consciousness
  global, 60
  higher, 28, 164, 187, 213, 227, 280, 290
  involution of, *see* involution
  Kosmic,
    see cosmic consciousness
  levels,
    see levels of development
  light as symbol, 72-73
  moral, *see* moral
  narrowing, 23
  nondual, 32, 172, 183, 185, 189, 200, 248-49, *see also* nondual, One Taste
  ontological status, 192, 197, 231,
  psychic, 32, *see also* mysticism, psychic, psychism
  pure, 86, 245, 305, *see also* pure consciousness event
  in Samkhya and Yoga, 162
  seat of, 256
  species, 170, 183, 197, 309
  states of, 17, 19, 24, 33, 45, 54-55, 76, 81, 152, 160, 217, 229, 279, 291, 304, 313
  subtle,
    see subtle level, mysticism
  transpersonal, 191, *see also* transpersonal experience
  ultimate, 32, 172, 200, 313
consciousness studies, 25, 284
constructivism, 238-39, 268, 284, 302, 311
contemplation, 164, 167, 179, 187, 208, 226, 234, 241, 252, 255, 260, 266, 284, 294, 295, 305
  eye of, *see* eye
  of ideal forms, 167
contexts of mystical experience, 10, 254-59, *see also* mysticism
contextualism, 78, 238, 253, 293, 306
Conversations with God, 222
conversion, 94, 169, 183, 241, 284, 307
cool
  mysticism, 254-59,
  traditions, 85, 148, 247, 275, 284
co-operation, 255, 259
cosmic consciousness, 17-19, 22, 23, 170, 174, 183, 188, 189, 191, 192, 197, 198, 200-02, 204, 208, 219, 225, 241-43, 248-49, 255, 284, 300, 304
  Bucke on, 17-19
  and higher self, 187, *see also* self
  and One Taste, 200-02, 249,
    see also One Taste
  origin of religion, 19
  and Oversoul, 19,
    see also Oversoul
  and psychic mysticism, 249
  and subtle level, 198, 200
  Walt Whitman, 19
Cosmic Consciousness, 17
cosmic game, 90-91
cosmic self, *see* self
cosmic synthesis, *see* psychosynthesis
cosmos, 193, 213, 218-19, 225, 256, 278, 294, 296, 303, 311, 314
  anthropic principle,
    see evolution
  and Kosmos, 202,
    see also Kosmos
counselling, 4, 87, 199, *see also* transpersonal counselling
creative illness, 83

creativity, 12, 21, 47, 48, 64, 74, 75, 80, 86-87, 100, 178, 182, 208, 251, 255, 259, 260, 286, 290, 292, 302, 312
  cocreation, *see* cocreation
  and dynamic ground, 34-35
crisis
  identity, 199, 287
  spiritual, 13, 83, 169, 179, *see also* spiritual emergency
cult, 13, 66, 76, 151, 175, 284
  of self, 128

daemon/daimon, 162, 254, 284
dark night
  and BPMII, 190
  of the self, 83
  of the senses, 207, 284
  of the soul, 46, 65, 66, 83, 86, 171, 179, 190, 261, 284, 294
  of the spirit, 171, 207, 284
  and the mystic way, 241
darkness (as symbol), 72-74, 90
D-cognition, *see* cognition: deficiency
death
  confronting, 86
  fear of, 18, 54
  instinct, 312, *see also* Thanatos
  process, 286
  and rebirth, 190, *see also* rebirth, reincarnation
  survival of, *see* survival
deep ecology, *see* ecology
deep empathy, *see* empathy
deep self, *see* self
deep unconscious, *see* unconscious
defence mechanisms, 73, 99-100, 122, 285, 304, 306
deficiency cognition, *see* cognition: deficiency
deficiency needs, 146, 156, 285
deities, 161, 207, 248, 280, 285, 289, *see also* God, Goddess
  blissful, 23
  wrathful, 23, *see also* demons
deity mysticism, *see* mysticism
deliverance ministry, 87, 94, 285
demons, 207, 216, 285
dependent arising/origination, 162, 285, 303

depression, 261, 284, 313
  and transformation, 84-86
descending current, 27-31, 33, 35, 37, 67, 69, 78, 210, 228, 268, 271, 272, 285
deserved harm, *see* harm
determinism, 156, 291
Devil, 89-90, *see also* demons, Satanism
devotion, 87, 246, 251, 281, 282
dharma, 285
dharma samtana, 162, 285
dialogic mysticism, *see* mysticism
Dionysian approach, 152, 285
disintegration, 305, *see also* dissociation
dissociation, 14, 52, 69, 124, 166, 167, 181, 199, 279, 281, 285, 295, 300
divination, 40, 285
Divine, 28, 53, 90, 169, 170, 188, 193, 197, 216, 218, 220, 224, 225, 240, 254-56, 259, 281, 285, 286, 288, 289, 290, 292, 294, 298, 300, 309, 311, 314, *see also* deities, God, Goddess
divine soul, *see* soul
divine spark, *see* spark
Doors of Perception, 22
double, 161, 164, 166, 173
dreams, 9, 182, 197, 279, 296
  big, 12, 282
  lucid, 44, 48, 165, 286, 296
  and soul, 165
  and subliminal self, 195
  working with, 4, 20
Dream Yoga, *see* Yoga
dreamless sleep, 279, 282
drops (in Buddhism)
  eternal indestructible, 52, 53, 287
  lifetime indestructible, 295
drugs
  LSD, 22, 46, 190, 260, 304
  MDMA, 260, 286
  mescaline, 22, 304
  nitrous oxide, 17, 22
  psilocybin 244, 260
  psychedelic, psychoactive, 17, 21-23, 86, 87, 156, 189, 243,

244, 260, 276, 286, 291, 304, 305
   treatment, 110
dualism, 78, 89, 168, 172, 201, 212, 245, 282, 285, 286, 311, *see also* Cartesianism
dynamic ground, 27, 34, 205-09, 285, 286, 303, 306, *see also* nonegoic core
Dzogchen, 172, 174, 223, 286, 307

Earth Mother, 29
Eastern mysticism, *see* mysticism
Eastern philosophies, 78, 209, 234, *see also* mysticism, religion
eclipse, 71
ecocentrism, 66
ecofeminism, 31, 35, 37, 286
ecology, 15, 29, 227, 267, 268
   deep, 35, 66-67, 97, 113, 285
   transpersonal, 66-68, 313
ecoromanticism, *see* romanticism
ecosphere, 66
ecstasy, 12, 21, 40, 53, 54, 64, 66, 75, 76, 78, 86, 151-52, 156, 167-71, 187, 190, 196, 207, 241, 251, 253, 254, 261, 286, 288
Ecstasy, *see* drugs:MDMA
Edinburgh, 16, 17
effectance, *see* hands
egg diagram (Assagioli), 186-87
ego, 29, 34, 69, 162, 168, 173, 195, 268, 285, 286, 293, 300, 301, 306, 308, 313, 314
   in Aurobindo's theory, 195
   and evil, *see* evil
   in Grof's theory, 190
   illusory, 242
   in Jung's theory, 180-84
   mature, 199, 207
   mental, *see* mental-egoic
   in psychosynthesis, 21, 186-87
   transcendence, 45, 92, 124, 144, *see also* self-transcendence
   in Washburn's theory, 34-35, 205-09
   in Wilber's theory, 199, 203
egocentrism, 7, 12, 66, 68-69, 76, 123, 124, 156, 212, 285, 286, 308, 310, 313, *see also* narcissism
   emancipation from, 36-37, 69,

113, 154, 184, 211, 267, 275, 286, 299, 300
   and evil, 103-04, 113-14
egoic
   consciousness, *see* self-consciousness
   identity, 12, 13, 69, 178, 205-09, 228-29, 286, 289, 297, 313, *see also* ego, mental-egoic, self
   phase, 34, 205-07, 285, 286
ego-self axis, 180-81, 286
Egyptian religion, *see* religion
EHE, *see* exceptional human experiences
elevationism, 31, 32, 34, 185, 286, 303
emancipation, *see* egocentrism, Ocean of Emancipation
embodiment, 9, 29, 78, 169, 208, 213, 214, 215, 265, 286, 290, *see also* body
embryonal experience, *see* fetal experience
emergence, *see* spiritual emergency
emotion, 65, 210, 282, 307
emotional self, *see* self
emotivism, 133-34, 138, 143, 286
empathy, 7, 12, 21, 64, 102-05, 109-10, 210, 213, 255, 275, 286, 292, 303, 311
   deep, 102, 252
   failure of, 7, 101, 102-06, 109, 113-14, 311
   span of, 8, 109, 113-14
empiricism, 8, 13, 14, 235, 274, 286, 302
   inner, 35, 293
   radical, 16, 305
   scientific, 235
emptiness, 86, 92, 171, 200, 245, 248, 249, 255, 280, 286, 311, 315, *see also* void
enchantment, 254
encounter groups, 24, 87, 152, 287, 308
encounters (UFO), *see* UFO experiences
energy, *see* subtle energy

enlightenment, 64, 68, 76, 152, 153, 255
  spiritual, 28, 36, 75, 76, 143, 147, 282, 287, 294, 296, 312
Enlightenment, the, 41, 133, 143, 287
enstasy, 86, 208, 287
entelechy, 118, 143, 148, 287,
  see also teleology
epiphany, 287
epistemology, 5, 24, 33, 37, 43, 287
  indigenous, 37,
    see also indigenous
  and mysticism, 235
  and science, 235
epithymia, 161
époche, rule of, 217, 287, 307
Eros, 228, 287
Esalen Institute, 24
esotericism, 2, 20, 81, 186, 189, 281, 287, 293, 310, 312
essentialism, 238-39, 287
eternal indestructible drop,
  see drops
eternal life, 18, *see also*
  immortality, survival
etheric body, *see* body
European Transpersonal Association (EUROTAS), 38
evangelism, 287, 307
evil, 7, 8, 88-114, 207, 275, 285, 289
  character, 7, 98-105, 113,
  concept of, 88-98, 107, 114, 161-62, 167
  denial of 76, 88, 91
  and ego, 7, 98-101, 114, 307
  Grof on, 90-92
  Jung on, 72-74, 89, 99-100
  psychological roots, 7, 65, 72-74, 98-107, 113, 181
  and quadrant model, 110-12
  social roots, 106-12
  solutions to 86, 91, 93, 106, 109-14
  transpersonal perspective, 112-13
  Wilber on, 89
evocation, 167, 287, 294
evolution, 19, 27, 29, 32, 52-53, 63, 112-14, 155, 198, 222, 228, 250,

281, 287, 290, 302, 303, 304, 309
  anthropic principle, 193-94, 280
  Aurobindo on, 193-97
  of consciousness,
    see consciousness
  spiritual, 193-97, 204, 247, 306
exceptional human experiences, 43, 286, 287
exegesis, 165, 287, 295
existential
  crisis, 83, 86, 199, 287
  identity, *see* identity
  psychology, 16, 264
  therapy, *see* therapy
existentialism, 65, 281, 287
  and self-actualization, 123, 129, 143
exorcism, 87, 88, 94, 287
exotericism, 288
exotic approach, 81, 82, 85-87, 227, 229, 230, 268, 288
experientialism, 35, 54, 76, 212, 213, 288
experimental psychology, *see* psychology
exteriorization, 43, 288
extinction of self, *see* self
extrapersonal, 47-50, 55, 288
extrasensory perception, 47, 56, 248, 304
  clairvoyance, 23, 44, 49, 191, 198
  precognition, 23, 42, 44
  remote viewing, 23
  sixth sense, 254, 262
  telepathy, 42, 44, 49, 54
extravertive mysticism,
  see mysticism
eye
  of contemplation, 235, 312
  of flesh, 312
  of reason, 312
  that cannot see itself, 168,
    see also witness

Facing Evil, 95
faith, 140, 223, 224, 226, 269-70, 279, 296
  loss of, 65, 83, 86, 261
fakirism, 47, 288
false self, *see* self

fana, 162, 288
fantasy, 80, 182, 255, 301
    guided, 4, 290
    of God, 222
fascinans, 246, 288
fascism, 93, 107
fear, 86
    of non-being, 108
female, *see also* gender differences
    perspective, 29, 270
    spiritual experience, 35, 78,
        210, 251, 301
    value sphere, 211, 228
feminism, 29, 231, 232, 268, 269-70,
    284, 286, 288
    transpersonal theory, 177,
        209-11, 227-28
    and Wilber, 210-11, 227, 271
fetal experience, 23, 46, 237
field of consciousness,
    see consciousness
fifth force, 264, 288
final cause, 288, 312
first force, *see* force
flatland, 67, 288
flow experience, 43, 86, 219, 255,
    260, 261, 288
focussing, 288
force
    first, 21
    second, 21, 308
    third, 21, 65, 74, 292, 312
    fourth, 21, 74, 289
    fifth, 264, 288
    vital, 283
formless consciousness, 32, 53, 80,
    171, 183, 185, 189, 191, 197, 199,
    200, 203, 204, 245, 248, 251, 282,
    283, 289, 291, 295, 305, *see also*
    consciousness
    and Jung, 183
formless self, *see* self
fourth force, *see* force
free will, 164
Freudianism, 74, 116, 287, 289,
    295, 304, 308, 310, 312, *see also*
    psychoanalysis
frontal self, *see* self
fulcrums, 198, 199, 289, 295
functionalism, 116, 289

fundamentalism, 57, 90, 218, 289

Gaia, 66, 289, 313
gender differences,
    see female, feminism, male
    Wilber's perspective, 271
gestalt
    psychology, 116
    therapy, *see* therapy
Gifford Lectures (William James),
    16, 17
Given, Myth of,
    see Myth of the Given
glimpse experience, 86, 289, 301
global consciousness,
    see consciousness
glossolalia, 309
Gnosticism, 28, 90, 162, 167, 179,
    289, 316
God, 18, 29, 89, 90, 109, 139, 140,
    169, 170, 216, 227, 233, 235-36,
    242, 245, 254-57, 280, 281, 282,
    283, 284, 285, 289, 294, 297, 300,
    303, 304, 307, 312
    archetype, 89, 180, 185, 220-23,
        289
    belief as functional, 139
    death of, 89
    defined negatively, 315,
        see also via negativa
    and Devil, 89-90
    final, 200, 295
    as ground, 52, 198
    Horned, 291, 298
    identity with, 170, 222
    and nondual, 172, 223
    as Other, 220-23, 260
    personal, 200, 289, 306
    remembrance of, 311
    two faces, 90
    union with, 28, 162, 170, 174,
        190, 218, 241-43, 248, 283,
        293, 310, 312
    Wilber on, 222-23
God mysticism, *see* mysticism
Goddess, 29, 109, 161, 185, 210,
    216, 220, 221, 227, 285, 289, 298
Godhead, 162, 171, 200, 255, 289
God-image, *see* God: archetype
good and evil, 7, 64, 91, 286,
    see also evil

dualism, 90, 93
potentials, 91, 99, 103
relativism, 89-91, 94-95
transcendence of, 89-91
transpersonal perspective, 113,
    114
good faith, 290
Good Friday experiment, 244
good life, 96, 135, 145, 155
goods and harms, 96, *see also* harm
grace, 74, 84, 86, 247, 290
Grace and Grit, 84
Great Chain/Nest/Holarchy of
    Being, 28, 29, 32, 64, 193, 198,
    224, 250, 290
Great Circle/Web of Being, 27-29,
    35, 290
Greek mythology, 284
gross realm, 162, 198, 201, 203,
    247, 249, 251, 290, 304
    and the low subtle, 55, 248
ground, 171, 197, 201, 242
    and nondual consciousness,
    172, 202
groundedness, 169, 283, 290
growth needs, 290
guardian angel, 147, 161, 173, 174,
    254, 290
guide, 12, 162, 168, 182, 183, 207,
    214, 284, *see also* spirit guide
guided fantasy, 4, 290
guru, 2, 188, 254, 290
Guru Yoga, *see* Yoga

hallowed resplendence, 208
hallucinogenics, *see* drugs
hands, 7, 103, 104, 106, 114, 278
harm, 103
    deserved, 97, 100, 107
    relative and universal, 96
    undeserved, 96-101, 107
hate, 103
Hatha Yoga, *see* Yoga
hauntings, 40, 166, *see also*
    apparitions
head, 7, 29, 103, 104, 109, 113, 114,
    278
healing, 23, 37, 48, 54, 87, 167, 283,
    287, 297, 309
    holotropic, 22
    primal wound, 83, 109

and self-knowledge, 109
spiritual, 44, 45
of splits, 30, 63-65
wounded healer, 315
heart, 7, 29, 103, 104, 109, 113, 114,
    171, 200, 213, 243, 252, 255, 266,
    278, 290, 293
    in Islam, 162
    and mysticism, 240
    as witness, 172
Hebrew Bible, 161
hedonism, 122, 290
    and self-actualization, 123, 129,
    148
hermeneutics, 15, 59, 276, 290
Hermeticism, 179, 290
hero, 136, 182
heterarchy, 29, 290
hexing, 23, 48, 290
hierarchical approach, 29, 34, 88,
    210, 227, 247, 251, 259, 265, 267,
    271, 290, 291, 295, 310,
    see also structural-hierarchical
        approach
    and feminism, 210, 251
    critique of, 212, 250-51
    in mysticism, 250, 251, 259
hierarchy of needs, 116, 117, 119,
    125, 140, 146, 154, 291, 303
    critiques of, 146-47
high causal, *see* causal level
high subtle, *see* subtle level
higher mind, *see* mind
higher self, *see* self
higher unconscious, *see*
    unconscious
Hinduism, 24, 28, 192, 223, 281,
    282, 291, 296, 299, 307, 311, 312,
    314
holarchy, 34, 63, 265, 272, 291, 295,
    see also holon
holism, 7, 10, 63-70, 116, 132, 178,
    225, 283, 291, 299
    all-quadrant, 7, 66-69
    new-age, 7, 64-65
    psychological, 7, 65-68
Holocaust, 74, 89, 106
holon, 32, 291, 297,
    see also holarchy

holotropic
    experience, 22, 23, 90, 291
    model, 177, 189-92
    therapy, *see* therapy
Holotropic Breathwork™, 22, 24,
    46, 190, 199, 290, 291
homunculus theory, 118, 291
horizontal path, 27, 29, 66-67, 69,
    228, 291
Horned God, *see* God
hot
    mysticism, 247, 254
    traditions, 85, 247, 256-57, 259,
    275, 292
human nature, 21, 74-75, 93, 99,
    114, 123, 179, 219, 220, 266, 283,
    297, 314
human potential movement, 24,
    75, 292
    critiques of, 77, 131, 307
humanism, 116, 292
    Christian, *see* Christianity
humanistic approach, 10, 41, 59,
    63, 228, 269
humanistic psychology, 3, 16, 25,
    264, 292, 308, 312
    agenda, 21, 74-75
    critiques, 26, 77, 80, 302, 307
    history of, 21, 24, 74, 296
hun, 162
hypnosis, 198

Idea of the Holy, 245
idealism, 78, 143, 292, 302
    Aurobindo's, 193
    Maslow's, 116
    mental, 167
    in transpersonal psychology,
    65
idealized self, *see* self
identification, 313, *see also* identity
    experiences of, 11, 22, 46, 191
    with mental ego, 51
    with nature, 66
identity, 47, 58, 108, 110, 147, 148,
    151, 166, 215, 237, 252, 255, 259,
    292, 314
    collective, 266
    crisis, *see* crisis
    egoic, *see* egoic
    ethnic, 105, 113

existential, 178, 198
expansion of, 32, 81
knowledge by, 197, 311
personal, 51, 52, 55, 204, 295
sexual, 105, 203
transcendence of, 49, 50, 51,
    125, 169, 308, *see also*
    self-transcendence
transpersonal, 160, 164, 175-76,
    178, 201, 213, 215, 258
with God, *see* God
ideology, 308
    good and evil, 106-07, 110-11
    in self-actualization, 134-36
    in transpersonal psychology, 1,
    13
I-I, 171, 200, 292, 306
I-It, 222
Iliad, 163-64
illness, 86
illumination, 12, 18, 20, 187, 198,
    207, 241, 261, 287, 292, 312
illumined mind, *see* mind
illusoriness of world, 295, 296, *see*
    also maya
imagination, 34, 52, 64, 80, 255,
    286, 301, 307, 309, 310, 315
    and subtle level, 32, 198
immanence, 10, 27, 29, 78, 210,
    228, 268, 285, 292
    psychic,
        see psychic immanence
immortality, 18, 161, 163, 165-66,
    169-70, 173-76, 179, 204, 281,
    see also survival
inauthenticity, 150, 157
inconscient, 193, 194, 195, 292
indigenous
    epistemology, 37
    religion, *see* religion
    spirituality, 35, 46, 52, 210, 211,
    250, 251, 268, 270
individualism, 27, 29, 133, 134,
    138, 149, 151, 156, 292
individuation, 20, 49, 74, 125, 143,
    181, 226, 265-66, 292, 293
ineffability, 91, 240, 242, 244, 245,
    253, 292, 300, 305

initiation, 293, 315
    into inner and outer reality,
        180-81, 293
inmost being, 194, 196
inner being, 194-96, 283, 293, 310
inner empiricism, 35, 293
inner world, 180, *see also*
    unconscious
inspiration, 9, 48, 75, 86, 168, 182,
    183, 188, 248, 255, 259, 260
instinctoid, 293
Institute of Noetic Sciences, 38
Institute of Transpersonal Psy-
    chology, 37
Integral
    approach, 15, 30, 33, 59, 67,
        264, 273, 276, 305
    practice, 88, 92, 203, 226, 293
    psychology, 160, 177, 192,
        263-64, 288, 293
    studies, 79
    therapy, *see* therapy
Integral Institute, 67
Integral Transformative Practice,
    293
Integral Yoga, *see* Yoga
integration, 63-70, 109, 203,
    207-08, 211, 213, 214, 219, 227,
    265, 266, 272, 293
    ascending and descending
        currents, 67, 69
    body, mind, spirit, 7, 64, 67,
        169, 283
    failure of, 185, 305
    of gender perspectives, 270-71,
        279
    higher order, 63, 65
    personal with transpersonal,
        69, 92
    psychological, 20, 21, 34, 52, 66,
        109, 113, 159, 181, 188,
        205-07, 214, 265, 271, 292,
        301, 305, 308
    of quadrants, 7, 59, 67, 203, 305
integrative life 203, 208, 214
interactionism, 239, 268, 293
inter-being, 251, 255, 256, 293, *see
    also* interconnection
interconnection 144, 227, 293, *see
    also* inter-being

inter-individual psychosynthesis,
    see psychosynthesis
Interior Castle, 171
internalization, 293, 300
*International Journal of
    Transpersonal Studies*, 38
interpretation (of mystical experi-
    ence), 257
intimate relationship
    as spiritual path, 82, 252-53,
    see also mysticism: sexual
*Intimations of Immortality from Rec-
    ollections of Early Childhood*, 52
introjection, 101, 125, 292, 293, 304
introspection, 35, 167, 199, 284,
    293
introversion, 23, 85
introvertive mysticism, *see*
    mysticism
intuition, 20, 21, 29, 52, 162, 164,
    168, 182, 188, 213, 235, 254, 293
    in Aurobindo's theory, 194,
        196, 197
    higher, 187
invocation, 167, 294
involution, 29, 198, 281, 292, 294
    in Aurobindo's theory, 193-95
Iron Age, 53
Islam, 28, 162, 224, 294, 311
I-Thou, 102, 113, 208, 220-23, 254,
    294

Jainism, 28, 162, 163, 294
jiva, 162, 163, 294
jivatman, 162, 194, 196, 197, 294
Jnana Yoga, *see* Yoga
John F. Kennedy University, 37
Journal of Consciousness Studies, 38
Journal of Humanistic Psychology,
    38
Journal of Transpersonal Psychology,
    21, 38, 217, 274
Judaism, 28, 224, 294, 311, 312
Jungian analysis, 87, *see also* ana-
    lytical psychology
Jungian psychology, *see* analytical
    psychology
just world, 107
justifiable harm, *see* harm

ka, 161, 163, 173

Kabbalah, 24, 162, 250, 294, 295
Kantian ethics, 133
karma, 53, 96, 162, 169, 170, 216,
    287, 291, 294, 309
Karma Yoga, *see* Yoga
kataphatic mysticism,
    see mysticism
khaibit, 161, 173
khu, 161, 163, 173
Kingdom of God/Heaven, 19, 36
Kosmic consciousness, *see* cosmic
    consciousness
Kosmos, 200, 201, 294, *see also*
    cosmos
kuei, 162
kundalini, 201, 294, 295
    awakening, 56, 167, 201, 262,
        295
Kundalini Yoga, *see* Yoga

ladder model, 28, 29, 268, 271, 295,
    see also structural-hierarchical
    approach
language mysticism, *see* mysticism
latah, 166, 295, 300
laughing gas,
    see drugs: nitrous oxide
Leeds University, 2
levels of development, 33, 34, 55,
    199, 202, 264, 295, 309, *see also*
    astral-psychic level, causal
    level, personal level,
    prepersonal level, psychic
    level, subtle level,
    transpersonal level, ultimate
    level
liberation, 167, 197, 211, 241, 282,
    294, 295, 299, 307, 316
    and Original Self, 183, 184
life after death, *see* survival
Life Divine, 193
life force, 287
lifetime indestructible drop, *see*
    drops
light, 190, *see also* illumination,
    illumined mind
    and darkness, 316
    inner, 167
    in near-death experience, 169,
        298

spiritual, 162, 292
    symbolism of, 72-75, 90
linear model, 209, *see also* hierar-
    chical approach, struc-
    tural-hierarchical approach
lines of development, 33, 295
lines of self, *see* self
Liverpool
    John Moores University, 4, 26,
        37, 277
    as pool of life, 3
logos, 161
logotherapy, 87, 88, 199, 295
longbody, 169, 295
loss of faith, *see* faith
love, 12, 21, 48, 64, 74, 86, 92, 103,
    117, 123, 207, 219, 227, 228, 288,
    290, 292, 294, 311
    B-love, 152, 153, 156
    conditional, 102
    and mysticism, 18, 170, 239,
        240, 242, 246, 248, 249,
        251-53, 255, 259, 260
    unconditional, 102, 279, 314
loving-kindness, 255, 297,
    see also metta
low causal, *see* causal level
low subtle, *see* subtle level
lower unconscious, *see*
    unconscious
LSD, *see* drugs
lucid dreams, *see* dreams

Machiavellianism, 149, 156
magic, 2, 4, 40, 44, 53, 78, 167, 191,
    234, 246, 247, 287, 288, 289, 290,
    293, 294, 296, 298, 307, 311, 312,
    315
    ritual, 23, 48, 87, 307
magical thinking, 52, 53, 56-57, 61,
    164, 296
Mahamudra, 172, 296
Mahayana Buddhism, *see*
    Buddhism
maintenance
    and descending current, 29,
        see also descending current
    in progress, 269
maithuna, 255, 296 *see also* mysti-
    cism: sexual

male, *see also* gender differences
    and evil, 74, 107
    perspective on transpersonal,
        29, 79, 209-10, 270, 280
    spiritual experience, 78
    value sphere, 211, 228
malevolence, 7, 103-09, 114
mana, 182, 254, 296
mana personality, 180-82, 185, 296
mandala, 182, 296
mantra, 296
Mantra Yoga, *see* Yoga
Many, the, 29, *see also* pluralism
maps, 67, 265
materialism, 15, 54, 60, 175, 218,
        270, 296, 308
    scientific, *see* scientific
        materialism
    spiritual, *see* spiritual
        materialism
materialization, 302
matriarchy, 29
matter, *see* involution, Great
    Chain/Nest/Holarchy of
    Being
mature ego, *see* ego
maya, 150, 296
MDMA, *see* drugs
meaninglessness, 65
meditation, 4, 21, 24, 45, 46, 50, 54,
        55, 81, 110, 151, 167, 172, 173,
        192, 201, 209, 226, 245, 248, 250,
        252, 253, 255, 261, 262, 276, 286,
        296, 299, 305, 307, 308, 312, 314,
        315, 316
    mindfulness, 297, 315, 316,
        see also vipassana, zazen
    and phenomenology, 230
    research on, 24, 66
    and siddhis, 55
    on suffering, 87
    and transformation, 60, 265
mediumship, 2, 23, 40, 44, 46, 48,
        182, 297
    Jung's investigation, 42
    mental, 297
    physical, 23, 48, 302
    trance, 41, 167, 313
mental body, *see* body

mental illness, 132,
    see also psychopathology
mental mediumship,
    see mediumship
mental mysticism, *see* mysticism
mental-egoic, 32, 51, 52, 164, 206,
        266, 297, 301, 303, 313
merging, 12, 48, 219
mescaline, *see* drugs
Mesmerism, 41, 297
metahuman, 219, 297
metamotivation, 21, 74, 125-29,
        149, 153-54, 156, 177, 178-79,
        219, 275, 297, 308
metaneeds, 126, 297
metapathology, 83, 297,
    see also psychopathology
metaphysics, 8, 9, 11, 14, 92,
        160-61, 175, 179, 189, 214,
        216-33, 297, 313, 314
    and Aurobindo, 193, 197, 204
    definition of, 232, 297
    and evil, 89-93
    and feminism, 227
    and Grof, 192
    and James, 229, 303
    and Jung, 89, 179, 183, 219-23,
        225, 229
    and Maslow, 219, 225
    and mysticism, 234-35, 239, 262
    and phenomenology, 173-75,
        230-31
    in psychosynthesis, 189
    and soul, 160-65, 174-76, 177
    and transcendence, 9, 89, 92
    and transpersonal psychology,
        45-47, 61, 78, 175, 197, 216-33
    and Washburn, 208
    and Wilber, 204-05, 223-26,
        229-30
metta, 87, 255, 297
middle unconscious,
    see unconscious
mid-life crisis, 181
mind, 18, 136, 171, 255, 285, 299,
        305, *see also* consciousness,
        psyche, unconscious
    bicameral, 163, 282
    and body, 52, 195, 212
    Cartesian, 173,

see also Cartesianism
distinction from soul and
  spirit, 163
and Great Chain of Being, *see*
  Great Chain/Nest/Holarchy
  of Being
higher, 162, 194, 196, 291, 292
illumined, 162, 194, 196, 292
and matter, 22, 23, 32, 47, 48,
  304
no mind, *see* no mind
and nondual, 172, 307,
  see also nondual
and the Real, 236, 296
and subtle, 198,
  see also subtle level
universal, 191, 300
mind mysticism, *see* mysticism
mindfulness meditation,
  see meditation
miracles, 40
mission, 123, 127, 129, 153
modes of mystical experience,
  see mystical experience
monasticism, 312
monistic mysticism, *see* mysticism
monotheism, 224, 294, 297
moral, *see also* morality
  consciousness, 98, 109, 114, 164
  development, 3, 110, 113
  effectance, 7, 8, 114
  evil, 96-97, 102, 114,
    see also evil
  relativism, 94-95, 133
  span, 113
morality, 92, 95, 99, 100, 108, 133,
  202, 203, 214, 242, 307
  and biology, 149, 155
  definition, 97
  and quadrant model, 114
  and self-actualization, 123, 132,
    142, 149
  and spirituality, 10, 20, 95, 242
  universal, 95, 109, 133
morphic field, 170, 297, 309
motivation
  Maslow's theory, 116-17,
    see also metamotivation
multidisciplinary approach, 273

mundane approach, 10, 69, 82,
  84-88, 229, 230, 232, 261, 268,
  298
muse, 168, 182, 255
'My Soul' (Whitman),
  see Oversoul
mysterium, 246, 259, 288, 298, 313
mystery cults, 234
mystery of being, 2, 36, 78, 80, 129,
  138, 211-12, 230-31, 232, 236,
  265-67, 298, 301
mystic way, 241, 298
mystical atheism, *see* atheism
mystical participation, 164
mysticism, 12, 19-24, 43, 45, 55, 56,
  75, 78, 81, 85, 86, 123, 131, 149,
  151-52, 162, 164-73, 178, 189,
  190, 192, 218, 219, 225-27,
  234-62, 282, 283, 284, 287, 289,
  293, 298, 299, 304, 305, 309, 311,
  312, 314
  5 x 5 model, 10, 85, 253-62,
    267-68, 285
  apophatic, 248, 280
  ascetic, 29
  casual, 82, 226, 227
  causal, 248, 250,
    see also causal level
  characteristics and types of,
    9-10, 235, 238, 239-62, 267,
    275, 284, 285, 289, 292, 293,
    298, 299, 304, 309, 312, 314
  in childhood,
    see transpersonal experience
  Christian, 17, 24, 46, 241, 261
  contexts, 10, 254-59
  cool, *see* cool
  definition of, 9, 234-39, 256,
    262, 298
  deity, 174, 198, 202, 203, 285,
    289
  dialogic, 10, 254, 257, 260, 285
  and drugs, 243, *see also* drugs
  Eastern, 241, 251, 294
  embodied, 29
  extravertive, 85, 243-45, 248,
    288, 304
  formless,
    see formless consciousness
  God, 242, 289

gross, 201
Happold on, 242
history of, 251
hot, *see* hot
Indian, 294
introvertive, 241, 243, 245, 246, 247, 252, 293
James on, 17, 240
Jewish, 46, 294,
    see also Kabbalah
kataphatic, 248, 294
of knowledge and understanding, 242
language, 256, 295
of love and union, 235, 240-42
mental, 10, 256, 297
and metaphysics, 234-35, 239, 262
mind, 174
modes, 10, 254-55, 257-59
monistic, 10, 241, 242, 243, 245, 247, 248, 250, 256, 297
nature, 10, 32, 174, 198, 199, 201-02, 227, 236, 237, 241-43, 248, 252, 254-57, 298, 300, 304, *see also* cosmic consciousness
nondual, 10, 32, 185, 199, 248-50, 255, 258, 259, 292, 300, *see also* nondual, One Taste
non-religious, 241
numinous, 10, 254, 257, 259
Otto on, 245-46
paradoxicality, 244
problem of ranking, 242, 250-51, 259
psychic, 200-02, 248-50, 254-56, 304
Rawlinson on, 246-47
and religious experience, 234, 236-39, 241, 245
serious, 82, 226, 227
sexual, 87, 90, 252, 253, 256, 258, 296, 308, 311
social, 10, 251-53, 256, 309
soul, 200, 203, 242, 243, 248, 309
Stace on, 243-44
subtle, 248, 249,

    see also subtle level
Sufi, 46
synergic, 10, 255, 258, 259
theistic, 10, 189, 199, 230, 241-48, 250, 256-57, 259, 312
and transpersonal experience, 51, 237
Underhill on, 240-41
unitive, 10, 235, 240-45, 255, 258, 259, *see also* spiritual marriage, unitive experience
Wainwright on, 244-45
warm, 247, 254-56, 258
Welwood on, 252-53
Western, 209, 251
Wilber on, 204-05, 247-51
of women, *see* female
Zaehner on, 241-42
Mysticism Scale, 237, 244
myth, mythology 14, 20, 23, 80, 138, 140, 141, 174, 182, 222, 227, 267, 284, 298, 314
and evil, 106-07, 110, 111
function of, 137-39, 141-42, 174
of the hero, *see* hero
as narrative, 8, 10
and self-actualization, 130-58
Myth of the Given, 230, 235, 298
mythical quest, *see* quest
mythical thinking, 52, 138-42, 164, 267, 298
mythmongering, 137, 142, 157, 217, 230, 298

nada, 167, 298
Nada Yoga, *see* Yoga
narcissism, 26, 103, 104, 122, 148, 239
    spiritual,
        see spiritual narcissism
narcissistic rage, 108, 298
Naropa University, 37
narrative understanding, 8, 10, 80, 136, 138, 155, 158, 267, 298
nature, 27, 210, 228, 254, 307, 313,
    see also cosmos, mysticism
nature mysticism, *see* mysticism
nature spirits, 254, 262
Nazism, 106, 112, 116
NDE, *see* near-death experience

near-death experience, 12, 23, 40, 44, 54, 56, 57-59, 169, 182, 188, 298
  evidence for survival, 58-59
  Jung's, 42, 179
  negative, 13, 83, 86, 298
  and transformation, 54, 57-59
nefesh, 161, 162, 163
negative experiences,
  see also shadow
  and transformation, 83-86, 207, 261
  working with, 84, 85, 312
negative NDE,
  see near-death experience
negative void, *see* void
Neolithic, 53
neopaganism, 289, 298, 315
Neoplatonism, 28, 161, 162, 173, 234, 241, 250, 299, 300, 302
neshamah, 162
neurophysiology, 15, 16, 25
neuropsychology, 25
neurosis, 199, *see also* psychopathology
  noogenic, 83, 299
new age, 3, 7, 13, 15, 47, 63-65, 69, 75, 76, 81, 96, 217, 234, 235, 290, 299, 302
new religious movements, 76, 270, 284, 298, 299
New Testament, 161
new-age holism, *see* holism
night sea journey, 83, 86, 207, 299
nirvana, 19, 28, 36, 86, 192, 299
nirvikalpa samadhi, *see* samadhi
nitrous oxide, *see* drugs
no mind, 183, 184, 200, 299, *see also* no self, nondual
no self, 160, 162, 173, 214, 279, 299, *see also* anatman/anatta, no mind, nondual
noesis, 235, 240, 242, 244, 299
nondual, 89-90, 162, 172, 183-85, 189, 196, 197, 199-202, 210, 223, 224, 226, 247-51, 253, 258, 259, 271, 279, 286, 296, 299, 300, 307, 313, *see also* One Taste
  consciousness,
    see consciousness, mysticism

level, 91-92, 202, 248-50, 265
  mysticism, *see* mysticism
  transcendence of good and evil, 89-91
nonegoic core, 34, 205-08, 272, 286, 299, *see also* dynamic ground
non-mystical experience, 260-61, 299
noogenic neurosis, *see* neurosis
noosphere, 60, 201, 294, 299
normative approach, 8, 10, 12, 13, 15, 24, 155, 277, 299
noumenon, 91, 93, 230, 299
noumenal self, *see* self
nous, 161, 162, 173
numerology, 42
numinous, 12, 185, 207, 244, 245-48, 253, 254, 257, 259, 300, *see also* mysticism

OBE, *see* out-of-body experience
object, 300, 304, 308
object relations, 4, 105, 300
occultism, 2, 41, 56, 192, 234, 245, 290, 300, 307
  Freud, Jung on, 20, 42, 179
Ocean of Emancipation, 36, 211, 300, *see also* egocentrism
oceanic experience, 123, 300
  and BPMI, 190
Odyssey, 164
Old Testament, see Hebrew Bible
olon, 166, 300
One, the, 28, 29, 162, 173, 299, 300
One Taste, 91-92, 172, 197, 199, 200-02, 204, 208, 214, 222, 248-49, 251, 255, 300, 313, *see also* nondual
  and cosmic consciousness, 200-02, 249
  and morality, 91-92
ontology, 5, 7, 11, 23, 92, 189, 190, 212, 216, 218, 220, 224, 231, 232, 239, 249, 296, 300, *see also* materialism, metaphysics
  and phenomenology, 174, 231
OOBE, *see* out-of-body experience
optimism, 75-78, 143
oracle, 40, 285, 300
original embedment, 206
Original Man, 162

Original Self, 36, 162, 163, 172-74, 183-84, 300
Other, 85, 169, 181, 220, 227, 246-47, 254-55, 257, 285, 292, 298
  concept of, 220
  soul-image 181,
    see also soul-image
other-worldly approach, 66-67, 69, 225, 228
outer being, 194-96, 283, 293, 300
out-of-body experience, 9, 44, 54, 166, 169, 201, 202, 212, 280, 298, 300
overmind, 162, 194, 197, 300
Oversoul, 19, 173, 191, 200-01, 300

Palaeolithic, 53
panenhenic experience, 241, 242, 243, 255, 300
panentheism, 300, 303
pantheism, 257, 300
paradoxicality, *see* mysticism
parallel universes, 23
paranormal, paranormal experience, 23, 32, 39-62, 81, 201, 234, 243, 245, 248, 295, 301, 302, 304, 309
  dangers of, 56-57
  definition, 300
  James on, 41-42
  and Jung, 42, 179
  and religion, 40-42
  and transpersonal, 6, 10, 39, 191, 275
  and transformation, 56, 57, 60-61
parapsychology, 4, 14, 277, 301
  in quadrant model, 59-60
  as science, 41, 43, 57-59, 62
  and transpersonal psychology, 6, 39, 57–61
parenting, 26, 87
  abusive, 105
  good enough, 102
participatory vision, 35-37, 45, 69, 78, 138, 177, 211-13, 230, 231, 239, 265, 266-68, 272, 283, 301
past-life experiences, 12, 23, 44, 46, 48, 56, 191, 198, 237
pathology, *see* psychopathology

patriarchy, 29, 35, 209, 251, 301
  and Wilber, 209, 226, 227, 251
PCE, *see* pure consciousness event
peak experiences, 21, 30, 43, 46, 64, 66, 74, 86, 124, 152, 178, 283, 287, 301, 302, 308, 313
  and cognition of being, 123, 178
  and self-actualization, 123-24, 127, 131, 151-52, 154, 156
  and self-transcendence, 125, 127
  and values of being, 124
peek experience,
  see glimpse experience
perennial philosophy, 19, 28, 78, 230, 238, 250, 256, 266, 270, 301, 312
  critiques of, 35-36, 137, 157, 211, 224-25
  post-axial version, 28, 32, 35, 78, 155, 197, 224
  pre-axial version, 27, 35, 78, 155
perennial psychology, 225
perennialism, *see* perennial philosophy, perennial psychology
perinatal experience, 22, 30, 190-91, 275, 301
permeability, 210, 214, 227, 229, 301, 303
permeable self, *see* self
persona, 72, 73, 99, 100-02, 150, 180-81, 297, 301, 308
  in transpersonal psychology, 74-81
Personal Construct Psychology, 3
personal level, 32, 34, 49-52, 112, 113, 198-99, 204, 209, 210, 265, 266, 271, 283, 301, 313
personal psychosynthesis, *see* psychosynthesis
personal self, *see* self
personal shadow, *see* shadow
personal unconscious, 180, 190, 195, 301
personality types, 33
Phaedrus, 165
Phantasms of the Living, 40

phantasy, 100, 301
    God as, 221, *see also* God
pharmacology, 273
phenomenal self, *see* self
phenomenological method, 301,
    307
phenomenology, 9, 26, 59, 61, 217,
    229, 230, 302, 307
    and Jung, 229
    and metaphysics, 173-75,
        230-31
    and mysticism, 19, 219, 239,
        240, 243, 244, 282,
        see also mysticism
phenomenon (cf. noumenon), 93,
    302
phylogenetic
    development, *see* evolution
    experience, 23, 46, 302
physical mediumship,
    see mediumship
physiosphere, 201, 294, 302
plateau experience, 86, 127, 302
Platonic forms, 167, 302
Platonism, 145, 162, 193, 286, 302
pleasure principle, 156,
    see also hedonism
pluralism, 10, 29, 36-37, 78, 80,
    211-12, 224, 231, 236, 266-68
pneuma, 161, 162, 173
po, 162
politics, 87, 108, 109, 112
Pollyanna paradigm, 64, 77, 302
poltergeist phenomena, 23, 48, 60,
    191
polytheism, 302
positive
    approach, 74-75, 83, 86, 292
    mental health, 21,
    see also self-actualization
positive psychology, 26, 65, 75,
    276, 302
positive shadow, *see* shadow
positive thinking, 64, 75, 302
positivism, 3, 59, 141, 283, 302
possession, 9, 13, 40, 44, 56, 86, 94,
    166, 212, 285, 302
post-axial traditions, 28-29, 32, 35,
    78, 135, 143, 155, 164, 197, 224,
    268, 302

postdualistic integration, 207
postmodernism, 94, 95, 143, 298,
    302, 306
practitioner-researcher, 277
practitioners, 276-78
pragmatism, 10, 142, 153, 303
prakriti, 303, 307
pratityasamutpada, 162, 303
prayer, 60, 151, 226, 245, 315
pre-axial traditions, 27-29, 35, 78,
    155, 164, 268, 303
precognition, *see* extrasensory
    perception
preegoic phase, 34, 205-06, 208,
    286, 303
premonitions, 42, *see also* extrasen-
    sory perception: precognition
pre/perm fallacy, 210, 303
prepersonal level, 31-32, 34, 46,
    51-53, 56, 61, 62, 112-13, 198,
    208-09, 210, 265, 271, 286, 296,
    303, 306, 307
prepotency, 116, 303
presence, 284
    in cosmic consciousness, 17-18,
        170, 200, 244, 245
    embodied, 169
    and numinous experience, 237,
        257, 259
    sensing a, 40, 42, 44, 166, 254
pre/trans fallacy, 31-32, 34, 51,
    208, 210, 286, 303, 305, 306
primal repression, 303
primal wound, 83, 101-02, 104,
    108, 114, 303
Primal Wound, 101
primary process, 52, 303
process theology, 193, 303
progress, 27, 29
    and maintenance, 269
projected authority, 76, 226, 303
projection, 304
    anima and animus, 182
    and evil, 72, 100-04, 107, 113
    mana personality, 182
    narcissistic, 103-04
    in religion, 20, 221-23
    shadow, 65, 72, 73, 99-100, 181
    soul-image, 182
    spirit, 32

prophecy, 44, 246, 254, 283
pseudo self, *see* self
psilocybin, *see* drugs
psyche, 161-62, 166, 173, 192, 218,
    280, 281, 304, 305, 308, 313, 314
    Assagioli's model, 20-21,
        186-89
    Aurobindo's model, 192-97
    as context of mystical
        experience, 254-56
    Grof's model, 190-92
    integration, 30, 207, 308
    Jung's model, 20, 72, 179-85,
        213, 222-23, 269
    Washburn's model, 205-09
psychedelic, *see* drugs
psychiatry, *see* transpersonal
    psychiatry
psychic, *see also* psychism
    energy, 34
    centres, 167, *see also* chakras
    experience, 39-56, 187, 190, 198,
        226, 250, 287
psychic being, 53, 162, 194, 196,
    197, 204, 214, 304, 308, 311
psychic immanence, 222, 304
psychic inflation, 199
psychic level, 32, 55, 78, 200-02,
    226, 251, 265, 304
psychic mysticism, *see* mysticism
psychical research, 17, 304
psychism, 2, 42-43, 48, 55-57, 78,
    86-87, 167, 192, 195, 199, 304,
    see also psychic
psychoactive drugs, *see* drugs
psychoanalysis, 20, 21, 184, 190,
    195, 205, 264, 289, 304,
    see also Freudianism
psychodrama, 24, 304
psychodynamic approach, 4, 65,
    285, 293, 300, 301, 304, 310, 314
    see also analytical psychology,
    psychoanalysis, psycho-
    synthesis
psychoid experiences, 23, 191, 198,
    304
psychokinesis, 23, 42, 44, 48, 60,
    191
    recurrent spontaneous psycho-

kinesis (RSPK), 48, *see also*
    poltergeist phenomena
psychological health, 139
    and hierarchy of needs, 119
    and self-actualization, 131-32
psychological holism, *see* holism
psychologism, 49, 110, 138, 141,
    142, 153, 157, 186, 304
    and Jung, 223
psychology, 3
    academic, 5, 3, 276, 283, 305
    experimental, 59
    Wilber's critique, 264
psychology of religion, 25, 305
    and transpersonal psychology,
        13, 50
psycholytic therapy, 87, 290, 305
psychopathology, 83-84, 297, 299
    in spectrum model, 198-99
    spirit attachment, 310
    spiritual emergency,
        see spiritual emergency
    and transformation, 83-84,
        207-08
psychosis, 199, 207, 305, 310,
    see also psychopathology,
    spiritual emergency
    and paranormal experience, 56
psychosurgery, *see* therapy
psychosynthesis, 20-21, 37, 105,
    159, 177, 186-89, 271, 280, 291,
    305, 314
    cosmic, 188, 284
    inter-individual, 188, 293
    personal, 21, 188, 301
    spiritual/transpersonal, 21,
        188, 310, 313
psychotherapy, 4, 15, 16, 20, 21,
    65, 87, 110, 272, 289,
    see also therapy
    Buddhist, *see* Buddhism
    Jungian, *see* analytical
        psychology
    logotherapy, *see* logotherapy
    object relations,
        see object relations
    psychoanalysis,
        see psychoanalysis
    psychodrama,
        see psychodrama

psychodynamic, *see*
    psychodynamic approach
psycholytic,
    see psycholytic therapy
psychosynthesis,
    see psychosynthesis
transpersonal, *see*
    transpersonal psychotherapy
ptf-1, 303, 305, *see also* pre/trans
    fallacy
ptf-2, 303, 305, *see also* pre/trans
    fallacy
puberty rites, 315
puella aeterna, 182, 305
puer aeternus, 182, 305
pure consciousness event, 78, 86,
    238, 245, 248, 255, 305
purgation, 241
purusha, 162, 305, 307

quadrant model, 6, 8, 32-33, 59, 78,
    79, 203, 264, 280, 288, 293, 305
    and good & evil, 110-12, 114
    and parapsychology, 59-60
    and transpersonal disciplines,
        59-60
    and transpersonal practice, 226
qualia, 15, 305
quaternity, 42, 305
quest, 8, 136, 142, 145, 158, 254,
    278
quietism, 87, 305

racism, 93
radical empiricism, *see* empiricism
Raja Yoga, *see* Yoga
Real, the, 9, 78, 89, 188, 189,
    235-37, 239, 244, 246, 251-62,
    267, 292, 298, 299, 306
    loss of 261-62
real self, *see* self
reality
    fundamental, *see* Real
    ordinary, 235
realized self, *see* self
rebirth, 52, 169, 183, 190, 204, 207,
    306, *see also* reincarnation
reductionism, 16, 32, 74, 150, 179,
    208, 303, 304, 306, 312,
    see also psychologism

regeneration in spirit, 34, 206, 208,
    266, 306
regression, 46, 51, 56, 61, 275
    in the service of transcendence,
        30, 34, 206-08, 306
reincarnation, 44, 169, 174, 182,
    197, 214, 216, 233, 291, 294, 306,
    see also rebirth
relativism, 36, 132, 306
    moral, *see* emotivism, moral
    and pluralism, 267
religion, 13, 19, 20, 27, 78, 161, 174,
    175, 223-24, 237, 266, 283, 285,
    287, 288, 289, 292, 293, 294, 297,
    298, 299, 301, 306, 312, 314
    comparative, 157-58, 246, 283
    defined, 306
    Eastern, 24
    Egyptian, 161, 163, 173
    and evil, 90, 107, 108, 110
    experiential foundations, 173
    Grof on, 90
    Indian, 28, 285, 287, 291, 294,
        316
    indigenous, 28, 29, 35, 46, 78,
        292, 309
    Jung on, 220-23
    major world, *see* Buddhism,
        Christianity, Hinduism,
        Islam, Jainism, Judaism,
        Taoism
    Maslow on, 220-21
    and mysticism, 234, 238, 241,
        see also mysticism
    neopagan, *see* neopaganism
    organized, 12, 28, 29, 268
    and paranormal, 40-42
    post-axial, *see* post-axial
        traditions
    pre-axial, *see* pre-axial
        traditions
    psychology of, *see* psychology
        of religion
    and the transpersonal, 11, 12,
        50, 226, 268
    and transpersonal psychology,
        175, 225, 232
    Western, 24
religious belief, 46, 139, 217-18,
    286, 292, 299

religious experience, 11, 23, 159, 229, 236, 270, 305
   James on, 16-17
   and mystical experience, 236-37, 245,
     see also mysticism
   and numinosity, 245-46,
     see also numinous
Religious Experience Research Centre, 20
religious studies, 15, 249, 269, 272-74, 277, 283, 306
remote viewing,
   see extrasensory perception
renewal process, 83
repression, 64, 99-100, 159, 181, 208, 301, 306
   of dynamic ground, 34, 205, 285, 303
   primal, 206, 303
   of real self, 121, 122
   of shadow, 73
researcher-practitioner, 277
retro-romanticism,
   see romanticism
return of the repressed, 73,
   see also repression
revelation, 169, 183, 196, 197, 247, 254, 294
Revelations of Divine Love, 294
ReVision, 38
Revisioning Transpersonal Theory, 35
revivalism, 260, 307
Rigpa, 172, 200, 255, 307
ritual, 60, 226, 237, 245, 288, 311, 314, 315
ritual magic, *see* magic
role self, *see* self
roles, 121, 150
romantic poets, 252, 255, 307
romanticism, 95, 261, 285, 307
   ecoromanticism, 67
   retro-romanticism, 32, 307
roots (as symbol), 29
Roots of Evil, 106
ruach, 161, 162, 163
rule of époche, *see* époche

sachchidananda, 162, 193, 194, 195, 197, 292, 307

sacredness, *see* numinous
sadism, 87, 103, 104, 106
sahu, 161, 173
salvation, 12, 18, 143, 193, 246, 247, 284, 285, 288, 289, 292, 295, 296, 307, 309, 312, 314,
   see also soteriology
   collective, 27, 78
   individual, 27, 28, 78 153
samadhi, 188, 305, 307
   nirvikalpa, 171, 248, 299
   savikalpa, 248, 255, 308
samatha, 87, 307
Samkhya, 162, 303, 305, 307
sandbox syndrome, 64, 77, 93, 307
Satanism, 2, 307
savikalpa samadhi, *see* samadhi
Saybrook Graduate School and Research Center, 37
scapegoating, 108-09
Schutz encounter, 308, *see also* encounter groups
science, 8, 15, 16, 139, 157, 217, 230, 232, 235, 308, *see also* transpersonal psychology
scientific materialism, 41, 308, *see also* scientism
Scientific and Medical Network, 38
scientific method, 13-14
scientism, 15, 308, *see also* scientific materialism
script analysis, 199
second force, *see* force
secondary process, 308
secularism, 12
self, 52, 53, 105, 108, 149, 172, 178, 182, 183, 249, 308
   as absolute, 241
   aiming at, 128, 144, 148, 152
   archetype, 20, 180-85, 292, 308
   body self, 150, 199, 206
   causal, 199, 283
   connected, 12, 29, 178, 209-10, 214, 255, 284, 295
   conscious, 187-88
   cosmic, 160
   deep, 159
   denial of, 299, 306,
     see also anatman/anatta

developmental origin, 14, 105, 121, 139
divine, 190, 191
emotional, 199
empirical, 162
existential, 173
expansion of, 66, 228, 229, 237, 286, 313
extinction, 162, 288
false, 101, 150, 292, 304, 311, 313
formless, 162, 163, 184
frontal, 203-04, 289, 295, 308
fulcrums, *see* fulcrums
as heart, 290
higher/highest, 20, 30, 47, 152, 159, 173, 179, 186-89, 208, 291, 313, 314
idealized, 121, 150, 292
integrated, 51, 80, 199
lines of, 199, 203, 308
loss of, 160, 253, 288,
  see also self-transcendence
no self, *see* no self
noumenal, 162, 168, 187, 299
objective, 168
ordinary, 61, 81, 147, 163, 232, 286, 288, 306, 308, 313
original, *see* Original Self
and Other, 52
outer, 195
permeable, 210-11, 214
personal, 45, 81, 113, 187
phenomenal, 162, 301
pseudo, 121, 150, 151, 156, 304
psychic, 199
real, 116, 118, 121-28, 139, 147-57, 173, 179, 187, 213, 306, 308, 313
as the Real, 236
realized, 109, 182,
  see also self-actualization, self-realization
role, 199, *see also* roles
sense of, 11, 22, 32, 47, 49, 51, 52, 98, 99, 101, 108, 181, 198, 218, 228, 232, 237, 303, 313
separate, 284
social, 101, 151, 155
somatic, 150

as spirit, 203
spiritual, *see* transpersonal self
streams, *see* self-streams
subjective, 172
subliminal, 194, 196
subtle, 199, 214, 311
transcendence of,
  see self-transcendence
transpersonal,
  see transpersonal self
true, 159, 183-84, 187, 242, 281, 313
ultimate, 162, 292
universal, 21, 214
whole, 73, 103, 109, 159, 181, 183
wider, 159
as witness, 171, *see also* witness
self-actualization, 3, 8, 21, 64, 66, 74, 115-58, 178, 275, 283, 290, 308
characteristics of, 120
concept of, 115-21, 124, 127, 128, 131-35, 140, 143-44
critiques of, 122-23, 125, 128-34, 139, 141-45, 148-51, 155-57
and existential choice, 118, 123, 125, 131, 147
and hierarchy of needs, 116-17, 146
Maslow's empirical research, 119-20, 123, 145
and metamotivation,
  see metamotivation
and morality, 123, 132, 142
and myth, 8, 130-58
and peak experiences, 123-24, 131, 151, 154, 156
as personality syndrome, 118-20
and psychological health, 119, 120, 132
and real self, 122, 125,
  see also self
and self-transcendence,
  see self-transcendence
and teleology, 134, 136, 138
transcending and non-transcending, 127-28, 154
and values of being,

see values of being
self-centredness,
    see egocentrism
self-centres, 8, 105, 308, 314
    empathic and benevolent, 109
    and evil, 105-09
    external and internal, 105, 109
self-concept, 101-02, 108, 181, 199,
    215, 297, 304
self-consciousness, 9, 18, 28, 31,
    163, 164, 168, 175, 183, 219, 281
    evolution of, 163, 282
self-inquiry (Ramana Maharshi),
    306
self-knowledge, 109, 241, 287, 314
selflessness, 36, 153, 212, 239, 267,
    294, *see also* self-transcendence
selfobject, 105, 308
self-realization, 3, 8, 42, 68, 109,
    110, 114, 118, 132, 187, 247, 265,
    283, 284, 287, 292, 305, 308, 316,
    see also self-actualization
self-renewal through trauma, 83
self-streams, 160, 203, 214, 289,
    308
self-system, 101, 105, 108, 308
    wounded, 114
self-transcendence, 46, 49, 51, 158,
    200, 275, 308
    and hierarchy of needs, 117,
        154
    and metamotivation,
        see metamotivation
    and self-actualization, 125-29,
        144, 153-55
sephiroth, 162
serious mysticism, 82, 226-27
Sermons of Meister Eckhart, 171
service, 37, 87, 203, 314
sex, 28, 82, 123, 253, 266, 287
sexual mysticism, *see* mysticism
shade, 161, 162, 164, 166, 169, 173,
    174
shadow, 7, 10, 64, 71-93, 180-81,
    185, 308
    accepting, 65, 73, 109, 113, 181
    acting out, 73
    archetype, 7, 71-73, 308
    collective, 74, 89, 93, 109, 283
    and evil, 73, 99-101, 107, 113

and persona, 74, 100
personal, 74, 93, 109
positive, 73, 100, 302
projected, 72, 73
repressed, 73
transforming, 84-88
transpersonal, 66, 93
in transpersonal psychology,
    71-93
shamanic crisis, 56, 83, 86
shamanic experience, 40, 44, 46, 53
shamanic journey, 167, 182, 191,
    209, 226, 309, *see also* vision
    quest
shamanism, 2, 24, 27, 37, 161, 163,
    166, 167, 246, 309
sheaths of Vedanta, 162
shen, 162
siddhis, 2, 23, 44, 48, 54, 55, 167,
    198, 248, 304, 309
silence, 171, 173, 200
sin, 18, 237
sixth sense, *see* extrasensory
    perception
skandhas, 162
Sky Father, 29
'sleep' (in waking consciousness),
    290
social mysticism, *see* mysticism
social self, *see* self
socialism, 115
socialization, 7, 101, 104, 156
Society for Psychical Research, 41,
    43
sociobiology, 126, 150, 309
sociology, *see* transpersonal
    sociology
solar eclipse, 71
somatic self, *see* self
soteriology, 12, 15, 37, 148, 193,
    224, 227, 267, 280, 309, 314,
    see also salvation
    structured, *see* structured path
    unstructured, *see* unstructured
        path
    via negativa, *see* via negativa
soul, 21, 47, 53, 159-76, 196, 199,
    204, 208, 213, 216, 242, 247, 250,
    255, 284, 294, 299, 304, 305, 309,
    310, 311

concept of, 8, 9, 147, 159-65,
     170, 173-76, 309
dark night of, *see* dark night
divine, 19, 162-64, 173, 174,
     175, 196, 214, 281, 314
Hillman's concept, 80, 84
immortal, 18, 161, 163, 165, 166,
     173, 174,
     see also immortality, survival
individual, 187, 233, 279, 294,
     299, 306, 308
as line of self, 199, 203-04, 308
longbody, *see* longbody
loss of, 166
Oversoul, *see* Oversoul
as psychic being, 204
in psychosynthesis, 186, 189
spark, *see* spark
World Soul, *see* World Soul
soul mysticism, *see* mysticism
soul-image, 180-82, 309
soul-making (Hillman), 80-81
space-time 22-23, 191
spark, spark-soul, 162, 166, 169,
     173, 194, 196, 197, 242, 309
speaking in tongues, 283, 309
species consciousness, 170, 183,
     197, 309
spectrum of consciousness, *see*
     spectrum model
Spectrum of Consciousnesss, 30
spectrum model, 30-32, 49, 53-56,
     88, 197-205, 264, 265, 271, 289,
     309, 310
Spiral Dynamics, 34, 309, 310
spiral-dynamic approach, 34-35,
     177, 205-09, 241, 268, 271-72,
     309
spirit, 1, 8, 29, 114, 160, 162, 167,
     188, 198, 199, 216, 242, 250,
     254-55, 256, 294
     concept of, 11, 19, 147, 159-65,
       170, 173-76, 196, 223, 229,
       236, 269, 280, 283, 309, 315
     dark night of, *see* dark night
     domain, 27, 32, 208, 222, 223,
       226, 229, 231
     guardian, *see* guardian angel
     as line of the self, 199, 203, 308
     regeneration in,
       see regeneration in spirit
spirit attachment, 86, 310
spirit entities, 46, 48, 161, 287, 290,
     310
spirit guide, 23, 48, 161, 179, 182,
     188, 198, 309, 310
spirit release therapy, *see* therapy
spirit world, 309, 315,
     see also spiritism
spiritism, 23, 40, 46, 48, 87, 297,
     310, *see also* spiritualism
spiritual body, *see* body
spiritual crisis, *see* crisis, spiritual
     emergency
spiritual emergency, 46, 56, 57, 83,
     84, 261, 310
spiritual experience, 11, 23, 24,
     226, 252, 275, 291, *see also* reli-
     gious experience, mysticism,
     transpersonal experience
spiritual friendship, 251, 294
spiritual life, 9, 179, 197, 214, 265
     and biology, 126, 149, 155
spiritual marriage, 170, 183, 202,
     203, 255, 258, 259, 310, 312
spiritual materialism, 68, 69, 76,
     81, 82, 154, 212, 310
spiritual narcissism, 36, 68, 69, 76,
     81, 212, 213, 310
spiritual practice,
     see transpersonal practices
spiritual psychosynthesis,
     see psychosynthesis
spiritual self, *see* transpersonal self
spiritual teachers, 76, 109, 197,
     260, 276, 282, 290
     Wilber on, 226
spiritual traditions, 15, 20, 36, 81,
     267, 273, 284, 292
     hot and cool, *see* hot, cool
     indigenous, *see* indigenous,
       religion
     problem of evaluating, 36, 203,
       212
spiritual ultimates, 211-12, 231,
     235, 297, 300
spiritualism, 2, 41, 234, 310,
     see also spiritism

spirituality, 2, 10, 12, 23, 68, 78, 80, 95, 178, 208, 209, 266, 288, 301, 310, *see also* religion, transpersonal
 female and male
  see female, male
 indigenous, *see* indigenous, religion
 non-religious, 269, 310
stages of life, 181, 293
states of consciousness, *see* consciousness
stigmata, 40, 44
structural-hierarchical approach, 34-35, 177, 197-205, 268, 271-72, 295, 309, 310, *see also* hierarchical approach
structured path, 85, 209, 226-27, 230, 275, 277, 310, 314
subconscient, 194, 195, 310, *see also* unconscious
sub-genius, 128
subliminal self, 194-97, 310
submission, 294
subtle body, *see* body
subtle Cartesianism, 212, 311, *see also* Cartesianism
subtle energy, 44, 47, 48, 167, 173, 207, 216, 283, 294, 311
subtle level, 32, 78, 80, 81, 89, 162, 198, 201, 202, 203, 222, 223, 226, 230, 247-51, 265, 310
 high, 49, 53, 55, 198, 248, 291
 low, 49, 53-56, 198, 200, 202, 248, 295, 304
subtle mysticism, *see* mysticism
subtle self, *see* self
suffering, 78, 90, 91, 251, 260, 262, 282, 295, 313
 and transformation, 83-88
Sufism, 17, 24, 162, 250, 251, 311
sunyata, 171, 200, 248, 255, 311
superconscient, 194, 196, 197
superconscious, 47, 185-89, 291, 311
supermind, 162, 194, 197, 311
supernatural, 27, 40, 256, 300, 309, *see also* paranormal
 beings, 284, 285, 290
superstition, 52, 56, 57, 296

Supreme Being, 193, 281, 286, 289, 291, 311, *see also* Brahman, God
 denial of, 282, 294
surface being, 196, 311
survival (of death), 14, 17, 18, 166, 169, 311, *see also* immortality
 evidence for, 57-58
survival personality, 101-02, 311
sustainable development, 269
symbiosis, 190, 252, 311
symbolic interactionism, 121, 139, 311
symbolic thinking, 136, 137, 139, 281, *see also* symbols
symbols, symbolism 20, 55, 138, 182, 237, 256, 297, *see also* symbolic thinking
synchronicity, 23, 42, 44, 48, 191, 311
synergic mysticism, *see* mysticism
synergy, 69, 116, 126, 259, 260, 311
Synthesis of Yoga, 193

Tai Chi, 87, 311
Talks with Ramana Maharshi, 172
Talmud, 294, 311
Tantra, 87, 251, 253, 271, 294, 296, 311, 314
Tao, 36, 311, 312
Taoism, 24, 123, 162, 253, 283, 311, 312
teleology, 133-38, 142, 155, 312
 in post-axial traditions, 135, 143, 155
 and self-actualization, 122, 134, 136, 138, 155
telepathy,
 see extrasensory perception
terrorism, 93, 192
tertiary cognition, 52, 208, 312
Thanatos, 99, 312
theism, 212, 223, 230, 235, 306
theistic mysticism, *see* mysticism
theology, 15, 46, 78, 89, 174, 202, 221, 228, 269, 273, 280, 284, 286, 289, 294, 312, 315,
 see also process theology
theory of mind, 14
Theosophical Society, 312

Theosophy, 2, 17, 19, 24, 28, 162, 250, 279, 280, 281, 282, 287, 297, 310, 312

therapy, 73, 109, 151, 276, 282, *see also* psychotherapy
  behaviour, 110, 281
  existential, 87, 199
  gestalt, 24, 289
  holotropic, 87
  integral, 203
  physical, 199
  regressive, 199
  spirit release, 87, 310

Theravada Buddhism, *see* Buddhism

theurgy, 312

third force, *see* force

this-worldly approach, 66-67, 69, 225, 228

three bodies of Vedanta, 162, 198, 202, 247

three eyes, *see* eye

Thus Spake Zarathustra, 76

thymos, 161

Tibetan Book of the Dead, 204

Tibetan Buddhism, *see* Buddhism

time, *see* space-time

timelessness, 204-05, 242, 245

token economy, 110, 312

tonglen, 87, 312

Torah, 294, 312

tradition, 78, 134, 294, *see also* spiritual traditions

tragedy, 65, 86, 96, 147
  and transformation, 83-84

trailing clouds of glory, 52, 204, 312

trance, 44, 166, 167, 171, 297, 307, 309, 313
  mediumship, *see* mediumship

'transcend and include', 51, 196, 266

transcendence, 27-30, 35, 45, 78, 129, 207, 210, 211, 216-33, 253, 280, *see also* Transcendent
  concepts of, 9, 23, 127, 216-33, 235, 313
  experiences of, 21, 152, 156
  feminist critique, 211, 227, *see also* feminism

and immanence, 228, 268, *see also* immanence

regression in service of, *see* regression

of self, 11, 51, 94, 124-27, 144, 153, 275, *see also* self-transcendence

of space or time, 22-23, 48

Transcendent, the, 7, 9, 45, 85, 89, 91, 92, 179, 218-33, 235, 283, 306, 313, *see also* transcendence

transcendent function, 20, 313

transcendent witness, *see* witness

transconceptual disclosures, 36, 211

transegoic, *see also* transpersonal
  phase, 34, 69, 206-08, 286, 313
  potentials, 207-08

transformation, 10, 12-13, 15-16, 20, 25, 27, 30, 32, 33, 50-62, 81, 138, 141, 171, 178, 213, 229, 230, 237, 247, 261, 277, 278, 293, 298, 299, 306, 313
  Aurobindo on, 194-97
  bodily, 44
  and the mundane, 50, 152, 252
  and mystical experience, 56, 60, 188, 240, 241, *see also* mysticism
  and near-death experience, 54, 57, 59, *see also* near-death experience
  and negative experiences, 7, 82-88, 169, 261, *see also* spiritual emergency
  and paranormal experience, 54-62
  of self, 12, 36, 49, 151, 211, 214, 229, *see also* self-transcendence
  and spiritual practice, 24, 38, 50
  taxonomy of experiences and practices, 85-87
  and transportation, 55, 82, 275

transmigration, 161, 196, 306, 313, *see also* rebirth, reincarnation

transpersonal, 21, 25, 38, 56, 75, 78, 80, 82, 113, 160, 191, 275
  American and European

perspectives, 78
concept and definition of,
  11-13, 39, 45-50, 54, 55, 68-69,
    81, 185, 216, 218-19, 229, 232,
    269
in everyday life, 36, 69,
    see also mundane approach
and extrapersonal,
    see extrapersonal
Grof's theory, 190-91
James on, 17
Jung on, 42, 185
and metaphysics,
    see metaphysics
and paranormal,
    see paranormal
and perinatal, *see* perinatal
and religion, *see* religion
shadow, *see* shadow
and spirituality, *see* spiritual
    experience, spirituality
women's experience, *see* female
transpersonal anthropology, 15,
  59, 60, 68, 265, 273
transpersonal counselling, 5, 15,
  25, 37, 276, *see also* counselling
transpersonal development, 30-37,
  178, 205, 280, 291
  Ferrer on, 212
  and psychosynthesis,
    see psychosynthesis
  spiral and ladder models, 268,
    309
  Washburn's theory, 34-35, 52,
    205-09
  Wilber's theory, 30-34, 197-205,
    226, 241, 265
  Wright on, 209-11, 227
transpersonal ecology, 35, 66-68,
  228, 231, 232, 265, 269, 272, 313
  critique, 67
transpersonal events, 13, 266, 270,
  283
  cocreated, 267,
    see also cocreation
transpersonal experience, 13, 23,
  53, 179, 229, 237, *see also* mysticism, religious experience,
  spiritual experience
  in childhood, 52, 53, 204, 261,

275
Grof on, 22-23, 46-48, 189-92,
  237
and paranormal experience,
  see paranormal
social-cultural influences on,
  68
varieties of, 7, 10, 12, 85-87
Washburn on, 207-09
in Wilber's model, 198-203,
  247-50
transpersonal level, 31-32, 34,
  51-52, 61-62, 112-13, 198-210,
  226, 266, 283, 286, 303, 306, 313
transpersonal pathologies,
  see psychopathology
transpersonal practices, 7, 25, 27,
  28, 50, 66, 68, 76, 78, 87-88, 109,
  110, 151, 188, 196, 215, 226, 238,
  275
  taxonomy, 7, 87-88
transpersonal psychiatry, 25, 265,
  272, 276
transpersonal psychology, 264,
  272, 313
  academic courses, 4, 5, 6, 26,
    37, 38, 263, 277, 278
  critiques, 7, 35, 65-66, 68, 74-82,
    93, 209, 228, 231
  debates in, 66-67, 79, 262, 265,
    268, 271
  definition of, 6, 13, 24, 39, 43,
    45-49, 217-18, 272-74
  future directions, 10, 69, 70,
    262, 263-78
  history of, 3, 6, 14–26, 41, 70,
    74, 115, 192, 249, 263, 289,
    296
  and integral approach, 33, 59,
    263-64
  and metaphysics,
    see metaphysics
  organizations, 6
  and parapsychology,
    see parapsychology
  and positive psychology,
    see positive psychology
  and related disciplines, 13, 24,
    25, 50, 68
  and religion, *see* religion

resources in, 6, 37-38, 276
as science, 5, 6, 9, 10, 13-16,
    24-25, 33, 37, 43, 58, 61-62,
    174-75, 197, 217, 230, 267,
    272-76
and transpersonal studies, 265,
    273-74
Wilber's defection, 30, 68, 263
Transpersonal Psychology Review,
    38
transpersonal psychosynthesis,
    see psychosynthesis
transpersonal psychotherapy, 5,
    25, 37, 87, *see also*
    psychosynthesis
transpersonal self, 8, 9, 21, 154,
    159-215, 291, 305, 313
    Assagioli on, 177, 186-89, 291
    Aurobindo on, 177, 192-97
    Ferrer on, 177, 211-13
    Grof on, 177, 189-92
    Jung on, 177, 179-85
    Maslow on, 177-79
    Vaughan on, 215
    Washburn on, 177, 205-09
    Wilber on, 177, 197-205
    Wright on, 177, 209-11
transpersonal shadow, *see* shadow
transpersonal sociology, 59, 60, 68,
    265, 273
transpersonal studies, 15, 67, 265,
    267, 273-74, 290, 313
transportative experience, 54-56,
    82, 240, 275, 313
trauma, 86, 101, *see also* primal
    wound, spiritual emergency
    self-renewal through, 83
Tree of Life, 228
tremendum, 246, 313
trough experience, 46, 48, 66, 86,
    313
true self, *see* self

UFO experiences, 23, 40, 43, 44,
    48, 49, 56, 191
ultimate consciousness,
    see consciousness
ultimate level, 55, 198, 222
unconditional love, *see* love
unconditional positive regard,
    102, 314

unconscious, 20, 29, 99, 173, 179,
    182, 183, 254, 282, 285, 293, 296,
    299, 301, 303, 304, 306, 308, 309,
    310, 313, 314
    collective,
        see collective unconscious
    deep, 34, 159, 206, 285, 303, 306
    Freudian, 99, 195
    higher, 20, 30, 186-87, 189, 191,
        196, 213, 291
    lower, 20, 186-87, 195, 295
    middle, 20, 297
    personal,
        see personal unconscious
    and shadow, *see* shadow
undeserved harm, *see* harm
unifying centre, 105, 186, 188, 214,
    314
union, 53, 55, 86, 162, 170, 171,
    182, 210, 240, 241, 242, 249, 253,
    255, 257, 258, 259, 261, 279, 288,
    294, 295, 296, 310, 312, 314,
    see also communion, mysticism,
        nondual, unitive experience,
        unity
    with God, *see* God, mysticism
    sexual, 258, *see also* mysticism
    symbiotic, 190
unitive experience, 12, 45, 170-71,
    183, 189, 197, 198, 202, 219,
    240-45, 258, 293, 314, *see also*
    mysticism, union, unity
unitive life, 171, 241, 266, 298, 314
unitive mysticism, *see* mysticism
unity, 18, 124, 197, 218, 243, 245,
    260, 288, 300, *see also* union,
    unitive experience
universal mind, *see* mind
universal self, *see* self
universal soul, *see* World Soul
universalism, 267-68, 284, 293,
    314, *see also* perennialism
unstructured path, 85, 227, 230,
    275, 314
Upanishads, 21, 255, 314
utilitarianism, 133, 314
utopianism, 64, 115-16, 307, 314

Vajrayana, *see* Buddhism
values of being, 124-26, 129, 131,
    153, 179, 213, 282, 287, 297, 314

value spheres (male and female)
211, 228
Varieties of Religious Experience, 16,
42
Vedanta, 2, 17, 78, 162, 171, 193,
209, 230, 241, 250, 279, 281, 282,
290, 306, 307, 310, 314
advaita, 212, 223, 224, 230, 241,
247, 250, 279, 306, 307
influence on Wilber, 198,
204-05, 223-24, 247-48, 250
three bodies,
see three bodies of Vedanta
Vedas, 314
vertical path, 27, 29, 66-67, 69, 228,
314
via negativa, 248, 280, 315
vipassana, 4, 315, *see also*
meditation
virtue, 135, *see also* morality
and vice, 103-04
vision quest, 87, 309, 315,
see also shamanic journey
visionary experience, 37, 42, 192,
213, 251, 266, 311
vision-logic, 268, 315
visions and voices, 40, 42, 86, 137,
163-64, 169, 170, 182, 190, 198,
207, 243, 245, 248, 249, 251, 254,
258, 260, 261, 302, 312, 315
visualization, 21, 60, 290, 315
vocation, *see* mission
voices, *see* visions and voices
void, 90, 171, 191, 200, 236, 243,
248, 255, 311, 315
negative, 86

warm mysticism, *see* mysticism
Western mysticism, *see* mysticism
Western philosophies, 78, *see also*
mysticism, religion
Wicca, 2, 24, 315,
see also witchcraft
wider self, *see* self
will to believe, 140-42
Will to Believe, 140
wings (symbol), 29
witchcraft, 2, 44, 315,
see also Wicca
witness, transcendent witness 32,
53, 78, 109, 168-73, 199-200,

214, 248-49, 255, 282, 283, 290,
309, 313, 315
eternal, 205
as line of self, 203-04, 308
witnessing, 189, 198, 245, 249, 315,
see also witness
women mystics, 251,
see also female
women's experience, *see* female
World Soul, 162, 201, 279, 300, 315
worldview, 33, 105, 203, 270, 308
and evil, 110-11
wounded healer, 83, 315

yang, 29, 162
yechidah, 162
yin, 29, 162
Yoga, 2, 4, 17, 23, 24, 46, 54, 55, 60,
162, 171, 189, 192, 193, 248, 294,
301, 304, 307, 309, 316
Bhakti, 87, 282
Dream, 286, 296
Guru, 251, 290
Hatha, 2, 290
Integral, 196, 293
Jnana, 294
Karma, 87, 251, 294
Kundalini, 87
Mantra, 295, 296
Nada, 298
Raja, 2, 20, 87, 186, 187, 301,
305
siddhis, *see* siddhis
Yoga Sutras, 305

zazen, 4, 87, 316,
see also meditation
zeitgeist, 74, 89, 316
of transpersonal psychology,
77-79
Zen, 36, 162, 163, 172, 183-84, 200,
223, 224, 299, 300, 316
and Jung, 183-84
Zoroastrianism, 161, 290, 316